MODERN RELIGIONS:
AN EXPERIENTIAL ANALYSIS
AND EXPOSÉ

by

Elliot Benjamin, Ph.D.

Natural Dimension Publications: 2013

Copyright 2013 by Elliot Benjamin, Ph.D.

ISBN 978-1-257-08261-2

TABLE OF CONTENTS

INTRODUCTION

This book is a collection of personal experiential essays about twenty four relatively new religious movements, which I refer to interchangeably as modern religions and new age spiritual organizations; an experiential analysis is included for twenty two of these groups. The first chapter, *A Tri-Perspective Experiential Analysis of Modern Religions*, can be viewed as a tri-perspective evaluation and analysis of my own subjective experiences in seventeen of these new age spiritual organizations. I describe my experiences in many of these new age spiritual organizations in a more personal way in my experiential essays in chapters 2, 3, and 4. Chapter 5 consists of a series of essays in which I put the pieces of my experiential essays together and discuss my perspectives on the phenomenon of both modern religions as well as religion in general. The five chapters in this book, each with its own set of self-contained footnotes, can essentialy be read in any order that the reader chooses, without detracting from the content of the book. I have put my tri-perspective experiential analysis as the first chapter primarily to give readers an initial relatively more objective informative perspective, as for many of these modern religions I have written experiential essays in the remainder of the book. I put my experiential essays written in the 1990s and 2000s as the second chapter to next convey my more recent experiences with modern religions, in this context referred to as new age spiritual organizations. Chapter Three describes my experiences with five modern religions in the 1970s, and Chapter Four describes my experiences with Scientology.

I would like to state clearly that my relatively more objective analysis in Chapter I, complete with numerical ratings of the cult dangers of twelve modern religions plus five philosophical/spiritual currently active organizations that I consider to be generally beneficial, is primarily still based upon my own experiences with all of these organizations, which is the main theme of this book. This book is not meant to be a scientifically researched historical presentation of the modern religions I have written about. The main theme of this book is that subjective experience is a primary means of learning about life, and can be a valuable means of conveying this knowledge to others. It is my expectation that you the reader will learn more about any of these new age spiritual organizations that interest you, through reading the many available accounts of them (see Chapter One Notes) as well as experiencing for yourselves what these modern religions are all about, though with much carefulness and caution along with an openness to authentic spiritual experience. My goal is simply to convey my own experiences through having thrown myself into an unusual number of personal encounters with a wide variety of modern religions throughout my life.

The motivation for writing Chapter I of this book was initially directly related to my involvement with Ken Wilber's extensive philosophical organization Integral Institute, for possible use in the integral study of new religions through Integral University [1]. Ken Wilber's Integral Four Quadrant model, which can be described as encompassing the realms of Intentional, Behavioral, Cultural, and Social, will be a prime ingredient of the analysis in Chapter I. The Intentional and Behavioral quadrants comprise the inner and outer dynamics within the individual, and the Cultural and Social quadrants can be thought of as the inner and outer dynamics of the individual in relation to his/her society. Wilber's Integral Four Quadrant model is described in detail in most of his more recent books [2]. In addition, I will be making use of the analysis of new religious movements given by Dick Anthony and Bruce Ecker, referred to as The Anthony Typology, and described in their 1987 book *Spiritual Choices*, which is edited by Dick Anthony, Bruce Ecker, and Ken Wilber [3]. I will also be utilizing the Cult Danger Evaluation Frame rating scale given by Isaac Bonewits in his 1971 book *Real Magic* [4], which will serve as a quantitative comparison of all the religious groups I will be discussing. However, as previously stated, although these philosophical research tools will be made use of, the basis of my analysis will remain my own subjective experience with the new religious movements that I am writing about [5]. I believe that there is a rich and special kind of learning about both the beneficial as well as dangerous ingredients inherent in modern religions that is available only through delving into one's personal experiences. As I have been a longtime explorer of modern religions as my own personal journey of spiritual seeking, my main purpose is to convey to people what I have learned through my personal experiences.

I strongly encourage you the reader to pursue your study of any of the modern religions I am describing that interests you, by engaging in your own experiences (when appropriate and relatively safe) and through reading further about them in books that are nowadays easily available, a number of which I list in the chapter notes. The modern religions that have had the most major impact upon me are Scientology, Avatar, Neopaganism, Conversations with God, and Reiki. Other modern religions that I have experienced and will be discussing include The Unification Church (The Moonies), Divine Light Mission, est, Gurdjieff, Eckankar, A Course in Miracles, and Self-Realization Fellowship. Holographic Repatterning and Beshara appear as experiential essays in Chapters 2 and 3 respectively, but are not included in the Chapter I analysis, as my experiences with them were not of a nature that warranted this kind of analysis. I will also be applying my tri-perspective experiential analysis to five organizations that although are generally not considered to be modern religions per se, may prove to be a highly valuable comparison with the modern religious groups that I will be analyzing. These five groups are Tikkun, which is an extremely liberal, inclusive, and peace oriented primarily Jewish organization, Omega Institute for Holistic Studies, which is a well known new age retreat center in New York State, Kripalu Center for Yoga & Health, which is a spiritually oriented yoga and retreat center in western Massachusetts, Twelve Step Support Groups, which are worldwide emotional/ spiritual peer support groups based upon the philosophy of Alcoholics Anonymous, and ICSA (International Cultic Studies Association), which is a worldwide cults awareness and information organization. In the Appendix I apply my Bonewits Cult Danger Evaluation Frame analysis to five more organizations that I believe serve as valuable comparisons to the modern religions I have previously experientially analyzed: Integral Institute, Acceptance and Commitment Therapy (ACT), Human Awareness Institute (HAI), the Center for Creative Consciousness (CCC), and Temple Heights Spiritualist Camp.

Perhaps the biggest obstacle in my way of seriously promoting my *Modern Religions* book is the danger of financial ruin threatened by the legal actions of some of the modern religions that I am writing about, especially Scientology. Scientology is widely known for taking legal action against ex-members and others who write about and promote their critical thoughts and negative experiences with Scientology. Scientology will take a person to court quite easily, as they are tremendously wealthy and have the mission of discouraging damaging public exposures and negative portrayals of their organization, through forcing would-be detractors to meet the financial burdens of expensive lawsuits whether or not Scientology thinks they can win the case. I therefore need to unequivocally make it clear that all statements expressed in this book, including the previous statement I just made about Scientology's motivation for taking legal action against individuals writing about Scientology, are merely my own opinions; in the case of Scientology this is based primarily upon my experiences with Scientology in the 1970s. But in regard to my experiential understanding of Scientology, what I have read about Scientology and discussed with others in more recent years is very secondary to the substantial personal learnings that I have experienced with this organization for two years in the mid 1970s.

I would also like to stress that when I use the term "cult" I am referring to a gradient scale of a number of different characteristics, as described by many authors, and I am specifically using the description by Isaac Bonewits in *Real Magic* (please see Figure 3 on page 18). It is not a matter of whether a particular modern religion is or is not a cult, but of where this modern religion places in what I will refer to as the Bonewits Cult Danger Scale. In this way a relatively objective description can be made of the characteristics that I will take to mean a high level of cult danger. Although the Bonewits Cult Danger scale, Anthony Typology, and Wilber Integral Model will all be utilized in this tri-perspective experiential analysis, I find that these three perspectives are addressing very different viewpoints in regard to describing the cult dangers of modern religions. Essentially I find that both the Anthony Typology and Wilber Integral Model are more based upon a comprehensive theory than the Bonewits Cult Danger Scale (the Wilber Integral Model is extremely comprehensive). However, the Bonewits Cult Danger Scale is exceptionally useful and organic for the purpose of giving a concrete illustration of the actual behaviors that take place in the modern religions I am describing.

For all three perspectives that I am using, I make the qualification "relatively objective" because although I am utilizing concrete rating scales in regard to specific behaviors of a modern religion, I am still relying upon my own experiential framework at the foundation, which is of course my own subjective experience. This combination of subjective experience and objective analysis is very much at the basis of Ken Wilber's Integral theory, and is at the cornerstone of what he describes as a "higher order science" in one of his earlier books, *Eye To Eye* [6]. Lastly, Wilber's Integral Model is intimately related to his Four Quadrant perspective of inter-connecting the Intentional, Behavioral, Cultural, and Social domains in the form of an Integral Transformative Practice (or ITP) [7]. However, it only makes sense to compare the modern religions I am writing about in regard to their high level, Four Quadrant ITP potential if they have a sufficient number of positive characteristics to begin with, and do not rate as a serious cult danger, especially on the Bonewits Cult Danger Scale. For otherwise I am afraid that their four quadrant ITP potential amounts to nothing more than what mathematicians like to refer to as the "empty set." In what follows I will briefly describe the three models that I will be using: the Anthony Typology, the Wilber Integral Model, and the Bonewits Cult Danger Scale.

The Anthony Typology is an eight cell matrix that represents interaction amongst three dual characteristics of new religious movements (in the terminology of Anthony, Ecker, Wilber; see Figure 1 on page 15). These three dual characteristics are Monistic/Dualistic, Technical/Charismatic, and Multilevel/Unilevel. A brief summary of these terms are as follows (see [8] for the following quotes and for more information):

The distinction between monistic and dualistic world views corresponds to a distinction between Eastern and Western religions. In Monistic world views, all individuals are inherently one with the Godhead and will ultimately enjoy that condition consciously. Dualistic world views, however, maintain that not all individuals ultimately achieve salvation; one must qualify by surviving a competitive salvational ordeal or selection process. Those who do not will receive eternal damnation. (p. 36).

In regard to the Technical/Charismatic dimension, Anthony and Ecker describe the distinction as follows:

These categories indicate the nature of a group's practice. In Technical groups, techniques—any repetitive mental or physical processes that can be taught through explicit articulation and instruction—are the basis of seeking spiritual transformation. Common examples include most forms of meditation (such as mantra meditation and visualization meditation), chanting, hatha yoga, and pranayama (breath yoga). In charismatic groups, spiritual attainment is sought primarily through direct, personal relationship with the leader. Because the leader is regarded as a direct link with or embodiment of divine authority, knowledge, and love, contact with such a person is itself considered transformative, particularly sustained contact involving devotion, love, remembrance, attention, and obedience. (p. 39).

Regarding the Multilevel/Unilevel dimension:

These terms describe a group's sensibilities regarding the nature of spiritual transformation and attainment....Unilevel groups err toward trivializing and misreading the nature of genuine spiritual transformation....groups with unilevel sensibilities confuse the attainment of authentic spiritual transcendence or realization with the attainment of mundane psychological satisfaction, inducement of special inner sensations or moods, commitment to a certain set of beliefs....Multlevel groups do not confuse mundane and transcendental consciousness and so foster genuine spiritual inner development. (p. 40).

For Anthony and Ecker, the most serious cult dangers are in the cell which represents Unilevel/Dualistic/Charismatic, in which they include The Unification Church, Synanon (authoritarian anti-drug program popular in the 1970s), and People's Temple (Jonestown tragic mass suicide/murder in the 1970s). On the other end of the spectrum, they expect generally favorable characteristics to be most common in the cells Monistic/ Multilevel/Charismatic and Monistic/Multilevel/Technical. It is interesting that a number of the gurus in these categories (for example Da Free John—also known as Adi Da and by other names, Chogyam Trungpa, Baba Muktananda, Meher Baba, Sri Chimnoy, etc.) have been the source of much negative publicity regarding both their spiritual practices as well as their ethical practices, especially in the cases of Trungpa and Da Free John/Adi Da [9]. It is also interesting that both Anthony and Ecker are devotees of Meher Baba, and the Charismatic dimension is considered by them to be of the highest context if an authentic guru can be found. Suffice it to say that I do not agree with them on this point, as I believe there are numerous problems and pitfalls with the Charismatic dimension, but I still find the Anthony Typology to be both informative and useful, in context and combination with other schemes.

Ken Wilber's Integral model is a very different kind of scheme from the Anthony Typology, as Wilber's Four Quadrant Integral model is designed to be all encompassing, although in Wilber's more recent development of his integral theory he has expanded his four quadrants into eight "perspectives" [10]. However, it appears that Wilber's Four Quadrant Integral model is highly consistent with the Anthony Typology in regard to describing the cult dangers of what Anthony, Ecker, and Wilber refer to as new religious movements [11]. The primary relationship of Wilber's Integral Model to a description of the cult dangers of new religious movements can be simplified by a generalization of Wilber's three general categories: pre-rational, rational, and trans-rational in the Intentional and Cultural domains. The generalization I have in mind is to add a fourth category in-between pre-rational and rational, which I will call "pseudo-rational." This new category is essentially not at all new in Wilber's original model, as it can be viewed as the mythic level of consciousness, which Wilber places in-between the magical level and the rational level, and would include our dominant religious institutions such as Judaism, Christianity, Islam, etc. (see [2]; in particular Wilber's book *Sex, Ecology, Spirituality*). I believe that my new category describes the modern religions that I have experienced as engaging in this kind of mythological thinking, though in a seemingly quite modern—or even "scientific" manner. However, the level of consciousness I am referring to is anything but scientific; in some cases it can be considered "pseudo-scientific," and in general I will refer to it as "pseudo-rational." Wilber discussed his ideas about confusing the pre-rational and trans-rational levels of consciousness in his essay *The Pre-Trans Fallacy* in his book *Eye To Eye* (see [6]), and he described in much more detail the specific stages of archaic, magical, mythic, rational, psychic (or vision logic), subtle, causal, and non-dual in many of his books (see [2]). In his subsequent work he has described levels of development in the Behavioral (individual) as well as Social dimensions, which interact with the Intentional (individual) and Cultural dimensions to comprise his Integral Four Quadrant model, and more recently his expanded Integral Eight Perspective model (see [2], [10]).

In regard to the most useful aspects of Wilber's Integral model for our purposes, we will use my generalization of Wilber's more simplified model, i.e. the pre-rational/pseudo-rational/rational/trans-rational spectrum to describe the levels of consciousness of the groups that I will be discussing. Wilber also discussed in his essay *The Spectrum Model* in *Spiritual Choices* [8], the likelihood that a beneficial authentic group, in addition to being trans-rational or "transformative," and not pre-rational (and I will take the liberty of adding "not pseudo-rational"), will anchor its "legitimacy" in a tradition as opposed to a sudden rise to power and prominence, and has an authority that is "phase-specific," meaning that the guru is a guide and mentor and has the goal of transferring his/her (mostly "his") authority to others, once the appropriate high level of consciousness is achieved by others [12]. In regard to Wilber's Four Quadrant Integral model, I will be making use of the ideas behind the four quadrant personal integration of an ITP (Integral Transformative Practice) as described in the book *The Life We Are Given* by George Leonard and Michael Murphy (see [7]), as well as by Wilber in *A Theory of Everything* (see [2]) and some of his other more recent books, to further evaluate the cult dangers of the modern religions that I have experienced. However, I will once again emphasize the stipulation that this ITP analysis only makes sense if the modern religion has a high enough rating on all three models to begin with. For example, after reading about Scientology in Chapter 4, you may ask yourself the following question: how well integrated is a Scientologist in regard to truly being part of the culture in which he/she lives aside from her/his specific Scientology involvement? Finally, in regard to a description of Wilber's four quadrant levels of the spectrum in his Integral model, I have taken the liberty of adding on the higher levels in the Intentional quadrant, as Wilber does not generally list these in his books (see Figure 2 on pages 16-17).

We now come to what will be pragmatically the most useful scheme to describe the cult dangers of the modern religions I will be discussing, which is Isaac Bonewits' Cult Danger Evaluation Frame, which I will refer to as the Bonewits Cult Danger Scale, as described in his book *Real Magic* (see [4] and Figure 3). This is a rating scale from 1 to 10 (1 is lowest and 10 is highest) for the level of agreement with 15 statements that describe characteristics of cults, including items such as internal control, dogma, recruitment, censorship, sexual manipulation, and endorsement of violence. There have been numerous articles and books written in the field of cult studies in the past 30 years [13], and a number of rating scales have been utilized to engage in research about cults. However, I find Bonewits' cult danger scale to be quite simple to use, and I believe it immediately gets to the heart of the matter in regard to the dangerous cult characteristics of a modern religion. *Real Magic* is by no means an anti-cult book; it is a classic book in the movement of Neopaganism, which is one of the modern religions I have written quite favorably about [14]. I find it refreshing to utilize a cult danger scale in a book whose primary purpose is not to expose the cult dangers of new religious movements. At any rate, I believe that the Bonewits Cult Danger Scale will be extremely useful in giving us an organic and concrete illustration of the cult characteristics of the modern religions I am describing.

I will be arriving at a cult danger "number" for each one of the modern religions I describe, based upon the average number rating across the fifteen cult danger characteristics on this scale. It is quite possible that a modern religion can be in one of the "safer" cells of the Anthony Typology, such as Multilevel/Monism, or be placed on the trans-rational level in Wilber's Integral Model, and yet display a number of serious danger rankings in the Bonewits Cult Danger Scale. From what I have read and seen about Da Free John/Adi Da (see [9]), I would say that Da Free John/Adi Da is a good illustration of this occurring, although certainly Da Free John/Adi Da would fail Wilber's criteria of anchoring its legitimacy in a tradition as well as being engaged in a phase-specific authority. But both the Anthony Typology and Wilber Integral Model give us useful theoretical models of how a study of the cult dangers of modern religions can be approached. Using them in conjunction with a model such as the Bonewits Cult Danger Scale, we have a dynamic interplay of criteria to measure in a relatively objective way how an individual experiences the cult dangers of a modern religion.

The remainder of this book covers two periods of time. The first time period is roughly the five years from the beginning of 1975, when I first became interested in Scientology, until the beginning of 1980, when I had completed recording my experiences in various recently formed religious organizations, as well as integrating these experiences into my own philosophy of life. The second time period is roughly the fifteen years from 1995, when I found myself in a romantic relationship with a devotee of Eckankar, to the present time when I am assimilating my explorations of a whole new set of recently formed religious organizations as well as revisiting my process of assimilating my explorations into my philosophy of life. The way in which I began writing about my experiences in what I refer to as modern religions occurred in the following way. From time to time I would find myself writing a cathartic essay in a stream of consciousness, not having any real purpose except to express myself, after a vivid and emotional experience with some kind of organization that I had gotten heavily involved with. My very first experiential essay, which I wrote in 1975, a few months after my high school teaching experience in the Black and Mexican-American ghettos of Houston, Texas, I called *The Natural Dimension and Society*. I asked myself what it meant to be a "natural" human being, a "natural" seeker of knowledge. I was gearing myself more as a teacher, thinking about how to educate our children, but I was in for quite a surprise. For this was the same time that I began to experience the most penetrating, challenging, mind-molding, and also exhilarating educational upheaval of my life. I am talking about the Church of Scientology of Boston. It was an incredibly stimulating experience for me; before I could even think about what I was doing, I found myself spending ten hours a day, six or seven days a week, studying the ideas of one man: L. Ron Hubbard. Everybody around me was fanatically believing everything they were being taught. And we were being taught some extremely unconventional and bizarre things (see Chapter 4). What kept me from totally losing my own unique selfhood, like so many of my fellow-Scientologists? I kept thinking about the "free mind," the mind that we were given to explore anything and everything under the sun, no holds barred. With this mind, one should not be afraid to delve into anything, including Scientology. With this frame of mind, I took the leap and dared all the forces of hell to warp my mind. With help from my "real" friends, especially my ex-wife Diane, I managed to retain my sanity, keep what I referred to as my "natural dimension" [15], and eventually reach a point of transcendence and assimilation of Scientology into my conscious awareness, integrating L. Ron Hubbard's unique philosophy into all that I had previously learned of life.

This integration began in January, 1977 with my first Scientology essays: *On Scientology* and *The Engram and the Dream*. From there, all my essays on Scientology just burst out of me, within a two day period. This was what I had been waiting for—for two years. I felt like publishing all my essays on Scientology right away, but something inside of me said to be patient. I applied to a doctoral psychology program at the Humanistic Psychology Institute, with the intention of writing a dissertation on the relationship of religion to psychology. I decided to seek out other modern religious movements, but this time with a firm purpose in mind: as a student of professional humanistic psychology. With this purpose I took Werner Erhard's est training in April, 1977 in New York. I became fascinated at how much of est was taken from Scientology. At this time I also recalled the experiences

I had had with Reverend Sun Myung Moon's Unification Church and Guru Maharajii's Divine Light Mission. I began to see various threads that united these seemingly diverse religious movements, and I became determined to put all the pieces together.

I moved to Berkeley, California to begin my doctoral psychology program, pursued my study of est, encountered "Moonies" on the streets, discovered Gurdjieff and Occultism in San Francisco, and became thoroughly familiar with the world of humanistic psychology. I finally decided that my free-style writing form was too dear to me to compromise in doctoral dissertation form and regulation, and I therefore decided to indefinitely postpone my goal of becoming a professional psychologist and I put all my energies into synthesizing the book that had been such a living part of me all those years. It was during this period of time, from the beginning of 1979 until the end of 1980, that I wrote most of the essays in Chapter 5 of this book: *The Phenomenon of Religion*, as well as my semi-autobiographical novel: *The Maturation of Walter Goldman*. Scientology related excerpts of my novel appear in Chapter 4 of this book: *Encounters with Scientology*. These excerpts are included because I believe that they illustrate in an authentic, dramatic, and nuts and bolts way my own experience of being immersed in Scientology. Walter, the hero in my novel, is essentially me. Walter's friend and initial mentor Zachary, who eventually succumbs to his own guru and cult indoctrinations, is in reality none other than my boyhood friend Richie, the source of all my writings about Guru Maharajji and Divine Light Mission in Chapter 3 of this book: *Encounters with Some Modern Religions in the 1970s*.

For a number of reasons I did not publish my book or any of my essays at that time. I actually did very little in regard to religion, modern or traditional, for the next fifteen years. I opened up my philosophy to the world in the form of a business venture and non-profit corporation: Natural Dimension Teaching Agency, became a father, got divorced, moved to Maine, bought a house, began my career as a mathematics professor at a small college in rural Maine, started doing pure mathematics research that eventually enabled me to earn my Ph.D. in mathematics, wrote my mathematics enrichment book: *Numberama: Recreational Number Theory in the School System* [16], conducted Numberama mathematics enrichment workshops in various places in the United States, and began a sequence of romantic relationships that lasted on the average a year or two. However, as fate would have it, one of these romantic relationships was the stimulation for me to return to the exploration of modern religions that I had begun in my twenties. In 1995 I became involved in a romantic relationship with a devotee of Eckankar, who was also a practitioner of Holographic Repatterning [17]. When this relationship ended in 1997, somehow my inner system was ready to re-explore modern religions, and I gave myself quite the crash course. Summer of 1997 I encountered A Course in Miracles, Self-Realization Fellowship, Avatar, Reiki, Conversations with God, and Neopaganism, and I decided to refer to my re-emergence as New Age Spiritual Explorations [18]. After my initial experience of Reiki in 1997, I attended Reiki sharing sessions for about a year, and then two years later I began a three year romantic relationship with a Reiki master that ended in 2004. This three year romantic relationship has been the source of most of my essays on Reiki. Both my Reiki source/ex-girlfriend as well as my son Jeremy helped me get relatively more current on Scientology, as described in my first essay in Chapter 2: *Scientology in the 21ˢᵗ Century.*

In January, 2005 I began a romantic relationship with the woman whom I am still very much involved with, in a wonderfully harmonious way for the past six years. In March, 2008 I enrolled in the Ph.D. psychology program at Saybrook University, which is the same school (with a different name) as the Humanistic Psychology Institute, which is the original doctoral psychology program that I was involved in for five months in 1977, thirty three years ago. My concentration is Consciousness and Spirituality, and I am presently working on my Ph.D. dissertation, which is an experiential exploration of the possibility of life after death though the ostensible communications of mediums with deceased persons.

I am currently teaching transpersonal psychology on-line at Akamai University, and in-person at a community college in Maine. I have twenty nine published article on Frank Visser's Integral World website (see [1]), and over fourty-five additional published articles in a variety of fields, including humanistic and transpersonal psychology, spirituality and the awareness of cult dangers, art and mental disturbance, pure mathematics, and mathematics enrichment.

The perspective that I am coming from in this book is that of an experiential philosopher and researcher. I very much believe that both philosophy and research needs to be experienced in the very core of our beings, not just in our intellectual minds [19]. I am in essential agreement with Ken Wilber in this regard, though I have mixed feelings about Wilber and his Integral World organization in regard to a number of other aspects [20]. The experiential essays that I have included in Chapters 2, 3, 4, and parts of Chapter 5, are examples of what has been described as "autoethnography" [21]. Autoethnography allows for a researcher to include her/his own thoughts, feelings, reflections, intuitions, insights, experiences, and personally engaged self when describing cultural phenomena, extending the more traditionally objective anthropological and sociological ethnographic studies of cultures and societies (see [21]). It is expected that an autoethnographic researcher write in a personal intimate way to reflect upon his/her own experiential learnings in the environments being explored, and my writings in the above mentioned chapters certainly fall under this heading. The personal exploratory nature of my writings also go hand-in-hand with the heuristic inquiry research of Clark Moustakas (see [21]). Heuristic inquiry is a way of engaging in what can be thought of as "extended science" research through methods and processes aimed at discovery; a way of self-inquiry and dialogue with others with the goal of finding the underlying meaning of important human experiences (see Moustakas' book *Heuristic Research* and [21] for the reference).

Some of the essays and experiential analyses in this book have been published in various journals or websites [22]. There are chapter notes after the Introduction and each of the five chapters, containing assorted references that include listings of recommended books for each of the new age spiritual organizations/modern religions that I have written about. This book is my way of essentially searching for God, thinking of the term God in a broad sense as First Cause, Primal Energy, etc., and I state my own view of the true meaning of religion in my last essay of this book: *Life Without Religion?* With this last essay I invite you to search and explore your own pure form of religion, but I also caution you to be extremely careful to not lose your real self and thereby fall into the temptations, manipulations, and serious dangers that I describe in a number of the pages of this book.

NOTE: The first part of the Appendix: *On Ken Wilber's Integral Institute: An Experiential Analysis*, has been added to the book in July, 2006. This is a continuation along the lines of my tri-perspective experiential analysis in Chapter 1, and is self-contained with its own references as it appears on the Integral World website and on the ICSA E-Newsletter, Vol. 6, No. 2, 2007 (http://www.integralworld.net and http://cultinfobooks.com.) The second part of the Appendix: *The Boundary Between Cultic, Benign, and Beneficial in Five Spiritual Groups* has been added to the book in May, 2008. This article is based upon my talk at the ICSA conference in Philadelphia in June, 2008, is also self contained with its own references, and includes the Bonewits Cult Danger Scale analysis for Conversations with God, Avatar, The Center for Creative Consciousness (CCC), Acceptance and Commitment Therapy (ACT), and Human Awareness Institute (HAI). The article appeared in the ICSA E-Newsletter, Vol. 7, No. 3, 2008. The third part of the Appendix: *An Experiential Analysis of the Cult Dangers of a Spiritualist Camp*, has been added to the book in November, 2010. This is an excerpt from my unpublished article that also includes the topics of extended science, auto-hermeneutics, and an experiential analysis of the possibility of life after death through the ostensible communications of mediums with deceased persons. The fourth part of the Appendix: *Neopagan Rituals: An Experiential Account*, has been added to the book in December, 2010. This article was published in Coreopsis: A Journal of Myth and Theatre, Vol. 2, No. 1, 2010.

FIGURE 1: THE ANTHONY TYPOLOGY

MULTILEVEL/MONISTIC/ TECHNICAL	MULTILEVEL/DUALISTIC/ TECHNICAL
MULTIILEVEL/ MONISTIC/CHARISMATIC	MULTILEVEL/DUALISTIC/ CHARISMATIC
UNIILEVEL/MONISTIC/ TECHNICAL	UNILEVEL/DUALISTIC/ TECHNICAL
UNILEVEL/MONISTIC/ CHARISMATIC	UNILEVEL/DUALISTIC/ CHARISMATIC

FIGURE 2: THE WILBER FOUR QUADRANT INTEGRAL MODEL

QUADRANT 1: UPPER LEFT INTERIOR-INDIVIDUAL (INTENTIONAL)	QUADRANT 2: UPPER RIGHT EXTERIOR-INDIVIDUAL (BEHAVIORAL)
PREHENSION	ATOMS
IRRITABILITY	MOLECULES
SENSATION	PROKARYOTES
PERCEPTION	EUKARYOTES
IMPULSE	NEURONAL ORGANISMS
EMOTION	NEURAL CORD
SYMBOLS	REPTILIAN BRAIN STEM
CONCEPTS	LIMBIC SYSTEM
CONCRETE OPERATIONAL	NEOCORTEX (TRIUNE BRAIN)
FORMAL OPERATIONAL	COMPLEX NEOCORTEX
VISION-LOGIC	SF1
PSYCHIC	SF2
SUBTLE	SF3
CAUSAL	(SF1, SF2, and SF3 are postulated as higher order exterior structures)
NON-DUAL	

QUADRANT 3: LOWER LEFT INTERIOR-COLLECTIVE (CULTURAL)	QUADRANT 4: LOWER RIGHT EXTERIOR-COLLECTIVE (SOCIAL)
PHYSICAL	GALAXIES
PLEROMATIC	PLANETS
PROTOPLASMIC	GAIA SYSTEM
VEGETATIVE	HETEROTROPHIC ECOSYSTEMS
LOCOMOTIVE	SOCIETIES WITH DIVISION OF LABOR
UROBORIC	GROUPS/FAMILIES
TYPHONIC	TRIBES (FORAGING)
ARCHAIC	TRIBAL/VILLAGE (HORTICULTURAL)
MAGIC	EARLY STATE (AGRARIAN)
MYTHIC	NATION STATE (INDUSTRIAL)
RATIONAL	PLANETARY (INFORMATIONAL)
CENTAURIC	

NOTE: In Wilber's model there is a generic correspondence between the interior and exterior quadrants for the individual and collective domains respectively; however, this correspondence is not an exact one-to-one correspondence, but rather a general indication.

FIGURE 3: THE BONEWITS CULT DANGER SCALE

1. **INTERNAL CONTROL**: amount of internal political power exercised by leader(s) over members.

2. **WISDOM CLAIMED**: by leader(s); amount of infallibility declared about decisions.

3. **WISDOM CREDITED**: to leaders by members; amount of trust in decisions made by leader(s).

4. **DOGMA**: rigidity of reality concepts taught; of amount of doctrinal inflexibility.

5. **RECRUITING**: emphasis put on attracting new members, amount of proselytizing.

6. **FRONT GROUPS**: number of subsidiary groups using a different name from that of the main group.

7. **WEALTH**: amount of money and/or property desired or obtained; emphasis on members' donations.

8. **POLITICAL POWER**: amount of external political influence desired or obtained.

9. **SEXUAL MANIPULATION**: of members by leader(s); amount of control over the lives of members.

10. **CENSORSHIP**: amount of control over members' access to outside opinions on group, its doctrines or leader(s).

11. **DROPOUT CONTROL**: intensity of efforts directed at preventing or returning dropouts.

12. **ENDORSEMENT OF VIOLENCE**: when used by or for the group or its leader(s).

13. **PARANOIA**: amount of fear concerning real or imagined enemies; perceived power of opponents.

14. **GRIMNESS**: amount of disapproval concerning jokes about the group, its doctrines or leaders(s).

15. **SURRENDER OF WILL**: emphasis on members not having to be responsible for personal decisions.

RATING SCALE

LOW   **HIGH**

1   2   3   4   5   6   7   8   9   10

INTRODUCTION NOTES

1) For information on Integral Institute, see www.integralinstitute.org, www.kenwilber.com, and www.integralworld.net. I did not become involved with Integral University; for more information about my perspective on Ken Wilber and Integral Institute, see my article: *On Ken Wilber's Integral Institute:An Experiential Analysis*, which is included in the Appendix (see Appendix: Part I).

2) See for example: *Sex, Ecology, Spirituality* (Boston: Shambhala, 1995), *Integral Psychology* (Boston: Shambhala, 2000), *A Brief History of Everything* (Boston: Shambhala, 2000), *The Eye of Spirit* (Boston: Shambhala, 2001), and *A Theory of Everything* (Boston: Shambhala, 2001).

3) Anthony, D., Ecker, B., & Wilber, K. (Eds.) (1987). *Spiritual Choices*. New York: Paragon House.

4) Bonewits, I. (1989). *Real Magic*. York Beach, Maine: Samuel Weisner (original work published 1971).

5) The focus upon a researcher's relevant subjective experiences as an important component of his/her research is controversial in mainstream psychology. However, there are a number of researchers in psychology who have advocated this approach, generally as part of what is referred to as "intersubjective" and "qualitative" studies that include the experiences of both the participants and the researchers. See in particular the books *Heuristic Research: Design, Methodology, and Applications* by Clark Moustakas (1990); London: Sage, and *Transpersonal Research Methods for the Social Sciences* by William Braud and Rosemarie Anderson (1998); London: Sage. In regard to my idea of utilizing a qualitative/quantitative experiential system to describe my experiences in various religious/spiritual/philosophical groups that I am experientially describing, I would like to thank Nori Muster, author of *Betrayal of the Spirit* (see [13] in Introduction

Notes for reference) for first suggesting this idea to me, after she wrote a book review for an earlier draft of *Modern Religions* (see back cover). I later co-facilitated a Spirituality and Cults workshop with Nori at an ICSA conference, and I found the portrayal of her experiences with the Hari Krishna movement, which she also described in her aforementioned book, to be fascinating.

6) Wilber, K. (2001). *Eye to Eye*. Boston: Shambhala (original work published 1983).

7) See George Leonard & Michael Murphy (1995), *The Life We are Given*; New York: Tarcher/Putnam, for a detailed description of an Integral Transformative Practice.

8) See *Part I: The Anthony Typology: A Framework for Assessing Spiritual and Consciousness Groups*; by Dick Anthony and Bruce Ecker, in *Spiritual Choices* (see [3] for reference).

9) See Geoffrey Falk (2005*), Stripping the Gurus* (www.angelin.com /trek/geoffreyfalk/blog/blog.hm) for a particularly scathing exposé of these groups and many others.

10) Wilber, K. (2006). *Integral Spirituality*. Boston: Shambhala.

11) See the *Editorial Commentary* (pp. 260-264) after Wilber's chapter *The Spectrum Model* in *Spiritual Choices* (see [3] for reference).

12) See *The Spectrum Model* chapter in *Eye to Eye* (see [6] for reference), and Wilber's (2005) book. *A Sociable God*. Boston: Shambhala (original work published 1983) for more explanation regarding the meanings and distinctions of all these terms.

13) See for example Margaret Singer & Janja Lalich (1996), *Cults in Our Midst*; San Francisco: Jossey-Bass; Steve Hassan (1990), *Combating Cult Mind Control* (Rochester, Vermont: Park Street Press; Steve Hassan, *Releasing The Bonds* (2000); Somerville, MA: Freedom of Mind Press; Nori Muster (2001), *Betrayal of the Spirit*; Chicago: University of Illinois Press; Michael Langone (editor) (1993), *Recovery from Cults*; New York: W.W. Norton & Co.

14) See my essay *On Neopaganism* in Chapter 2, reference [77] in Chapter One Notes, the section on Neopaganism in Chapter 1, and my 2010 Coreopsis journal article *Neopagan Rituals: an Experiential Account*, which comprises Appendix: Part 4.

15) For more information about my philosophy of natural dimension, see my 2006 Integral World essay: *My Conception of Integral* (www.integralworld.net)

16) Benjamin, E. (1993). *Numberama: Recreational Number Theory in the school system*. Swanville, ME: Natural Dimension Publications.

17) See my essays *On Eckankar* and *On Holographic Repatterning* in Chapter 2, as well as the Eckankar section in Chapter 1.

18) For all of these new age spiritual organizations, see Chapter 2 for experiential essays and Chapter 1 for a tri-perspective experiential analysis.

19) See Bentz, V. M., & Shapiro, J. J. (1998). *Mindful inquiry in social research*. London: Sage, as well as my essay *My Conception of Integral* (see [15] in Chapter One Notes for reference).

20) See my essay: *On Ken Wilber's Integral Institute: An Experiential Analysis* in the Appendix; this essay has appeared as published articles in the ICSA E-Newsletter and the Integral World website (see www.icsahome.com and www.integralworld.net).

21) See Chang, H. V. (2008). *Autoethnography as method (Developing autoethnographic inquiry)*.Walnut Creek, CA: Left Hand Press; Ellis, C. (2009). *Revision: Autoethnographic reflections of life and work (Writing Lives)*. Walnut Creek, CA: Left Hand Press; Moustakas, C. (1990). *Heuristic research: Design, methodology, and applications*. London: Sage.

22) The journals and websites where I have published articles related to experiential essays and analyses in this book are: Coreopsis: A Journal of Myth and Theatre (http://sites.google.com/site/mythandtheatre/), the Ground of Faith journal (http://homepages.ihug.nz/~thegroundoffaith/issues), PagaNet News (www.paganet.org), ICSA E-Newsletter (www.icsahaome.com), Inner Tapestry journal (www.innertapestry.org), Integral World website (www.integralworld.net), Integral Science website (www.integralscience.org), and the Rick Ross website (www.rickross.com).

CHAPTER 1

A TRI-PERSPECTIVE EXPERIENTIAL ANALYSIS OF MODERN RELIGIONS

SCIENTOLOGY

In Chapter 4: *Encounters with Scientology* I have described my own personal experiences with the religion of Scientology in the 1970s in a collection of twelve essays written during that time period, two of which were written a few years after I left Scientology. In that chapter I have also included some excerpts from my semi-autobiographical novel *The Maturation of Walter Goldman*, where the main character gets caught up in a fictional Scientology organization. In addition, in Chapter 2: *New Age Spiritual Explorations In The 1990s and 2000s*, I have included an essay I wrote in 2002 describing my relatively more recent mini-explorations of Scientology in Los Angeles and Maine. What I will do in the Scientology part of this chapter is to analyze Scientology in regard to the measurement vehicles of the Anthony Typology, the Wilber Integral Model, and the Bonewits Cult Danger Scale, based upon what I have learned about Scientology from my own experiences with them in the 1970s, as described in Chapter 4. The interested reader can easily find out more information about Scientology [1].

To begin with, in the Anthony Typology Scientology is placed in the Monistic/Unilevel/Charismatic cell, with overlap into the Monistic/Unilevel/Charismatic cell. However, based upon my own experiences with Scientology I do have some concerns about both of these classifications. This classification scheme becomes rather vague and not especially illustrative for a number of reasons. Scientology claims to be open to all people, and they certainly proselytize to the world—quite successfully for that matter. However, I believe they also very much belong in an Us vs.Them category of Scientology vs. non-Scientology, one illustration of which can be seen by their term "wog," an abbreviation meaning "wise old gentleman," used as a derogatory condescending label for a non-Scientologist [2]. Scientologists all have the potential to go "Clear" and 'OT" (Operating Thetan) [3], whereas non-Scientologists are doomed to live their lives governed by their "reactive minds" and chained by their "engrams." Does this not seem like the makings of a modern religion that smacks of Dualistic in the extreme? Which is it—Monistic or Dualistic? Perhaps the choice of category itself is the problem here, as Anthony and Ecker concede when they initially place Scientology in the Technical cell, stating that there is also overlap in the Charismatic cell. And they are quite correct, as along with the overpowering and overwhelming amount of Scientology technical materials there is the awe-inspiring continuous presence of Scientology founder and guru L. Ron Hubbard, whose picture is all over the Scientology surroundings, constantly watching over each and every Scientologist in his/her Scientology endeavors. Until his death in the mid 1980s, Hubbard would furnish the whole Scientology organization with continuous detailed memos full of instructions on how a Scientologist should behave in both personal as well as Scientology ways. Yes—extremely high technology and extremely high charisma; these are the hallmarks of Scientology. And I certainly do agree in general with Anthony and Ecker that Scientology belongs in the cell of Unilevel as opposed to Multilevel, signifying that what one experiences from Scientology is not authentic spirituality, but rather a psychological catharsis that is on a lower level than true spiritual realization. However, although I would not argue with this general classification, in all fairness I must question exactly where one can draw the line here. As much as I have written about the dangers of Scientology, I cannot honestly claim that it is not possible for someone experiencing a cathartic release of engrams in the process of "auditing" (Scientology growth therapy) [4] to experience a more spiritual state as well. My main point is that at least for the case of Scientology, something more concrete and revealing than the Anthony Typology is needed to accurately describe its cult dangers.

In examining the Wilber Integral Model for Scientology, the first question is: where exactly is Scientology in the pre-rational/pseudo-rational/rational/trans-rational continuum? Certainly Scientology engages the rational mind in an impressive display of heightened intellectual activity [5]. However, is this embracing of the rational mind truly what Wilber refers to when he writes about the logical/rational level of consciousness? Free logical/rational inquiry is epitomized by the extensive high level logical thought processes exhibited by for example mathematicians, scientists, philosophers, and lawyers. When it comes to having ideas other than those espoused by Scientology, from my experience there is a Scientology ruling that these ideas are not allowed to be expressed, and are even monitored by the Hubbard E-Meter, a type of Scientology lie detector and auditing physiological machine [6]. So does Scientology engage on the rational level of consciousness? In my experience, although Scientology is rational up to a point, it goes rather backwards to more primitive mythological levels of consciousness.

Some of the descriptions of the O.T.post-Clear levels do sound to me like quite far-fetched science-fiction accounts of stories of other galaxies, but unfortunately many people spend thousands of dollars to gain these levels of experience [7]. As I understand it, the essential way to distinguish between pre-rational and trans-rational is to determine if the rational mind is fully engaged and "transcended" [8], or instead bypassed and regressed into a lower level of consciousness. I contend that it is this lower regression quality that Scientology practices, but to be generous and give Scientology the benefit of the doubt for its undeniably strong focus upon the mind, I shall put Scientology in the pseudo-rational category and not the pre-rational category. The overwhelming success which Scientology has experienced throughout the world in the first half century of its existence may be substantial evidence that many people do not view Scientology as a pre-rational level of consciousness (of course a Scientologist does not view Scientology as a pseudo-rational level of consciousness either). But for any free mind who has been through and out of Scientology, I believe it is quite evident that Scientology is a very obvious example of what I have defined to be a pseudo-rational level of consciousness. In regard to Wilber's other criteria, I believe the picture is even more clear. In my opinion, the legitimacy of Scientology is something that was invented by L. Ron Hubbard and not part of any continuing tradition. The name "Scientology" itself suggests modernism in its very core. And Wilber's category of phase-specific authority is quite obviously completely violated in the case of Hubbard and Scientology. Hubbard's writings are the gospel of Scientology, beginning with his first book in 1950: *Dianetics: The Modern Science of Mental Health* (see [1]) that launched Dianetics as the precursor of Scientology. L. Ron Hubbard died in the mid 1980s, but he is now worshipped as a bona-fide perfect human being in the company of Jesus and Buddha [9].

When we examine Scientology regarding the Bonewits Cult Danger Scale, the picture finally becomes quite concrete. As I promised in the Introduction, we shall emerge with an actual mathematical number to describe the cult dangers of Scientology and to compare it to the cult dangers of the other modern religions that I am writing about. Of course this is based upon my own ratings of Scientology, which is based primarily upon my subjective experiences with them in the 1970s, but it will at least give us a sense of how a more relatively objective concrete description of the cult dangers of a modern religion can be made. Based upon my own experience and knowledge of Scientology, here are my ratings; once again the ratings are from 1 to 10 with 1 the lowest and 10 the highest; see Figure 3 in the Introduction for a verbatim description by Bonewits (1971/1989) of his Cult Danger Evaluation Frame as listed in *Real Magic* (p. 215) (see [4] in Introduction Notes for reference).

Internal Control	10
Wisdom Claimed	10
Wisdom Credited	10
Dogma	10
Recruiting:	10
Front Groups	8
Wealth	10
Political Power	7
Sexual Manipulation	5
Censorship	10
Dropout Control	8
Endorsement of Violence	5
Paranoia	10
Grimness	10
Surrender of Will	7
TOTAL	**130**
AVERAGE	**8.7**

NOTE: The average ratings will all be approximated to one decimal place.

We thus have our first numerical cult danger score. Scientology comes in at the extremely high cult danger rating of 8.7, though a few words of explanation may be in order for how I rated Scientology in some of these categories. All the "10" ratings clearly demonstrate my perceptions of Scientology in these categories. The "8" rating for Dropout Control refers only to those dropouts who do not publicly voice their complaints about Scientology; for dropouts who go public with exposés, the rating is 10+. In regard to the "5" rating on sexual manipulation, although I am not aware of any blatant sexual manipulations in Scientology, it is drilled into Scientologists that a non-Scientologist needs to be converted, especially one whom you are married to (once again from my own experiences with Scientology). In regard to Endorsement of Violence, actual physical violence is not something that has been concretely linked to Scientology, only alluded to and investigated. But mental violence in regard to lawsuits, harassment, and spreading of false rumors with the intent of destroying a person's reputation as well as mental health (from my own experiences as well as readings about Scientology) would be a 10+. Surrender of Will is also a tricky category, as Scientology certainly supports its celebrity stars in continuing and extending their careers, such as John Travolta and Tom Cruise, as this strongly serves to benefit Scientology. However, the common practices of Scientology, in my involvement with the organization in the 1970s, was to encourage Scientologists to join their staff and serve two and a half and five year contracts, in which surrender of will to Scientology and L. Ron Hubbard was very much at the crux of what transpired [10] (once again from the perspective of my own experiences). In regard to the "8" rating for Front Groups, Scientology does have a number of front groups, such as Hubbard business colleges (see [9]) and the Scientology take-over of the Cults Awareness Network (from what has been reported in ICSA), but there are modern religions that I believe promote the front group orchestration even more fully, such as The Unification Church. I would make a similar statement comparing The Unification Church to Scientology in regard to Political Power; however, there are forms of political power, such as Scientology's attacks upon the profession of psychiatry, in which they most certainly deserve a 10+ rating (in my opinion). But enough said about Scientology, as we shall now proceed to our second modern religion for relatively objective analysis, which is Werner Erhard's est (officially spelled with small letters) organization, prominent in the 1970s and 1980s.

est

I did the est training in New York City in 1977, a few months after I left Scientology. Werner Erhard, the founder of est, had himself explored Scientology, and we can find a number of ingredients of Scientology in the est training, as I describe in my est essays in Chapter 3, and which can be found in more depth in a number of other books [11]. est was one of the early successful LGATs (Large Group Awareness Trainings), and this new age large group format has become increasingly more common in recent years [12]. In *Spiritual Choices* there is a recorded interview with Werner Erhard [13], quite a rare occurrence from what I understand. In this interview there is much friction and differences of opinion between Erhard and his more open-minded interviewers, as Erhard highlights the philosophy of est, maintaining that virtually everyone who does the est training experiences "enlightenment" as a result of the two weekend est training, in the company of 250 to 300 strangers in hotel ballrooms. The form of this enlightenment experienced is the realization that you are already perfect exactly as you are, and there is nothing you need to attain or seek in life in order to become happy.

In the Anthony Typology est is placed primarily in the Unilevel/Monistic/Technical cell, but this placement is not at all strict, as the authors also show that est could be in the Multilevel/Monistic/Technical cell (which is one of the two most favorable cells, according to Anthony and Ecker). The editors of *Spiritual Choices* certainly have mixed feelings about est, as they discuss in their commentary after the Werner Erhard interview. Essentially their conflict revolves around the question of does est give people the experience of authentic spirituality, or does it merely promote the psychological well-being feeling along with a reinforcement of worldly attainment. I can well understand their conflict, as I myself felt quite conflicted after doing both the est training and two-thirds of a graduate est seminar in San Francisco, as can be seen from my est essays in Chapter 3. Once again, as in the case of Scientology, est does not seem to fit conveniently into any one category. I would have to agree with the editors of *Spiritual Choices* that there were aspects of est that focused upon authentic spirituality as well as aspects that focused upon more ordinary psychology and worldly concerns; i.e. aspects that were Multilevel and aspects that were Unilevel. I would also agree with the editors that est was

2

essentially Monistic and not Dualistic; i.e. est was truly open to all people and did not seem to act in the extreme Us vs. Them condescending superior manner in which I described Scientology, which was the reason I argued for Scientology being in the Dualistic cell. In regard to the Technical/Charismatic distinction, I find the picture to be more complicated than Anthony, Ecker, and Wilber have described. The *Spiritual Choicse* editors placed est in the Technical cell, and it is true that there is certainly a heavy concentration of psychological processes and stimulating philosophical material presented in the course of the two weekend est training. However, it is also true that Werner Erhard was a magnetically charismatic guru figure to his est followers [14]. Putting all this together we find that est can be described to be Multilevel as well as Unilevel, and Technical as well as Charismatic. It seems that as in the case of Scientology, it is necessary to look at our other models in order to gain more understanding of the cult dangers of est.

In regard to the Wilber Integral Model, I would certainly place est in a less negative category than Scientology. From my own experience of having done the est training, I must say that est does engage in completely utilizing the rational mind (to the point of mental exhaustion, intentionally and skillfully orchestrated by the est trainers) and then supercedes the rational mind with an experience that goes beyond the rational [15]. This was my own experience after the second est weekend when I completed the est training. Whether all 250 people taking part in the est training actually experienced this "beyond rational" state as Erhard claims, is something we will never know, as the original form of est ended in the 1980s. I certainly am doubtful of this claim, but it still must be recognized, in my opinion, that est does focus its intentions relatively high on Wilber's pre-rational/pseudo-rational/rational/trans-rational continuum (with my own addition of "pseudo-rational" added to Wilber's original abbreviated continuum). I would put est somewhere in-between the rational and trans-rational levels of consciousness.

In regard to Wilber's criteria of anchoring its legitimacy in a tradition, once again this is a difficult question to answer. Erhard certainly paid tribute to the traditions of the East, especially that of Buddhism, but his origination of est is chock full of modern jargon and a high level sales pitch [16]. All things considered, the end result packaging of est has very little similarity to any tradition whatsoever, even though one could argue that the underlying themes of est do go back to Eastern philosophy and spirituality. As far as Wilber's category of phase-specific authority is concerned, there was no indication of Erhard ever intending to step down from his guru role and give his authority to high level est leaders in the est organization. Indeed when Erhard finally did step down from his active guru role in est, he did so through dissolving the whole est organization—out of financial pressures. We thus certainly do get quite a mixed message for est in the Wilber Integral Model as well as in the Anthony Typology. In one sense est seems to have been truly engaged towards the trans-rational level of consciousness, but there were also causes of alarm in regard to the controlling guru aspects of its leader and originator, Werner Erhard.

We now examine est in the context of our more concrete evaluation: the Bonewits Cult Danger Scale. Once again, the evaluation scores on the fifteen characteristics utilized are based upon my own experience, this time with est in the late 1970s. Based upon my experiences, I will assign the following ratings to est.

Internal Control	5
Wisdom Claimed	5
Wisdom Credited	8
Dogma	9
Recruiting	8
Front Groups	3
Wealth	7
Political Power	3
Sexual Manipulation	2
Censorship	1
Dropout Control	2
Endorsement of Violence	1
Paranoia	1
Grimness	1
Surrender of Will	5
TOTAL	61
AVERAGE	**4.1**

I must say that I am somewhat surprised est has not gotten a less favorable numerical rating by me on the Bonewits Cult Danger Scale. But as I look over the ratings I gave est on the various characteristics and compare them with Scientology, it is clear to me that what we have here is a relatively benign organization in regard to serious cult dangers. An average score of 4.1 is not conveying that there are no cult dangers, but rather that these cult dangers are relatively mild (see *Concluding Survey and Discussion of Results* at the end of this chapter for a more detailed interpretation of the average score rankings). From my experience with est, there were never any hints of violence, paranoia about studying other disciplines, or inhibitions of jokes and lightness about the est material. My highest ratings show the dogma of est's whole philosophy that in two weekends everyone would become "enlightened" in a hotel ballroom, the high esteem and guru fascination that est followers displayed for Werner Erhard, and the rather obnoxious emphasis put on bringing "guests" to the est seminars that I experienced in the Be Here Now graduate est seminar [16]. Surrender of Will, Internal Control, and Wisdom Claimed all received intermediate ratings of "5," demonstrating that there were certainly cult dangers of getting overly enmeshed in the est organization and influence of Werner Erhard, but that these dangers were not nearly as severe as the dangers involved in Scientology. I was not aware of Front Groups per se in est, other than perhaps smaller groups being involved in the Hunger Project, which was essentially the one major political focus that I was aware of est being involved in.

Although est did place a strong emphasis on recruiting new people to take the est training, I was not aware of any focused activity to prevent or return dropouts, other than the general recruiting strategy to attract all people to est. Werner Erhard certainly became very wealthy through his mass marketing LGAT est training, but the individual costs for taking the est workshops were not something I could say were unreasonable in comparison to the costs of other new age workshops that were commonly available at the time. In fact I would say that the costs of doing est workshops were virtually "cheap" in comparison to Scientology as well as to Avatar [17]. One of the current leaders of the International Cultic Studies Association (ICSA) cults awareness organization [18] is an ex-est workshop facilitator who had been heavily involved with the est organization for a number of years. This ICSA leader certainly considers est to have been a major cult involvement for her, and I am by no means discounting her experience by the relatively mild cult danger score I have come up with for est on the Bonewits Cult Danger Scale. However, putting all three evaluation models together, it certainly does appear to be the case that there were some cult dangers in est, but in the grand scheme of things these cult dangers were not particularly alarming.

Given that all three of our cult evaluation models have demonstrated some positive characteristics of est (or at least a lack of severe cult danger characteristics), I would like to conclude this analysis of est by briefly examining the potential that est might have offered for engaging in an ITP, i.e. a four quadrant Integral Transformative Practice [19]. As already pointed out in my discussion of est in the Wilber Integral Model, est did focus upon the levels of consciousness beyond rational. This focus upon levels of consciousness beyond rational appears to me to show positive potential for the individual Intentional practice of an ITP. The est practices of "going into your space" and "be here now," as well as their focus upon personal experience, is very consistent with the meditative and contemplative traditions described in the book *Transformations of Consciousness* [20]. However, it also must be emphasized that in the essays by Brown and Engler in this same book, and especially in the book *Cults in Our Midst* by Margaret Singer and Janja Lalich (see [13] in Introduction Notes), it is cautioned that the benefits of meditation can easily be turned into detrimental effects for individual meditators, particularly when the meditation is done in a large group atmosphere as opposed to the time honored Eastern tradition of meditating under the individual tutelage of an esteemed meditation master who has meditated and studied for many years. At any rate, when it comes to the Cultural and Social quadrants of Wilber's Four Quadrant Integral model, it is quite clear that est was primarily focusing upon persuading people to take further est seminars and becoming increasingly more involved with the est organization [21]. Although est did not particularly try to take away people's lives outside of est, neither did they particularly encourage people to develop themselves in their wider extended potential in the four quadrants. There was virtually no emphasis put upon the individual Behavioral dimension, other than the occasional outdoor vigorous hiking retreat offered as a special kind of est seminar. Thus although est does not appear to have portrayed serious cult dangers, neither does it appear to have portrayed any particularly beneficial Integral Transformative Practice. Indeed it was quite possible for est graduates to become self-indulgent in their own introspective, perhaps initially trans-rational processes, while gradually allowing Werner Erhard and the est organization to take up more and more of their Cultural and Social quadrant activities. I do believe that this is what happened to a large number of est graduates, and this is why there was certainly cult dangers present in est. But in comparison with Scientology, as well as in comparison with our next modern religion to be analyzed, Reverend Moon's Unification Church, in my opinion est is most definitely in the "mild" cult danger category.

THE UNIFICATION CHURCH

Reverend Sun Myung Moon's Unification Church became both popular and notorious in the 1970s, and was at the forefront of the controversy over "deprogramming" of Unification Church members (widely known as "Moonies"). Deprogramming involved trying to persuade members to leave the church through kidnapping them against their will in order to help them see how brainwashed they were by the extremely detrimental cult tactics of Reverent Moon and his organization. Steve Hassan, who is recognized as one of the world's leading cult experts and cult counselors, is an ex-Moonie who was successfully deprogrammed in this way, and he describes his experiences in fascinating detail in both of his books [22]. There are many books and exposés readily available about The Unification Church [23]. The church, with Reverent Moon still its supreme ruler, is extremely wealthy and powerful, and politically active today. The Unification Church owns a major newspaper in Washington D.C., has enjoyed favorable personal relations with United States presidents, and there are suspicions of illegal associations with various military organizations and financing of weapons to combat communism in various parts of the world. It certainly is relevant today to examine the cult dangers of The Unification Church, and we shall once again begin with the Anthony Typology.

Unlike the cases of Scientology and est, Anthony and Ecker display no ambiguity about which cell to place The Unification Church in. The Unification Church is placed in the most serious cult danger cell: Unilevel/Dualistic/Charismatic. I am in substantial agreement with Anthony and Ecker in regard to their placement, though my agreement in this case is based upon what I have read and heard about the Unification Church over the past few decades in addition to my own personal experiences with them in the 1970s, as described in my

Unification Church essays in Chapter 3. Essentially The Unification Church, through the authoritarian decrees and writings of Reverend Moon [24], engages in a belief that Reverend Moon is actually the Second Messiah, and that it is necessary to accept Reverend Moon as your supreme "father" in order to achieve peace in this lifetime and go to heaven. To succeed in this mission, much social and political ramifications take place. The crux of the spiritual basis of the church, which I do believe is completely warped and not at all authentic, is distilled into mundane long hours of tedious street-working activities, such as selling flowers and candy bars [25]. The other side of this disturbing picture is the fabulous wealth that Reverend Moon himself lives in, his evasion of government income taxes for which he spent a year in jail, his regimented caste system of Unification Church members based upon country and origin (Korea first, Japan second), and his alleged criminal/military illegal activities [26]. In summary, lack of authentic spirituality describes the Unilevel classification; continuous proselytizing to accept Reverend Moon as the heavenly father with the devil corrupting everyone else describes the Dualistic classification; and complete non-rational or pseudo-rational faith in Reverend Moon as the Second Messiah describes the Charismatic dimension. Yes—Anthony and Ecker have every reason to be concerned about the cult dangers of The Unification Church, although they do not see these cult dangers as likely to end up in extreme tragedy, such as the mass suicides and murders that occurred in the People's Temple in Jonestown in the 1970s. Their viewpoint in this regard is based primarily on their perspective that The Unification Church does not see the world as its enemy but rather as merely ignorant of the one and only spiritual truth, and in need of being converted.

When we look closely at The Unification Church through the Wilber Integral Model, it is clear that The Unification Church is operating at a level of consciousness below rational. From my own experience with listening to The Unification Church lectures and having read Reverend Moon's main book *Divine Principle* (see [24]), I would say that there is most definitely an appeal made to initially convince people through their reasoning capacity of the truth of what Reverend Moon claims [27]. However, the historical parallels made use of to lead to the conclusion that the Second Messiah is walking the Earth today, is from Korea, and is in fact none other than Reverend Moon himself, is an illustrative example of the pseudo-rational level of consciousness, in a similar way to much of the science fiction and pseudo-psychological doctrines of Scientology. Of course it is well known that The Unification Church also engages in a great deal of highly manipulative emotional bonding activity such as "love bombing," in order to recruit people into their church [28]. In regard to anchoring its legitimacy in a tradition, in one sense it can be viewed that Reverend Moon represents a longstanding tradition of Korean spirituality. However, the specific way in which Reverend Moon has devised his Second Messiah scheme and placed himself as the supreme leader of the world is way past the continuity of any authentic tradition, regardless of whatever spiritual Korean ancestors Reverend Moon may claim to have had. As far as phase-specific authority is concerned, Reverend Moon is now in his eighties, and is as much in control of The Unification Church as he was when I first encountered The Unification Church over thirty years ago. There are no "phases" here and no concrete plan to turn authority over to others. When Reverend Moon dies I imagine The Unification Church will continue its influence through the leadership of one of the higher-ups in the organization, but this is not at all what Wilber means when he talks about phase-specific authority [29]. Putting these pieces together, we find that the Unification Church is operating at the pseudo-rational level of consciousness, is not anchoring its legitimacy in a tradition, and does not engage in phase-specific authority. We thus see that the alarm of the cult dangers through the Wilber Integral Model reinforces the high level of cult danger concerns from the Anthony Typology.

We now examine the cult dangers of the Unification Church from the perspective of the Bonewits Cult Danger Scale. The ratings that follow are taken from both my own personal experiences with The Unification Church in the late 1970s, as well as from all that I have learned about them (non-experientially) over the years. Since the social dynamics and inner workings of The Unification Church are now public knowledge, I have decided to include this public knowledge in the following Cult Danger ratings.

Internal Control	10
Wisdom Claimed	10
Wisdom Credited	10
Dogma	10
Recruiting	10
Front Groups	10

Wealth	10
Political Power	10
Sexual Manipulation	8
Censorship	8
Dropout Control	6
Endorsement of Violence	5
Paranoia	8
Grimness	10
Surrender of Will	10
TOTAL	135
AVERAGE	**9.0**

Once again I am somewhat surprised at the outcome of the Bonewits Cult Danger Scale quantitative results, as I did not expect to rate the Unification Church even higher than Scientology regarding their level of cult dangers. But the evidence speaks for itself; for ten of the fifteen cult characteristics I gave the Unification Church the highest rating of "10." There is no doubt about their supreme cult dangers regarding their many front groups, internal control, wisdom claimed, wisdom credited, recruiting, dogma, political power, and surrender of will. To explain some of my other ratings, although the sex lives and marriages of Unification Church members are directly controlled by Reverend Moon and the Unification Church leaders, my rating of "8" reflects the fact that unlike some other notorious gurus, I do not believe that Reverend Moon has engaged in explicit sexual relations with his followers [30]. My ratings of "8" on Censorship and Paranoia reflect the fact that although there is an extreme paranoia over communism per se and the influence of the "devil" as represented by alternative viewpoints to that of Reverend Moon, there is also a willingness to go out in public to confront this and engage in dialogue at conferences—both Unification Church sponsored conferences and others, such as ICSA conferences. My rating of "6" on Dropout Control reflects my understanding that although The Unification Church will try to prevent and return dropouts to a significant extent, I do not believe that they resort to the extreme financial ruin legal tactics to accomplish this in comparison to the well publicized disclosures about Scientology [31]. In regard to my rating of "5" for Endorsement of Violence, there are certainly serious concerns and suspicions about Reverend Moon's association with violent international military groups (see [28]), but as I am not aware of actual concrete proof of this it seems appropriate to give a moderate rating in this category. But the end result is definitely cause for extremely serious concern regarding the high level of cult dangers of The Unification Church, as from my experiences along with the public information available about them, all three of our evaluation models reinforce each other in this regard. Certainly there is no way we can entertain the notion of a Four Quadrant Integral Transformative Practice for Reverend Moon's Unification Church. Perhaps our next modern religion, Guru Maharajji's Divine Light Mission, will fare better.

DIVINE LIGHT MISSION

Guru Maharajji's Divine Light Mission is a modern religion that I became acquainted with through the proselytizing excitement of my boyfriend friend Richie [32], and this modern religion is still in existence today. Anthony and Ecker place Divine Light Mission in the Unilevel/Monistic/Charismatic cell, which indicates they have a significant concern regarding cult dangers in the Anthony Typology. The most obvious part of this three-way classification is the Charismatic dimension [33]. As I describe in my Divine Light Mission essays, there is essentially no logical rational reason to accept Guru Maharajji as the lord and savior of the universe. This is completely a function of Maharajji's personal charisma, although it is rather mind baffling how the 14 year old plump Indian kid who came on the American scene in 1971 managed to enthrall thousands of relatively intelligent young adult Americans to follow him. At any rate, I wholeheartedly agree with Anthony and Ecker that Divine Light Mission belongs in the Charismatic cell. In regard to the Unilevel dimension, this is certainly a reasonable choice, though not quite as obvious to me as the Charismatic dimension choice. Margaret Singer and Janja Lalich in their book *Cults in Our Midst* [34], described how gurus engaging in such physical demonstrations on group members as pushing on the eyeballs and pressing on the ears, resulted in the group members seeing visions and hearing sounds that were explained to them as being "Divine Light" and "Divine Harmony." This is where the name "Divine Light Mission" originally comes from, and the physiological explanations for these supposedly "divine" experiences is part and parcel of the Unilevel dimension.

However, just to be open-minded and to engage in the benefit of the doubt, I will consider the possibility that through the disciplined practice of meditation, a devotee of Guru Maharajji (known as a "Premi"), also may be experiencing a more authentic form of spiritual practice, and that this may cross over into the Multilevel dimension. In regard to the Monistic classification, once again I will concur with Anthony and Ecker. Although there is a fair amount of proselytizing efforts being made by Premis to their family and friends, Divine Light Mission by no means engages in the bitter "Us vs. Them" mentality that we have seen in both Scientology and The Unification Church. The initiation experience of "Receiving Knowledge" is looked upon as a highly spiritual and special experience, but people who do not have this experience are not viewed with animosity and condescension [35]. Putting Divine Light Mission in the Monistic cell seems to be a fair classification. Thus from an analysis via the Anthony Typology, it appears that Divine Light Mission may have some cult dangers to be concerned about, but that these cult dangers are in the low to moderate range, mild by comparison to Scientology and the Unification Church, perhaps somewhat comparable to those of est.

When we examine Divine Light Mission in the context of the Wilber Integral Model, the immediate observation is that there is very little rational thought going on here. The way that Guru Maharajji becomes the guru to his devotees is not by means of pseudo-rational logical explanations, as in the cases of Scientology and The Unification Church. Rather, the mind is looked upon as being a misguided means of understanding the world's "real" phenomena, and it is therefore stressed that the mind must be set aside in favor of the heart, in order to experience authentic spiritual realization [36]. Therefore I must place Divine Light Mission on the pre-rational level in Wilber's pre-rational/pseudo-rational/rational/trans-rational continuum. However, it is important to keep in mind here the distinction between "pre-rational" and "trans-rational," which is essentially that "trans-rational" makes full use of the rational mind and then "transcends" it—or in Ken Wilber's language "transcends and includes" it [37], whereas "pre-rational" never involves the rational mind to begin with [38].

In regard to anchoring its legitimacy in a tradition, here we have a much more favorable classification than any of the modern religions we have thus for encountered: Scientology, est, or The Unification Church. For Guru Maharajji does come from a long line of Hindu spiritual masters, an age-old tradition that insured the blessed divinity of Guru Maharajji from the time that he was born (although this family tradition was quite shattered when Guru Maharajji married an American girl at age 19). Indeed this is how he managed to begin his spiritual guru career in America at age 14. In regard to Wilber's third category, phase specific authority, we return to a "no phase" observation, as Guru Maharajji's leadership and complete control of Divine Light Mission is a life-long mission that I believe would be inherited by one of his children. Putting these observations together, we have a modern religion that is operating on the lowest level of Wilber's level of consciousness continuum and does not at all engage in phase-specific authority, but does anchor its legitimacy in a tradition. The complete bypassing of the mind, together with a life-long leadership role, does bring forth a serious degree of cult dangers to consider. However, the anchoring of its legitimacy in a tradition tends to lessen some of these cult dangers, as there is a bona-fide historical religious tradition to follow that would hopefully put some limits on the extremity of unethical individual behavior that a number of gurus seem to have engaged in [39].

Finally, through the Bonewits Cult Danger Scale we are able to see in a relatively more concrete way how these low to moderate cult dangers as suggested by both the Anthony Typology and Wilber Integral Model come into play. From my experiences with Divine Light Mission in the late 1970s, here are my numerical ratings on the Bonewits Cult Danger Scale.

Internal Control	6
Wisdom Claimed	10
Wisdom Credited	10
Dogma	10
Recruiting	5
Front Groups	6
Wealth	7
Political Power	2
Sexual Manipulation	2
Censorship	2
Dropout Control	2
Endorsement of Violence	1
Paranoia	2
Grimness	3
Surrender of Will	8

TOTAL   76
AVERAGE   **5.1**

As expected, we see that Divine Light Mission, with an average score of 5.1 on the Bonewits Cult Danger Scale, although somewhat higher than est in regard to cult dangers, is not on the high cult danger end of the spectrum—especially in comparison to Scientology and the Unification Church. The complete authority and high regard in which Guru Maharajji is held by his devotees is represented by my "10" ratings in Wisdom Claimed, Wisdom Credited, and Dogma. My Intermediate ratings of "5" and "6" for Recruiting, Internal Control, and Front Groups reflect that there is a fair amount of emphasis put in these realms, but it does not reach the excessive proportions that we have already encountered elsewhere. Although Guru Maharajji is extremely wealthy and lives in luxury, his "7" rating is not higher than this because as far as I know, Divine Light Mission does not procure its wealth through the donations or course purchases of its ordinary members. The high rating of "8" for Surrender of Will reflects the loss of personal identity on the part of a Premi, and the transferring of this identity to that of Guru Mahrajji. However, it does appear to me that the use made by Divine Light Mission of this surrender of will to Guru Maharajji is relatively non- detrimental (in comparison with the major representatives of high cult dangers) and therefore I did not give Divine Light Mission an even higher rating in this category. The remaining categories were all given low ratings of "1," "2," or "3," and in many cases a "2" was given instead of a "1" only to allow for the possibility of activities going on that I am not aware of. But in summary, we see that Divine Light Mission, although possessing a number of definite cult danger aspects, is not on the high cult danger end of the scale in comparison with some other modern religions that we have considered. On the other hand, Divine Light Mission does appear to be of a significantly higher cult danger risk than est, and I will therefore consider Divine Light Mission to have a moderate level of cult danger. Once again there does not seem to be sufficient integral positive characteristics here to describe Divine Light Mission in regard to being an Integral Transformative Practice. This brings us to the last modern religion that I have experienced in the 1970s for which I will apply my tri-perspective experiential analysis: the occult school of George Gurdjieff.

GURDJIEFF

George Gurdjieff was undoubtedly one of the most interesting, creative, and multi-talented leaders of a modern philosophical/spiritual group that the world has ever known. Unlike most of the modern religions that I am writing about, Gurdjieff originated his philosophy and gathered a following in the first half of the twentieth century, traveling throughout holylands in the East in search of primordial wisdom. His teachings became popular in the United States in large part through the book *In Search of the Miraculous* by P.D. Ouspensky [40], and various Gurdjieff schools became established in the 1960s and 1970s; the Gurdjieff movement is still quite popular in new age circles today. These Gurdjieff schools were considered to be "occult schools," practicing esoteric teachings that were not easily obtainable other than by taking part actively in a Gurdjieff group. My own experience of briefly taking part in a Gurdjieff group in 1977, is described in my Gurdjieff essays in Chapter 3, particularly in my essay *Occult School*. My intuitive evaluation of the Gurdjieff schools, which from now on I shall simply refer to as simply "Gurdjieff," is somewhat along the lines of est, in the sense that there are some definite dogmatic cult dangers, but in the whole scheme of things these cult dangers are comparatively mild, and there are also positive benefits to being involved in a Gurdjieff group. But let us begin our tri-perspective analysis and see how everything fits together.

To begin with, Anthony and Ecker place Gurdjieff (which they refer to as "The Gurdjieff Work") in the Multilevel/Technical/Dualistic cell. At first glance this is somewhat surprising to me to see Gurdjieff placed in the Dualistic cell, as out of the four modern religions that I have thus far written about, only The Unification Church is also placed in the Dualistic cell by Anthony and Ecker (recall that Anthony and Ecker put Scientology in the Monistic cell even though I disagreed and took the liberty of placing Scientology in the Dualistic cell). However, as I consider Anthony and Ecker's reasoning in this placement, it does accurately describe the dynamics of a Gurdjieff group. Essentially Anthony and Ecker claim that there is much severity and harshness in the atmosphere of a Gurdjieff group, where each group member is working on his/her self adamantly to surpass the ordinary sleep state of the machine like "normal" person, thereby attaining the heightened integrated spiritual state of awareness known as "Number 4 man," surpassing the separate states that are preoccupied with the body, emotions, and mind

[41]. In the process of this severe working on oneself, anyone who is considered to be on one of the lower levels of experience is looked down upon and challenged in a quite ferocious encounter group setting, to overcome their weaknesses and deal successfully with the material world in order to finally transcend it. This severity and harshness to those who are not considered to be on the higher levels of the Gurdjieff work, together with a haughty condescension toward the "normal" people not engaging in the Gurdjieff work, does merit the placement of Gurdjieff into the Dualistic cell, and I will go along with Anthony and Ecker on this point.

In regard to their placement of Gurdjierff in the Technical category, I will also essentially agree, as the dominant focus of a Gurdjieff group is certainly upon the techniques of working on yourself, the severe direct encounter with the other group members, and the required bodywork that accompanies all the focus on the mind and emotional self-discipline. However, it is also the case that the "teacher" of the Gurdjieff group holds the group together by his/her presence and effect of awe upon the group members, which certainly has some interplay with the Charismatic dimension [42]. In regard to the Multilevel classification, although the deeper focus of a Gurdjieff group is to promote an authentic spiritual awareness, Anthony and Ecker do point out that there are definite dangers of a Gurdjieff group falling into Unilevel temptations. Essentially this is because much of the Gurdjieff work involves dealing with the mundane world in order to eventually surpass it, and it is not uncommon for Gurdjieff aspirants to become stuck in this mundane world and never reach the higher spiritual states. We thus see that the picture from the Anthony Typology in regard to evaluating the cult dangers of Gurdjieff is not at all a clear one. We have the negative cult danger cell of Dualistic operating with the generally beneficial characteristics cell of Multilevel, plus the fact that the classification itself is not particularly strict or concrete, either from Anthony and Ecker's perspective or my own perspective.

When we turn our attention to the Wilber Integral Model, the picture becomes somewhat more clear. To begin with, I would say that Gurdjieff is operating on a similar level of consciousness to that of est, i.e. somewhere in-between the rational and trans-rational levels on the continuum. Gurdjieff's mental acrobatics are impressive, even if there are places I believe he goes overboard in assuming the truth of, such as for example his complicated and expansive notions about astrology (see [40]). However, unlike Scientology or The Unification Church, I do not see Gurdjieff's philosophy as being based essentially on false or pseudo-rationality. Gurdjieff's focus of working on yourself to integrate your mind with your body and emotions, and to eventually reach a place of transcendence and authentic spiritual awareness, most certainly puts Gurdjieff in the higher consciousness levels in Wilber's scheme of things. In regard to anchoring its legitimacy in a tradition, Gurdjieff himself spent many years building his philosophy from esoteric traditions within Eastern Orthodox Christianity, Sufism, and Zoroastrianism (see [40]). The philosophy and teachings he emerged with represent his own creative assimilations, but it is also true that the basics of the Gurdjieff philosophy are anchored in a number of religious traditions. In regard to phase-specific authority, I do not think that Gurdjieff had any plans of stepping down from his leadership role toward his followers. However, neither do I think that Gurdjieff had any kind of grandiose schemes to convert the world to his philosophy, such as is the case with Scientology and The Unification Church (with my frequent reminder that this is all in my own opinion). Rather, Gurdjieff's philosophy was meant only for the relatively few "super-capable" (in the Gurdjieff teachers' estimations) people who had the ability and motivation to go beyond the ordinary sleep state that most people lived their lives in. Certainly the cult dangers here do not reach into the masses in the way that the other groups I have written about have done. This is why Gurdjieff is considered "Occult Philosophy," even though there may be not much left today in our modern technological society that is "occult" anymore. But in considering the cult dangers of Gurdjieff via the Wilber Integral Model, these cult dangers seem to me most certainly to be relatively mild.

Let us now examine Gurdjieff in the context of my numerical ratings from the Bonewits Cult Danger Scale. Here are my ratings, once again from my experience in the late 1970s with Gurdjieff, as described in my Gurdjieff essays in Chapter 3.

Internal Control	6
Wisdom Claimed	5
Wisdom Credited	5
Dogma	9
Recruiting	3
Front Groups	5
Wealth	5

Political Power	2
Sexual Manipulation	2
Censorship	5
Dropout Control	2
Endorsement of Violence	2
Paranoia	2
Grimness	8
Surrender of Will	4
TOTAL	65
AVERAGE	**4.3**

As my intuitive feelings predicted, from my own experiences Gurdjieff does have some relatively mild cult dangers attached to it, and is quite comparable to est in this regard. The cult danger highest ratings I assigned to Gurdjieff were a "9" for Dogma and an "8" for Grimness. The intermediate ratings of a number of "5"s and one "6," represent the wide variability of many Gurdjieff groups currently in existence without one central authoritarian figure directing the large group of Gurdjieff aspirants. There are a number of front groups that bring people into the Gurdjieff school, such as the Theatre of All Possibilities described in my essay *Occult School*, and the performance of "sacred dances" described in my essay *Eden West* (see Chapter 3). However, I do believe that there is not anywhere near the extreme emphasis put upon front groups that one would find through diligently investigating this phenomenon in The Unification Church and Scientology. Internal Control, Censorship, Wealth, Wisdom Claimed, and Wisdom Credited similarly are largely a function of the severity of a particular Gurdjieff group and teacher. For example, I was quite disturbed at the $200 a month fee charged to be part of the Gurdjieff group at the Theatre of All Possibilities, and I was quite relieved to hear that the Eden West Gurdjieff group charged no fee at all to engage in the Gurdjieff work [43]. In general though, I think it is more common for Gurdjieff groups to operate under a strict authoritarian Gurdjieff "teacher" who does exert a fair amount of control over members' lives, though not nearly to the extremes of The Unification Church or Scientology. From my own limited experience in a Gurdjieff group, there was no pressure whatsoever put upon me to remain in the group; it was only "my" sense of partial regret that I felt upon deciding to not continue in the Gurdjieff work (see my essay *Occult School* in

Chapter 3). For all the remaining categories I gave very low cult danger ratings of "2," except for a rating of "3" for Recruiting and a rating of "4" for Surrender of Will. My rating of "3" for Recruiting is based upon bringing in the public through artistic performances, as I have described my own experience of being approached by an attractive young woman on a bus with an offer to see a free play [44]. My rating of "4" for Surrender of Will represents the dual aspects of Gurdjieff groups of encouraging individual personal responsibility and effective decision making on the one hand, while on the other hand there is an authoritarian Gurdjieff group leader who is in charge of making decisions that significantly affect the lives of the members of the Gurdjieff group. The only reason my "2" ratings are not "1"s is because of the many diverse Gurdjieff groups in existence, allowing for the possibility that there are groups that do engage in negative behaviors such as violence, sexual manipulation, etc. But the summary of my numerical ratings on the Bonewits Cult Danger Scale does support the essentially mild level of cult danger concerns that we found from the Wilber Integral Model, and the Anthony Typology does not contradict this evaluation.

　　In regard to applying the ideas of an Integral Transformative Practice (ITP) to Gurdjieff, one aspect of the Gurdjieff work does stand out as a significant reason to at least make an attempt at this kind of analysis. This aspect is the reliance on bodywork that is a central part of the Gurdjieff work. I was attracted to the bodywork on the acting stage in the Theatre of All Possibilities, as well as to the "Tarzan Grunts" of the sacred dances I saw at Eden West (see [41]). This focus upon the body is part and parcel of Gurdjieff's way of assimilating the body state into the mind state and emotions state to form the higher spiritual level aware individual. But this focus upon the body also becomes significant as an integrated spiritual practice that considers the body to be an important part of its overall development work. This is certainly an effective balance of the two upper quadrants in Wilber's Four Quadrant Integral Model: the individualized Intentional and Behavioral quadrants [45]. In terms of the two lower quadrants, representing the Cultural and Social domains, there is primarily the context of the Gurdjieff group itself. A Gurdjieff group member is part of a close-knit social group that is constantly engaging in many hours of challenging, assertive, confrontational encounter group work. There are certainly cultural mores to be followed, as well as social patterns of interaction. I don't think that Gurdjieff group members are particularly discouraged or prevented from taking part in wider groups of their interest, but it is also true that much of their free time (and sleep) is taken up in these Gurdjieff groups. Once again, in a somewhat similar way to est, there are ingredients here that hint at the possibilities of an Integral Transformative Practice, but the essentially dogmatic nature of a Gurdjieff group, together with all its social expectations, make this kind of an ITP into something much less meaningful than either Wilber, or Leonard and Murphy were writing about.

And this concludes my tri-perspective experiential analysis of the modern religions which I experienced in the 1970s, while in my twenties. We resume next after a fifteen year break, with the modern religion of Eckankar, which I experienced through my involvement in a romantic relationship in 1995.

ECKANKAR

Eckankar is a modern religion that was founded in 1965 by Paul Twitchell. In Twitchell's books [46] he claims that Eckankar has a long line of spiritual masters in a tradition that is thousands of years old. However, this claim of long-lasting history has been repudiated by the research of David Lane that became publicly available in a popular book in the early 1980s [47], demonstrating that much of what Twitchell wrote about was filled with plagiarism, false statements about the history of Eckankar, and false statements about himself. Although this caused quite a stir in the Eckankar community and induced a number of Eckists to leave the organization, Eckankar is still a prominent new age spiritual organization that has thousands of followers throughout the world. My introduction to Eckankar happened by way of a romantic relationship, as I describe in my essay *On Eckankar* in Chapter 2. In the present chapter I will continue the tri-perspective experiential analysis I have been doing for the modern religions that I experienced in the 1970s, and see how this analysis holds up for Eckankar.

From this point on we are now on our own in regard to the Anthony Typology, as Anthony and Ecker do not discuss any of the remaining modern religions that I am writing about, some of which did not come into existence until after *Spiritual Choices* was published in 1987. From my own perspective, I can see placing Eckankar in two difference cells in the Anthony Typology, namely the Multilevel/Charismatic/Monistic cell and the Multilevel/Technical/Monistic cell.

It should be noted that both of these cells are considered to be the cells with the most favorable authentic spirituality and non-cult characteristics. I do believe that the prime motive of Eckankar is the authentic spiritual quest in the form of experiencing one's soul; this is certainly a Multilevel context. Eckankar focuses upon peace, love, and harmony, and there is very little animosity or condescension toward others who have a faith different from Eckankar; thus we are in the Monistic cell as opposed to the Dualistic cell. In regard to the Charismatic vs. Technical dimension, here the distinction is much less clear. As I recall the pictures of Harold Klemp, the current "Living Eck Master," all over my ex-girlfriend's house [48], I remember how important it was to an Eckist to feel the cohesiveness and spiritual bond with the Living Eck Master; thus the Charismatic dimension. But it is also true that Eckankar has specific teachings and exercises, largely revolving around sound vibrations with meditation, to enable a person to establish his/her experience of soul connection; thus the Technical dimension. However, in either the Charismatic or Technical dimension we are still in quite a relatively safe cell in the Anthony Typology as far as cult dangers are concerned. We shall need to look elsewhere to find cult dangers in Eckankar.

When I examine Eckankar in the Wilber Integral Model, I am once again struck by the problem of where to put Eckankar in the levels of consciousness continuum. At first glance it may appear that Eckankar is operating somewhere in-between the rational and trans-rational levels, in a similar place to that of est and Gurdjieff. However, after surveying the research of David Lane (see [47]), it appears that much of the original writings by Eckankar founder Paul Twitchell were fabricated, resulting in people joining Eckankar under false pretenses. Although the crux of Eckankar centers around the experience of "soul travel" (i.e. leaving your body), it is still true that many people initially became interested in Eckankar through reading Twitchell's books. Taking this into consideration, it seems most appropriate to place Eckankar in the pseudo-rational level of the continuum. In regard to anchoring its legitimacy in a tradition, we have the same issue at stake. Twitchell claims a long-lasting historical religious tradition going back thousands of years. Lane claims this long-lasting tradition is complete fabrication, with Eckankar being little more than the creative invention of Paul Twitchell (see [47]). My own personal inclination is to agree with Lane here, and therefore I will conclude that Eckankar does not anchor its legitimacy in a tradition, at least not a tradition that has a significant degree of historical truth attached to it. In regard to phase-specific authority, since 1965 there have been three Eck Masters. Paul Twitchell died in 1971, at which point Darwin Gross took over the Living Eck Master role, until he was dishonorably discharged in 1981. From 1981 until the present time, the Living Eck Master role has been maintained by Harold Klemp. This is meant to be a life-long position, and there is no "phase" to the authority of a Living Eck Master. Putting these ingredients of the Wilber Integral Model together, we can now see prospective cult dangers much more clearly than we could see from the Anthony Typology. The falsifications and misrepresentations of Eckankar by Twitchell do raise some red flags for us in regard to possible cult dangers.

Based primarily upon my personal Eckankar experience for a year and half in the mid 1990s, here are my ratings of Eckankar on the Bonewits Cult Danger Scale.

Internal Control	2
Wisdom Claimed	9
Wisdom Credited	9
Dogma	10
Recruiting	4
Front Groups	2
Wealth	2
Political Power	1
Sexual Manipulation	1
Censorship	3
Dropout Control	2
Endorsement of Violence	1
Paranoia	5
Grimness	5
Surrender of Will	5
TOTAL	65
AVERAGE	**4.3**

We thus see that Eckankar has the exact same overall score on the Bonewits Cult Danger Scale as Gurdjieff, and I shall put Eckanakar also in the mild cult dangers category. However, the particular scores for Eckankar are quite different from those of Gurdjieff. Eckankar has very high scores of "9" and "10" on the items focused directly on the guru phenomenon, namely Wisdom Claimed, Wisdom Credited, and Dogma. On the other hand, Eckankar has a number of very low scores of "1" and "2" in the areas of Internal Control, Front Groups, Wealth (membership costs are relatively inexpensive), Political Power, Sexual Manipulation, and Violence. I gave Intermediate scores of "5" for Paranoia, Grimness, and Surrender of Will. For Censorship and Recruiting I have given respective scores of "3" and "4," which are not causes of significant alarm. Indeed the only cause of serious alarm seems to be the extreme focus of total divinity given to the Living Eck Master. From my own experience, I would say that the Living Eck Master of the past twenty three years, Harold Klemp, appears to be an essentially benevolent peaceful guru to his followers. However, it is not difficult to see how a less ethical Living Eck Master could influence and control Eckankar followers in a much more detrimental fashion. This complete reliance upon the guru in the form of the Living Eck Master is what I find to be the most series cult danger of Eckankar. But it must also be acknowledged that as of this point in time, Eckankar has not gone into anything even remotely approaching the glaring negative cult activities of The Unification Church or Scientology (i.e. negative cult activities from my experiential tri-perspective analysis).

Thus in all fairness, it seems that it would be appropriate to see how Eckankar fares as an Integral Transformative Practice. Of course the first obstacle is the question of do we have an authentic spiritual practice to begin with here? Giving Eckankar a major benefit of the doubt, from my own experience I will say that regardless of the fact that many people may have become Eckists based upon false information, there is still authentic spirituality in the sound vibrations and meditation exercises. We shall therefore consider these exercises to be of authentic spiritual value in Wilber's Intentional quadrant, but we do not have any particular body oriented activities in Eckankar to include in the Behavioral quadrant. In regard to the Cultural and Social quadrants, we primarily have Eckankar meditation and spiritual meeting groups, Eckankar literature, and Eckankar conferences. In short, the Cultural and Social quadrants are completely taken up with Eckankar itself. Like a Four Quadrant ITP for est and Gurdjieff, a Four Quadrant ITP for Eckankar leaves much to be desired. We may not have major cult dangers to be concerned about here, but neither do we have an effective form of an Integral Transformative Practice. Lets move on to one of the five new age spiritual organizations that I first encountered in the summer of 1997; Self-Realization Fellowship.

SELF-REALIZATION FELLOWSHIP

Summer of 1997 was the launching pad of my second stage of explorations of modern religions. My exploration of Self-Realization Fellowship began with my reading of the popular new age book *Autobiography of A Yogi* by Self-Realization Fellowship founder and guru Paramanahansa Yogananda [49]. Like Gurdjieff, Self-Realization Fellowship began in the first half of the twentieth century, and has remained popular in new age circles today. My own experience is that Self-Realization Fellowship appears to be fairly innocuous regarding cult dangers, but let's begin our tri-perspective experiential analysis and see what we come up with.

In the Anthony Typology the first placement that occurs to me is the Monistic cell as opposed to the Dualistic cell. Through the instructional practice of Kriya Yoga, Self-Realization Fellowship members are encouraged to attain heightened spiritual peaceful states. However, there does not seem to be an Us vs. Them mentality, and all people are viewed as deserving of peace and love, regardless of whether or not they are followers of Yogananda. In regard to the choice of the Technical or Charismatic cell, once again we have quite the toss-up here. The "energization" part of the Kriya Yoga exercises are certainly quite technical, involving the tensing and releasing of many particular body parts. However, there is also a tremendous emphasis upon identifying one's self not only with Yogananda, but also with the direct line of his ancestors, including Krishna as well as Jesus Christ. A typical Self-Realization Fellowship meditation shrine has six pictures to meditate upon. Yoganada, his three direct lineage gurus, Krishna, and Christ [50]. Yogananda was very much the benevolent adored guru to his followers, and his mystique has been successfully continued for nearly half a century since his death. Thus Self-Realization Fellowship has at least as much, if not more, reason to be placed in the Charismatic cell as it does to be placed in the Technical cell. In regard to the Multilevel vs. Unilevel distinction, there is not much doubt in my mind that Self-Realization Fellowship is operating on the Multilevel dimension. Yogananda brought his spiritual practices and beliefs to the United States from India, and he seems to have kept the highest levels of his spiritual practices intact. We thus see that we have the exact same placement in the Anthony Typology for Self-Realization Fellowship as we had for Eckankar; Multilevel/Charismatic/Monistic or Multilievel/Technical/Monistic (once again from my perspective), representing the best possible cell placement regarding being free of serious cult dangers. Although I had concerns about assuming these positive implications too easily for Eckankar, and some cult concerns did become evident through the perspectives of the Wilber Integral Model and the Bonewits Cult Danger Scale, I feel more comfortable in the case of Self-Realization Fellowship that the Anthony Typology cell placement is fairly representative of the positive aspects of this modern religion. As we proceed with our other two evaluations, we shall see if this optimistic viewpoint is warranted.

For the Wilber Integral Model once again we need to decide where to put a modern religion, in this case Self-Realzation Fellowship, on the levels of consciousness continuum. In *Autobiography of a Yogi* there are many events described that seem quite preposterous to me; from the five hundred year old guru Babaji who often appears as a young man in the hills of the Himalayas, to the claimed ability of some Yogi adepts to appear at two different locations at the same point in time (cf. [49]). However, the crux of the actual practice of Kriya Yoga is essentially a meditation, going along with a packet of "lessons" to practice affirmations leading toward a deeper more peaceful and spiritual state of consciousness (cf. [50]). I will give Self-Realization Fellowship the benefit of the doubt that their program of spiritual elevation through this combined yoga, meditation, and affirmations is essentially a legitimate spiritual practice. Although I believe that many of the claims in *Autobiography of a Yogi* are greatly exaggerated and fabricated, I do not view the essential foundations of this modern religion as being based upon the artificial creations of the founder/guru, as I believe was the case in Eckankar. Even though Yogananda is certainly greatly revered with much devotion by Self-Realization Fellowship members, this appears to be of a much more mature and independent quality and very different from the totally mindless (in my opinion) Lord of the Universe mentality that we have seen in both The Unification Church and Divine Light Mission. Therefore I shall give Self-Realization Fellowship the benefit of the doubt and utilize the same placement in Wilber's level of consciousness continuum as I did for est and Gurjieff; namely in-between the rational and trans-rational levels of the continuum.

In regard to anchoring its legitimacy in a tradition, we now have a bona-fide long historical and cultural tradition handed down to us, with Yogananda maintaining much respect and allegiance to his Eastern lineage and heritage. However, once again we see there is no "phase" here for phase-specific authority. Yogananda was a life-long guru, and his successor Daya Mata kept her leadership role in Self-Realization Fellowship for nearly half a century. But at least in comparison with other modern religions and other gurus, the leadership of Self-Realization Fellowship does appear to me to be essentially benevolent. I make this statement in spite of the dissatisfied accounts given by some ex-members of Self-Realization Fellowship who have experienced living in Self-Realization Fellowship ashrams for a period of time [51]. Once again it is a matter of viewing things in a relative manner; compared to Scientology and The Unification Church we do not seem to have much cause here to be concerned about cult dangers (in my opinion).

To complete our tri-perspective experiential analysis of Self-Realization Fellowship, I will now engage in the ratings for the Bonewits Cult Danger Scale, basing these ratings upon my own experiences with Self- Realization Fellowship for a year or two in the 1990s.

Internal Control	5
Wisdom Claimed	8
Wisdom Credited	10
Dogma	8
Recruiting	3
Front Groups	2
Wealth	3
Political Power	2
Sexual Manipulation	1
Censorship	1
Dropout Control	1
Endorsement of Violence	1
Paranoia	1
Grimness	3
Surrender of Will	7
TOTAL	56
AVERAGE	**3.7**

We thus have our lowest average score on the Bonewits Cult Danger Scale that we have yet seen. However, there are still some high individual cult danger scores that need to be understood. The score of "10" on Wisdom Credited reflects the essentially total reliance and worship that Self-Realization Fellowship members have upon the teachings of Yogananda. The scores of "8" on Wisdom Claimed and Dogma reflect the high degree of belief by Yogananda in his own pronouncements, but also allow for some flexibility and humility in this guru's nature. The score of "7" on Surrender of Will reflects the easy readiness many followers have to give up their own individual will to their feeling of identification with and devotion for Yogananda and the other Self-Realization Fellowship gurus, although not quite to the extent of Divine Light Mission followers, and certainly not to the extent of Unification Church followers. The intermediate score of "5" for Internal Control represents the distant control of members through intensified and prolonged individualized meditation activities, as members identify themselves with both Yogananda and Self-Realization Fellowship. There are a number of scores of "1," reflecting my strong sense that Self-Realization Fellowship is essentially free of some of the worst cult dangers, such as Sexual Manipulation, Violence, Censorship, etc. Self-Realization Fellowship does enjoy wealthy luxurious surroundings in its central location through gifts and voluntary donations from its wealthier members. However, the expense for the ordinary Self-Realization Fellowship member is quite reasonable to receive the Lessons (see [48]), and to attend retreats and conferences. All things considered, based upon my analysis in all three perspectives, I am inclined to give Self-Realization Fellowship a relatively neutral rating regarding cult dangers. In other words, although I do not consider Self-Realization Fellowship to be a particularly beneficial authentic spiritual growth organization, neither do I have much concern that there are any significant cult dangers here.

We can certainly try out a Four Quadrant ITP (Integral Transformative Practice) for Self-Realization Fellowship. If one accepts all the quite extravagant claims in *Autobiography of a Yogi* with a grain of salt (see [49]), then the experiences of Yoga, meditation, and affirmations through Kriya Yoga can indeed be a reasonable spiritual discipline in the Intentional quadrant of Wilber's Four Quadrant Integral Model. There is a danger though of becoming overly immersed in these meditation exercises, and a number of authors have addressed the dangers of engaging in meditation to an excessive degree [52}. Although Kriya Yoga does involve a physical focus on the body, this is not what I believe warrants a significant balancing activity in the Behavioral quadrant. The emphasis upon the inner spiritual domain may very well be rather lopsided in Self-Realization Fellowship. In regard to the Cultural and Social quadrants, through the Self-Realization Fellowship retreats and conferences there is much opportunity to interact with others who have a similar state of mind regarding their desire to attain high spiritual states through the practice of Kriya Yoga, as well as enhancing peace in the world. There is encouragement in Self-Realization Fellowship to allow your higher spiritual state to emerge in the world and contribute to enhanced possibilities for world peace. We thus see that although there are certain lacks in the ITP potential, most notably in the Behavioral quadrant along with an excessive emphasis upon meditation and individual subjective states, we do have some potential here for an Integral Transformative Practice, especially if the Behavioral quadrant is addressed and one is cautious to not engage in the meditative activities beyond what is conducive to one's overall development as a spiritual being. Our next modern religion to examine, A Course in Miracles, I will venture to guess may have an overall similar evaluation to that of Self-Realization Fellowship.

A COURSE IN MIRACLES

A Course in Miracles is considered to be the information "channeled" by Helen Schucman in the 1970s through an entity that gradually emerges through her channelings as a combination of the Holy Ghost and Jesus Christ. The textbook for A Course in Miracles is over a thousand pages of deep difficult esoteric reading with much Christian biblical overtones [53]. However, the more simple basic message of A Course in Miracles is the attainment of inner spiritual peace through experiencing "miracles," which in this context are essentially transcendental states of being along the lines of the trans-rational levels of consciousness in the Wilber Integral Model. At any rate, this is my own perspective of A Course in Miracles, from having read the entire textbook plus their bi-monthly journals for a few years, and having participated in a number of Course in Miracles discussion groups. The Course in Miracles organization sponsors yearly worldwide conferences and other retreats, in what appears to be quite a similar way to Self-Realization Fellowship. Let us see in my continued tri-perspective experiential analysis if A Course in Miracles can also be designated as a "Neutral" modern religion, as I have categorized Self-Realization Fellowship, relatively free of any serious cult dangers.

In the Anthony Typology it is quite clear to me that A Course in Miracles does belong in the Multilevel cell. The focus of A Course in Miracles is certainly the attainment of authentic higher level spiritual experience. Although I found it quite difficult to understand this focus from reading the Course in Miracles text directly, one of the most current popular new age writers and teachers, Marianne Williamson, has translated the essential messages of A Course in Miracles in her own words, and has reached many more people than the original versions of A Course in Miracles was able to do [54]. The success and popularity of A Course in Miracles does not appear to me to be a function of the charisma of any guru who has directed the movement. From what I have learned in my Course in Miracles discussion groups (see also [55]), Helen Schucman hardly had the personality to be considered any kind of a guru, and the subsequent leaders of the Course in Miracles organization do not appear to be acting in a guru capacity. There are numerous spiritual meditation and affirmation exercises in the Course in Miracles textbook (actually one for each day of the year; see [53]); there is no doubt that A Course in Miracles is in the Technical cell. In regard to the Monistic/Dualistic dichotomy, clearly A Course in Miracles is open to all people without prejudice or condescension, and "forgiveness" is considered to be one of their most fundamental spiritual principles. We thus see that A Course in Miracles, from my placement in the Multilevel/Charismatic/Monistic cell in the Anthony Typology, is in the most favorable cell regarding being relatively free of cult dangers.

As we now examine A Course in Miracles from the perspective of the Wilber Integral Model, as we remarked above we immediately see that A Course in Miracles is somewhere along the lines of the trans-rational level of consciousness in the Wilber continuum. However, it is also true that there is much Christian biblical context in which this trans-rational focus is given, much of which is quite foreign to me personally. Although the essential deep message behind the words did reach me, I would say that the Christian biblical context and words takes away from the genuine transcendental message it is based upon. Putting this all together, I would place A Course in Miracles in-between the rational and trans-rational levels of consciousness in Wilber's continuum, in a similar way to what we have seen for est, Gurdjieff, and Self-Realization Fellowship. In regard to the context of anchoring its legitimacy in a tradition, we certainly have a rich historical religious tradition of Christianity here. There may be innovative and even radical interpretations of Christianity in A Course in Miracles, but the historical foundations of Christianity are still very much present. As far as phase-specific authority is concerned, unlike all the modern religions we have thus far explored, we finally encounter a modern religion that does appear to be operating under phases of authority. Helen Schucman herself was not at all a controlling guru figure, and the subsequent leaders of the Course in Miracles organization have not taken on this role either. There has not been one central figure who controls this organization, but rather a number of people who lead Course in Miracles workshops, write popular new age books based upon A Course in Miracles principles, and contribute regularly to the Course in Miracles journal [56]. The authority in A Course in Miracles does seem to be phase-specific both in the amount of time different people devote to the leadership of A Course in Miracles, as well as to the variety of people involved in different roles of leadership in the organization. We thus see that A Course in Miracles fares extremely well in the Wilber Integral Model, in addition to the Anthony Typology.

We now examine A Course in Miracles through the perspective of the Bonewits Cult Danger Scale, based upon my own knowledge of and experience with A Course In Miracles for a year or two in the 1990s and 2000 [57]. The following are my Bonewits Cult Danger Scale ratings.

Internal Control	2
Wisdom Claimed	10
Wisdom Credited	5
Dogma	10
Recruiting	3
Front Groups	2
Wealth	2
Political Power	2
Sexual Manipulation	3
Censorship	1
Dropout Control	1
Endorsement of Violence	1

Paranoia	1
Grimness	3
Surrender of Will	7
TOTAL	53
AVERAGE	**3.5**

We see that A Course in Miracles has an even lower cult danger number on the Bonewits Cult Danger Scale than that of Self-Realization Fellowship. However, there are two scores of "10" in these ratings for the categories of Wisdom Claimed and Dogma. This reflects the total belief of Helen Schucman that what she wrote in A Course in Miracles was "channeled" from up above and therefore must be followed as it was given to her. However, the "5" score for Wisdom Credited reflects the fact that although the Course in Miracles material is considered by Course in Miracles followers to be sublime wisdom, there is not a particular guru who is credited with having this sublime wisdom (other than Jesus); certainly not Helen Schucman herself. Much of the emphasis of A Course in Miracles is upon surrendering your personal will and self to the "Holy Spirit," but once again there is not a particular person acting as guru to surrender yourself to (once again, other than Jesus); thus I rated Surrender of Will as a "7." The remaining scores are all relatively low scores of "1," "2," or "3." The "3" score in Sexual Manipulation represents an emphasis upon spiritual attainment and "holy encounter" that could have an effect upon one's sexual relationships, though quite possibly in a beneficial way. Putting our three perspectives together, we see that A Course in Miracles has received the best ratings from me on each of the three perspectives in our analysis for any of the modern religions we have thus far encountered. Certainly A Course in Miracles appears to be relatively free of cult dangers and to be at least in the Neutral category regarding being a favorable new age spiritual organization; however, there are also critical and skeptical viewpoints concerning A Course in Miracles [58]. Let us see if A Course in Miracles has any reasonable ITP potential in the Wilber Four Quadrant Integral Model.

Clearly the Intentional quadrant of the Wilber Four Quadrant Integral Model is the dominant focus of A Course in Miracles. The extent of deep meditative spiritual exercises with exact words for affirmations to repeat to yourself many times throughout the day is quite accentuated, to say the least. For many people this kind of recommended structure may be useful and welcome, although it is certainly not my own chosen path of spiritual development. But let us be flexible here and give A Course in Miracles a satisfactory rating in the Intentional quadrant of Wilber's model. However, it is quite obvious that there is a serious lack in the Behavioral quadrant in A Course in Miracles. Indeed there is virtually no emphasis whatsoever placed upon the body in a Course in Miracles. The body is portrayed as being the lower level accessory to the spirit, and is second only to the "ego" as being full of danger that can detract one from authentic spiritual pursuits (see [53]). The body can be controlled by the spirit and put to beneficial use, but there is hardly a respect and appreciation here for the body that is central to the philosophy of an Integral Transformative Practice. In regard to the Cultural and Social quadrants, A Course in Miracles fares somewhat better, as there is a cultural emphasis placed upon doing good in the world, forgiving others, and contributing toward world peace. The Social quadrant is primarily engaged through participating in Course in Miracles small study groups, and going to the larger Course in Miracles conferences. Involvement in other social groups is not at all discouraged in A Course in Miracles, but the central idea of an ITP regarding extensive balancing of activities in the Intentional, Behavioral, Cultural, and Social quadrants does not appear to be particularly well represented in A Course in Miracles. We shall thus leave A Course in Miracles in "Neutral" territory alongside Self-Realization Fellowship, in-between modern religions that possess significant cult danger characteristics and modern religions that are primarily beneficial to overall spiritual development. However, this Neutral category should by no means be taken for granted, as we investigate our next two modern religions that are based upon a very similar philosophy: Conversations with God and Avatar.

CONVERSATIONS WITH GOD

Conversations with God was originated by Neale Donald Walsch in the early 1990s as a popular new age book of the same title, followed within the next few years by the remaining two books in the initial Conversations with God trilogy [59]. Walsch has written a number of "With God" books since then [60] and has established a worldwide Conversations with God organization with a number of different subsidiary organizations [61]. After having read Walsch's major books I experienced being with Walsch in a Conversations with God conference in Oregon that included nearly a thousand people. I ended up having quite mixed views about Walsch himself, but I concluded that Conversations with God was not a dangerous cult (see [61]). Let us now see how my experiences and views about Conversations with God translate into my current tri-perspective experiential analysis of modern religions.

The essential messages of Conversations with God are that all your answers are "within," and that "you" can "choose" what you want to experience in life through looking deeply into your own self, which for Walsch takes the form of having a literal conversation with God. In my Conversations with God essays in Chapter 2, I do give Walsch the benefit of the doubt to being sincere in his beliefs. Therefore when we examine Conversations with God in the context of the Anthony Typology, I would place Conversations with God in the Multilevel cell, representing the assumption that this modern religion (or synonymously new age spiritual organization) is based upon high level authentic spiritual realizations. In regard to the Technical vs. Charismatic dimension, once again the category becomes rather blurred. Certainly there is much technical advice by Walsch in his books regarding going deeply inward, the idea of there being no right or wrong, individual choice and intention, highly evolved beings from other planets, God being within you, etc. However, after attending the Humanity's Team conference (a subsidiary organization of the Conversations with God Foundation) and seeing Walsch in action with large groups of people and his effect upon them, I must place Conversations with God in the Charismatic cell ([61]). In regard to the Monistic/Dualistic dichotomy, it is clear that Conversations With God belongs in the Monistic cell, as its whole current emphasis is upon transforming the world through eliminating hierarchies in religious beliefs of right and wrong [62]. In summary, we see that Conversations with God, from my placement in the Multilevel/Charismatic/Monistic cell, is in a generally favorable cell regarding potential cult dangers. However, the Charismatic cell in which I placed Conversations with God may very well be a red flag that needs to be addressed in our other two perspectives.

For the Wilber Integral Model, based upon my analysis for the Anthony Typology, I will once again give Conversations with God the benefit of the doubt and place it in-between the rational and trans-rational levels of consciousness in Wilber's continuum, as I have done with a number of other modern religions that we have thus far explored. However, in regard to anchoring its legitimacy in a tradition, Conversations with God has virtually no tradition whatsoever to fall back upon. Walsch makes the statement that traditional religious beliefs and practices are not only irrelevant but also can be quite dangerous and destructive (see [62]). Walsch advocates forming a completely new perspective in understanding and experiencing God, a perspective that is not based upon any historical religious traditions [63]. As far as phase-specific authority is concerned, once again we see that there is no phase here. Walsch runs the Conversations with God organization in what I consider to be a benevolent authoritarian manner. He is most definitely a guru figure to his followers, and he does not appear to have any intentions of phasing out his total authority in the Conversations with God organization. I will also say that in my opinion, he has not abused his power and authority in any kind of serious negative way, but of course this kind of abusive guru danger is always present, and is an obvious cause of concern (see [61]).

I will now give Conversations with God my ratings on the Bonewits Cult Danger Scale, based upon my 2003 experience at the Conversations With God Humanity's Team conference in addition to my previous learnings about Conversations with God.

Internal Control	2
Wisdom Claimed	8
Wisdom Credited	7
Dogma	8
Recruiting	4
Front Groups	4
Wealth	4
Political Power	5
Sexual Manipulation	2
Censorship	2
Dropout Control	2
Endorsement of Violence	1
Paranoia	3
Grimness	1
Surrender of Will	3
TOTAL	**56**
AVERAGE	**3.7**

Once again I come up with a relatively low score on the Bonewits Cult Danger Scale, actually the same average score as that of Self-Realization Fellowship. We also see that there are no ratings for Conversations with God greater than "8." The two ratings of "8" are for Wisdom Claimed and Dogma, representing the fact that although Walsch does have strong powerful beliefs in the validity of his ideas being told to him personally by God, he is also somewhat flexible in his interpretation of these ideas (see [61]). The trust and admiration for him from his followers is quite high, but my "7" rating in Wisdom Credited shows that this trust and admiration does not go past reasonable limits in regard to listening to everything Walsch says without thinking for oneself. There are a number of intermediate ratings of "4" for Recruiting, Front Groups, and Wealth, and "5" for Political Power, representing that there is a fair amount of emphasis in these categories, but does not reach inappropriate or excessive proportions. For example, there was a definite push when I was at the Humanity's Team Conference for people to seriously consider signing up for the Leadership program, the "fast track" option being done in three months for a cost of $12,500. In my opinion this is an exorbitant sum of money for three months of training, but there was not undo pressure put upon us to sign up for the Leadership training or any of the other Conversations with God workshops or retreats, which was in marked distinction from both Scientology and Avatar [64]. For all remaining categories I gave relatively low ratings of "1," "2," or "3." Although much of the Conversations with God philosophy is based upon taking responsibility for your actions and for your life, there is also the aspect of surrendering yourself to your higher power or "God." Walsch is quite the theatrical comedian on stage, and my rating of "1" for Grimness reflects this lightness and humor which Walsch brings to his retreats as well as to his writings. There is no endorsement of violence whatsoever, and no obvious sexual manipulations, though the Walsch philosophy of complete individual freedom could have sexual overtones regarding being bi-sexual or even multi-sexual in romantic relationships. Walsch also displays some serious concerns about the dangers of traditional religions that do not share his views of non-hierarchy and openness. However, all things considered we seem to once again have a modern religion here that is in Neutral territory regarding being susceptible to cult dangers vs. being a "favorable" new age spiritual organization. As I concluded in my last Conversations with God essay [65], Neale Donald Walsch does have a strong ego and charismatic personality, but Conversations with God is not a dangerous cult.

Given that we once again have a Neutral classification for my tri-perspective experiential analysis of a new age spiritual organization, let us see if Conversations with God can be considered to be a legitimate ITP in Wilber's Four Quadrant Integral Model. As we have seen for a number of other modern religions examined in this way, the Multilevel and trans-rational contexts of Conversations with God certainly appear to fulfill a quality place in the Intentional quadrant of Wilber's model for an Integral Transformative Practice. In regard to the Behavioral quadrant, although there are not specific practices advocated in Conversations with God, there is an emphasis upon being in the world in a harmonious balanced way, especially through expressing yourself in loving sexual ways with others. Thus the body is by no means ignored in the context of a spiritual practice in Conversations with God. As far as the Cultural and Social quadrants are concerned, I must say that Conversations with God demonstrates the most extensive and forceful focus on these quadrants that we have thus far seen. In addition to all the Conversations with God study groups, retreats, and conferences, the Conversations with God subsidiary organization Humanity's Team has the goal of changing the world for the better through striving for world peace regardless of religious beliefs or perspectives. There is much emphasis upon working with prison inmates, underprivileged populations—both in our own country as well as in third world countries, and in general with virtually all segments of social structure: education, law, politics, ecology, business, medicine, etc. (see [61]). Yes—the Cultural and Social quadrants emphasized in Conversations With God are indeed quite impressive. Aside from the rather limited focus on the Behavioral quadrant, I would say that Conversations with God does appear to have some solid potential for people to engage in a bona-fide Integral Transformative Practice. Deep meditation and self-analysis can be interpreted as a conversation with God or as simply the experiences of higher self along the lines of many spiritual writers [66]. One can certainly add one's own Behavioral quadrant activities such as yoga, Tai Chi, dance, etc. to round out an effective Conversations with God ITP.

However, it is also important to not forget the dangers that we have seen from both the Anthony Typology and the Wilber Integral Model. This is one time that the Bonewits Cult Danger Scale does not adequately reflect the red flag of the guru phenomenon dangers, since in comparison to other gurus and leaders of new age spiritual organizations with serious cult dangers, Neale Donald Walsch cannot be considered to be a serious threat to individual freedom and ethics. However, the Charismatic cell placement in the Anthony Typology and the lack of anchoring of its legitimacy in a tradition and phase-specific authority in the Wilber Integral Model do remind us that Conversations with God is run in an authoritarian charismatic new age way by one powerful magnetic person, and it is important to monitor this one person's continued presence and activity in Conversations with God. We shall find that it is even more important to keep this kind of careful monitoring in mind as we examine our next new age spiritual organization, whose philosophy is very similar to that of Conversations with God and began a few years earlier; I am referring to Avatar.

AVATAR

Avatar is a new age spiritual organization founded in the late 1980s by Harry Palmer, and has a somewhat similar philosophy to Conversations with God in regard to a person being able to "choose" what he or she wants to experience in life. Avatar successfully markets itself by promising to enable people to learn how to actualize their dreams and gain a heightened experience of being alive. I had reached the level of "Assistant Avatar Master" and spent over $8,000 to gain this dubious honor [67]. As I describe in my Avatar and Conversations with God essays in Chapter 2, Avatar gives much more cause for alarm regarding cult dangers than does Conversations with God. Through my tri-perspective experiential analysis we shall see which perspectives of my analysis accurately reflect these cult dangers.

In the Anthony Typology I would once again have to utilize the Multilevel cell placement. I do believe that there is a bona-fide spiritual experience available in Avatar, described as going into "source," from where the inner power to make substantive changes in your life is cultivated. The "Feel-Its" exercises, Creation affirmations, and Dis-Creation initiation (see [67]) are all dealing with authentic spiritual states that belong in the Multilevel cell. There are a number of deep impactful techniques learned in Avatar that are fairly simple to apply [68]. Although Avatar founder Harry Palmer is certainly viewed as a guru to Avatar members, and through his personal charisma induces people to spend exorbitant sums of money on Avatar [69], I would still place Avatar in the Technical cell because of the enormous focus of the primary spiritual drills and exercises. In regard to the Monistic/Dualistic choice, from my perspective Avatar does not discriminate in an Us. vs. Them mentality and is open to all people doing the Avatar training. I would place Avatar in the Monistic cell on this basis, which puts Avatar in the most favorable cell in the Anthony Typology: Multilevel/Technical/Monistic. However, I contend that as we have seen before, there is something missing in this Anthony Typology placement, and hopefully we will discover what is missing as we go through our two other perspectives.

In the Wilber Integral Model, once again based upon my Multilevel placement of Avatar in the Anthony Typology we seem to have a level of consciousness that is in-between the rational and trans-rational levels in Wilber's continuum. Some of the exercises and drills may be less than totally authentic for some people, but all things considered I do find Avatar's techniques that are designed to bring forth an authentic spiritual state to be quite effective (see [67]). However, when it comes to anchoring its legitimacy in a tradition, we have a similar situation to what we had in Conversations with God. There is no tradition to fall back upon; Avatar is Harry Palmer's creation from new age bits and pieces that he experienced in life (including Scientology). Similarly, there is no phase-specific authority, as Palmer takes on a similar benevolent authoritarian guru role to his Avatar followers as Neale Donald Walsch does to his Conversations with God followers. There are no plans to phase out Harry Palmer's complete control of the Avatar organization. We thus see that in the Wilber Integral Model the cult dangers picture for Avatar is not quite as rosy as it appears to be in the Anthony Typology. However, we still very much need to see the specifics of the cult dangers of Avatar, and hopefully we shall see this through the perspective of the Bonewits Cult Danger Scale.

My ratings on the Bonewits Cult Danger Scale are based upon my involvement in Avatar from 1997 through 2001.

Internal Control	5
Wisdom Claimed	9
Wisdom Credited	9
Dogma	10
Recruiting	6
Front Groups	1
Wealth	10
Political Power	1
Sexual Manipulation	2
Censorship	5
Dropout Control	5
Endorsement of Violence	1
Paranoia	7
Grimness	5
Surrender of Will	5
TOTAL	81
AVERAGE	**5.4**

Avatar's score of 5.4 on the Bonewits Cult Danger Scale is the third highest score we have seen thus far, only Scientology and The Unification Church having higher scores (although both Scientology and The Unification Church do have significantly higher cult danger ratings than Avatar does on the Bonewits Cult Danger Scale). On this basis it certainly does appear that Avatar presents a moderate degree of cult danger concerns, in a somewhat similar capacity to that of Divine Light Mission. I gave Avatar ratings of "10" in two categories: Dogma and Wealth, and ratings of "9" in two categories: Wisdom Claimed and Wisdom Credited. There is no deviating from the exact ways that Palmer set forth for his exercises to be done (see [68]), and no differences of opinion tolerated regarding Palmer's philosophical views. However, Palmer does not claim to be an all knowing "perfect master" and his followers do not see him in this totalistic way either; rather he is a more human guru, therefore deserving of ratings of "9" rather than "10" in the Wisdom Claimed and Wisdom Credited categories. However, when it comes to Wealth there is no doubt that Avatar deserves the top score of "10." All roads lead eventually to the Avatar "Wizards" course in Florida, a thirteen day course that costs $7,500 plus all the extras for hotels, food, and transportation. And the expensive prices of the Avatar courses (the cheapest is the first nine day course for $2,300 plus the above extras) is heavily marketed to anyone who shows preliminary interest in Avatar or who graduates from the initial Avatar training course or the Avatar Masters' course (see [69]). I gave relatively high scores of "6" or "7" and intermediate scores of "5" in the categories of Internal Control, Recruiting, Censorship, Dropout Control, Paranoia, Grimness, and Surrender of Will. When you complete the Avatar Masters' course you are required to sign a lengthy contract stating, among other things, that you will not divulge any Avatar secrets. Avatar does take legal action against ex-members who make public their negative views of Avatar. Recruiting is a full-fledged business activity, and Palmer's book *The Masters' Handbook* is primarily a marketing tool for Avatar Masters who want to find their own paying Avatar students (see [69]).

When one appears to drop out of the Avatar scene, both personalized mailings and phone calls are made to try to bring this person back to Avatar. Influence and control of Avatar members' lives is frequently done for the purpose of persuading Avatar members to sign up for their next level Avatar courses (each course has a course fee of at least a few thousand dollars plus the extras (see [67]). Questioning of financial Avatar matters or disagreeing with particular Avatar exercises is looked upon with suspicion by Avatar leaders and is grounds for not granting a successful completion certificate for higher level Avatar courses [70]. Although taking personal responsibility for life is focused upon in Avatar, surrendering your will to "source" is considered to be of fundamental importance. Although on a major part of the Avatar drills there is much joking and laughter going on as part of the drill, this joking and laughter must stay in its proper place and not be addressed toward disagreeing with the Avatar structure or philosophical principles, in order to be successful on an Avatar course. Avatar is run completely as a business, and Harry Palmer makes no pretenses about covering up his marketing strategies and course prices. I am not aware of any Front Groups in Avatar, endorsement of violence, or interest in political power (to all of which I have given ratings of "1"). Sexual Manipulation received a rating of "2" from me, as the focus upon individual choice and freedom may have an effect upon decisions in regard to one's romantic and sexual involvements.

All things considered, we can see from the Bonewits Cult Danger Scale that Avatar's cult dangers cannot be ignored. We have here a very expensive new age spiritual organization with a highly organized and effective recruitment and marketing strategy. Although the leader/guru has not gone over the edge in terms of blatantly destructive practices for his followers, the dogma, recruitment focus, and high prices of Avatar courses are in themselves enough reason to be very much on guard with this new age spiritual organization. The philosophy of Avatar may be in some ways similar to that of Conversations with God, but the similarity ends there. Avatar has been described as "the new est," and there is truthfulness in this description. We see another LGAT (Large Group Awareness Training Program) at work here, as we have seen in est, and one that also focuses upon individual freedom and choice, but has no reservations about charging very expensive prices for their courses right away. What is alarming is how successful Avatar has been in getting people to pay these very expensive prices for their courses, myself included. Needless to say, we will not be examining Avatar's potential for engagement in an Integral Transformative Practice. But it is also true that there is a world of difference between Avatar and Scientology or the Unification Church in terms of degree of cult dangers. For our next new age spiritual organization, Reiki, I believe we will also find a world of difference from Avatar regarding degree of cult dangers, but in the direction of having significantly less cult dangers and moving closer to being a "Favorable" new age spiritual organization.

REIKI

Reiki has various interpretations to it according to one's orientation, ranging from the universal energy rediscovered by Mikao Usui in Japan in the early 1920s and "channeled" by way of "attunements" through his lineage, to the continuity of Tibetan hands-on healing methods over thousands of years [71]. However, the interpretation that I choose to bring to Reiki is far more modest and simple. From my own experience with Reiki, as I have described in my Reiki essays in Chapter 2, I view Reiki as "meditation with touch" [72]. This may sound like a rather mundane way of describing the Eastern mystical context of universal energy for which Reiki is known. But it has the advantage of not attributing false or unsubstantiated claims to Reiki, simultaneously maintaining the healing spiritual benefits that deep meditation coupled with the sensitive laying on of hands can bring forth. As I have experienced peacefulness, relaxation, and personal insightful awareness repeatedly when being given this kind of "meditation with touch," I expect that Reiki will fare comparatively well in my tri-perspective experiential analysis. There are loose associations of Reiki practitioners linked through Reiki sharing sessions as well as the internet. This Reiki association can be considered a new age spiritual organization, and the emphasis on the spiritual state experienced through Reiki, together with the Reiki precepts and techniques handed down from Reiki founder Usui [73], certainly justifies Reiki to be viewed in the context of a modern religion. Let us begin our tri-perspective experiential analysis and see if we finally end up with a modern religion that we can place in the "Favorable" category, on the other side of cult dangers.

In the Anthony Typology it is quite clear that Reiki belongs in the Multilevel cell, as the central emphasis in Reiki is on receiving the universal healing energy, which we may think of as experiencing a heightened sense of awareness through deep meditation and generally the laying on of hands. However, it is also quite common for Reiki practitioners to not actually touch the person but rather lay their hands within a person's "energy fields," or even put their intention into giving distant healing, generally using specific Reiki symbols that have been given to them in their "attunements" [74]. The impact on people receiving Reiki in these ways can be interpreted via subtle sensitivities or psychic connections, as well as through "expectations" or the "self fulfilling prophesy" [75]. However, no matter how one chooses to interpret the experience of receiving this kind of meditation with (or without) touch, it seems quite clear that we are talking about an authentic spiritual experience here that belongs in the Multilevel cell. In regard to the Technical or Charismatic cell, although there is certainly a mystique and a guru phenomenon associated with Usui, I believe that the emphasis upon the techniques of giving attunements, hand positions, symbols, Reiki precepts, and various other specialized techniques place Reiki in the Technical cell. There is no doubt in my mind that Reiki belongs in the Monistic cell as opposed to the Dualistic cell, as Reiki practices love and harmony to all people, and the emphasis upon receiving a Reiki attunement is not done in a condescending hierarchical way in regard to those who have not received these attunements [76]. We thus once again have a classification by me which represents the most favorable cell in the Anthony Typology: Multilevel/Technical/Monistic. However, there are also aspects of Reiki that may not be completely as idyllic as Reiki appears to be in the Anthony Typology, and this is where our other two perspectives will serve us well.

In the Wilber Integral Model, once again I am comfortable placing Reiki on the trans-rational level of consciousness based upon my Multilevel cell placement from the Anthony Typology. However, the tremendous variety of Reiki orientations and the rather farfetched claims by many of these orientations persuade me to keep to the same continuum level placement that I have often been making, in-between the rational and trans-rational levels of consciousness [77]. It is interesting to compare Reiki to Divine Light Mission, in the sense that in order to "Receive Knowledge" in Divine Light Mission one must first accept Guru Maharajji as Lord of the Universe [78]. But one can receive Reiki healings and attunements regardless of whether or not one believes in the universal energy transmission perspective of Reiki or any other Reiki perspective. This is one reason that I have put Divine Light Mission on the pre-rational level of consciousness while I am placing Reiki on a much higher level of consciousness in the continuum.

In regard to anchoring its legitimacy in a tradition, the picture becomes much more blurry, as it depends upon what orientation of Reiki we are using. Certainly the Tibetan Reiki orientation basing its continuity on an unbroken lineage for thousands of years is very much steeped in anchoring its legitimacy in a tradition. This is much less the case for the traditional Reiki heritage that stems from Usui's "rediscovery" of Reiki in the 1920s, although even this perspective involves the context of Reiki being an ancient universal energy that was always available. However, there are also much more exotic and closer to science fiction versions of Reiki that have little or no historical tradition associated to them. As far as phase-specific authority is concerned, once again the picture gets somewhat blurry. Focusing upon the Reiki lineage from the time of Usui (most of the other Reiki orientations have very little factual information for us to say much about), we can view this as initial phase-specific authority. This is essentially because Usui only lived for five or six years after his revelation Reiki experience, and his direct lineage evolved in a few different directions with a number of individuals taking on leadership roles in Reiki. Aside from Usui, who can be considered the primary Reiki guru but a short-lived one who seems to have been an essentially progressive uplifting teacher, we do not have any absolute authority figure in Reiki, but rather different phases where various individuals have taken on Reiki leadership roles. We thus see that Reiki also fares quite well in the Wilber Integral Model, the slight red flag perhaps being the lack of historical legitimacy in a tradition for followers of Usui and especially for the more modern ad hoc Reiki groups.

I now complete my tri-perspective experiential analysis of Reiki through my ratings on the Bonewits Cult Danger Scale, based upon my experiences in Reiki from 1997 through 2004.

Internal Control	3
Wisdom Claimed	9
Wisdom Credited	9
Dogma	8
Recruiting	3
Front Groups	3
Wealth	5
Political Power	2
Sexual Manipulation	2
Censorship	3
Dropout Control	1
Endorsement of Violence	1
Paranoia	3
Grimness	3
Surrender of Will	7
TOTAL	62

AVERAGE   4.1

I must say that I am somewhat surprised that Reiki did not receive more favorable ratings from me on the Bonewits Cult Danger Scale. Let us examine some of these ratings and see what they might mean. The highest ratings of "9," "8," "7," and "5" occur respectively in the categories of Wisdom Claimed, Wisdom Credited, Dogma, Surrender of Will, and Wealth. The beliefs in the universal Reiki energy and the transference or channeling of this universal energy through attunements and healings are quite rigidly adhered to, with a great deal of reverence being given to the Japanese Reiki founder Usui. However, there also seems to be a certain degree of humility in the personality of Usui, as well as differences of opinion and discussion amongst Reiki practitioners regarding some historical details; for this reason I gave the Wisdom Claimed and Wisdom Credited categories ratings of "9" instead of "10," and Dogma a rating of "8." There is a strong emphasis upon leaving behind the rational mind and entering the Reiki flow, which can certainly be considered a surrender of will, but this surrender is not given to any particular individual but rather to the universal Reiki energy (which I interpret as the person's deepest layer of self); thus I rated the Surrender of Will category as a "7." There are some Reiki masters who charge very large sums of money to give people attunements, as much as $10,000 for the Masters' attunement, but for the most part receiving three levels of Reiki attunements to become a Reiki master will run around a thousand dollars, or perhaps a few hundred more. This still seems quite high-priced to me, given that from my perspective people are frequently paying over a thousand dollars for simply "meditation with touch" (or without touch).

Reiki healings are generally given for similar fees as massage and counseling, and there do exist Reiki masters who offer all their services for very small fees and occasionally even for no charge [79]. All things considered, I gave the Wealth category the intermediate rating of "5." For all the remaining categoriesmI gave relatively low ratings of "1," "2," or "3"; most of the "3" ratings are not "1"s or "2"s primarily because of the variety of modern ad hoc Reiki groups that bring in both outlandish ideas as well as harsher perspectives toward other Reiki practitioners with different points of view [80]. It should also be noted that a number of states in this country have put rather severe legal restrictions on Reiki. There may be valid reasons why Reiki practitioners in these states feel a degree of threat from their society. But in summary, if there are lingering cult dangers in Reiki they are certainly on the quite mild side. In fact, I will give Reiki the benefit of the doubt, given its positive ratings in the Anthony Typology and Wilber Integral Model, and place Reiki in the Neutral category regarding cult dangers vs. favorable practices. I believe that the high cult danger ratings in the categories of Wisdom Claimed, Wisdom Credited, and Dogma are effectively tempered by the relatively low cult danger ratings in the categories of Recruitment, Censorship, Dropout Control, Paranoia, Grimness, and the remaining categores.

Given that I am placing Reiki in the Neutral category for cult dangers, we can certainly examine its potential for an ITP in the Wilber Four Quadrant Integral Model, from my Reiki perspective of "meditation with touch". In my meditation with touch perspective it is clear from my Multilevel cell placement in the Anthony Typology and my in-between rational and trans-rational consciousness level placement in the Wilber Integral Model, that I believe Reiki has high quality spiritual activity to offer in Wilber's Intentional quadrant. In regard to the Behavioral quadrant, we have a similar situation to that of Conversations with God, in that one would need to add one's own working with the body to balance out the Reiki meditation state. Some of the more modern ad hoc Reiki orientations may actually incorporate more of this Behavioral quadrant through activities such as "Reiki Dance," but this is by no means a common occurrence in Reiki. In regard to the Cultural and Social quadrants, we see a much more comprehensive and balanced approach. Reiki advocates peace in the world through giving people the healing Reiki energy. This extends both to Reiki sharing groups as well as to the general public in all kinds of social structures, most especially in hospitals and childbirths [81]. There are Reiki practitioners who went to Ground Zero in New York City after 9/11/2001 to give Reiki to the firemen working in the rubble, and Reiki practitioners who went to Russia to give Reiki to Russian people who could not afford to pay for Reiki. There is a healthy and inspiring balance of the individual receiving the Reiki energy and then giving it to others in a variety of cultural and social contexts. We thus find, as we did in the case of Conversations with God, that Reiki does appear to have positive potential for an ITP, especially if a balancing physical activity is engaged in for the Behavioral quadrant. However, Reiki is definitely not my own chosen path of spiritual practice or ITP (and neither is Conversations with God for that matter), as the traditional beliefs of Reiki that I have taken many pains to reinterpret are extremely rigid, from my own perspective. Our next modern religion to examine from my tri-perspective experiential analysis, Neopaganism, is much closer to heart for me personally, and may very well prove to be our first modern religion that I can legitimately place in the "Favorable" category.

NEOPAGANISM

As I have described the nature of my tri-perspective experiential analysis in the Introduction, my goal is not to give a comprehensive objective portrayal of the groups that I am writing about. The tri-perspective experiential analysis I have embarked upon is my way of organizing, analyzing, and quantifying my own personal experiences in seventeen new age spiritual organizations. It is in this spirit that I will apply my tri-perspective experiential analysis to Neopaganism, i.e. based upon my own experiences with Neopaganism from 1997 through 2004. My Neopaganism essay in Chapter 2 captures the gist of my experiences [82], but there have been other Neopagan workshops and festivals that I have attended, and they have not all been as positive as the Starwood festival which I wrote about in my essay. However, most of my experiences with Neopaganism have been personally fulfilling and engaging while being free of manipulation and coercion. I do believe that Neopaganism belongs in the "Favorable" modern religion category, clearly on the other side of cult dangers. But then again, I had these expectations for Reiki, only to find that Reiki barely made it into Neutral territory. This is where the benefits of an experiential tri-perspective analysis make itself strongly known, as we will continue to see as I begin my tri-perspective experiential analysis of Neopaganism.

There are numerous philosophies and perspectives in the Neopagan movement [83], and my own definition of earth-based spirituality Neopaganism refers simply to "people in modern times who consider themselves to be practicing Paganism with present day adaptations." [84]. My experience of Neopaganism is taken primarily from all the workshops, rituals, and bonfires I have attended through the Starwood, Rites of Spring, and Twilight Covening festivals and workshops (see [82]). There was one other weekend Pagan gathering, near where I live in Maine, that I participated in. This weekend gathering was not a positive experience for me, as I found it to be rather crass and lacking depth, not at all what I consider to be an authentic spiritual experience. Thus when it comes to deciding whether to put Neopaganism in the Multilevel or Unilevel cell in the Anthony Typology, it is not an automatic or easy decision to make. The truth is that it can go in either direction, based upon what a person is seeking and which particular Neopagan group a person experiences. There is plenty of worldly fun and entertainment at the Starwood Pagan festival (see [82]), but there is also opportunity for deeper spiritual experience. For me, the dancing around the nightly bonfires had all the ingredients to furnish me with an altered state of consciousness, as did a number of the rituals of Starwood, Rites of Spring, and Twilight Convening (see [82]), plus a few afternoon and evening Pagan events that I attended in California with my son. Putting all this together, I feel justified in placing Neopaganism in the Multilevel cell in the Anthony Typology, with the understanding that the Multilevel potential is there for those who are seeking it.

In regard to the Technical vs. Charismatic choice, this is much easier. I have found very little guru directed activity in my exploration of Neopaganism, and the practices of meditation, dance, drumming, yoga, massage, breathwork, etc. clearly place Neopaganism in the Technical cell. Similarly, there is no doubt that Neopaganism belongs in the Monistic cell as opposed to the Dualistic cell. Neopaganism is open to all people and all religions, and does not alienate itself or act condescendingly toward those who think differently. Of course not every Neopagan lives up to these standards completely, but for the most part this has been the crux of my experience with Neopaganism for the seven years that I was attending Neopagan workshops and festivals. We thus see that Neopaganism, like the past few modern religions that I have experientially analyzed, is in the most favorable cell in the Anthony Typology: Multilevel/Technical/Monistic (once again based upon my own experiences).

As we become more accustomed to this tri-perspective experiential analysis, it becomes clear that the Wilber Integral Model level of consciousness that accompanies the Multilevel cell in the Anthony Typology will fall in-between the rational and trans-rational levels of Wilber's continuum. In the case of Neopaganism, the variety of worldly vs. spiritual kind of experiences available certainly give this in-between rational and trans-rational placement appropriate justification. In regard to anchoring its legitimacy in a tradition, once again this is not an easy question to answer. Some Neopagans very clearly trace their heritage back to the Celts or Druids or other early Pagans. On the other hand, some Neopagans make no pretenses about their religion being made from scratch in the 20th century, such as the Church of All Worlds, founded by Oberon Zell, which is based upon

Robert Heinlein's popular science fiction novel *Stranger in a Strange Land* [85]. There is no clear answer here, and we can only say "it depends on who you are asking." In regard to phase-specific authority, here we can comfortably say that whatever authority is exercised in the Neopagan community is quite phase-specific. There is no central guru or authority figure in Neopaganism, and the local authority figures in Pagan covens and gatherings, i.e. the priests and priestesses, generally alter their leadership based upon which rituals are being done. We thus find quite a loose flexible social structure for a modern religion or new age spiritual organization; certainly the most flexible and least authoritarian group we have thus far explored.

I now give my ratings for Neopaganism on the Bonewits Cult Danger Scale, based upon my experiences with Neopaganism from 1997 through 2004.

Internal Control	3
Wisdom Claimed	2
Wisdom Credited	4
Dogma	2
Recruiting	2
Front Groups	2
Wealth	1
Political Power	1
Sexual Manipulation	3
Censorship	1
Dropout Control	1
Endorsement of Violence	1
Paranoia	5
Grimness	1
Surrender of Will	3
TOTAL	32
AVERAGE	**2.1**

Clearly we have a horse of a different color here. The Bonewits Cult Danger Scale has furnished us with a good deal of certainty that Neopaganism belongs in the "Favorable" modern religion category, clearly on the other side of cult dangers. This is reinforced by the Anthony Typology as well as the Wilber Integral Model, and

Neopaganism's score on the Bonewits Cult Danger Scale puts it strikingly in a class by itself in comparison to any of the other modern religions we have explored. There are no ratings above "5"; the highest rating of "5," for Paranoia, reflects the realistic danger that Neopagans feel in our society at the way their religion is misrepresented and negatively thought of, being unfairly linked with Satanism. The next highest score of "4," for Wisdom Credited, reflects the general respect and trust that many Neopagans do feel toward their workshop and ritual leaders, though this is a respect and trust that is realistic and earned. The ratings of "3" for Internal Control, Sexual Manipulation, and Surrender of Will demonstrate a degree of influence of Wiccan and Pagan priests and priestesses in covens, a not uncommon occurrence of Polyamory (i.e. having more than one sexual partner as a way of life), and a temporary surrender of will to nature and ancestors in the context of an altered state of consciousness. The remaining scores are all "1"s and "2"s, and it is noteworthy how different these ratings are for Neopaganism compared to nearly all the other groups we have explored, in the categories of Wisdom Claimed, Dogma, Recruiting, Wealth, Political Power, Censorship, Dropout Control, and Grimness. Yes—it appears that we finally have encountered a new age spiritual organization that we can safely say is free of cult dangers, at least in regard to the context of my own experiences with Neopaganism over a seven year period of time.

In regard to Neopaganism's potential for an ITP in Ken Wilber's Four Quadrant Integral Model, the most immediate quadrant that stands out to me is actually the Behavioral quadrant. Neopaganism is exceptionally strong in focusing upon the body, in terms of dance, drumming, yoga, martial arts, massage, Tai Chi, etc. The Intentional quadrant certainly has the potential of being expressed in a constructive manner, but once again this is entirely dependent upon the aspirations of the individual person. Meditation and altered states of consciousness are very much part of Neopaganism if one chooses to partake of these experiences. In regard to the Cultural quadrant we have a widespread Pagan source of community, once again for those who seek it. There is much opportunity to partake of many different Pagan communities all year round, all over the world. The Social quadrant goes hand in hand with the Pagan cultural community, especially nowadays with our modern technology and Internet access. However, this Cultural and Social Pagan community orientation does not necessarily go beyond the Pagan community itself. Neopagans may certainly decide to engage themselves in Social causes beyond their Pagan communities, and many of them do, but this kind of going beyond the Pagan community is not particularly emphasized in Neopaganism. Unlike the world peace oriented social emphasis of both Reiki and Conversations with God, there is no comparable social ethics or practices like this in Neopaganism. The freedom of the individual is considered to be sacred, and organizing into social groups to accomplish "good" things for the world is not considered particularly important or even necessarily appropriate in Neopaganism. I see this Cultural and Social perspective as being rather loose and lacking, especially given the grave perils our world is currently living in. I would therefore say that there is certainly reasonable potential to engage in a beneficial ITP through Neopaganism, but one would need to formulate one's own Cultural and Social practices beyond the Neopagan community, as well as focus upon the higher level spiritual context that can be found in Neopaganism. We thus see that even though Neopaganism most certainly is in the land of Favorable modern religions, it might have gone too far in the realm of focusing upon the individual without taking into account the urgent needs of the society in which the individual lives.

For the remainder of this chapter, I will examine five additional new age spiritual organizations, each one of which I have found to be beneficial and personally meaningful in different ways. My main purpose in these final explorations is no longer specifically to describe a group's cult dangers, although I will continue with my tri-perspective experiential analysis for purposes of continuity and comparison, and actually one of these five new age spiritual organizations that I have found to be personally meaningful does end up with my classification being in the Mild cult danger category. But my more fundamental purpose is to bring forth an extensive philosophical exploration of new age spiritual organizations from an experiential research perspective [86]. This experiential research perspective looks at all of life and describes phenomenologically what it sees. What are the ingredients of new age spiritual organizations that can give people support in their life journeys and stimulate authentic spiritual insights and meaning in their lives? The next new age spiritual organization we will examine can be described as a modernized form of Judaism, but without the "chosen people" syndrome; this is the modern religion of Tikkun.

TIKKUN

Tikkun is a modern largely Jewish peace oriented organization founded by Michael Lerner in the late 1980s. I first became acquainted with Tikkun from reading Micahel Lerner's book *Spirit Matters* in 2002 [87], and I attended a one day Tikkun workshop in Massachusetts that same year, followed by a five day Tikkun conference in 2003 in Washington D.C. that was focused upon peace in the Middle East. At both events I was quite impressed with the self-assured and effective but yet modest leadership of Michael Lerner, who is a Ph.D psychologist as well as a rabbi, and the peace oriented inclusive idealistic Jewish philosophy which Tikkun represented [88]. Tikkun is a highly political organization, and we ended up in the halls of congress in Washington D.C., speaking to our U.S. senators and congressmen about a Tikkun platform for peace in the Middle East, focusing upon a combined Palestinian/Israeli state. However, for the purposes of our experiential tri-perspective analysis of new age spiritual organizations, although I have no doubt that Tikkun is free of cult dangers, it remains to be seen if Tikkun can qualify as a favorable modern religion and offer an effective Integral Transformative Practice in Wilber's Four Quadrant Integral Model.

The first question that must be decided upon is where to put Tikkun in regard to the Multilevel/Unilevel choice in the Anthony Typology. At first glance it may seem that of course Tikkun belongs in the Multilevel cell, as most of the modern religions we have examined have ended up in the Multilevel cell; even some of the ones with a modest degree of cult dangers attached to them. From reading *Spirit Matters* one certainly gets the message from Michael Lerner that Tikkun wants to embrace both the spiritual as well as the material world, merging spirituality into business, politics, law, education, medicine, etc. However, after attending the Washington D.C. Tikkun conference I must say that I found this element of spirituality in Michael Lerner's writings to be severely lacking in actual practice. The focus was almost entirely on the social/political arena, and there was virtually no time set aside for meditation and spiritual nourishment, in spite of what was described in *Spirit Matters*. I therefore must conclude from my own experience of Tikkun that we have a courageous, dedicated, and idealistic organization that I have much agreement with personally [89], but I am not able to say that Tikkun offers an authentic spiritual practice per se when it comes down to how they set their priorities in their workshops. Based upon these considerations I must place Tikkun in the Unilevel cell.

In regard to the choice between the Technical and Charismatic cell, although Michael Lerner is certainly quite influential and has his own personal Jewish brand of charisma, the extensive philosophical principles upon which Tikkun is based and represented in various articles in the Tikkun journal (see [88]) appeal predominantly to the liberal and intellectually minded person. Tikkun reaches people through logic and reason, focusing upon their sacred convictions of peace in the world and in Israel through being open to all people and all faiths, eliminating the "chosen people" doctrine of Judaism. I will therefore place Tikkun in the Technical cell. In regard to the Monistic/Dualistic choice, here we have an easy decision, as Tikkun's basic philosophy is non-judgmental openness to all people in a tremendously extensive and liberal-minded perspective of Judaism; certainly Tikkun belongs in the Monistic cell. We thus see that Tikkun has the placement of Unilevel/Technical/Monistic in the Anthony Typology, based upon my own experiences with Tikkun.

In regard to the Wilber Integral Model, as we saw in the Anthony Typology we have a similar choice to make in placing Tikkun on the appropriate level of consciousness in Wilber's continuum. Certainly Tikkun is at the height of rationality, exhibiting extreme logic and intelligence in all of its philosophical premises and arguments. However, can we justify placing Tikkun on a level beyond rational, i.e. in-between the rational and trans-rational levels of consciousness? For the same reasons as my Unilevel placement of Tikkun in the Anthony Typology, I must place Tikkun on the rational level of consciousness in the Wilber Integral Model. In regard to anchoring its legitimacy in a tradition, here we can give a resounding affirmative as Tikkun is based quite heavily upon Jewish foundations, even though many aspects of Judaism are liberally interpreted and/or radically transformed. In regard to phase-specific authority, once again I will answer in the affirmative. From my own experience, Michael Lerner is an authentic teacher figure, but has no desire or need to be in lifelong control of Tikkun. Michael Lerner is the editor in chief of Tikkun magazine [90], and shares the leadership of the Tikkun related political organization The Network of Spiritual Progressives with Cornel West and Sister Joan Chittister. We thus see that in both the Anthony Typology and the Wilber Integral Model, Tikkun fares quite well, with the exception that a bona fide authentic spiritual focus is talked about and written about, but was not present from my own experiential perspective.

We now examine Tikkun from the perspective of the Bonewits Cult Danger Scale; my ratings are based upon my experiences at the Tikkun conferences that I attended in 2002 and 2003, and also upon some interesting personal e-mail interactions I have had with Michael Lerner in 2007 and 2010 [91].

Internal Control	4
Wisdom Claimed	5
Wisdom Credited	4
Dogma	6
Recruiting	4
Front Groups	4
Wealth	3
Political Power	10
Sexual Manipulation	1
Censorship	1
Dropout Control	3
Endorsement of Violence	1
Paranoia	6
Grimness	3
Surrender of Will	1
TOTAL	**57**
AVERAGE	**3.8**

I am somewhat surprised that Tikkun's rating on the Bonewits Cult Danger scale is not lower than it is, but we see that Tikkkun's rating is comparable to that of Self-Realization Fellowship, A Course in Miracles, Conversations with God, and Reiki, all of which I placed in the Neutral category, in-between modern religions with cult dangers and favorable modern religions. The rating that particularly stands out for Tikkun on the Bonewits Cult Danger Scale is the "10" rating for Political Power. Tikkun's tremendous focus upon influencing U.S. senators and congressmen to support Tikkun's Middle East peace platform, and the various political figures, including 2004 Democratic Presidential aspirant Dennis Kucinich, who spoke at the Tikkun Washington D.C. Middle East peace banquet that I attended, demonstrate the intensive social/political focus of Tikkun. The upper level intermediate scores of "6" for Wisdom Claimed and Dogma represent Tikkun's strong liberal-minded philosophical peace-oriented beliefs, although there is also plenty of dialogue and discussion in Tikkun regarding the specifics of these beliefs. The score of "6" in Paranoia represents the strong fear of the influence of traditionally minded pro-Israeli lobbyist organizations, as well as the fears of alienating Jewish people with different points of view. The lower intermediate scores of "4" for Internal Control, Wisdom Credited, Recruitment, and Front Groups demonstrate a moderate level of cohesiveness in the Tikkun organization but not excessive allegiance to its leaders, with a fair amount of recruitment efforts to bring other people into Tikkun, through a variety of group activities that may or may not utilize the name Tikkun. The scores of "3" for Wealth, Dropout Control, and Grimness demonstrate a small but not insignificant level of membership fees, frequent mailings to keep Tikkun members in the organization, and a healthy respect for the organization but one that does allow for humor. The score of "1" for Surrender of Will highlights the extreme focus on purely rational decision making, and the scores of "1" for Endorsement of Violence, Sexual Manipulation, and Censorship testify to the high level of ethical responsibility in Tikkun. It is clear from my tri-perspective experiential analysis that based upon my own experiences with Tikkun, I can confidently say that although Tikkun is a strong-minded liberal cohesive organization, there is relatively no cult dangers attached to it. From the lack of authentic spirituality based upon my own experience with Tikkun, together with its neutral level score on the Bonewits Cult Danger Scale, I will place Tikkun in Neutral territory—in-between the Favorable and Mild Cult Danger categories of modern religions.

In regard to evaluating Tikkun's potential for an ITP in Wilber's Four Quadrant Integral Model, the lack of authentic spirituality is an obvious sign that there will be problems here. In addition to Tikkun not being represented well in Wilber's Intentional quadrant, there is also little body oriented activity in the Behavioral quadrant. There was a bit of Jewish dance activity at the Washington D.C. Tikkun conference that I attended, but a focus on the individual Intentional and Behavioral quadrants was sorely lacking, from my own experience. Where Tikkun shines is in the social and political arena, which translates into the Cultural and Social quadrants in Wilber's model. Here we have a multitude and rich variety of opportunity for all kinds of involvement in social and cultural causes and groups, both within Tikkun, in our society, and in the world. If one were able to sustain one's own balanced spiritual practice—both in the Intentional and Behavioral quadrants, perhaps one could maintain an effective ITP while benefiting from the tremendous Cultural and Social quadrant potential involvement with Tikkun. However, this does seem like quite the stretch to me, and far too easy for the individual Intentional and Behavioral quadrants to get swallowed up by Tikkun's extremely active Cultural and Social quadrants. Thus I am not able to conclude that Tikkun fares particularly well for its ITP potential in Wilber's Four Quadrant Integral Model. Let us see how all of this fits together in our next candidate for another favorable new age spiritual organization in addition to Neopaganism; our next candidate is Kripalu Center for Yoga & Health.

KRIPALU CENTER FOR YOGA & HEALTH

Kripalu Center for Yoga & Health originated in the early 1970s as a disciplined guru-centered yoga retreat center; the name Kripalu is based upon the name of the Indian guru to whom the yoga center was dedicated, Swami Kripalvanandji. The history of Kripalu is quite interesting, as the founder of Kripalu, Yogi Amrit Desai, who was a disciple of Swami Kripalvanandui, became involved in sexual liaisons with members of the Kripalu community, which was completely contradictory to the philosophy of Kripalu that this leader espoused. However, unlike many other spiritual communities that tolerate and excuse ethical misconduct on the part of their leaders, Kripalu took the initiative of demanding that their leader leave Kripalu [92]. This resulted in Kripalu expanding their network into a variety of new age course offerings in addition to their Kripalu style of yoga, with a democratically based leadership that has functioned both effectively and ethically for the past seventeen years. I have participated in five Kripalu workshops since 1998, and my tri-perspective experiential analysis of Kripalu will be based upon my Kripalu workshop experiences [93].

To begin with, I am quite comfortable with placing Kripalu in the Multilevel cell in the Anthony Typology. Kripalu never loses its authentic spiritual focus, as the Kripalu teachers emphasize that the essential basis of Kripalu yoga is its spiritual essence. The five workshops I have done at Kripalu were quite varied and included workshops with three well-known new age teachers: Julia Cameron, Jonette Crowley, and Cyndi Dale [94]. Although some of these workshops became extremely mystical and involved elements that I took with quite the grain of salt (in particular the workshops with Cyndi Dale and Jonette Crowley; see [94]), I can confidently say that things did not get out-of-hand in regard to these teachers overstepping their boundaries in regard to their personal influence of students at the workshops. The spiritual essence of Kripalu was maintained at all my Kripalu workshops, and this spiritual essence was reinforced outside of the workshops by deep meditation while practicing the yoga postures, silent meal time in the mornings, and a generally quiet contemplative atmosphere throughout the Kripalu surroundings. The transformation from guru leadership to democratic group leadership plus the high level instructional yoga practices certainly place Kripalu in the Technical cell as opposed to the Charismatic cell. Kripalu has a genuine orientation to helping all people find their true spiritual path, and very much represents the Monistic cell as opposed to the Dualistic cell. We thus see that based upon my experiences at five Kripalu workshops, I have placed Kripalu in the most favorable cell in the Anthony Typology: Multilevel/Technical/ Monistic.

In regard to the Wilber Integral Model, Kripalu is our first modern religion or new age spiritual organization that I can place squarely in the trans-rational level of consciousness in the Wilber continuum. The spiritual emphasis in Kripalu is quite profound, and those who attend Kripalu workshops generally find their deeper spiritual selves emerging. Kripalu does not compromise itself with materialistic perspectives, but keeps its focus on the spiritual state that transcends the mind while simultaneously acknowledging the mind as one of our important and worthwhile attributes. This is why I will place Kripalu on the trans-rational level of consciousness in Wilber's continuum. Although Kripalu does have its own particular spiritually based style of yoga, its general yoga tradition has a long Eastern heritage, and I do believe that Kripalu satisfies Wilber's criterion of anchoring its legitimacy in a tradition. Kripalu's democratic leadership insures that it engages in phase-specific authority. We thus see that Kripalu has excellent ratings on both the Anthony Typology as well as the Wilber Integral Model.

We now examine Kripalu's ratings on the Bonewits Cult Danger Scale, based upon my experiences with Kripalu from 1998 through 2010.

Internal Control	1
Wisdom Claimed	5
Wisdom Credited	5

Dogma	5
Recruiting	3
Front Groups	1
Wealth	3
Political Power	1
Sexual Manipulation	1
Censorship	1
Dropout Control	1
Endorsement of Violence	1
Paranoia	2
Grimness	5
Surrender of Will	5
TOTAL	**39**
AVERAGE	**2.6**

On the Bonewits Cult Danger Scale we see that Kripalu rates very low in regard to cult dangers, second only to Neopaganism in the modern religions that we have thus far examined. Kripalu's highest rating is "5," which I have given for the categories of Wisdom Claimed, Wisdom Credited, Dogma, Grimness, and Surrender of Will. Kripalu has a firm spiritual philosophy of yoga that is at the basis of all its activities, but this spiritual yoga-based philosophy is not rigid or authoritarian, but open to constructive changes through discussion and practice by its practitioners. This spiritual focus encourages people to engage in deep meditation where one may very well experience the feeling of surrender of will, but there is also much grounding experiences available at Kripalu, especially the combined dance and yoga activity originally called "dancekinetics" (see [92]), to keep this meditative surrender of will from becoming too excessive. Kripalu does have a somewhat serious and subdued atmosphere, but this is a function of the inner spiritual focus rather than a serious harsh nature of any of the Kripalu leaders. My ratings of "3" for Recruitment and Wealth show a mild and reasonable recruiting effort resulting in a comfortable financial arrangement for both Kripalu and its workshop participants. For all the remaining categories I gave ratings of "1," representing from my perspective a highly ethical and non-coercive new age spiritual organization. On the basis of the excellent ratings I have given Kripalu on the Anthony Typology and the Wilber Integral Model, and its quite favorable rating on the Bonewits Cult Danger Scale, I will place Kripalu in the Favorable new age spiritual organization category, alongside of Neopaganism.

In regard to Kripalu's potential for an effective ITP in Wilber's Integral Four Quadrant Model, I believe we have found our most promising possibility for an Integral Transformative Practice. Kripalu yoga is a bona fide spiritual meditative practice that encompasses both the Intentional and Behavioral quadrants in Wilber's model in a balanced harmonious way. The emphasis on the body in practicing yoga postures is central to a yoga practice, but in Kripalu yoga an equal emphasis is given to the inner spiritual state. Kripalu has reached out to communities and workplaces all over the world, especially through its Kripalu Yoga Teacher Training program. Kripalu has part of its mission to spread the spiritual discipline of yoga throughout the world, and it engages in various work barter and scholarship programs to help accomplish its mission. Through becoming involved in Kripalu's outreach focus in a variety of areas, one has much potential to be in community with others, embracing the Cultural and Social quadrants in Wilber's model. We thus find that Kripalu offers an effective means of Integral Transformative Practice in Wilber's Four Quadrant Integral Model. Our next new age spiritual organization to consider, Omega Institute for Holistic Studies, is in many ways similar to Kripalu, but without the centrality of Kripalu's spiritual yoga focus. It will be interesting to see if Omega is able to join Kripalu in the category of Favorable new age spiritual organization.

OMEGA INSTITUTE FOR HOLISTIC STUDIES

Omega Institute for Holistic Studies is one of the most popular and extensive new age retreat centers in the world. Numerous and various personal growth, healing, physical well-being, spirituality, and related workshops are offered on a continuous basis throughout the year, especially during the Spring, Summer, and Fall months [95]. Omega began in the early 1970s, as did Kripalu, but unlike Kripalu, Omega has always operated without the presence of any particular guru figure or any one particular model of spiritual practice as its central basis. I have done six weekend workshops at Omega in the 1990s and 2000s [96], and my tri-perspective experiential analysis of Omega will be based upon my experiences at these workshops.

Our first criteria of Multilevel vs. Unilevel cell placement in the Anthony Typology is by no means as easy a decision to make as it was for Kripalu. Omega certainly has the exploration of authentic spirituality at the core of many of its workshops as well as in its central philosophy. However, my experiences at Omega does not reflect the kind of pure spiritual essence atmosphere in the way that I have described Kripalu. Omega is much more of a new age "vacation" atmosphere and less of a new age spiritual retreat atmosphere than Kripalu, from my own experience. When I am at Omega, it feels to me like I am with people who are generally quite successful in society and looking for the highs of a get-away weekend in a new age context. In comparison, when I am at Kripalu, it feels to me like I am in an atmosphere that truly encourages people to alter their lives in authentic spiritual directions, minimizing the focus upon materialistic and society success. There are certainly exceptions to these general descriptions of both Kripalu and Omega, but in terms of my own experience with the dominant mindset of Omega, I must place Omega primarily in the Unilevel cell in the Anthony Typology. Certainly Omega caters to personal growth, holistic healing, physical well-being, creativity and artistic development, etc. But in regard to the deeper levels of authentic spirituality, I do find Omega to be lacking, based upon my actual experience with the people who generally attend the Omega workshops. On the other hand, many of the Omega workshop leaders and a number of the workshop participants exhibit a similar authentic spiritual state of consciousness to that of Kripalu, and it can be argued that Omega deserves a secondary Multilevel cell placement.

In contrast to the challenge of the Multilevel vs. Unilevel cell placement, the other two cells in the Anthony Typology will be much easier to pinpoint for Omega. There are no gurus or cherished leaders at Omega; Omega undoubtedly belongs in the Technical cell as opposed to the Charismatic cell. Omega is a fine example of catering to all people without prejudice or condescension, and certainly belongs in the Monistic cell as opposed to the Dualistic cell. We thus see that Omega has the dominant classification of Unilevel/Technical/Monistic with the secondary classification of Multilevel/Technical/Monistic in the Anthony Typology, reflecting the somewhat less than authentic spiritual atmosphere generated by many of the people who attend Omega workshops, once again from my perspective.

In regard to the Wilber Integral Model, we have a very similar problem to consider in terms of where to place Omega in Wilber's levels of consciousness continuum. However, the inclusion of the secondary Multilevel cell placement in the Anthony Typology indicates that Omega does place beyond the rational level of consciousness, though certainly not squarely in the trans-rational level in the way that Kripalu did. I shall place Omega in-between the rational and trans-rational levels of consciousness, as I have done for a number of new age spiritual organizations that we have examined. In regard to anchoring its legitimacy in a tradition, once again this is not an easy question to answer. In one sense Omega focuses upon the tradition of Eastern meditation and contemplation, going back thousands of years. However, there is no particular tradition of heritage that Omega is based upon, but rather Omega has been formulated as a new age mixture of many spiritual and personal growth disciplines, both Eastern and Western. In terms of how I view Wilber's criteria, I must say that I do not believe that Omega anchors its legitimacy in a tradition, certainly not in the sense of Kripalu's yoga tradition, Tikkun's Jewish tradition, or Neopaganism's Pagan tradition. For Wilber's third category of phase-specific authority, we can immediately respond in the affirmative, as Omega chooses its leaders in a democratic temporal fashion with virtually no danger of any person assuming excessive authority. We thus find that Omega does have generally favorable ratings in both the Anthony Typology as well as the Wilber Integral Model, but that these ratings are not quite as impressive as they have been for either Kripalu or Neopaganism.

We now examine Omega on the Bonewits Cult Danger Scale, based upon my workshop experiences at Omega in the 1990s and 2000s

Wisdom Claimed	5
Wisdom Credited	5
Dogma	9
Recruiting	3
Front Groups	5
Wealth	5
Political Power	2
Sexual Manipulation	2
Censorship	5
Dropout Control	2
Endorsement of Violence	2
Paranoia	2

Grimness	8
Surrender of Will	4
TOTAL	35
AVERAGE	**2.3**

We find that Omega has an extremely low score on the Bonewits Cult Danger Scale, lower than even Kripalu, and a second only to Neopaganism in terms of being safe from cult dangers. Like Kripalu and Neopaganism, I gave Omega no ratings higher than "5." Omega's "5" ratings for Wisdom Claimed and Wisdom Credited reflect their solid Eastern/Western personal growth and spirituality basis, but without significant dogmatic or rigid proportions, evidenced by the lower "3" rating for Dogma that I have given them. My "5" rating for Wealth represents the successful materialistic business enterprise that Omega immerses itself in, complete with new age cruises, etc., but their successful finances do not stem from exorbitant workshop fees and do not result in the extreme wealth of its leaders. Omega does have a solid program of Recruiting through its extensive and attractive seasonal catalogues and featured workshop descriptions (see [95]), on a somewhat higher level than Kripalu, which accounts for my "4" rating, and this Recruiting activity very much contributes toward Omega's financial well-being. There are some workshops at Omega where Surrender of Will is experienced to some extent, but there is also much social grounding at mealtimes and other activities, which accounts for my "3" rating in this category. My "2" rating for Internal Control allows for the occasional possibility of extended contact with workshop leaders past the workshops, though this is by no means a common or strong feature of the Omega experience. All the other categories received ratings of "1," and we thus see from the Bonewits Cult Danger Scale that Omega is a highly safe and respectable new age spiritual organization in terms of cult dangers for its participants. Though from my perspective its authentic spiritual context is not at the level of either Kripalu or Neopaganism, in my opinion Omega does bridge the gap of going beyond the Neutral classification in regard to cult dangers, and deserves to be placed in the category of Favorable new age spiritual organization.

In terms of Omega's potential for an ITP in Wilber's Four Quadrant Integral Model, I believe that we have reasonable potential for an effective Integral Transformative Practice, but one that does require a significant degree of individual effort to go beyond what Omega specifically offers. Both the Intentional and Behavioral quadrants are well represented in Wilber's model. Recall that my description of lacks of authentic spirituality at Omega were not based upon my experiences with the workshop leaders but rather with many of the workshop participants. The workshop leaders at Omega for the most part do offer a genuine opportunity for authentic meditative spiritual practice, and this is well-balanced with a variety of body-oriented activities including yoga, massage, Tai Chi, dance, tennis, etc. However, in regard to Omega's ITP potential in the Cultural and Social quadrants, we do not have anything like the solid and extensive cultural/social emphasis of Kripalu or the intensive social/political emphasis of Tikkun. Omega caters much more to the individual than it does to any cultural or social involvements. However, there is certainly the opportunity to become engaged in the Omega community, both as a frequent workshop participant (if your finances allow for it) as well as through joining the Omega staff (see [95]). Beyond the Omega community, Omega participants would need to take their learning experiences from being at Omega workshops and build upon this through their own cultural extensions into social groups that have a connection to their Omega experience. I do not believe that this is something which happens very often or easily for people, and for this reason I will say that Omega's ITP potential is definitely lacking in the Cultural and Social quadrants of Wilber's model. Omega has a tendency to cater to what has been referred to as "new age narcissism" [97]. However, it is also true that Omega offers a balanced rich variety of experiences for the individual in the Intentional and Behavioral quadrants, and it is certainly quite possible for the individual to form his/her own community connections in the Cultural and Social quadrants to engage in an effective Integral Transformative Practice.

We have thus far found three new age spiritual organizations that I have been able to place in the Favorable category, on the other side of cult dangers: Neopaganism, Kripalu Center for Yoga & Health, and Omega Institute for Holistic Studies. However, it remains to be seen if either of our two remaining new age spiritual organizations in my tri-perspective experiential analysis will furnish us with another "Favorable" example, as we examine our next new age spiritual organization: Twelve Step Support Groups.

TWELVE STEP SUPPORT GROUPS

We come now to a rather unusual new age spiritual organization and modern religion: Twelve Step Support Groups. These groups originated in the middle of the 20th century with Alcoholics Anonymous, but gradually extended itself to a variety of Twelve Step groups using the identical format, including groups for codependency, Alanon (for family and friends of alcoholics, codependents, etc.), sex and love addiction, etc. [98]. The Twelve Step groups that I am most familiar with are the groups that focus upon codependency, which can be defined as being overly affected by the feelings and behaviors of another person to the point of giving up fundamental parts of your own self (see [98]). Keeping with the main theme of this book, I will therefore be basing my tri-perspective experiential analysis upon my experiences with Codependency related Twelve Step Support Groups, including Alanon groups. The groups that I have participated in have been primarily in the Belfast, Maine area in the 1990s and 2000s. There is a very definite spiritual ingredient in the Twelve Step process, as "letting go and letting God" is a primary motto that describes the basic principles of these groups, whether it be focused upon alcoholism, codependence, love & sex addiction, or any other addictive type of behavior (see [98]). Let us now see how Twelve Step Support Groups fare in regard to cult dangers utilizing my tri-perspective experiential analysis.

In my own experience, the focus upon spirituality in the Twelve Step Support Groups is essentially both authentic and central to the whole program. The way in which this spirituality is tapped is through a combined form of prayer and meditation, but in a non-doctrinaire manner that is left entirely up to the individual regarding what meaning spirituality and God has for her/him. I therefore feel quite comfortable that Twelve Step Support Groups belong in the Multilevel cell in the Anthony Typology. There is relatively very little control exercised by Twelve Step Support Group members, as the whole format is designed to prevent any individual from becoming a continuous leader in the program. There are individuals who tend to monopolize the amount of personal sharing that takes place in these groups, but the twelve steps of the program are always adhered to, no matter what type of Twelve Step Support Group is taking place (see [98]). Certainly Twelve Step Support Groups belong in the Technical cell as opposed to the Charismatic cell in the Anthony Typology. The whole Twelve Step Support Group movement opens itself to anybody and everybody to take part in these groups, with a sincere empathy toward the plight of people who are suffering and have not engaged in Twelve Step Support Groups. There is no doubt that Twelve Step Support Groups belong in the Monistic cell in the Anthony Typology. We thus see that I have placed Twelve Step Support Groups in the most favorable cell in the Anthony Typology: Multilevel/Technical/ Monistic.

As we examine Twelve Step Support Groups in the context of the Wilber Integral Model, we immediately see from my Multilevel cell placement in the Anthony Typology that we are dealing with a level of consciousness beyond rational in Wilber's continuum. However, there is much variety in the authenticity of individual Twelve Step Support Group members' spiritual experiences, and what I believe is most appropriate is to place Twelve Step Support Groups in-between the rational and trans-rational levels of consciousness in Wilber's continuum. In regard to anchoring its legitimacy in a tradition, here we most definitely have very little to hold onto. The tradition upon which Twelve Step Support Groups is based is primarily that of Alcoholics Anonymous, which can hardly be seen as a longstanding tradition in the way in which Wilber is viewing this category. Perhaps one can stretch this somewhat and also use Christianity partially as a tradition, as there are occasional biblical references and a generic Christian moral focus to the whole program (see [98]). However, it is obvious that Twelve Step Support Groups do not have a firm longstanding tradition that anchors its legitimacy, certainly not in the way that some of the other modern religions we have explored do have. As far as Wilber's category of phase-specific authority is concerned, here we are safe to conclude that Twelve Step Support Groups have an extremely effective program in preventing anyone from entering into a position of authority that is not both limited and temporary. We thus see that although Twelve Step Support Groups fare reasonably well in the Wilber Integral model, they do not have the same flying colors that they have in the Anthony Typology. Perhaps there are some lurking cult dangers hidden in Twelve Step Support Groups after all, and we shall see if our third perspective from the Bonewits Cult Danger Scale uncovers anything here.

The following ratings are from my experiences of participating in codependency and Alanon groups in the Belfast, Maine area in the 1990s and 2000s.

Internal Control	5
Wisdom Claimed	8
Wisdom Credited	5

Dogma	10
Recruiting	2
Front Groups	1
Wealth	1
Political Power	1
Sexual Manipulation	6
Censorship	1
Dropout Control	1
Endorsement of Violence	1
Paranoia	8
Grimness	8
Surrender of Will	8
TOTAL	66
AVERAGE	**4.4**

As I hinted might be the case, the Bonewits Cult Danger Scale does indeed demonstrate some mild cult danger signs for Twelve Step Support Groups. I gave four ratings of "8" for Wisdom Claimed, Paranoia, Grimness, and Surrender of Will, and a rating of "10" for Dogma. The basic philosophy and doctrines of Twelve Step Support Groups are completely dogmatic, basing their ideas and format on the beliefs and principles stemming from Alcoholics Anonymous, with no deviations or differences of opinion being considered in regard to the philosophical framework of the groups. Although there are no formal leaders or gurus, the Twelve Step Support Group members who have been regularly attending these groups for many years are quite convinced about the truth of the groups' philosophical principles, and earn a healthy respect from newer members, though not in an unfaltering guru kind of way, as shown by my rating of "5" for Wisdom Credited. The oath of anonymity is a highly serious and required agreement made at the beginning and end of every Twelve Step Support Group meeting, and is based upon a high degree of paranoia regarding what the "outside world" may think of someone who attends these groups. There is much emotional outpourings in these groups, and although light socializing is common before and after the actual groups meet, the basic principles and philosophy of Twelve Step Support Groups are considered sacred and not to be joked about.

Surrender of Will, as the phrase "let go and let God" implies, is an essential part of the whole program, but the person is also expected to take responsibility for his/her actions, which does somewhat temper this surrender of will. For Sexual Manipulation I gave an upper intermediate rating of "6," which conveys that much of the group sharing is revolved around the topic of sex, and there are strong though sometimes subtle influences to withhold from being sexual in one's life until one does enough work on one's self. In a similar way, there is a fair amount of influence in the life choices that Twelve Step Support Group members make, which is conveyed by my "5" rating for Internal Control. There is very little direct recruitment efforts made, although there are often basic times and locations for Alcoholics Anonymous and Alanon meetings given in the local papers, which is why I gave Recruiting a "2" rating as opposed to a "1" rating. The rest of the categories all received "1" ratings from me, as Twelve Step Support Groups are extremely inexpensive financially (a dollar donation is requested at each meeting), and there is virtually no dropout control, censorship, endorsement of violence, political power, and front groups. All things considered, I do not think that Twelve Step Support Groups present any serious cult dangers, but there seems to be enough indications of concern to place it in the Mild Cult Danger category, along with est, Gurdjieff, and Eckankar. I can recall some people attending five or six Twelve Step meetings a week, replacing practically all their significant social interactions by these meetings. Yes—there is most definitely some level of cult danger here, although there is no powerful unethical dangerous guru attempting to control the lives of Twelve Step Support Group members. The cult dangers are mild, but there does not appear to be much outward extension of the acknowledged authentic spiritual element, aside from participating in the Twelve Step Support Groups themselves. For this reason, I do not believe that Twelve Step Support Groups have much to offer in regard to an Integral Transformative Practice in the context of the Wilber Four Quadrant Integral Model.

As we approach the end of the new age spiritual organizations I am experientially tri-perspectively analyzing, our last group is also a rather unusual inclusion, as it is a group that has its central mission that of studying the dangers of cults themselves; this group is known as ICSA, an abbreviation for International Cultic Studies Association. Perhaps one might assume that a group that studies the cult dangers of other groups cannot have any characteristics of cults themselves? Let us proceed open-mindedly and see what my final experiential tri-perspective analysis reveals about ICSA (originally named AFF, an abbreviation for American Family & Friends; the name was changed to ICSA in 2005).

INTERNATIONAL CULTIC STUDIES ASSOCIATION (ICSA)

ICSA, the abbreviation for the International Cultic Studies Association, the spiritual cults awareness and information network founded in 1979 as AFF (American Family & Friends), is admittedly a stretch to be included in this book as a new age spiritual organization or modern religion. However, I believe it will be instructive to examine ICSA in my experiential tri-perspective analysis, taking into account the factor that ICSA in no way claims to have any spiritual component per se in its organization. Although this is certainly a legitimate reason for excluding ICSA in my study, there is also an argument that perhaps an organization whose main purpose for existing is to promote awareness of cult dangers of other organizations should have some kind of spiritual foundation itself in order to justify their assessment of authentic vs. cultish levels of spirituality in other organizations. This kind of spiritual foundation is indeed the case with Ken Wilber's Integral Institute organization. Wilber's Integral Model has been tremendously useful in my tri-perspective experiential analysis, and Wilber's levels of consciousness is a primary part of the spiritual foundations upon which Integral Institute has been built [99]. My experiential tri-perspective analysis of ICSA will be based upon the associations that I have had with this organization over the past seven years, particularly the five day cults awareness conference that I attended in Edmonton, Canada in 2004, my ICSA conference presentations in 2006 and 2008, and my interactions with various ICSA leaders concerning the publications of some of my writings [100].

Based upon what we have already acknowledged concerning the intentional lack of any central spiritual component in ICSA, I must place ICSA in the Unilevel cell in the Anthony Typology. From my own initial experience of being at the ICSA cults awareness conference in 2004, it was very obvious to me that there was generally a strong reluctance for ICSA members to embrace any kind of organizational spiritual component, as their fears of organized spirituality leading to cult involvement were very real to them. There was an openness by ICSA leaders for me to co-facilitate a future ICSA workshop for people to discuss their own individual post-cult spiritual lives, which I subsequently did in 2006, but this still is entirely different from ICSA having a genuine spiritual component as part of their philosophy. ICSA is very much a scholarly philosophical organization with many workshops and books about cults available [101]. The leaders of ICSA are in their positions for temporary time periods, and there is no doubt that ICSA belongs in the Technical cell as opposed to the Charismatic cell in the Anthony Typology. Although ICSA is essentially open to all people and for legal reasons has had no choice but to allow members of spiritual organizations widely recognized as dangerous cults (see [101]) to attend their public conferences, there is also an ingredient of condescension toward people who are presently members of spiritual organizations that possess significant cult characteristics. There is a definite anti-cult philosophical basis in ICSA, which I happen to share personally, and there is much variability in the level of acceptance vs. animosity toward people who are still actively involved in new age spiritual organizations with strong cult characteristics. For this reason I must give ICSA a dual placement that can go either in the Monistic cell or Dualistic cell in the Anthony Typology. We thus see that ICSA can be put in two possible categories in the Anthony Typology: Unilevel/Technical/Monistic or Unilevel/Technical/Dualistic. The Unilevel/ Technical/Dualistic cell is considered to be one of the most alarming cells for possible cult dangers in the Anthony Typology.

As we consider ICSA in the context of the Wilber Integral Model, it is quite clear that ICSA is operating completely at the rational level of consciousness in Wilber's continuum, for the same reasons that I have placed ICSA in the Unilevel cell in the Anthony Typology. When it comes to anchoring its legitimacy in a tradition, there is not a whole lot that can be offered. Although I very much admire and respect ICSA's philosophical framework, intelligence, and courage in promoting cults awareness, there is certainly no longstanding tradition that it is based upon. Perhaps one can think of the tradition of freedom and democracy in America, but this is stretching things beyond what I believe Wilber was referring to for this category. As far as phase-specific authority is concerned, here we are completely safe to say that people who are in positions of authority in ICSA have attained their influence in a democratic way, and that these positions of authority are most definitely temporary and phase-specific. But I must admit that ICSA is not winning any awards for being free of cult dangers from my ratings on either the Anthony Typology or the Wilber Integral Model. Lets see if something can be salvaged as we examine ICSA from the perspective of the Bonewits Cult Danger Scale.

My ratings for ICSA on the Bonewits Cult Danger Scale are based upon my associations with ICSA from 2004 through 2011, and in particular from my experiences at the ICSA cults awareness conferences in 2004, 2006, and 2008.

Internal Control	5
Wisdom Claimed	8
Wisdom Credited	5
Dogma	8
Recruiting	2
Front Groups	1
Wealth	1
Political Power	3
Sexual Manipulation	2
Censorship	2
Dropout Control	1
Endorsement of Violence	1
Paranoia	8
Grimness	3
Surrender of Will	1
TOTAL	**51**
AVERAGE	**3.4**

I must admit that I am more than a little relieved to see that ICSA has a reasonably low score on the Bonewits Cult Danger Scale. ICSA's score of 3.4 on the Bonewits Cult Danger Scale is a slightly lower score than A Course In Miracles (3.5), which is the lowest score on the Bonewits Cult Danger Scale of all the groups that I have thus far placed in the Neutral category, in-between the placements of Mild Cult Dangers and Favorable modern religions. I shall thus place ICSA in this same Neutral category, along with A Course in Miracles, Self-Realization Fellowship, Conversations With God, Reiki, and Tikkun. One of the most striking ratings for ICSA in the Bonewits Cult Danger Scale is the rating of "8" for Paranoia. There is no doubt that ICSA is extremely fearful regarding the threat and power of its perceived enemies, which are the modern religions and new age spiritual organizations that have strong cult characteristics. This is a fear that I myself very much share, as I have already made quite clear in my experiential tri-perspective analysis of Scientology [102]. I think this fear is very real and completely justified, and it is the reason for the "8" rating (and not a higher rating) in the category of Paranoia. The "8" ratings for Wisdom Claimed and Dogma reflect the strong anti-cult philosophical stance at the basis of the ICSA organization, which again is a stance that I share personally with ICSA. There are intelligent insightful cogent arguments set forth by brilliant professionals in ICSA to present this stance (cf. [13] in the Introduction Notes), but I must objectively give high ratings in the Wisdom Claimed and Dogma categories to represent this ICSA perspective, although the philosophical arguments of these ICSA leaders are still open to discussion of other points of view, which is why these ratings are not higher than "8." The "5" ratings I gave for Internal Control and Wisdom Credited reflect the moderate degree of influence on ICSA members of its leaders who write the anti-cult books, an influence that does make a strong impression on ICSA members. However, from my own reading of these books and attending workshops by their authors, I can confidently state that ICSA does not manipulate people or cater to any kind of undo attention or guru effect. For all the remaining categories I gave "1," "2," or "3" ratings; the "3" ratings for Political Power and Grimness reflect a relatively small but existing interest in legal matters regarding the gaining of rights for people fighting cults, and a healthy respect for ICSA leaders with an appropriate and reasonable degree of humor.

There is very little actual recruitment, though if one does find the ICSA website there is much information and promotion to buy ICSA books, subscribe to the ICSA newsletter and journal, and attend ICSA conferences (see www.icsa.com for ICSA website information). There is virtually no censorship, although some people (for example, Scientologists in particular) may consider ICSA's perspective that the Cult Awareness Network (CAN) as of 1996 has become a Scientology sponsored organization and should be regarded as a dangerous organization, is a form of censorship. However, personally I am quite thankful to ICSA for publicizing this knowledge, and I am most happy to join ICSA in their work to promote awareness of modern religions and new age spiritual organizations that may have dangerous cult characteristics. But we see that ICSA, although I do believe they have avoided the temptation to enter into any significant cultish behaviors themselves in their promotion of cults awareness of other organizations, does not appear to have genuine spiritual foundations of their own as an organization. For this reason I do not believe that ICSA offers any kind of reasonable Integral Transformative Practice in Wilber's Four Quadrant Integral Model. However, ICSA does offer a wonderful opportunity to engage oneself in the cultural and social quadrants of Wilber's model through working to spread awareness of cult dangers throughout our social institutions, and this is an opportunity that I personally am in the process of developing. With this in mind, let us now summarize what we have learned in regard to the relative cult dangers and the favorable aspects of the seventeen modern religions or new age spiritual organizations that I have done my tri-perspective experiential analysis on.

SUMMARY OF RESULTS
AND CONCLUDING STATEMENT

Before giving the summary of all the experiential data that we have accumulated concerning the cult dangers of various modern religions and new age spiritual organizations, I would briefly like to describe the philosophical basis upon which I will be interpreting my results; this is in the context of what I refer to as an "experiential analysis." This philosophical basis is described both brilliantly and simply by Ken Wilber in his books *Eye to Eye* and *The Marriage of Sense and Soul* (see [99] in Chapter One Notes; and [21] in Introduction Notes for related heuristic and autoethnographic experiential research references). In *Eye to Eye* Wilber defined three modes of knowledge, which can be described simply as the eye of the senses, the eye of reason, and the eye of contemplation. The eye of the senses refers to direct scientific knowledge of the world that can be perceived with our senses and the scientific extensions of our senses, such as microscopes, telescopes, etc. The eye of reason refers to the logical activity of the mind and includes the realms of logic, philosophy, and mathematics. The eye of contemplation refers to immediate spiritual experience, awareness, or illumination through meditation, prayer, or any activity of life that results in a transcendental state of awareness. Wilber astutely described how these three eyes of knowledge have been misused to represent one another, with disastrous consequences for our modern society. In particular he focused his attention upon the "narrow science" view that incorporates all knowledge primarily into the eye of the senses, with leeway given to the eye of reason only in the form of mathematics. In *The Marriage of Sense and Soul*, Wilber made the impactful argument that if we move toward "deep science" in place of "narrow science," then the enormous gap in modern society between science and religion could be effectively merged.

In order to accomplish this feat, Wilber defined science in general as encompassing the three stages of instrumental injunction, direct application, and communal confirmation (or rejection). What Wilber means by these stages is first the actual practice or experiment, second the direct experience or apprehension of the data, and third the checking of the results with others who have adequately completed the injunction and apprehension strands. Thus a scientific experiment must be capable of duplication with identical results before it is regarded as scientific knowledge. A proof in mathematics must be corroborated by a community of capable mathematicians before it is accepted into the mathematical literature. And the crucial point for the prospective merger of science and religion is that the same must hold true for spiritual experience. In other words, spiritual experience needs to go through these three stages of Wilber's generic science formulation, and if and only if it succeeds in doing this it can be construed as "deep science." The first stage involves engaging in the actual experience or practice, whether it be yoga, prayer, Zen, Scientology auditing, Reiki attunements, etc. The second stage accumulates the insights and awareness of the first stage experience, and in the third stage we compare our results with others who have been through the first two stages in this realm. In the aforementioned books, Wilber proposed that science extend its domain to incorporate the study of spirituality and religion in this way, and that religion eliminate its mythological beliefs that have no deep science basis of truth, embracing its authentic spiritual experience through the three stages of deep science confirmation. If this model is applied to the eye of contemplation, as it has begun to be applied in recent years in the developing fields of parapsychology and transpersonal psychology [103], then Wilber's proposed merger of science and religion is indeed an idealistic notion that I believe has possibilities of making itself known in our concrete modern world [104].

It is in this context of "deep science" that I have embarked upon my tri-perspective experiential analysis of modern religions/new age spiritual organizations. What I mean by "experiential analysis" in this context is the immersion in the eye of contemplation, followed by the reasoning capacity applied to all of the sensory, mental, and transcendental realms in the new age spiritual organizations and modern religions that I have experienced. Keeping this perspective in mind, here is a summary of the results that I have found. For ease of presentation I will make use of the following abbreviations.

Anthony Typology:	Mu:	Multilvel	U:	Unilevel
	T:	Technical	C:	Charismatic
	Mo:	Monistic	D:	Dualistic

Wilber Integral Model:	PrR:	pre-rational
	R:	rational
	PsR:	pseudo-rational
	TR:	trans-rational
	R/TR:	in-between rational and trans-rational

	L:	anchors its legitimacy in a tradition
	NL:	does not anchor its legitimacy in a tradition
	P:	phase-specific authority
	NP:	no phase-specific authority

Bonewits Cult Danger Scale:	the number between 1 and 10 refers to the average score on the 15 categories of the Bonewits Cult Danger Scale.

For a number of the modern religions I have given more than one possible category placement in the Anthony Typology or the Wilber Integral Model, which will be simply illustrated with the preposition "or." I will abbreviate our three perspectives as follows:

AT: Anthony Typology

WIM: Wilber Integral Model

BCD: Bonewits Cult Danger Scale

For our first modern religion, Scientology, I explain these abbreviations in detail as follows:

Scientology: AT: U/T/D or U/C/D or U/T/Mo or U/C/Mo

WIM: PsR   NL   NP

BCD: 8.7

This conveys the ambiguity of Scientology in the Anthony Typology as having the four possible cell placements of Unilevel/Technical/Dualistic or Unilevel/Charismatic/Dualistic or Unilevel/Technical/Monistic or Unilevel/Charismatic/Monistic, once again from my perspective. In the Wilber Integral Model, Scientology in on the pseudo-rational level of consciousness in Wilber's continuum, does not anchor its legitimacy in a tradition, and does not engage in phase-specific authority (again from my perspective). The average score of 8.7 that I gave Scientology on the Bonewits Cult Danger Scale is extremely high, signifying very serious concerns of cult dangers.

Using this same classification scheme, the summary of data for our remaining sixteen modern religions are as follows:

est: AT: U/T/Mo or Mu/T/Mo or U/C/Mo or Mu/T/Mo

WIM: R/TR   NL   NP

BCD: 4.1

The Unification Church: AT: U/C/D

WIM: PsR   NL   NP

BCD: 9.0

Divine Light Mission:	AT:	U/C/Mo or Mu/C/Mo		
	WIM:	PrR	L	NP
	BCD:		5.1	

Gurdjieff:	AT:	Mu/T/D or Mu/C/D		
	WIM:	R/TR	L or NL	NP
	BCD:		4.3	

Eckankar:	AT:	Mu/C/Mo or Mu/T/Mo		
	WIM:	PsR	NL	NP
	BCD:		4.3	

Self-Realization Fellowship:	AT:	Mu/C/Mo or Mu/T/Mo		
	WIM:	R/TR	L	NP
	BCD:		3.7	

A Course in Miracles:	AT:	Mu/C/Mo		
	WIM:	R/TR	L	P
	BCD:		3.5	

Conversations with God:	AT:	Mu/C/Mo		
	WIM:	R/TR	NL	NP
	BCD:		3.7	

Avatar:	AT:	Mu/T/Mo		
	WIM:	R/TR	NL	NP
	BCD:		5.4	

Reiki:	AT:		Mu/T/Mo	
	WIM:	R/TR	L or NL	P or NP
	BCD:		4.1	

Neopaganism:	AT:		Mu/T/Mo	
	WIM:	R/TR	L or NL	P
	BCD:		2.1	

Tikkun:	AT:		U/T/Mo	
	WIM:	R	L	P
	BCD:		3.8	

Kripalu Center for Yoga & Health:	AT:		Mu/T/Mo	
	WIM:	TR	L	P
	BCD:		2.6	

Omega Institute for Holistic Studies:	AT:		Mu/T/Mo	
	WIM:	R/TR	NL	P
	BCD:		2.3	

Twelve Step Support Groups:	AT:		Mu/T/Mo	
	WIM:	R/TR	NL	P
	BCD:		4.4	

International Cultic Studies Association:	AT:		U/T/Mo or U/T/D	
	WIM:	R	NL	P
	BCD:		3.4	

In regard to interpreting this data, it seems clear that we have a generic classification that can be described in the five categories of High Cult Danger, Moderate Cult Danger, Mild Cult Danger, Neutral, and Favorable, which will be abbreviated respectively as H, Mod, Min, N, F. Based upon the above data, it seems reasonable to me to make the following classification:

H: Scientology, The Unification Church

Mod: Divine Light Mission, Avatar

Min: est, Gurdjieff, Eckankar, Twelve Step Support Groups

N: Self-Realization Fellowship, A Course in Miracles, Conversations with God, Reiki, Tikkun, ICSA

F: Neopaganism, Kripalu, Omega

Of course these classifications are not airtight in all cases; for example, we have seen that Reiki could have gone into Min or N, Omega could have gone into N or F, etc. But given that this whole experiential analysis is based upon my own personal experiences in all of these modern religions, i.e. my first two stages of Wilber's "deep science," it is quite clear that in my experience there is a sharp differentiation regarding the categorization of the cult dangers of nearly all the new age spiritual organizations that I have experienced. In regard to the feasibility of engaging in an Integral Transformative Practice through these modern religions, it is also quite clear that approximately half of them have some reasonable ITP potential, namely the modern religions in the Neutral and Favorable categories. Who are the winners and losers in this experiential analysis? The data speaks for itself; from my tri-perspective experiential analysis based upon my personal experiences in these new age spiritual organizations, we can see for example the extremes of cult dangers that I have experienced in Scientology and The Unification Church vs. the highly beneficial spiritual support network that I have experienced in Neopaganism and Kripalu. But all the data and interpretations that I have been able to accumulate and formulate for these modern religions are based upon my own very personal experiences in them for over thirty-five years. This is Ken Wilber's first two stages of deep science, which I have formulated as my tri-perspective experiential analysis of the modern religions that I have described in this first chapter. Please read on to gain a deeper understanding of the inner workings of modern religions from my personal experiential essays that convey my experiences in a number of the modern religions/new age spiritual organizations that I have described in this chapter, plus a few additional ones.

CHAPTER ONE NOTES

Scientology Notes

1) See for example Paulette Cooper (1971), *The Scandal of Scientology*; New York: Tower; Robert Kaufman (1972), *Inside Scientology*; New York: Olympia; Russell Miller (1987), *Bare Faced Messiah: The True Story of L. Ron Hubbard*; Great Britain: Penguin Books Ltd.; Bent Corydon & L. Ron Hubbard Jr. (1987), *L. Ron Hubbard: Messiah or Madman*; Sebaucus, NJ: Lyle Stuart; Joe Atack (1990), *A Piece of Blue Sky: Scientology, Dianetics, and L.Ron Hubbard Exposed*; New York: Lyle Stuart. See current Scientology news and materials at various cults awareness websites; in particular International Cultic Studies Association (ICSA): www.icsahome.com, Freedom of Mind Resource Center: www.freedomofmind.com, and the Rick Ross website: www.rickross.com. There are also generic Scientology books by L. Ron Hubbard readily available at local bookstores; for example *Dianetics: The Modern Science of Mental Health* (Los Angeles: The American Saint Hill Organization, 1975; original work published 1950); Scientology: *The Fundamentals of Thought* (Los Angeles: Bridge, 1999; original work published 1983), and *Scientology: A New Slant on Life* (Los Angeles: Bridge, 1997; original work published 1988).

2) See *A Comparison of Scientology and Judaism* in Chapter 5 of this book (in all future notes a chapter reference will mean a chapter in this book unless otherwise indicated).

3) See Chapter 4 and/or the Scientology books listed in [1] in Chapter One Notes for detailed descriptions of all the Scientology terms used here.

4) See my essay *Sample Dianetic Auditing Process and Concluding Statement* as well as *Excerpts from "The Maturation of Walter Goldman"* in Chapter 4 for illustrative accounts of preliminary level Scientology auditing.

5) See my essay *The Misunderstood Word* in Chapter 4 for a rather humorous account of this.

6)   See my essays *The Misunderstood Word, Ethics, The E-Meter, Sample Dianetic Auditing Process and Concluding Statement,* and *Excerpts from "The Maturation of Walter Goldman"* in Chapter 4.

7)   See the books *A Piece of Blue Sky* and *Inside Scientology* (see [1] in Chapter One Notes for references) for particularly vivid accounts of some very strange past-life auditing experiences.

8)   See any and all of Ken Wilber's writings on transcending and including lower "holons" into higher holons, and in particular his essay *The Pre/Trans Fallacy* in his book *Eye To Eye* (see [6] in Introduction Notes for reference).

9)   See my essay *Scientology in the 21st Century* in Chapter 2.

10) See my Scientology essays in Chapter 4.

est Notes

11) See for example Adelaide Bry (1976), *est: 60 Hours that Can Transform your Life*; New York: Avon Books; Steven Pressman (1993), *Outrageous Betrayal: The Real Story of Werner Erhard, from est to Exile*; Emeryville, CA: St. Martins Press; Carl Frederick (2003), *est: Playing the Game the New Way*; New York: Synergy International of The Americas, Limited.

12) See my Avatar essays in Chapter 2 and the section on Avatar in this chapter for a current example of a successful and financially demanding LGAT.

13) See *The est Training: An Interview with Werner Erhard* in *Spiritual Choices* (see [3] in Introduction Notes for reference).

14) See my essay *On Werner Erhard* in Chapter 3 for a glimpse of Werner Erhard's charismatic guru effect on his est followers.

15) See my est essays *est: Part 1: The Human Zoo* and *est: Part 2: The Message of the East* in Chapter 3.

16) See my est essay *est: Part 3: Religion and Big Business* in Chapter 3.

17) See my Scientology essays in Chapter 4 and my Avatar essays in Chapter 2.

18) See the section in this chapter on ICSA for more information about this organization.

19) See the Introduction for the definition of an ITP.

20) Ken Wilber, Jack Engler, and Daniel P. Brown (editors) (1986); *Transformations of Consciousness*; Shambhala: Boston; see in particular the essays by Brown and Engler.

21) This increasing involvement and deceptive form of est intimacy was the motivation behind my essay: *est: On Pseudo-Intimacy* in Chapter 3.

Unification Church Notes

22) See Steve Hassan's books *Combating Cult Mind Control* and *Releasing the Bonds* (see [13] of Introduction Notes for references).

23) See for example Irving Louis Horowitz (editor) (1978), *Science, Sin, and Scholarship: The Politics of Reverend Moon and The Unification Church*; Cambridge, MA: The MIT Press; Alan Tate Wood & Jack Vitek (1979), *Moonstruck: A Memoir of My Life in a Cult*; New York: William Morrow & Co; Barbara Underwood & Betty Underwood (1979), *Hostage to Heaven: Four Years in the Unification Church by an Ex-Moonie and the Mother who Fought to Free Her*; Portland, OR: Clarkson N. Potter; Josh Freed (1980), *Moonwebs: Journey into the Mind of a Cult*; Toronto, Ontario: Dorset Publishing; Steve Kemperman, (1981), *Lord of the Second Advent*; Ventura, CA: Regal Books; Erica Heftmann (1982), *The Dark Side of the Moonies*; Australia: Penguin Books; Nansook Hong (1999), *In the Shadow of the Moons*; New York: Little Brown.

24) See in particular Reverend Moon's book *Divine Principle* (1973), New York: The Holy Spirit Association for the Unification of World Christianity.

25) See the books above by Steve Hassan in [22] in Chapter One Notes, as well as my essay: *An Ex-Moonie Speaks* in Chapter 3.

26) See the Unification Church references in Steve Hassan's book *Releasing the Bonds* (see [13] of Introduction Notes for reference).

27) See my essay *On the Unification Church* in Chapter 3 for the details of this reasoning argument.

28) See the Unification Church references in [23] in Chapter One Notes, and my essay *An Ex-Moonie Speaks* in Chapter 3.

29) See Wilber's chapter *The Spectrum Model* in *Spiritual Choices* (see [3] of Introduction Notes for reference).

30) See Geoffrey Falk's book *Stripping the Gurus* (see [9] of Introduction Notes for reference) for a particularly disturbing extensive description of the commonality of this kind of sexual violation occurring by many gurus.

31) See any of the Scientology references listed in [1] of Chapter One Notes.

Divine Light Mission Notes

32) See my Divine Light Mission essays in Chapter 3.

33) See for example Jeanne Messner (1976), *Guru Maharaj Ji and the Divine Light Mission*, in Charles V. Glock & Robert N. Bellah (editors), *The New Religious Consciousness*; Berkeley: University Of California Press; Ronald Enroth, *Divine Light Mission* chapter in *Youth, Brainwashing, and The Extremist Cults*; Grand Rapids, MI: Zondervan; James V. Downton, Jr. (1979), *Sacred Journeys: The Conversion of Young Americans to Divine Light Mission;* New York: Columbia University Press; David V. Barrett (2001) *Elan Vital* chapter in *The New Believers*; London: Cassell & Co.

34) Singer & Lalich, *Cults in Our Midst* (p. 136) (see [13] in Introduction Notes for reference).

35) See my Divine Light Mission essays in Chapter 3 and the above references in [33] for more information about Receiving Knowledge.

36) See my Divine Light Mission inclusion *Letter from Richie* in Chapter 3, the section *Alienation* in *Excerpts from "The Maturation of Walter Goldman"* in Chapter 4, and the above references in [33] for descriptive accounts of this "heart over mind" experience.

37) See any of the books in [2] in Introduction Notes.

38) See Wilber's essay *The Pre/Trans Fallacy* in his book *Eye to Eye* (see [6] in Introduction Notes for reference) for an illustrative and extensive formulation of the Pre/Trans Fallacy. See also the book

Ken Wilber in Dialogue (1998), edited by Donald Rothberg & Sean Kelly; Wheaton, Illinois: Quest Books, for some alternative views to the Pre/Trans Fallacy.

39) Once again see Geoffrey Falk's book *Stripping the Gurus* (see [9] of Introduction Notes for reference) for many disturbing accounts of the unethical behavior of a number of gurus.

Gurdjieff Notes

40) For the seminal book on Gurdjieff, see P.D. Ouspensky (1949), *In Search of the Miraculous*; New York: Harcourt; see also books written by Gurdjieff, the most popular of which are *All and Everything: Beezlebub's Tales to his Grandson* (New York: Arkana, 1992, first published in 1950) and *Meetings with Remarkable Men* (New York: Dutton, 1969). Informative Gurdjieff books by other authors include Thomas & Olga de Hartmann (1976), *Our Life with Mr. Gurdjieff*; New York: Penguin Arcana; Kathleen Riordeen Speeth (1976), *The Gurdjieff Work*; Los Angeles: Jeremy P. Tarcher; Jacob Needleman & George Baker (Editors) (1996), *Gurdjieff Essays and Reflections on the Man and his Teachings*; New York: Continuum Press.

41) See my Gurdjieff essays in Chapter 3 for a further account of this description of "working on oneself" as discussed by Anthony and Ecker.

42) See my Gurdjieff essays in Chapter 3; in particular my essay *Occult School*.

43) See my related Gurdjieff essays *Occult School* and *Eden West* in Chapter 3.

44) See *Occult School* in Chapter 3.

45) Gurdjieff's integration of the body with the mind and emotions also has parallels with the "Centaur" level of consciousness as described by Ken Wilber in his books listed in [1] of Introduction Notes.

Eckankar Notes

46) See for example Paul Twitchell (1969), *Eckankar: The Key to Secret Worlds*; Minneapolis, MN: Eckankar Publications; see also any of the books by current Living Eck Master

Harold Klemp; for example *The Language of the Soul* (Minneapolis, MN: Eckankar Publications, 2003).

47) See David Lane (1983), *The Making of a Spiritual Movement: The Untold Story of Paul Twitchell and Eckankar*; Del Mar, CA: Del Mar Press; see also R.E. Olson (1995), *Eckankar: From Ancient Science of Soul Travel to New Age Religion* in T. Miller (Editor), *America's Alternative Religions*; Albany, NY: S.U.N.Y. Press.

48) See my essay *On Eckankar* in Chapter 2.

Self-Realization Fellowship Notes

49) See the seminal book by Paramahansa Yogananda (1993), *Autobiography of a Yogi*; Los Angeles: Self-Realization Fellowship (original work published 1946).

50) See my essay *On Self-Realization Fellowhip* in Chapter 2.

51) See in particular Geoffrey Falk's description of his own experiences in a Self-Realization Fellowship ashram in *Stripping the Gurus* (see [9] of Introduction Notes for reference).

52) See for example the chapters by Engler, and Engler & Brown in *Transformations of Consciousness* (see [20] of Chapter One Notes for reference).

A Course in Miracles Notes

53) Foundation for Inner Peace (1996). *A Course in Miracles*. New York: Penguin Books (original work published 1975).

54) Marianne Williamson (1996), *A Return to Love*. New York: Harper Perennial.

55) See Helen Schucman's preface in the 2007 third edition of *A Course in Miracles* authored by Helen Schucman and published by the Foundation for A Course in Miracles.

56) See for example Wapnick, K. (2004). *Ending Our Resistance to Love: The Practice of A Course in Miracles*. Foundation for A Course in Miracles: Temeculo, CA.

57) See my essay *On A Course in Miracles* in Chapter 2.

58) For a skeptical and critical view of A Course in Miracles see the section on A Course in Miracles in Martin Gardner,

Weird Waters & Fuzzy Logic: More Notes of a Fringe Watcher (Amherst, NY: Prometheus Books, 1996).

Conversations with God Notes

59) See Neale Donald Walsch, *Conversations with God: An Uncommon Dialogue: Book 1* (New York: G.P. Putnam & Sons, 1995)*; Conversations with God: An Uncommon Dialogue: Book 2*. (Charlottesville, VA: Hampton Roads Publishing Co., 1997); *Conversations with God: An Uncommon Dialogue: Book 3* (Charlottesvile, VA: Hampton Roads Publishing Co., 1998).

60) See for example *Friendship with God: An Uncommon Dialogue* (New York: Putnam & Sons, 1999); *Communion with God* (New York: Putnam & Sons, 2000); *The New Revelations: A Conversation with God* (New York: Atria Books, 2002); *Tomorrow's God: Our Greatest Spiritual Challenge* (New York: Atria Books, 2004); *Conversations with God for Teens* (Charlottesville, VA: Hampton Roads Publishing Co., 2001); *The Little Soul And the Sun* (a children's book) (Charlottesville, VA: Hampton Roads Publishing Co., 1998).

61) See my Conversations with God essays in Chapter 2 and my essay *On Conversations with God* in the ICSA-E-Newsletter, 2004, Vol. 3, No. 2, http://cultinfobooks.com

62) See in particular *The New Revelations* (see [60] in Chapter One Notes for reference).

63) See *The New Revelations* as well as *Tomorrow's God* (see [60] in Chapter One Notes for reference).

64) See my Scientology essays in Chapter 4 and my Avatar essays in Chapter 2.

65) See my essay *Humanity's Team: Part II* in Chapter 2.

66) See for example any of the books by Ken Wilber in [1] of Introduction Notes; Roger Walsh (1999). *Essential Spirituality.* New York: John Wiley & Sons; Deepak Chopra (2000). *How to Know God.* New York: Harmony Books; Carl Jung (1933), *Modern Man in Search of a Soul* (New York: Harcourt, Brace & World, Inc., 1933).

Avatar Notes

67) See my Avatar essays in Chapter 2 and my essay *On Avatar* in ICSA E-Newsletter, 2005, Vol. 4, No. 2, http://cultinfombooks.com.

68) For some examples of these techniques see Harry Palmer's books *Living Deliberately* (Altamonte Springs, Florida: Stars' Edge International, 1994) and *Resurfacing* (Altamonte Springs, Florida: Stars' Edge International, 1994).

69) See Harry Palmer's book *The Avatar Masters' Handbook* (Altamonte Springs, Florida: Stars' Edge International, 1997) for an illustration of Avatar's business promotion practices.

70) See in particular my Avatar essay *Assistant Avatar Master* in Chapter 2.

Reiki Notes

71) There are many books on Reiki currently available; see for example Bodo J. Beginski & Shalila Sharanmon (1988), *Reiki: Universal Life Energy*; Mendocino, CA: Life Rhythms; William Lee Rand 1991), *Reiki: The Healing Touch*; Southfield, MI: Vision Publications; Diane Stein (1995), *Essential Reiki: A Complete Guide to an Ancient Healing Art*; Freedom, CA: Time Crossing Press, Inc.; Libby Barnett, Maggie Chambers, & Susan Davidson (1996), *Reiki Energy Medicine: Bringing the Healing Touch into Home, Hospitals, and Hospice*; Rochester, VT: Healing Arts Press; Hiroshi Doi (2000), *Modern Reiki Method for Healing*; Coquitham, British Columbia, Canada: Fraser Journal Publishing.

72) See in particular my last Reiki essay in Chapter 2: *Reiki: Meditation with Touch*.

73) See in particular Hiroshi Doi's book *Modern Reiki Method for Healing* (see [71] above for reference).

74) See my Reiki essays in Chapter 2.

75) See for example the often cited article by Spanos, N. P. (1986). Hypnotic Behavior: A Social-psychological interpretation of amnesia, analgesia, and "trance logic." *The Behavioral and Brain Sciences*, *9*(3), 449-467.

76) See my first Reiki essay in Chapter 2: *On Reiki Healing*.

77) For examples of some of these "farfetched" Reiki claims, a survey of Reiki on the internet will bring forth a number of rather unusual Reiki beliefs, involving reincarnations of Usui and various sprits and angels as well.

78) See my Divine Light Mission essays in Chapter 2.

79) See my essay *On Becoming Involved with a Reiki Master* in Chapter 2.

80) To give an example of one of these "harsher perspectives," there is a well-known Reiki master who has trademarked her own brand of Reiki attunements and legally threatens other Reiki masters who have studied with her and received her attunements, and then go on to utilize what they have learned from her in combination with their own practices in their work with their own Reiki clients.

81) See in particular the book *Reiki Energy Medicine. Bringing the Healing Touch into Home, Hospitals, and Hospice* (See [71] above for reference).

Neopaganism Notes

82) See also my essays *On Neopaganism* and *Spirituality, Cults, and Neopaganism* in PagaNet News, Beltane editions 2004 and 2005, Virginia Beach, VA: www.paganet.org; and my article *Neopagan Rituals: An Experiential Account* in Coreopsis: A Journal of Myth and Theatre, 2010, Vol. 2, No. 1, which is Appendix: Part 4 in this book.

83) Some of my own favorite books about Paganism and Neopaganism are the following: Isaac Bonewits (1989), *Real Magic*; (York Beach, Maine: Samuel Weiser; original work published 1971); Starhawk (1979), *Spiral Dance: A Rebirth of the Ancient Religion of the Great Goddess*; (San Francisco: HarperCollins); Margot Adler (1979), *Drawing Down the Moon*; (New York: Penguin Group); Marion Zimmer Bradley (1981), *The Mists of Avalon* (New York: The Ballantine Publishing Group); Donald Michael Kraig (1988), *Modern Sex Magic* (St. Paul, MN: Llewellyn Publications, 1988); Gavon Frost & Yvonne Frost (1999), *The Magic Power of White Witchcraft*; (Paramus, NJ: Prentice Hall); Phyllis Curot (1998), *Book of Shadows: A Modern Woman's Journey into the Wisdom of Witchcraft and the Magic of*

the Goddess; (New York: Broadway Books, 1998); and Phyllis Curot (2001), *Witch Crafting: A Spiritual Guide to Modern Magic*; (New York: Broadway Books, 2001).

84) See my essay *On Neopaganism* in Chapter 2.

85) See the seminal science fiction novel by Robert Heinlein (1961), *Stranger in a Strange Land*. New York: G. P. Putnam & Sons; for information about the Church of All Worlds see http://www.caw.org

86) See [5] and [21} in Introduction Notes.

Tikkun Notes

87) Michael Lerner (2000*)*, *Spirit Matters*; Charlottesville, VA: Hampton Roads Publishing Co.

88) See the Tikkun journal: Tikkkun: A Bimonthly Jewish Critique Of Politics, Culture & Society (San Francisco: www.tikkun.org) as well as Michael Lerner's book *Healing Israel/Palestine: A Path to Peace and Reconciliation* (San Francisco: Tikkun Books, 2003).

89) See my essay *Current Spiritual Involvement: 2004/2005 (with 2008 and 2010 Afterwords)* in Chapter 5.

90) In 2005 the co-chairs of Tikkun were Michael Lerner, Cornel West (Black intellectual leader and author of *Race Matters* (New York: Vintage Books, 1994), and Susannah Heschel. At this present time, November, 2010, much of the political activity of Tikkun has transformed to the Network of Spiritual Progressives (www.spiritualprogressives.org).

91) In 2007, after Michael Lerner responded condescendingly and in a rather harsh and non-humanistic manner to me in regard to my anti-war article that I had submitted to Tikkun magazine, he subsequently sincerely apologized to me after I honestly communicated to him my hurt and disappointment. In November, 2010, I dialogued with Michael Lerner about my ideas to promote anti-war activity related to Afghanistan, after I took part in a Network of Spiritual Progressives conference call that Michael Lerner initiated, facilitated, and gave an inspiring talk at. This resulted in my writing another anti-war article*: Integrated Politics: Libertarians and Liberals Against the War in Afghanistan*, which subsequently got published on the Integral World website

(www.integralworld.net). I submitted my article to the Tikkun blog, but unfortunately the Tikkun blog has been discontinued, for I believe financial reasons. However, shortened versions of my article have been published in three peace-oriented journals in which I have previously published anti-war articles (see [37] in Chapter Five Notes).

Miscellaneous Notes

92)   See *Stripping the Gurus* (see [9] of Introduction Notes for reference) for more information about the history of Kripalu as well as a number of fascinating accounts of unethical behavior on the part of various well-known gurus.

93)   See my essay *Spirituality and Cults: An Experiential Analysis* in Inner Tapestry Journal, April-May, 2005, Vol. 3, No. 6 (www.innertapestry.org). See the Kripalu journal (www.kripalu.org) for a description of the current Kripalu workshops and activities offered, with all financial costs, logistics, etc.

94)   See Cyndi Dale's books *The Subtle Body: An Encyclopedia of Your Energetic Anatomy*; (Boulder, CO: Sounds True, 2009) and *Illuminating the Afterlife: Your Souls' Journey through the Worlds Beyond*; (Boulder, CO: Sounds True, 2008); see Jonette Crowley, *The Eagle and the Condor: A True Story of an Unexpected Mystical Journey*; (Greenwood Village, CO: Stone Tree); see Julia Cameron, *The Artist's Way: A Spiritual Path to Higher Creativity*; (New York: Tarcher, 1992). For more information about my Kripalu workshop with Jonette Crowley, see Part 3 of the Appendix, which is my article *The Boundaries Between Cultic, Benign, and Beneficial in Five SpiritualGroups*; (ICSA E-Newsletter, 2008, Vol. 7, No. 3); see in particular the section on Crowley's organization The Center for Creative Consciousness, which includes my Bonewits Cult Danger Scale ratings for this organization.

95)   See the Omega journal; information can be found at www.omega.org (Rhinebeck, New York) for workshop descriptions with all financial costs, logistics, etc.

96)   The last workshop I did at Omega was in October, 2009, which was a workshop on "soul survival" and featured well-known speakers including Raymond Moody and Brain Weiss, who did a great deal to promote the study of (respectively) near-death

experience and past-life regression. See Raymond Moody's (1975) book *Life after Life* (Covington, GA: Mockingbird Books), and Brian Weiss' (1988) book *Many Lives, Many Masters* (New York: Simon & Schuster). For a personalized description of my Soul Survival workshop at Omega see my 2010 Integral World article: *Integrated Metaphysical Reflections*: (www.integralworld.net).

97) See Ken Wilber's books *A Theory of Everything* (Boston: Shambhala, 2001) and *Boomeritis* (Boston: Shambhala, 2003).

98) See for example Melody Beattie (1987), *Codependent No More* (Center City, MN: Hazelden); Melody Beattie (1990), *The Language of Letting Go* (Center City, MN: Hazelden); Pia Mellody (1989), *Facing Codependence* (San Francisco: HarperCollins); Pia Mellody (1992), *Facing Love Addiction* (San Francisco: HarperCollins); Co-dependents Anonymous, Inc.(1995), *Co-dependents Anonymous* (Phonnix, AZ: author); The Augustine Fellowship (1986), *Sex and Love Addicts Anonymous* (Norwood, MA: author).

99) See Ken Wilber's books *Eye to Eye* (Boston: Shambhala, 2001) and *The Marriage of Sense and Soul* (New York: Broadway Books, 1998), as well as my essay *Spiritual Involvement: 2004/2005 (with 2008 and 2010 Afterwords)* in Chapter 5, and my essay *On Ken Wilber's Integral Institute: An Experiential Analsyis*, which comprises Appendix: Part 1.

100) See in particular my essays *On Conversations with God* and *On Avatar* (see [61] and [67] in Chapter One Notes for references), and my essays *On Ken Wilber's Integral Institute: An Experiential Analysis* and *The Boundaries Between Cultic, Benign, and Beneficial in Five Spiritual Groups* in Appendix: Part 1 and Part 2. I have also received feedback on a draft of this book from a few ICSA leaders, and Nori Muster, author of *Betrayal of The Spirit: My Life Behind the Headlines of the Hare Krishna Movement* (see [13] of Introduction Notes for reference) has written an informal book review for *Modern Religions* (see [5] of Introduction Notes and the *Modern Religions* back cover).

101) See [13] of Introduction Notes for a small sample of some of these books written by ICSA leaders.

102) See my Scientology essays in Chapter 4, in particular my Scientology postscript essays entitled *Scientology on Trial* and

Scientology and Fear. Scientology, The Unification Church, and Hare Krishna were all well represented at the 2004, 2006, and 2008 ICSA cults conference.

103) See for example Ken Wilber, Jack Engler, Daniel P. Brown (Editors), *Transformations of Consciousness* (Boston: Shambhala, 1986); Stanley Krippner, *Song of the Siren: A Parapsychological Odyssey* (New York: Harper Colophen Books, 1977); Roger Walsh & Francis Vaughan (Editors), *Paths Beyond Ego: A Transpersonal Vision* (New York: Penguin, 1993); Tony Schwartz, *What Really Matters: Searching for Wisdom in America* (New York: Bantam, 1995); Imants Baruss, *Alterations of Consciousness* (Washington DC: American Psychological Association, 2003); Harry Irwin & Carolyn Watt, *An Introduction to Parapsychology* (London: McFarland, 2007); Charles Tart, *The End of Materialism: How Evidence of the Paranormal is Bringing Science and Spirit Together* (Oakland, CA: Noetic Books, 2009); and also see the precursor for all the above books: William James, *The Varieties of Religious Experience* (New York: New American Library, 1958; original work published 1902).

104) See the Integral Institute website (www.integralinstitute.org) for Ken Wilber's current efforts in regard to bringing the merger of science and religion into the realm of possibility in our society.

CHAPTER 2

NEW AGE SPRITUAL EXPLORATIONS IN THE 1990s AND 2000s

SCIENTOLOGY IN THE 21ST CENTURY

(7/23/02)

A quarter of a century later and I have learned a bit more about Scientology. A few months ago I visited my son Jeremy, who is now a twenty-year-old engineering student at the University of Southern California at Los Angeles. He had been telling me how Scientology is tremendously popular and widespread in Los Angeles, but I did not think a whole lot about it. One day as we were driving through the downtown area, we saw a sign on a building saying "Hubbard College of Business Administration." Jeremy said this must be a Scientology place as L. Ron Hubbard was the founder of Scientology, but I was not at all convinced, thinking that the name must just be a coincidence. However, something in my curiosity made me park the car, and the two of us went into the building, with butterflies in my stomach. Sure enough, the founder of this college of business administration was none other than L. Ron Hubhard himself. Lots of Scientology books were on public display, and the man behind the counter had a dark business suit on and looked deeply into our eyes in a way that I knew all too well. I felt these shivers of coercive and manipulative memories telling me to get the hell out of this place as soon as possible, but I also felt this dedicated curiosity and almost responsibility to find out what was currently going on in Scientology. I managed to ask the guy a few generic questions, and obtained the sixty page college brochure. I could feel my exploratory excitement being rekindled as I thumbed through the booklet. Yes—one could obtain a two year college degree at L. Ron Hubbard's accredited business school, paying nearly $35,000 a year tuition. There were all sorts of business certification programs and general public education business courses and workshops offered. The more I read the more I became reacquainted with L. Ron Hubbard's whole educational system that I experienced back in the 1970s, from individualized competency-based education to the "Misunderstood Word" technology to professional salesmanship and marketing techniques in order to bring people into a Church of Scientology [1]. Hubbard's techniques of training Scientologists to package and market Scientology so successfully to the world were now formulated into a bona fide business college! And this business college was not just a unique college in Los Angeles; these colleges were all over the world, as there were close to twenty of these colleges established as subsidiary organizations of the Church of Scientology. This was both amazing and scary to me, as there was no doubt in my mind that anyone taking part in Hubbard's business college was simultaneously being manipulated into becoming a Scientologist as well as a business executive, especially as there were a number of Scientology churches in Los Angeles only a few blocks away from this business college. And thus the fire of curiosity became rekindled in me, as Jeremy and I went on what we referred to as "Scientology Hunting" as we drove down Hollywood Boulevard.

We soon passed a massive structure of adjoining buildings that Jeremy said was the major Scientology church in Los Angeles. There was a large banner advertising a celebration for L. Ron Hubbard's birthday in two weeks in the Los Angeles Shrine Auditorium. I knew it was time for me to once again enter a church of Scientology, this time with my twenty year old son. I felt both frightened and excited as we made our way into the church. I had told Jeremy that we should give them false names and telephone numbers, as I did not want them to be able to have us on their marketing lists. The more things change the more they remain the same—as we immediately got offered a free personality test, a free invitation to L. Ron Hubbard's birthday celebration, numerous Scientology brochures and pamphlets, and were invited to watch a half hour film about Scientology. There were lots of Scientology books now available to the public, and Jeremy and I went into the small auditorium to watch the Scientology film--just the two of us. It was all there—just as I wrote in my essays back in the 1970s (see [1] in Chapter Two Notes)—but greatly expanded, as the brochures included a complete list of all the Hubbard colleges of Business Administration throughout the world.

Scientology has been steadily growing and becoming richer over the years. They have a multitude of large churches as well as small missions in over 130 countries in the world—and millions of people have now been involved in Scientology. They won their many court battles over accusations of being a counterfeit religion, and are now legally established as a bona fide religious institution, along with non-profit status. They presently advertise, in both their film and brochures, their Celebrity Centers in Los Angeles and New York, with pictures of Tom Cruise, John Travolta, Kristi Alley, and Chick Corea in the celebrity forefront. One of their immediate future massive marketing plans include large Scientology billboards in major cities all over the world, targeting people on the streets, as recruiting people in dire straits for initial free auditing (Scientology therapeutic processing, see [1] in Chapter Two Notes) has the potential of producing quite the dedicated future Scientologists. Their hatred and paranoid fears of psychologists and psychiatrists has reached massive proportions, as they continuously stress the dangers and harmful effects of engaging in any other kind of professional therapy—aside from Scientology auditing. Yes—Scientology is all too alive and well in the 21st century. L. Ron Hubbard died back in the 1980s, and the Church of Scientology now worships him as an enlightened spiritual being in the company of Jesus and Buddha. The list of his claimed amazing accomplishments and achieved expertise in numerous professions and hobbies is indeed staggering. As I remember writing in my Scientology essays in the 1970s, Hubbard is a brilliant man and there is much we can learn from Hubbard and Scientology [2]. But make no mistake about it; the 100 per cent doctrine has not changed, meaning that Hubbard professes that 100 per cent of the time everything he utters is infallibly the way things are, and neither has the serious danger changed of becoming a member of a self-destroying manipulative new age spiritual organization [3].

Well—after stopping into a smaller Scientology information center and feeling like the attractive bookstore receptionist was seeing right through me and my acting attempts to be the naive newcomer to Scientology, I had enough of "Scientology Hunting," in Los Angeles, anyway. As I had recently been thinking about trying to make another go of my Spirituality & Cults course, I felt like I got the shot in the arm that I needed to once again initiate my venture. I forced myself to read through two Scientology books available in my local bookstore, and read through all the material on ARC (an acronym for affinity, reality, and communication), the tone scale, the dynamics, engrams (similar to the "traumatic experiences" of psychoanalysis), Dianetics (L. Ron Hubbard's precursor to Scientology that was designed to relieve people of their engrams), etc., and even some generic descriptions of auditing procedures (see [1] in Chapter Two Notes). The list of Scientology churches and missions throughout the world was unbelievable. There were over thirty-five churches and missions and centers in Los Angeles alone! But I noticed that there was also a Scientology mission not too far from where I live in Maine. It was in Brunswick, just a forty-five minute drive from the town in which for the past year I have been spending a lot of time with the woman in my life—Bobbi. Bobbi is a Reiki master who has recently opened up her own Reiki Center, and it has extended into offering herbal consultation, family math, and new age spirituality explorations, as I have become quite involved in Bobbi's Center [4]. I knew that I needed to check out Scientology in Maine, but as Bobbi had listened to all my Scientology essays she was quite concerned about me going there by myself, and she insisted that she go with me. I had serious qualms about Bobbi being in a Church of Scientology, but I also appreciated her concern for me. I realized that I was dealing with something that had tremendous personal impact upon me. And thus Bobbi and I went together to the Brunswick, Maine Church of Scientology.

And now my essay about Scientology in the 21st century takes on a bit of a humorous twist. To backtrack a little, after Jeremy and I ventured into the Scientology central headquarters in Los Angeles, I became determined to find out what the current costs of Scientology were, as my information was all from twenty-five years ago. But in none of the Scientology literature or books was there any mention at all of how much either auditing or training costs. I did manage to ask the financial question at the second Scientology place we stopped into when in Los Angeles, but I felt very nervous about making us seem suspicious to these Scientologists. I knew that it was way past my comfort and safety zone to set foot in the Scientology churches in Boston and New York again, and I figured that the least I could do was to check out the Scientology website. Sure enough the Scientology website contained the same kind of information as the brochures--full of praise and promise for Scientology and L. Ron Hubbard, but no mention of the costs. Bobbi had mentioned to me that she knew of someone through her internet Reiki correspondences who had been a Scientologist a few years ago, and she gave me the person's e-mail address. But this person wrote back to me claiming that he had never been a Scientologist and referred me to someone else who might be able to help me out. But this second person wrote back saying that he did not remember what the costs were and suggested that I contact Scientology directly. Bobbi and I began to wonder if Scientologists could possibly be afraid to divulge this information to me. I felt too uncomfortable to call the Church of Scientology, and though Bobbi offered to do this herself for me, I did not think it was safe for her to do either. But once I found out that there was a Scientology mission so close to us, I could no longer avoid taking the risk, and thus it occurred that Bobbi and I paid a visit to the Scientology mission in Brunswick, Maine.

I knew that a mission was a small church, but I was not at all prepared for how different this mission was from the Scientology churches I had been to in Boston, New York, and Los Angeles. The mission was in an ordinary two-story house with a small sign on the door, and after ringing the door bell and no-one answering for a minute, we were about to leave, figuring that Scientology in Brunswick, Maine was pretty low key if they were not even home in the middle of a weekday. But just as we were leaving, a rather ordinary looking middle-aged man came to the door and invited us to come in. We thus entered the house and found ourselves passing by a musical band/drums set and into a homey and cozy living room, where a woman sat behind a desk, looking rather bored. We sat ourselves down on an old comfortable couch and the man sat in an easy chair directly opposite us; he was both relaxed and friendly, and did not at all seem threatening or manipulative to us. There was a stack of the usual Scientology books in the bookshelve, and occasionally Scientology students on their courses would walk by from the upstairs rooms. But the relaxed and friendly atmosphere was almost embarrassing to me, as I had warned Bobbi so much about all the dangers of actually setting foot in a Church of Scientology. Bobbi and I had our lines all prepared, as Bobbi set us up as "Karen and the Professor." Not only did we give ourselves fictitious names, but Bobbi took on the hilarious identity of this ditsy woman Karen, as we pretended to be a married couple, me being the patient professor and Karen talking a mile a minute about utter nonsense. Many times I was afraid that Bobbi was overdoing her act, and that the guy would realize we were secret agents and an awful scene would take place. I had to control my inner laughter tremendously as Bobbi would say things like: "I don't need my books audited," "Does being on the E-Meter (Hubbard's physiological thoughts and emotions measuring device; see [1] in Chapter Two Notes) hurt?", "There is nothing wrong with me—I just want to change people's attitudes," "I'm a natural person—I don't like electronic devices," etc. Even the guy let out a smile and said "Come on" when Bobbi asked him if the E-Meter could electrocute you. But somehow the guy began to look deeply into Bobbi's eyes as he questioned her, trying to reach who she really was. Bobbi did not succumb or give up her Karen act, but she said afterwards how penetratingly deep and invasive this guy's captivating stare was. Yes—TRs (an acronym for Training Routines to dilate a Scientologist's eye pupils and "capture" people through their deep eyeball stares, see [1] in Chapter Two Notes) was alive and well in Brunswick, Maine.

I managed to keep my naive inquisitive professor act up, and I succeeded in finding out the information I came there to find out. It turns out that for only $500 you can become a Dianetics auditor without utilizing the E-Meter. Of course the great emphasis is on becoming a full E-Meter Scientology auditor afterwards, but the guy said that one would need to go to Boston to learn this as they were not equipped to do E-Meter auditing in Brunswick. When he talked about the priceless benefits of going Clear (the Scientology goal of relieving people of all their engrams and achieving the first stage of inner peace, (see [1] in Chapter Two Notes), I asked him if there were levels beyond Clear. Bobbi became concerned that he would become suspicious of my thinking about this, but he answered me directly, admitting that each post-clear level (the Operating Thetan levels) cost a few thousand dollars. I remembered how back in the 1970s there were about a dozen Operating Thetan levels. How much would it cost to go Clear? Around fifteen or twenty thousand dollars if done on the E-meter. It would be cheaper without the E-meter, but virtually no-one did it this way because it takes too long. Somehow this guy was so nice and calm that in spite of all my background and our being such wonderful actors, Bobbi/Karen actually became interested in buying a book and even momentarily thinking about the $100 Introductory course the guy told her about, which could help her learn to change people's attitudes through becoming skilled at observing what

Scientology describes as the "tone scales" people are on (see [1] in Chapter Two Notes. And I actually found, in my imagination, the prospect of becoming a Dianetics auditor to be rather tempting. Yes--I was very glad that Bobbi was with me, and I decided against buying the book, as Karen told the guy that I controlled all our finances. I think that the guy thought I had a lot of potential to make a fine Scientology auditor, and making a Scientology auditor is still the essential ingredient that allows Scientology to survive and prosper.

And so I have fulfilled my responsibility to learn more about Scientology. By the time we left, at least two hours from when we entered the Scientology mission, Bobbi was quite impressed with the impact that the Brunswick Church of Scientology had upon her. She said that if she were by herself and had never met me, she would have definitely signed up for the Introductory course and would have been at their mercy. Their course schedule is so much more convenient and lighter than the way it used to be back in Boston in the 1970s, as two or three evenings a week is enough to enroll on a course here in Brunswick, Maine [5]. Dianetics auditing at the mission could be done at $30 per hour. The emphasis is still on twelve and a half hour intensives, and following up with the more expensive E-Meter auditing is expected, but for an initial investment this was certainly most reasonable. This was not hard core salesmanship—this was laid back small town Maine friendliness. And it was alarmingly effective, as the dangers and traps are the same as they were twenty-five years ago. Take one step and you are hooked—you would be in the Boston Church of Scientology before you know it. But as my understanding of the frightening versatility and variety at which Scientology procures its victims is now current, at this point I shall conclude my explorations of Scientology in the 21st century [6].

ON ECKANKAR

(9/1/97)

And modern religions continue for me—after a seventeen year break—while I am now living in a small town in rural Maine. Many years of reality—learning how to be stable, hold down a job as a mathematics professor at a small college in Maine for twelve years, be a homeowner for nine years, and a devoted father for sixteen years. But something has been coming over me the past few months, as I am now forty seven, smack in the middle of what society labels a "mid-life crisis." Only for me, it is in actuality a return to my questioning exploration of my younger years, not altogether different from Hermann Hesse's Siddhartha [7], who returned to his spiritual meditative state after spending twenty years in the business world. My heroine is no longer my ex-wife Diane, as I have now been divorced for twelve years, and I'm afraid there is not much idealism left between me and Diane. But I have been given a reminder of what Natural Dimension is all about, as I fell in love again—at age forty four. As fate would have it, the woman I fell in love with, Sue, decided to go back to her husband—but for the past three years our deep miraculous connection has somehow been preserved. I introduce Sue now, only because the way I encountered Eckankar was directly related to my agonizing break-up with Sue, back in 1995.

I once remarked that I have a propensity for discovering new religions by meeting women I feel an attraction to. This is how I discovered Scientology, The Unification Church, Gurdjieff, and Neopaganism [8]. Well, a few months after my break-up with Sue, I met Ms. X; I am not using the real name of this woman in order to protect myself from any possible legal entanglement, as Ms. X subsequently threatened to file a law suit against both me and the Belfast, Maine Adult School, where I had been offering my course on Spirituality and Cults, if I promoted both this essay and my essay *On Holographic Repatterning* in this chapter. Ms. X had been an Eckist (devotee of Eckankar) for over fifteen years. Ironically, I had actually been to an introductory session about Eckankar in 1979, just around the time Ms. X joined this religion. Eckankar was founded in the mid 1960s by Paul Twitchell. Twitchell's book *Eckankar: The Key To Secret Worlds* is the foundational book upon which Eckankar is based [9]. Twitchell was the Eck Master (guru of Eckankar) for seven years, until his death, followed by Darwin Gross, who was the Eck Master for ten years, until his dismissal for rumored "unethical" behavior. For the past sixteen years the Eck Master has been Harold Klemp.

I have read a number of Eckankar books, and have been to a few Eckankar services and Eckankar workshops. The spiritual basis of Eckankar is "soul travel," complete with all the spiritual inner worlds, through the various levels of higher awareness and "subtle bodies" (see Cyndi Dale's books in [94] of Chapter One Notes). Twitchell goes into tremendous detail describing the intricacies of the soul progressing through its many layers toward God realization. He encompasses angels, reincarnation, leaving your body in dreams, and various kinds of extrasensory perceptions, especially sound (see [9] of Chapter Two Notes). The essential Eckankar technique to initiate soul travel is to chant the sacred word "Hu." This chanting of "Hu" is considered to be uttering the sacred sound of God, which releases the universal Eck energy throughout your system—not too different from the Buddhist energy of kundalini or prana, or the Reiki energy [10].

What distinguishes Eckankar from Buddhism, and from my perspective causes it to have some mild cult dangers [11], is its extreme reliance on the guru in the form of the living Eck Master. The living Eck Master is considered to be the supreme spiritual being on our planet—in the same way that Jesus was in his day, and in the same way that the followers of Divine Light Mission view Guru Maharajji and the followers of the Unification Church view Reverend Moon [12]. Ms. X had pictures of Harold Klemp all over her house; he was the source of her strength and comfort, though she had never met him. At first it was enticing to me to be involved in a romantic relationship with a bona fide "cultist." After all, Eckankar did seem relatively harmless to me, in comparison to Scientology and est and The Unification Church [13]. There is not any emphasis upon exorbitant financial demands, severing your relations with people who are not Eckists, or recruiting new members into the Eckankar organization. But I can remember how overwhelmingly sick I felt after listening to speaker after speaker extol their relationships to all the Eck Masters, past and present, as it is claimed that there is a long line of Eck Masters from India going back thousands of years [14]. It was very obvious to me that all these people were living under the auspices of their Eck guru, and swallowing the dictates of the modern Eck Masters held in devotional regard—Paul Twitchell and Harold Klemp. It was a phenomenon worthy of study for me, but could I actually spend the rest of my life in a romantic relationship with an Eckist?

Ms. X and I got into our first major fight—over Eckankar. Somehow we worked through it, and eight months later I went to another Eckankar workshop with her. I started to get used to seeing the same people, and I started to feel less uncomfortable being around Eckists. They certainly seemed harmless enough, even if I did consider them to be deluded cultists. I began to look upon it as Ms. X was an Eckist, just as someone else was a Jew or a Christian, believing in things that were just as foreign to me as Eckankar. There is some beautiful spiritual music from Eckankar, including a piano songbook that Ms. X and I used to like to sing from. Eckankar did have some kind of spiritual effect upon me; it went straight to my heart. But the guru aspect of it was something that I always felt repelled by. I could not be in Ms. X's bed and have Harold Klemp staring at me. Ms. X and I finally did break up—around six months ago. But I must say that the major impetus for our breaking up was not Eckankar. Actually it had to do with Ms. X's other major cultish involvement (see *On Holographic Repatterning* in this chapter). And so I leave Eckankar as a relatively pleasant harmless spiritual trap—not the truth, but not the supreme danger either [15].

ON CONVERSATIONS WITH GOD

(8/20/01)

As I think about new age spiritual organizations and cults, Neale Donald Walsch, the author of the *Conversations with God* books and founder of the new age spiritual organizations Conversations with God and Recreation Foundation, strikes me as a good example of a person who is truly conveying his deep mystical experience of God to the world without falling into the temptation of becoming yet another guru and masterminding yet another cult-like spiritual organization. Walsch has written a number of books which extend his first three books *Conversations with God: Books 1, 2, and 3*, including *Friendship with God*, *Communion with God*, and various booklets on diverse topics such as relationships, right livelihood, children's spirituality, etc. (see [59] and [60] of Chapter One Notes). He conducts workshop retreats all over the world, and there are CWG (Conversations with God) centers and study groups all over the world as well. Walsch's books continuously make the best seller lists, as they have become some of the most popular new age spirituality books of the last decade. Essentially Neale Donald Walsch claims to have the experience of speaking directly with God, and he can be viewed as being a medium or channel for a higher spiritual force, in a somewhat similar way in which I view Helen Schucman being a channel of higher spiritual energy when she wrote *A Course in Miracles* (see [53] and [55] in

Chapter One Notes). Personally I don't view either of these two spiritual experiences as involving an external God or communion with Jesus (in the case of Helen Schucman), but rather as their deep level spiritual experiences within their own selves. Ken Wilber described these experiences as the subtle, causal, and non-dual levels in his book *Sex, Ecology, Spirituality* (see [2] in Introduction Notes). But this difference in interpretation does not seem to me to be a significant obstacle in attaining comfort, guidance, and support in maintaining my own spiritual framework, particularly in the case of Neale Donald Walsch's interpretation of God as one of a universal Buddhist kind of force that is both within and without, part of each and every human being, representing the deepest and noblest parts of who we are.

The essence of Walsch's teachings involve total freedom to follow your own deepest and noblest instincts and inclinations, and does not seem very different to me from my own conception of what it means to live in a "natural dimension" (see [15] of Introduction Notes). A cornerstone of his philosophy is that your experiences follow from your beliefs, and this is the same exact basic philosophical premise at the foundation of Avatar, Harry Palmer's spiritual/personal growth organization which I have found to be quite financially exorbitant and far more cultish than either Conversations with God or A Course in Miracles (see my Avatar and Course in Miracles essays in Chapter 2, and the related sections for these groups in Chapter 1). I have been to a Conversations with God study group and informal Recreation gathering, and have had a few telephone conversations with some of the Conversations with God leaders. Everyone I have met and/or spoken with has struck me as being sincere, non-coercive, and non-manipulative. In fact, I was quite impressed that even though the leader of the CWG Recreation Foundation, Portland, Maine gathering I recently attended was intent on forming a CWG center, he had no problem with me writing and circulating an essay about CWG and forming a spiritual discussion group where I would share the knowledge and experiences that I have gathered about the Conversations with God network. This is completely and strikingly different from the secrecy and legal binds that Avatar has placed upon me, or rather has attempted to place upon me, as Avatar is going to become a prominent part of my new age spirituality/cults discussion group, whether they like it or not [16].

Neale Donald Walsch is doing a weekend workshop at Omega Institute in New York State in October, 2001, and I had thought about attending and gaining more experience about this new age spiritual leader and his organization. But my pragmatic priorities do not seem to be adding up to me doing this. Thus my initial experience with the Conversations with God Recreation Foundation as an organization is quite limited at this point. I subscribe to the CWG monthly journal, and perhaps the most serious concern I have about CWG, which Walsch is quite aware of himself, is that Neale Donald Walsch does have a rather large ego and has to be continuously careful to not fall into the trap of being made into a guru by his many ardent followers. He seems to have an inspiring and harmonious relationship with his wife Nancy, and he is extremely involved with various new age spiritual leaders—including Marianne Williamson and Deepak Chopra, in forming a global network to work toward world peace and universal elevation of spirit. There are strong connections with the synchronicity ideas of James Redfield (*The Celestine Prophesy)* as well as the mind over matter prayer ideas of Larry Dossey (*The Recovery of the Soul)* [17]. There are also fascinating accounts of "highly evolved beings" (HEBs) in *Conversations with God: Book 3* (see [60] in Chapter One Notes), and the whole series of books is filled with a kind of humor and wit and unpretentiousness which has reached the hearts of millions of people. I have much praise and respect for Neale Donald Walsch for what he has created, and I eventually do want to attend a CWG retreat, and have the experience of being with him in person. If you want the feeling of community in a non-threatening and non-coercive way, with a minimum of rules and regulations and a constant reminder to search inward for your own spiritual inspiration, then based upon what I have thus far learned about Conversations with God, I recommend exploring the Conversations with God Recreation Foundation. However, for me, Conversations with God and the Recreation Foundation is too much based upon the ideas and experiences of this one person, even though I believe that Walsch has successfully withstood the guru temptation. I don't want to become a follower of Neale Donald Walsch; rather I want to learn from and assimilate Neale Donald Walsch's teachings into my own philosophy and spiritual experience. I feel far more comfortable with identifying myself with Neopaganism when I feel the need for a community support network; and my next essay shall be entitled *On Neopaganism* (see [82] and [84] of Chapter One Notes). But as far as legitimate and non-threatening new age spiritual organizations go, at this point I believe that Conversations with God and the Recreation Foundation is a noteworthy contribution to an ethical and valuable spiritual endeavor in a world-wide organizational network.

HUMANITY'S TEAM: PART 1

(6/30/03)

Is Neale Donald Walsch a guru? Is Conversations with God a cult? Here I am in Oregon at the retreat setting of the Living Enrichment Center in the middle of the first ever Humanity's Team conference. This weekend conference was attended by nearly 1,000 people, and 135 people—including myself, have opted to pay the additional $650 to spend a few extra intensive days with Neale Donald Walsch to be instructed in the "New Spirituality" on a higher level; this is called the "Teaching the Teachers Tutorial." The cost of this retreat is actually quite reasonable, as it includes food and lodging in a beautiful rustic Oregon setting. The Living Enrichment Center is widely known as the brainchild of Reverend Mary Morrisey, an inspiring author and speaker in her own right. But I need to stay on track here and try to answer the questions I began with. Is Neale Donald Walsch a guru? Is Conversations with God a cult?

When people ask me if a particular spiritual organization is a cult, I try to explain to them how the term "cult" is not an all or nothing thing, but rather a gradual continuum of behaviors that range from exceedingly dangerous to quite mild. There are a number of cult description scales in use, and one of the most comprehensive and useful scales I have seen can be found in Neopagan leader Isaac Bonewits' book *Real Magic* (see [83] in Chapter One Notes). Using this scale, I would put Scientology in the upper portions of the cult danger scale, Avatar somewhere in the middle, and Conversations with God, at least at this time of being smack in the middle of my full workshop, in the quite mild side [18]. The behaviors I am focusing upon in these classifications include overpowering ego of a charismatic leader, authoritarian control by this same leader, exorbitant financial demands, coercive pressures to recruit new members, alienation from those who are not members of the spiritual organization, adversity and animosity to other viewpoints, dogmatic beliefs in the absolute truth of everything the leader says, and a number of other variables (see [18] in Chapter Two Notes). Certainly

Scientology and its founder L Ron Hubbard rank in high danger utilizing the above variables on Bonewits' cult danger scale; however, Avatar and its founder Harry Palmer are more difficult to classify, as although there is certainly the authoritarian control, high financial costs, pressure to recruit new members, and dogmatic beliefs, these are not in the extreme levels of Scientology, and there is not the same kind of fear of other viewpoints and alienation of outsiders (see [18] in Chapter Two Notes). The cult dangers of both Scientology and Avatar are described in my related essays [19], but my previous Conversations with God essay of two years ago concludes that Conversations with God is a beneficial and safe spiritual philosophy and organization that is certainly not a spiritual cult. I had written that Neale Donald Walsch does have an ego problem to deal with, but that he is aware of this and works on keeping himself from becoming a dangerous guru to his many followers who would be all too ready to make him into one.

I actually met Neale Donald Walsch a few weeks ago at Michael Lerner's Tikkun conference in Washington D.C., as Walsch was one of the main speakers at this predominantly Peace in the Middle East conference. The Tikkun conference was an amazing combination of spirituality and politics, and I most certainly will write an essay about Tikkun and my further exploration of Judaism [20]. But for now, suffice it to say that Tikkun is an example of a spiritual organization that has all the positive characteristics of being the opposite of a cult, i.e. inspiring and stimulating but open to other viewpoints, safe, nurturing, and financially reasonable. I would put the Neopaganism I experience at my annual Starwood festival in this category as well (see [82] and [84] of Chapter One Notes), and I have high hopes that Barbara Marx Hubbard's Foundation of Conscious Evolution also belongs in this category [21]. But once again getting back to Neale Donald Walsch and the Conversations with God Foundation (which has gone back to its original name from the Recreation Foundation), the picture becomes more complicated as I find myself in the midst of the upper echelons of the entire organization.

Yes—Walsch has a big ego and is most definitely a theatrical charismatic leader who loves to be on stage. Yes—Conversations with God is run by Walsch in an essentially authoritarian manner. And yes—I must also admit that what I consider to be beyond reasonable high costs have recently been instituted in some Conversations with God programs. For example, their Leadership Education program costs nearly $10,000 over a three year period or $12,500 on a "fast track" three months special deal. This does not sit well with me; neither does the recent increase in prices of the "Recreating Yourself" and "Being It" workshops from $300 or $400 to $1,250. I honestly did not expect to be confronted with these financial blocks to go further in the Conversations with God organization, but I immediately found this to be an unpleasant surprise when I arrived at this conference. Humanity's Team is Walsch's passionate and brilliant worldwide effort to bring peace to the world. It is a subsidiary organization of Conversations with God Foundation, and is tremendously extensive in its ramifications, exposure, influence, and preliminary connections with like-minded organizations. The philosophical basis for Humanity's Team is described primarily in Walsch's most recent book *The New Revelatons*, and is further described in his earlier series of books *Conversations with God: Books 1, 2, 3*, as well as in *Friendship with God* and *Communion with God* (see [59] and [60] in Chapter One Notes). The essential ideas are tolerance and openness to others' spiritual/religious points of view, an openness to the idea that there are new things to learn on our spiritual paths, God is a universal energy force that is within all of us, there is no such thing as Heaven and Hell, there is no intrinsic right or wrong, and we are souls who survive the death of our bodies. With the exception of Walsch's belief in the absence of intrinsic right and wrong, and my long held spiritual agnostic perspective regarding souls that survive the death of our bodies, I am quite comfortable with these basic guidelines for what he calls the "New Spirituality."

Walsch firmly believes that the way to heal the world and save our species is to promote this New Spirituality to as many people as possible. He is certainly on target when he talks about the urgency of doing something to heal the world: witness September 11th, 2001 and the terrorist bombers as starters. And now I am expected to become one of Neale Donald Walsch's messengers. The expectations and hopes for us to take this New Spirituality home to our communities have been made repeatedly by Walsch and some of the Humanity's Team leaders at the conference. But my question is: are these expectations and hopes going to turn into coercive and manipulative pressures to bring others into the official organization Humanity's Team, and the Conversations with God Foundation? Is the expectation that I make the moderate financial commitment to become an official member of Humanity's Team going to be shoved down my throat by Neale Donald Walsch the next few days? Right now, in my mind Conversations with God can go in either direction. On a cult description scale I would place it somewhere in the middle of Avatar and Tikkun. By all standards, the cult dangers of Conversations with God are certainly relatively mild, but can I put it into the positive safe beneficial spiritual organization classification exemplified by Michael Lerner in Tikkun [22]?

I think of the amazing seventy-three-year old Barbara Marx Hubbard; every fiber of her slight physical being exudes intelligence, realness, purity, and lack of ego involvement. Or Duane Elgin, famous author of *Voluntary Simplicity* and humble leader of his own spiritual organization [23]. Or Dennis Weaver, popular ex-actor (Chester on Gunsmoke) who founded his own Econologics organization to find a balance between Ecology and Economics. The simple and humorous and forthright idealism of Dennis Weaver has won me over, as it apparently did everyone else at this Humanity's Team gathering. It is an interesting aside that Dennis is a follower of Paramahansa Yogananda's Self-Realization Fellowhip, a spiritual organization that I consider to have essentially positive safe beneficial characteristics with some mild follow the guru ingredients that are most definitely too limiting to my own tastes [24]. I think of Ilchi Lee, the honorable Korean spiritual leader playing his flutes in his fun-loving way and getting across his philosophy of controlling our bodies and brains with our spirits in such a simple, dignified, and beautiful (though for me neither stimulating nor inspiring way; and see [25]). And Mary Morrisey's self-revealing talk, describing her challenging beginnings and courage to believe in the power of her inner spiritual faith to overcome her own personal obstacles and establish the Living Retreat Center [26]. Or Daphne Rose Kingman sharing her personal story of her uncle in such an unassuming manner as she described her vision of a mature and open-ended way of loving (see [26] in Chapter Two Notes). Perhaps the most encouraging aspect of this whole Humanity's Team conference is that Neale Donald Walsch has surrounded himself with all these people to co-create Humanity's Team along with them. These people do not appear to me to have the ego/guru problem and personality challenges that Walsch has. But will Walsch listen to these people when it comes time to make the important decisions that truly distinguish a positive safe beneficial spiritual organization from a dangerous manipulative spiritual cult? It was so touching to me how Barbara Marx Hubbard honestly admitted that Neale Donald Walsch has an ego problem and that she sees part of her own role in Humanity's Team as offering a feminine balance to Walsch's overwhelming powerful masculine nature.

Yes—Neale Donald Walsch has the good sense to surround himself with truly enlightened spiritual beings who have been able to allow the real and pure essence of the New Spirituality to permeate their inner state of being without the need of on-stage theatrics. At the Tikkun conference Walsch shared the stage of being a main speaker with Michael Lerner, Deepak Chopra, Marianne Williamson, Cornell West (intellectually respected Black leader and Tikkun co-chair, and Jim Wallis (well known Christian peace activist), all of whom exemplify this ultra-high spiritual way of being [27]. So what is the verdict here? Well, as I said when I began this essay, I am smack in the middle of the Humanity's Team conference. Quite frankly, I am concerned that all of Walsch's true spiritual colleagues who serve the purpose of minimizing the detrimental effects of his big ego, will not be at the second half of this conference. He has his small group of devoted followers who carry out his instructions to organize Humanity's Team and will be with him for the rest of the workshop. But these people are by no means the kind of people who I consider to be independent thinkers and inspiring spiritual beings. To be honest, I am somewhat scared. I have heard that Walsch intends to primarily lecture us for many hours non-stop, and this is not how I assimilate material in a good way. It is not my intention to start a Humanity's Team Center in Maine. Rather, I see myself as moving in the direction of promoting my writings about new age spiritual organizations, and my course which I now call "Spirituality and Cults."

Yes—Humanity'sTeam and Conversations with God will certainly be a prominent part of my course, and I still hope that I will be able to offer Humanity's Team to people as a positive safe beneficial spiritual organization to explore, along the lines of Tikkun but without the primarily Jewish base. How much pressure will I receive to make the financial investment to officially join Humanity's Team, an investment that is difficult for me right now as I transition from math professor to counselor? I am so thankful for the supportive reminder I received from a fellow spiritual explorer at the conference who will also be here the next few days for the second half of the conference, reminding me that I do have the choice of taking time to think through everything and not make any immediate commitments, financial or otherwise. The inspiration and idealism and supportive community are also here; the wonderful feeling of being part of a noble cause to literally save humanity. But how daring and outspoken and authentic am I willing to be with Neale Donald Walsch—both in private (if the opportunity arises) and in this 135 person social setting? As it is now time to begin the second half of this Humanity's Team conference, I do think that I shall be writing a third essay about Conversations with God in the immediate future.

HUMANITY'S TEAM: PART 2

(7/02/03)

And the immediate future is occurring a few days later in Detroit, as I wait for my airlines connecting flight back to Maine. The advanced part of the Humanity's Team conference is over, and I am still in one piece. Unlike the way I finished the Avatar Masters' course two years ago [28], I did not go through being grilled by the Conversations with God leaders or receive a second class Humanity's Team classification. And if anything, I have been more outspoken at this Conversations with God gathering than I was at the Avatar Masters' Workshop. Yes—Neale Donald Walsch has passed my test and I conclude at this point that he is not a dangerous guru and Conversations with God is not a manipulative cult. But make no mistake about it—Neale Donald Walsch is tremendously powerful, has an enormous ego problem that he needs to confront (which he admits), and is overwhelmingly flamboyant, theatrical, controlling, and impactful. It makes sense that these are the qualities which have enabled him to have gathered such a massive following for his Conversations with God movement. But my initial sense of Walsch from the Tikkun converence in Washington D.C. a month ago has remained with me. I do believe that Neale Donald Walsch is deeply genuine and authentic on the inside, and that he truly believes he has received the divine inspiration and message of God. And for all I know, this has as much chance of being true as not true.

Walsch loves to lecture and tell spontaneous jokes for hours upon end, sharing whatever comes into his mind at the moment. His ability to capture the audience through prolonged intellectual stimulation mixed with taking people through deep individual processes reminds me of the powerful abilities and demonstrations of the est trainers I encountered back in the 1970s [29]. But when all is said and done, Conversations with God is far more gentle and humanistic then est or Avatar, and in no way resembles the stark cult dangers of Scientology. Yes—the prices of the Leadership Training seem unnecessarily high to me, and thirty or forty people have already registered for this training from my conference. And yes—Walsch did make a number of forceful sales pitches to persuade people to make the commitment to do this Leadership Training. But it stopped there, as it did not reach the point of being obnoxious and shameful to me, the way it did in Avatar (see [28]). However, what really won me over to Walsch's side was a rather daring step I took relatively early on in the training. I have always disagreed with Walsch's belief that there is no right or wrong, i.e. on the deeper level of the soul everything is good, and I even had a telephone conversation with one of the higher level CWG administrators about my problems with this dictum, two years ago when I first attended my Conversations with God gathering in Maine. Hitler and Nazi Germany are enough reason for me to believe in evil and the existence of right and wrong, and I do not choose to believe otherwise. As Walsch began lecturing non-stop for many hours and went on and on about his right/wrong philosophy, I found myself becoming quite low-key and disillusioned with Neale Donald Walsch, Conversations with God, and Humanity's Team. But during the meal breaks people would always ask me how I was doing, and I found myself honestly conveying to people how I felt and what I thought. Various people induced me to express my views to Walsch, either privately or in front of the group. However, it was challenging enough obtaining the microphone to ask a question, as Walsch does tend to dominate the stage, to say the least. And it felt quite terrifying to me when I thought of telling Neale Donald Walsch that I disagree with one of his major new revelations, but I still want to consider myself to be part of Humanity's Team and practicing the New Spirituality, in front of 135 people when Walsch is the public theatrical master and I am shy speaking up in large groups.

But I finally did it—and I must say that I was quite surprised by Neale Donald Walsch's immediate response. Walsch was highly sensitive to the emotion in my voice, and he immediately said that I did not need to agree with everything he said to be on Humanity's Team and practice the New Spirituality. And I witnessed all the inner turmoil immediately leave me, as Neale Donald Walsch and I stared at each other, with an openness and mutual understanding that I never dreamed would take place. And this is when I made the decision that Neale Donald Walsch, egocentric and overpowering as his outward personality may be, is not a dangerous guru and Conversations with God is not a manipulative cult.

And thus the rest of the training passed without any more major conflicts for me. I did not like having to witness the whole philosophical perspectives demonstration of why Hitler went to Heaven, the most controversial statement that Walsch has made in all of his writings. But I kept telling myself that it was O.K. for me to disagree with this and still be a part of Humanity's Team. Actually the most interesting and significant part of the training for me occurred when Walsch all of a sudden offered to include willing participants as writers in a book about Humanity's Team, which he would write the foreword and afterword to. The prospective publisher of this book was one of the training participants, and it was quite exciting for me to entertain the possibility of contributing a chapter in the book, based upon my essays on Conversations with God. I did not seem to bat much of an eyelash at the $3,000 or $3,500 it would cost me to do this, but I was not thinking very realistically about what I would actually be sending in for my chapter. How in my right mind could I think that Neale Donald Walsch would allow what I have written about him to go into print under his own auspices? I don't believe that his ego is balanced enough to allow this to happen, but then again I didn't think that he would respond the way he did to my right/wrong question. I would need to condense my writings into 1500 - 1800 words, but perhaps the basics of my very first essay of two years ago: *On Conversations with God*, with some kind of safe brief afterword about the Humanity's Team conference, would be worth pursuing. If it doesn't get accepted I would get my money back, and quite frankly this kind of opportunity to promote myself as a philosopher and bring Natural Dimension closer to seeing its day is one that I know I must at least be open to [30].

But in conclusion, I can now say that I have experienced Conversations with God on a much deeper level than I did in my original essay of two years ago, and I still encourage people to explore Neale Donald Walsch's Conversations with God organization as well as the New Spirituality and Humanity's Team. Walsch has given the 135 participants in this training—including myself, a private e-mail address to correspond with him. I take this to be quite an honor, and quite an opportunity [31]. In spite of all his faults, I have learned much from Neale Donald Walsch and I very much appreciate his willingness to make himself so available and vulnerable to us. I don't know how much further Natural Dimension and Conversations with God can travel together, but I do feel that I should at least be open to the possibility of extending myself in this direction. What does this mean in terms of me at some point in time writing yet another essay about Conversations with God? If you haven't guessed by now, there is actually quite a good possibility that this will happen—but certainly not in the next few days. For now, I do believe that I have a plane to catch.

NOTE: It has been interesting for me updating my Conversation with God essays in December, 2010, nearly seven and a half years after I wrote my last CWG essay *Humanity's Team: Part II*. In this seven year timeframe I have been regularly receiving mailings from Conversations with God, Humanity's Team, and Neale Donald Walsch, but there have been absolutely no pressures for me to respond in any way, and I have chosen to not respond. However, as I am still waiting (as of 1/4/11) to see if Michael Lerner and Tikkun will post my essay *Integrated Politics: Liberals and Libertarians Against the War in Afghanistan* on their blog (see [91] in Chapter One Notes), in all fairness to Neale Donald Walsch and Conversations with God, I am thinking that perhaps I should send my essay to CWG as well. If I do this and I receive a positive response, perhaps I will write yet another essay about Conversations with God.

ON A COURSE IN MIRACLES

(11/25/2000)

A Course in Miracles—finally I will say a few words about this "course." I first encountered A Course in Miracles soon after I moved to Maine—in 1986. I remember someone passing around this bible type of book and everyone taking turns reading a passage out loud, with occasional references to Jesus coming up. I did not think a whole lot about it, other than it was kind of interesting, but too Christian-oriented for my comfort zone, even to study as another "modern religion." Over ten years later I went to another Course in Miracles group—this time at Silo Seven Bookstore in Bangor, Maine in the summer of 1997, the same summer that I discovered Conversations with God, Avatar, Reiki, Self-Realization Fellowship, and Neopaganism [32]. Somehow this time the readings and discussions had more impact upon me, and I got into a heated argument with the discussion leader about the extent to which Jesus was figured prominently in the course, as from my perspective it was essentially Jesus who was "channeling" the course material. She lent me a tape describing the origins of the course, and I listened to it, realizing that we both probably had valid points of view. I decided to buy the foundational Course in Miracles book, went to a few more discussion groups from time to time, began reading the exceedingly deep and difficult and long spiritual text (see [53] and [55] in Chapter One Notes), and finally put it all aside.

Perhaps a year later I read a book by Marianne Williamson: *Return to Love* (see [55] in Chapter One Notes), and I felt a strong sense of impact and connection. As Marianne Williamson had originally been a devout teacher of A Course in Miracles and was still a loyal adherent to the course, I gradually found myself continuing to read chapters from the Course in Miracles book. Another year or two passed while my reading progress was quite minimal, and then in May 2000 I went to a workshop with Marianne Williamson at Omega Retreat Center in New York State [33]. When I realized in a personal way how much value Marianne Williamson had received from A Course in Miracles, I decided to take it more seriously. And so I have actually finished reading this book—1250 pages of deep Jesus-filled writing, written by Helen Schucman in the form of God, Jesus, and the Holy Ghost speaking directly through her (see [51] and [53] in Chapter One Notes). But I must confess—it has had impact upon me.

The central notions of transcending the ego, finding forgiveness inside your self, and forming "holy" encounters and relationships, are very beautiful notions indeed. For many Christian people, the basic framework of A Course in Miracles is one of enhanced freedom, as the Christian dogmas from the bible are largely removed, and the emphasis is upon your own experience, devoid of organizational rituals. It is rather ironic that both the source writer of A Course in Miracles, Helen Schucman, and the most famous promoter of A Course in Miracles, Marianne Williamson, were both originally Jewish, as I myself am. But I still have much trouble with all the Jesus references. I have gone back to a few more Course in Miracles study groups, and I do find the groups to be both intellectually stimulating and emotionally calming. There is something beneficial for me going on here [34], and I feel comfortable that there is no proselytizing being done. In fact, I now subscribe to a a newsletter that I get every two months: The Holy Encounter, and I am quite impressed with the maintained idealism of A Course in Miracles as a humanistic organization. But I constantly need to translate (within myself) the language of A Course In Miracles into a format that I am comfortable with. It is not my deepest way, but it is a way that I seem to receive benefit from, at least on an occasional basis. There does not appear to be anything that is particularly harmful here. I suppose that some people might claim that the repeated urgings to not look upon the day-to-day world as "real" may induce some people to make poor decisions regarding how they conduct their day-to-day lives. But I do not see this as essentially very different from the person steeped in his or her art form, who must get through day-to-day life while holding to deeper and higher visions of what his or her life is all about. And A Course in Miracles offers the continued support of ongoing study groups, a nurturing organization, and frequent large group workshops all over the world.

Thus in conclusion, though I have my spiritual blocks and disagreements with the Christian basis of A Course in Miracles, it strikes me as one of the more benign of the new age spiritual organizations that I have experienced, and it may very well have spiritual benefit for people of all spiritual persuasions [35].

ON SELF-REALIZATION FELLOWSHIP

(1/2/98)

Follow the guru and find your "self." Sound familiar? Paramahansa Yogananda is the founder of Self-Realization Fellowship (SRF) and author of the best-selling book *Autobiography of a Yogi* (see [49] in Chapter One Notes), which came out in the late 1940s, a few years before Yogananda's death. Self-Realization Fellowship has been around since Yogananda first came to the Unites States from India, in the early 1920s. The guiding force behind Self-Realization Fellowship is Kriya Yoga, a specialized form of spiritual/physical yoga that was handed down to Yogananda from a series of Indian gurus. There are six gurus that are worshipped in SRF: Yogananda, his three direct gurus in the ancestor line, the ancient Hindu Indian guru Krishna, and Jesus Christ. Yes—Jesus is embraced as well, as Christianity is welcomed as a merging of East and West, along with an embracing of Western science and technology. And I must admit that

Yogananda certainly does appear to be a rather gentle good-natured Indian guru, who writes in an exceptionally inspiring manner.

I have attended a few meditation/devotional SRF services in Portland, Maine, and have been receiving the specially designed SRF Lessons written by Yogananda and intended to train SRF students to eventually receive Kriya Initiation from one of the SRF monks. There is an annual seven day convention in the national headquarters in California, where people from all over the world gather together and receive Kriya Initiation, hundreds at a time. There is also the opportunity to go on SRF retreats in many cities in the U.S. and the world. The whole nature of Self-Realization Fellowship reminds me in many ways of Divine Light Mission, except for the fact that Yogananda is a much more palatable guru figure to me than Guru Maharajji [36]. However, I'm afraid that my personal barriers to following a guru have remained as intact as ever.

Yogananda goes through much inspiring devoted descriptions in his autobiography of his total dedication to his own guru—Sri Yaktaman. His lineage is traced back to Bibaji, reputed to appear to select initiates in the Himalayas as an Indian youth in his early twenties, though he is actually over five hundred years old. There are all kinds of miraculous events taking place in Yogananda's Indian world, and even Mahatma Gandi supposedly becomes a devotee of Kriya Yoga. From my reading of the SRF Lessons, Kriya Yoga involves a highly conentrated form of structured meditation, where one tenses and then relieves the tension in around thirty or forty different body parts. Although I welcome and appreciate general meditative states, it is all much too structured and formalized for my taste. It especially goes against my grain to be staring at pictures of the six SRF gurus before and after I meditate, which is the standard practice at the SRF meditation/workshop services [37]. But SRF is involved in much humanitarian and good-will activities throughout the world. The woman who presently leads the organization, Sri Daya Mata, has been the head of SRF for over forty years, and appears to me to be a wise, venerable, warm spiritual leader [38]. There are numerous books and tapes put out by SRF, as Yogananda was quite a prolific writer, and books are available by Yogananda disciples as well, including Sri Daya Mata. There are chants that are recommended for meditation practice, and these are also available through SRF. The cost of being an SRF member is refreshingly nominal, a welcome change of pace from some of the other modern religious organizations that I have been involved with.

But I must confess—I'm starting to get bored. I'm feeling like SRF has run its course for me. I get lessons every other week (in the mail) plus an eighty page SRF journal that comes out four times a year. And SRF is extremely diligent in sending its members frequent inspiring odds & ends in addition to the lessons and journals. They sponsor get-togethers for teenagers at their annual conventions. But it's just not me. Of course they embrace the soul that survives the body's death and reincarnates into another being. I can well understand how comforting it must be to believe all of this and to accept Yogananda as your guru, following his disciples through experiencing Kriya Initiation. But I could never "Receive Knowledge" in Divine Light Mission (see my essays on Divine Light Mission in Chapter 3), and for the same reason I could never receive Kriya Initiation in Self-Realization Fellowship. For it is necessary to wholeheartedly accept the guru as YOUR guru—until the end of time, to be allowed to experience this kind of initiation. So I'm afraid that all of this wonderful warm fellowship is not for me. Sometimes I wish it were, but I seem to have a different path in life. My immersion in and development of my contemplative life is meaningful and rewarding to me, especially the knowledge and experience I am assimilating through my continuous intensive studies in the world of mathematics. My own style of meditation is involved with playing classical piano while I absorb my morning's mathematical study and insights. My life theme seems to revolve around merging all my creative needs and artistic/mathematical expressions into a bona fide love relationship with a woman. And I am still captivated by one of the other modern religion explorations that I did the summer of 97—besides Self-Realization Fellowship. This other modern religion exploration I am referring to is Avatar—but that's a whole other essay [39]. For now, I do believe that I have learned all I want to from Self-Realization Fellowship. Relatively harmless and docile compared to Scientology, est, and the Moonies—but not for me [40].

NOTE: I would like to thank Geoffrey Falk, author of *Stripping the Gurus* (see [9] in Introduction Notes), for pointing out to me that in his experience of having spent nine months in a Self-Realization Fellowship ashram, the tensing and releasing of body parts that I have described in

Kriya Yoga is actually part of the preliminary Energization Exercises and was not part of the Kriya Yoga technique itself. Falk has a much more critical perspective toward Self-Realization Fellowship and former SRF leader Sri Daya Mata (who died in December, 2010) than I have given above, and I encourage people to read his book to gain more knowledge about what it is like to actually experience day-to-day life in a Self-Realization Fellowship ashram.

ON AVATAR

(1/2/98)

At long last I will try to convey something of my experience of Avatar—summer of 97. I became introduced to Avatar at an evening workshop at Silo Seven bookstore in Bangor, a wonderful environment for various spiritual/psychological presentations. There were only three people (including myself) attending this event, and one of the people described what he heard as the "new est." [41]. I must say that there seems to be more than a little truth to this pronouncement. Avatar was started in 1986 by a psychologist/ex-hippie named Harry Palmer—known to all Avatar students as simply "Harry." Palmer professes to not be a guru, but I'm afraid that I do not entirely agree with him on this point. For Palmer has a quite similar effect upon his followers that Erhard had upon his followers in est (see [41] of Chapter Two Notes). And Palmer is an exceptional businessman who has made a fortune with Avatar. The costs of doing Avatar are quite unbelievable, and I am somewhat embarrassed to tell you how much money I have spent to do the nine day Avatar training. But I will tell you anyway. Not including traveling around 1,000 miles in my car over the 9 days, the cost of tuition was $2,300. Yes—that's right—and this is in rural Maine! But around half of the ten people attending the workshop were from out of state, and many of them were reviewing the workshop, having taken it before (reviewing an Avatar workshop is done either for free or for a relatively small fee—well is $200 relatively small?). The workshop leaders are called Avatar Masters, and they all spend an additional $3,000 (not including the extra travel and motel costs, etc.) for an advanced Masters' workshop. There is also the Avatar Professional course, $2,500 plus extras, and the supreme experience to be with the "most enlightened beings on the planet"—the Avatar Wizards' course, which cost $7,500 plus extras.

So as you can see—Harry Palmer is quite the businessman. Over eighty thousand people have taken the Avatar training, and it is being offered in over sixty countries all over the world. He has not written very much, and his writing style is quite terse—but also quite impactful, as his books have been translated into a number of different languages. His primary book is *Living Deliberately* and his follow-up book is *Resurfacing*, which describes the first section of the three section Avatar nine day training course (see [68] of Chapter One Notes). Recently he has written *The Avatar Masters' Handbook* (see [69] in Chapter One Notes), which is presently available only to Avatar graduates, and I am considered to be one of these enlightened beings. *The Masters' Handbook* is chock-full of excellent business advice on successfully selling Avatar and becoming a professional Avatar Master (see [69] in Chapter One Notes). It is also of interest to me that Palmer is an ex-Scientologist. Indeed, his marketing and salesmanship abilities do remind me of L. Ron Hubbard's style, not to mention many philosophical/spiritual/psychological similarities as well [42].

But I'm getting way ahead of myself here. You see, this is by no means my final essay on Avatar. There were a lot of good things that I got out of the Avatar training. Summer of 97 was a time of much personal exploration for me. I needed some kind of personal support system, and I must admit that I did get this from Avatar. Was it worth $2,300? I honestly don't know. I know that I don't want to go any further in Avatar, other than possibly reviewing the Avatar training, as I did not completely finish the whole course. I had actually considered becoming an Avatar Master and leading trainings myself. But that's not right for me, and not just because of the financial costs. There is a great deal of secrecy about what goes on in the Avatar training. If word got out that I am disclosing what I am planning to disclose about Avatar, I have no idea how they will respond to me. I know that Avatar is not nearly as vicious as Scientology, but they are a relatively young organization, and I don't think they've had much experience with an ex-Avatar graduate doing an exposé about Avatar. But I'm going to give them the benefit of the doubt. I'm tentatively planning on reviewing the Avatar training next summer. Part of what I gained from Avatar was my intention to truly become a philosopher—in my own natural dimension (see [15] in Introduction Notes). And writing about Avatar is part and parcel of my philosophy of life. Lets see—how did it go now? Anything in the world should be open to being studied by the free natural mind. And so, I am now studying Avatar. It is in my natural dimension—so to speak. I can see that I am not yet ready to really describe the processes I went through in the Avatar training last summer, but not because I am hesitant to reveal any Avatar secrets. The reason is that it was all so deep and meaningful for me, and I still have not assimilated it to enough of an extent to write about it. It's taken me four months to even be able to write this initial essay about Avatar. So I will have to let this essay stand as merely my introduction to Avatar. But at least it's a beginning.

NOTE: As of 3/1/06, Harry Palmer's "psychologist" credentials were subsequently investigated in Florida, and he no longer uses this title in the state of Florida.

ON AVATAR: PART 2

(11/25/2000)

It's hard to believe that nearly three years have passed since I wrote my last essay, which happens to be *On Avatar*. I don't know why exactly I am writing again, but writing some more about Avatar seems to be as good a place to start for me as any. I did end up doing a review and completion of the Avatar course in July 1999, two years after I originally did the Avatar course. It once again had much impact on me. What do I like the best about Avatar? I would have to say that it is the way they encourage and support and train you to not give up on your dreams. They call it "primaries," and if the course goes well you end up feeling like you are capable of attaining the deepest goals, dreams, and desires that you have in life. The emphasis is very much upon going into your deepest spiritual self, referred to in Avatar as going into "source." This is not very different from the notion of empty mind, or Buddha consciousness achieved through meditation. The Avatar techniques to achieve this state of mind are actually quite simple and pleasant, having to do with feeling and noticing what is in your environment through a series of exercises called "feel its." Once this state of calm and relaxation is achieved, it is time to learn how to put total intention into overcoming the barriers of attaining your cherished goals, the barriers being called "secondaries." So the Avatar process can be described as going into source to eliminate your secondaries in order to attain your primaries. The bottom line of Avatar is that "you" decide how you feel and what you experience. In other words, you have the capability to control what you experience in life, through coming from a place of source, and visualizing what you want. This basic Avatar technique has philosophical similarities to the essential beliefs in both Neale Donald Walsch's Conversations with God philosophy, as well as Helen Schucman's A Course in Miracles, and various other new age belief systems [43]. But the nine day training grounds of Avatar is tremendously powerful and effective, and extremely intensive.

I must also give credit to Avatar for not interfering in what a person decides his or her primary to be. For me, I was in the midst of wanting to believe that the new relationship I was involved in was going to be the beautiful lifelong relationship I so much wanted to experience. The Avatar masters at first tried to gently convey to me that the lack of communication in this relationship was a very poor sign for attaining my primary in this particular relationship. But I was so stubborn and persistent that I refused to be open to what they were obviously seeing more clearly than I was. But true to Avatar form, they let me continue to work on making this my dominant primary and finding ways to attain it, though they did convince me to leave a little room for openness in case it turned out that this was not the relationship for which I had been praying for such a long time. When this relationship did finally end—about six months later for much of the reasons my Avatar Masters saw in advance, I felt a strong appreciation to Avatar for allowing me to have my experience in the Avatar course (i.e. choose to experience this—in Avatar language) in the way that I needed to at the time.

But what happens after the nine day Avatar training ends? Well—there are the regular mailings every two months or so of the Avatar journal—full of inspirational writings by Harry Palmer and various Avatar graduates, Masters, and Wizards. And there are new books and tapes put out by Harry Palmer. But the real emphasis is for the Avatar graduate to take the next step—to do the Avatar Masters' course and become an Avatar Master him/herself. Aside from the extreme expenses of doing this (see my first Avatar essay), my basic feeling is that I have already gotten what I wanted to get out of Avatar. There are some valuable tools in the Avatar training—make no mistake about this. But the follow-up courses in Avatar are financially exorbitant, and I can see the dangers of becoming addicted to Avatar if I were to succumb to these temptations. I would not rule out some time in the future doing another review of the original Avatar course, but this is starting to feel old hat to me. I know now what to expect—there would be no real surprises, and I do not particularly want to put myself in the whole world of being stimulated by Avatar again to go on to their Masters' course. There are other somewhat similar philosophies, like Conversations with God, that seem much less threatening for me to explore, and for which I may find value in. But then again there is a jolt I got from Avatar that I have not experienced from anywhere else in quite the same way. All things considered, there are for more dangerous modern religions—or new age spiritual organizations as I now prefer to call them, out there than Avatar. If you have between fifteen and twenty thousand dollars to spend, you might give serious consideration to becoming a "Wizard," and see if your dreams come true [44].

A LETTER WRITTEN WHILE ON THE AVATAR MASTERS' COURSE

(5/28/01)

Dear Barbara,

Funny that I find myself writing to you of all people—a woman I have not even met who is already quite involved with someone. But I am remembering what I promised you, which was also a promise to myself.

I said that I would not lose my "personal magic" as you eloquently put it. Avatar is most definitely a cult.

Somehow I have entered the upper echelons of the organization. Well, rather the training grounds for the upper echelons. They are tremendously careful about who they allow to enter their ranks—for good reason. I might already have ruined my opportunity to teach Avatar, as I have been quite outspoken about my concerns and discontentment about how expensive it is for people. But I once again find myself immersed in all the psychological processes, and finding it valuable. I do well with their actual psychological/ philosophical/spiritual material and could even see some day teaching it—in my own style. But in order to teach Avatar you have to sell Avatar, obtaining your own students. It really is like this other-worldly climate here, with the elite few Avatar leaders watching everybody very carefully, as they will decide who gets to have a full teachers' license (called Masters' license), who gets a provisional license (needing to do a further "internship"—most common type of license), and who gets essentially no license and is required to review the Masters' course (my course). There really is not much more I can do other than be myself and see how everything develops. I keep thinking about how I earn my living—teaching people math in a forced pressured grading atmosphere, and this motivates me to stay open to Avatar and see if there is any way that I can retain my "personal magic" and develop in Avatar at the same time....

Elliot

ASSISTANT AVATAR MASTER

(6/9/01)

Oh well—I did the Avatar Masters' course—five thousand dollars including hotel, food, and transportation; luxurious setting in Coronado, California. Why did I do it? I suppose I was ready to take a plunge into something uplifting and self-supporting after going through an extremely upsetting personal experience in a romantic relationship that involved losing important aspects of my self. And it was most certainly a plunge; two hundred people, many of these Avatar masters reviewing the course—from all over the world. There were six Stars' Edge trainers and three assistant Stars' Edge trainers running the course—the elite of Avatar. And we even got a surprise visit from none other than Harry Palmer himself, and his quite intense wife Avra. But notice the title of this essay: "*Assistant*" *Avatar Master*, which means I did not quite make the grade of "Avatar Master." So I am not granted the right to teach Avatar to others, and I would need to do a review of the Masters' course to upgrade my status, which means a few thousand more dollars for hotel, food, and transportation, even though the review course is free. But what actually happened on this course? Well, as you might not be surprised to hear, I got myself into a heap of trouble with the Stars' Edge trainer who appeared to have the most power and influence over who was given the status of becoming an Avatar Master and consequently allowed to teach Avatar. I was quite outspoken in my concern over the expense of Avatar, the emphasis on selling Avatar to find your own students, and I freely questioned the Stars' Edge trainers on how much money they were making for delivering the Masters' course. The particular Stars' Edge trainer I had my difficulties with took offense at my brazenness, and became suspicious that I was taking the course for fraudulent purposes, actually asking me if I was a reporter for the New York Times. He gave me various self-repair processes to work on, but I have no doubt that in the end he was not willing to trust me to deliver Avatar to others.

I was actually being open to becoming a truthful and bona-fide Avatar Master, and had even formulated a plan to co-deliver Avatar with a woman from Cincinnati who was a professional sales/marketing director. She was going to do the marketing/sales part and I was going to lead the actual teaching, as we planned on together doing the Section 1/Resurfacing part of the course in Cincinnati on a weekend in August, 2001. But all of this fell by the wayside once they gave me my Assistant Master status. It is true, as they tried to explain to me, that my status could have been lower, as there were some students who got no license at all. The only benefit of my status compared to no license is that I am allowed to "assist" a "Qualified Master" (official status with many Avatar requirements) on an Avatar course, which I would need to pay for unless I bring my own students. I was one of the first ones to finish the actual course, I got many compliments on how I was working with other Avatar students/masters, and many people further behind me were given the higher licensing status of "Intern Master," which enables them to teach the Section 1/Resurfacing weekend. I felt extremely hurt, embarrassed, and dejected when they told me my status, and my efforts to persuade them to reconsider fell upon deaf ears. And this was less than a week ago.

Deep down I know that there is a good higher reason for this, and that it is a signal to me that I am not supposed to be taking the easy way out and become a bona fide Avatar Master, feeling the comforts and comraderie of being part of a new age spiritual organization, learning how to be a successful new age businessman, selling Avatar to the world, etc. I chose to be myself at the Masters' course, and I got what I got. It is frustrating to me that I spent over $5,000 of money I did not have—maxed out my credit cards, etc, and got essentially nothing out of this to make back any of the hard-earned money that I spent on this course. Sure—I could spend even more money and do a Masters' course review in Germany or Korea (I would not go back to California and put myself under the authority of the Stars' Edge trainer whom I ran into my difficulties with), but there is no guarantee that the same kind of thing would not happen to me; and even aside from this, the truth of the matter is that I am by no means cut out to be a businessman. I have enough trouble selling my own Numberama ideas to the world [45], much less the ideas of another human being, especially when I have so many problems with the financial ethics, and even feel uncomfortable with some of the philosophical basics and exercises. I think back to my essays on Scientology—the problems with the 100 per cent technology, i.e. following 100 per cent the ideas and techniques of the person in charge [46]. And I realize that Avatar is essentially no different from Scientology in this regard. Like Hubbard, Palmer has come up with some impactful and effective ideas and techniques to help people actualize their dreams. But the procedures are repeated verbatim according to Palmer's instructions, from Source List to the Creation Handling Procedure to the Initiation Session. The verbatim repetition most certainly reminds me of the Dianetic Auditing sessions of Scientology, and I have no doubt that it is far more than a mere coincidence that there are these similarities of procedure between Scientology and Avatar, as Palmer himself is an ex-Scientologist [47].

So the viewpoint I "choose" to adopt (in Avatar language) is that my low status of "Assistant Avatar Master" has enabled me to make a narrow escape from yet another new age spiritual organization. I have signed a contract stating that I will not disclose any of the Avatar confidential materials to others—and I have likely already violated this contract by making both this essay and my previous Avatar essay public. This is no small matter, as Avatar has taken successful legal action against people who have done similar things to what I am doing. But I have been through something not very different from this a few years ago, in regard to conveying my experiences with Eckankar [48]. The lawyer I consulted assured me that I had the constitutional rights of "freedom of speech" on my side. Perhaps what I need to do is make a clean break with Avatar first—legally speaking. That is, I probably need to find a way to remove myself from the legal implications of my contract before making my essays on Avatar public. Once I do this, it seems to me that living in a free country should give anyone the right to speak freely upon any subject that one wishes to speak upon. I have now spent around $8,000 on Avatar. I have learned so much—both about Avatar and about the dangers of new age spirituality in the 2000s. As the first statement on the Avatar Source list says: "I am happy to be me." And this "me" is telling me that it is time to go back into action—not to do any more coursework on Avatar and not to teach Avatar officially to others—but to offer to others what I have learned about Avatar as well as all my other new age spirituality studies, and to facilitate heart-felt dialogue and discussion surrounding the search for authentic spiritual truth.

ON HOLOGRAPHIC REPATTERNING

(9/13/97)

The differences between religion and transpersonal psychology are often quite blurred [49]. Moreover, when one is exploring the realm of new age spiritual organizations, these distinctions may become nearly nonexistent. In this light, I would like to convey my experience with Holographic Repatterning.

Holographic Repatterning, which I will often refer to by its abbreviation of HR, was founded by Chloe Wordsworth in the late 1980s. My exposure to Holographic Repatterning is due to the same woman who exposed me to Eckankar—my ex-girlfriend whom I will once again refer to as Ms. X (see my essay *On Eckankar* in Chapter 2). I would occasionally call Ms. X my "double cultist," to her strongly adverse reaction. As I mentioned in the ending of my essay *On Eckankar*, my break-up with Ms. X was largely over our conflicts related to Holographic Repatterning. So why did her involvement in what may considered to be a transpersonal psychology organization have so much more of a negative impact upon me than her involvement in a modern religious organization?

When I met Ms. X, a little over two years ago, she was predominantly involved in Eckankar. She had recently graduated from a four year training program in Psychosynthesis—a branch of transpersonal psychology founded by Roberto Assagioli in the early 1900s [50]. Assagioli was a psychologist whom I have much respect and admiration for, and I do not by any means consider to be the founder of a spiritual or psychological cult. However, immediately after graduating from the Psychosythesis Institute, Ms. X began to take workshops in Holographic Repatterning. When I met her, she had been working in the realm of HR for about a year, occasionally using it with clients in her private practice as a therapist. She wanted to use it with me, and it gradually became our major vehicle of communication about difficult issues in our relationship. Whenever there was a conflict between us, Ms. X wanted to schedule an HR session for us, and I generally agreed to it, as I realized that this was the only way that was real to Ms. X in which she could deal with our issues and conflicts. At first it was a humorous kind of game to me. I learned the ins and outs of HR from Ms. X, and I must confess—I also learned how to manipulate the HR process to my own satisfaction. Not unlike Scientology, there are undoubtedly some valuable tools in Holographic Repatterning, and there is also the 100 per cent doctrine of the authoritarian teacher phenomenon (see [42] in Chapter Two Notes)—in the form of Chloe Wordsworth. I once met Chloe Wordworth—and I found her to be tremendously stimulating, intelligent, magnetic, and energetic. She has all the markings of a guru, and I contend that she is exactly this to her followers.

Wordsworth's HR materials focus upon transforming the vibrational frequencies of the level of functioning of a person, removing obstacles and resistances to a person's natural flow of energy [51]. Once again, this is not unlike Scientology's removal of painful engrams in the reactive mind, allowing a person to achieve the state of "Clear" [52]. There is even a physiological indicator of a person's mental/emotional state, as there is in Scientology [53]. HR makes use of the techniques of "muscle-checking." The basic premise of muscle-checking is that if you are comfortable with a statement and believe in it, then your natural flow of energy will be light and easy, whereas if you have a resistance to something then you will experience some kind of physical blockage. So Ms. X and I would continuously muscle-check each other after doing our HR sessions, through moving our arms against the pressure of the other person's hand. Ms. X was so adept at muscle-checking that she would quickly and nimbly muscle-check herself through moving one of her fingers through the opening between two fingers on her other hand; she would spend hours and hours doing HR sessions on herself in this fashion.

I must say that for nearly a year, Ms. X and I would always end our HR sessions feeling a sense of resolution, relief, and lightness. The way resistances are removed in HR is through the "healing modalities." Ms. X had a whole conglomeration of these healing modalities—including color torches, musical prongs, intoning equipment, Bach flower remedies, breathing exercises, etc. Holographic Repatterning pays a lot of attention to the Chakra system—i.e. the Eastern theory of the meridians (see Cyndi Dale's books in [94] in Chapter One Notes) and to astrological phenomena as well. After the healing modalities, a positive action would be assigned to us—which ranged through setting aside time for communication, massage, walking, recreational activity, lovemaking, etc. It was always so crystal clear to me that the reason Holographic Repatterning was effective was because my initial upset feelings would eventually get addressed through some part of the HR session. I needed to have the utmost patience to let Ms. X work through the hours of structure that the HR process dictated, but I knew that if I stayed in touch with my feelings we would eventually get through it. And we generally did.

The ingredient of Holographic Repatterning that finally came between me and Ms. X was the blind faith guru aspect of it. You see, the way Ms. X got her information concerning what issues, processes, and healing modalities a person needed to be working on, was through muscle-checking on herself a series of numbered items in Chloe Wordsworth's HR source book. I was constantly appalled at how Ms. X would arbitrarily decide upon what another person should be working on, through numbers in a book that were written by Chloe Wordsworth. Ms. X and I once went to an HR session conducted by a friend of hers, to work on my resistances to becoming a genuine part of Eckankar. I argued and argued over the arbitrary nature of what her friend told me was going on, through her muscle-checking of Chloe Wordswoth's numbered items. In the end, we somehow resolved things, and I can only understand it as HR followers supposedly are picking up some kind of subliminal energy flow through a psychic connection between themselves and Chloe Wordsworth. But it does seem preposterous to me, and often Ms. X would come out with issues for me to work on that I knew were not what was going on for me. Gradually Ms. X became less and less patient with my skepticism and resistances to HR. Gradually I became less and less patient and tolerant with Ms. X's total belief in everything Chloe Wordsworth said to do. I tried to encourage Ms. X to take the good aspects of HR and create her own unique blend of Psychosynthesis, HR, and other things that she had studied. But she was not able or wanting to do this. We even discussed the idea of doing couples' counseling together, but of course we could not agree upon a format. I finally realized that I was in a relationship with a bona-fide cultist, and yes—even a "double cultist."

It is interesting that Chloe Wordsworth is a devotee of an Eastern guru who was the founder of Sant Mat, which is considered to be a sister religion to Eckankar [54]. The basic premise of the sanctity of vibrational sound is at the heart of both Eckankar and Holographic Repatterning, as it also is in the religion of Sant Mat. Yes I had gotten re-initiated into modern religions—by way of a romantic relationship. Ms. X and I were supposedly quite seriously involved—we even discussed getting married. But somehow deep inside, I knew that Natural Dimension still lived. I did share many of my essays and much of my semi-autobiographical novel, *The Maturation of Walter Goldman* [55], with Ms. X, but it did not make much of an impression upon her. She could not understand why I had such immense resistance to following a guru. I would continuously share my true feelings with Sue—the woman I had been involved with before Ms. X (see my essay *On Eckankar* in Chapter 2). When I shared my real feelings with Sue, I knew that Natural Dimension was still alive and well, and I had been only "studying" both Eckankar and Holographic Repatterning. And so, six months ago Ms. X and I and ended our relationship, and I am finally able to assimilate my involvement in the spiritual/transpersonal realms that I encountered through her. I am now currently immersed in other spiritual/transpersonal realms, as I am actively studying/experiencing Self-Realization Fellowship, A Course in Miracles, Reiki, and most especially Avatar. I have also been exploring both polyamory and Neopaganism, but these are whole other essays (see [82] and [84] in Chapter One Notes, and Appendix: Part 4: *Neopagan Rituals: An Experiential Account*). For now, let me close by acknowledging that I am presently smack in the middle of being captivated by yet another transpersonal organization--it is Avatar, founded by Harry Palmer in 1986 (see [67] in Chapter One Notes). I'm quite mature now, fairly well established as both a mathematics professor and a father to my sixteen year old son, but my search for metaphysical awareness has been re-kindled. Maybe Ms. X and her corresponding impact upon me of Eckankar and Holographic Repatterning has reactivated my longing for getting back to the ultimate questions of life. Maybe my experience of falling in love with Sue at age forty-four has rekindled the basics of Natural Dimension that I had experienced with my ex wife Diane when I was nineteen. Maybe my son Jeremy turning sixteen and growing into a fine young man has given me the go-ahead to re-emerge myself in the spiritual realm. Whatever the reason, there is one thing that I do know for sure: I am back!

ON REIKI HEALING

(11/25/2000)

One of the currently popular new age spiritual practices is Reiki healing. Originating in Japan around the beginning of the 20th century,

Reiki has become an apparently rather harmless and non-threatening way for many people to experience a deep sense of calm and relaxation, along with a release of various physical ailments (see [71] in Chapter One Notes). I first experienced a Reiki healing around the same time I first encountered Avatar, back in the summer of 1997. Essentially you are lying on a massage table fully clothed, and the Reiki practitioner is gently and lightly touching you in completely non-sexual ways. This is by no means massage, but simply the laying on of hands. My first Reiki session did not last more than twenty or thirty minutes, was free of charge, and I left the session feeling peaceful and calm after having gone into the session with a great deal of anxiety over a personally threatening situation that I had to deal with. I had similar experiences in the next few Reiki sessions I did, and I decided to try out becoming a Reiki healer myself, as the training sessions were amazingly non-expensive. I learned that not all Reiki trainings were as cheap as the one I had found, but for the most part the expenses are reasonable. The one exception I heard about was a particular form of Reiki that charged as much as $10,000 to become a Reiki Master, but this was quite rare and not at all the dominant thrust in Reiki.

So how does Reiki really work? I can't say exactly, but I believe it has a lot to do with the level of intention a Reiki practitioner is putting into his or her (mostly her) practice. There are various Japanese Reiki symbols learned as part of your "attunement" when you train to become a Reiki practitioner; these symbols are given to you as part of the second level Reiki training (see [71] in Chapter One Notes). I have done the first two levels of Reiki training—there are two more levels, including the teaching level, with a few other symbols introduced. The idea is to visualize these symbols to accentuate the healing of the person you are doing Reiki on. You can also do Reiki upon yourself, though this is not something that clicks for me to do upon myself. I have been to a number of Reiki sharing sessions, where a group of three or four people take turns in giving each member of the group a Reiki healing session, the Reiki practitioners working in unison upon the person who is on the Reiki/massage table. For me, it has generally been quite comfortable and relaxing receiving a Reiki healing. I seem to go into my space in a calming way, and get in touch with how I am feeling and what I need to be doing with my life. Perhaps it is the gentle presence of sensitive women which nourishes this self process in me, though I have also experienced this with men being part of the group. When I would be giving a Reiki healing—which I have only done as part of a group, it always is a bit tricky to avoid touching a woman (especially one who is attractive to me) in any way that can even remotely be construed as being of a sexual nature. The one or two times I have done Reiki with a man on the table, I felt less comfortable and more guarded about touching the man—but these are my own individual Reiki healer issues.

Reiki is most definitely a system of healing, and a Reiki practitioner believes that many physical ailments and diseases (of people and animals) can literally be "cured" through the simple techniques of laying on of hands through Reiki, and this may also include keeping the hands in the energy field of the body without touching (see the books by Cyndi Dale's in [94] in Chapter 1 Notes), and even "distant healing" of people and animals many miles away. Although I am skeptical about the extent to which this is true, I do understand that there is an intimate and intricate relationship between the mind and the body, and when one attains a state of calm and peacefulness, it quite clearly may have advantageous effects on the body [56]. Unlike the bulk of new age spiritual organizations that I have explored, Reiki seems to have very little organizational pressures or inducements to spend exorbitant sums of money. All things considered, Reiki appears to me to be a nurturing and supportive spiritual practice [57]. It is a nice change of pace for me to take a break from my mind and get in touch with my feelings and spiritual center—in the Reiki atmosphere. I am quite open to experiencing more of Reiki—as both a Reiki practitioner and as a client. It is refreshing to finally not have to feel on-guard while experiencing a new age spiritual organization.

ON BEING INVOLVED WITH A REIKI MASTER

(7/26/02)

How difficult and challenging it is to be writing another essay about Reiki while being involved in a romantic relationship with a Reiki Master. My girlfriend Bobbi, the heroine of my recent essay *Scientology in the 21st Century* [58], is extremely involved in Reiki, to the point of opening up her own Reiki Center and going to an international Reiki conference in Toronto in September. Bobbi continuously does Reiki on herself, telling me how she is able to rise above her constant physical pains, heal her cuts and bruises much more quickly, connect up with spirit guides through channeling Reiki, and contact a deep source of universal energy. But for me, though I have received a number of Reiki healings and attunements from Bobbi in the year that we have been together, my experience of Reiki is pretty much the same as I wrote about in my previous essay of twenty months ago: *On Reiki Healing.* Reiki is a calming and relaxing form of meditation for me that is somehow connected up with other people. Am I contacting a deep source of universal energy when I am receiving Reiki? Perhaps I am. Through Reiki I do get in touch with my thoughts and feelings in a deeper sense, but I am not generally focusing upon physical ailments when receiving Reiki. For me, Reiki is the same deeper experience of self found in the Kundalini or Chi energy, the spirit of Christ, Buddha consciousness, the experience of "Source" from Avatar, going "Clear" from Scientology, "Receiving Knowledge" from Divine Light Mission, "Getting It" from est, etc. [59]. It seems to me that most of the new age spiritual organizations I have written about have the goal of enabling the spiritual aspirant to attain this transcendental state of being. Ken Wilber described this comprehensively in his books, in particular *Sex, Ecology, Consciousness* (see [2] in Introduction Notes), as he illustrated the psychic, subtle, causal, and non-dual states of being. Wilber himself engages in yoga as a daily practice, and I am entirely open to his way of contacting the divine. But the aspect of experiencing yoga as a daily practice requires a discipline and lifestyle that seems to me to be at the root of attaining these states of being (see [6] in Introduction Notes). My own daily discipline involves my early morning pure mathematics experience, followed by my experience of classical piano assimilation. This serves the purpose of continuously centering me, and I have learned long ago that this is my own unique way of putting myself in a higher state of being.

But here I go, almost giving in to the temptation to write about my own way, when this is supposed to be my second essay on Reiki. You see, writing about Reiki goes hand-in-hand with revealing some difficult conflicts in my relationship with Bobbi. But Bobbi is a very private person, and there is no way she would feel comfortable about me reading or letting other people read this essay—especially at our Spiritual Explorations in the 20/21st Century group at her own Reiki Center. But this in itself is going to be a problem for us—for I cannot stop Natural Dimension from speaking to me. For Natural Dimension is my own form of experiencing the universal energy, and it is telling me to once again open up my mind and assimilate what I have learned about Reiki the past year through being involved with Bobbi. To be quite candid, I am afraid that reading this essay to Bobbi would have the effect of ending our relationship. Perhaps you are wondering why—as I have not said anything negative about Bobbi's Reiki involvement. Well, aside from already revealing things about her Reiki experience that are very personal to Bobbi, I am afraid that the financial costs of becoming a Reiki Master are troublesome to me. Bobbi and I have already been through some agonizing conflicts over this, and I fear that if I continue writing this essay it can become the straw that breaks the camel's back. But I am now in my tent at Starwood Pagan festival, the place of freedom and magic that I have written about in my essay *On Neopaganism* (see [14] in Introduction Notes). Being at Starwood calls to Natural Dimension to emerge from its mature practical cautious state of trying to preserve a romantic relationship through holding back thoughts and feelings. No—I know this would only result in a slow ending of our relationship for me and Bobbi if I clog myself up. And so I shall continue to write and let the chips fall as they may.

For three hours I was dancing around the bonfire last night. My body moved in a wisdom of its own to the various drumming and singing rhythms as I became increasingly unconcerned about all the people on the sidelines who were socializing while watching the strange looking dancers, many of whom were either skyclad (i.e. naked) or painted up in magestic pagan displays. I did invest in a colorful sarong, which is the closest I feel comfortable to being skyclad at Starwood, aside from the Church of All Worlds' skyclad water ritual, which I participated in last night, as I had previously done a few years ago (see [14] in Introduction Notes). Anyway, here I go again—I seem to be having a lot of trouble saying much more about my involvement with a Reiki Master. As I question various Reiki Masters at Starwood about their financial perspectives on Reiki, I do realize that Bobbi's Reiki fees are probably somewhere around the average going rate. Yes—some people give Reiki attunements for very minimal amounts; but for someone trying to make their living as a Reiki Master in our society, it is understandable that one must charge somewhat more for attunements than for healings, and sequentially more for each level of attunement. In most Reiki systems there are three levels of attunement to become a Reiki Master (in Bobbi's system there are four). I myself was given the first two levels, but to actually teach Reiki, i.e. to give other people attunements and symbols, you must receive the third level (or fourth in Bobbi's system) called Master's attunement, which is how you become a Reiki Master. It is not unusual for the prices to jump from a few hundred dollars for the first two attunements to a thousand dollars or more for the third level Master's attunement. But this feels intrinsically wrong to me—especially here in rural Maine. Bobbi is just starting out in her Reiki Center, and she may very well find that the public will respond better to her if she cuts her current cost of $800 for a level four Masters' attunement with manual to half that amount. But I suppose the bottom line is that I am acknowledging the need to charge a significant amount of money to receive Reiki and become a Reiki Master.

The way in which Bobbi is offering her Reiki services to the public is completely different from the highly sophisticated and profitable financial schemes of either Scientology or Avatar. But I must admit that I feel quite concerned about the fees charged at the International Reiki Conference in Toronto that Bobbi is going to in September in order to receive her Master's level attunement in a different Reiki style—from a Japanese Reiki Master who traces his line in a short direct route from the Reiki founder Usui [60]. We're back in the thousand dollar range, and this is for a second form of Reiki. It makes me wonder where it all ends. I think about this high level Japanese Reiki Master likely making fifteen or twenty thousand dollars for two days of giving Reiki attunements to people, and I get images of another high priced guru. Obviously this is a source of contention between me and Bobbi. If I chose to receive the third level attunement in the Reiki style that I originally experienced (at quite minimal costs), I would be designated as a Reiki Master. I purposely have not done this—because I do not see Reiki as the supreme healing experience that Bobbi and other Reiki Masters feel that it is. But as I gradually become accustomed to the lower key natural Reiki perspective of both Reiki healers and other spiritual people whom I am connecting up with here at Starwood, I actually am feeling more open to the possibility of eventually becoming a Reiki Master myself. For these Starwood people Reiki is truly one of a number of ways of contacting the deeper universal energy that we are capable of experiencing. But they perceive Reiki in a similar way to Bobbi—channeling some kind of universal force to others. Perhaps I needed to make these Reiki connections here at Starwood in order for me to be more open to the way in which Bobbi experiences Reiki. For there are so many amazing and fascinating deeper level connections of consciousness being transmitted in the world. Whether you call it magic, psi phenomena, synchronicity, Kundalini, Reiki, or God, the reality of these connections are becoming increasingly clear to me [61]. Is it just natural coincidence that I am in a romantic relationship with a Reiki Master? Could there be some deeper reason for the involvement that Bobbi and I have with each other? Who knows—it is not inconceivable that we could even be living out some kind of past lives karma [62].

Well—enough musings for me this morning. I do believe that I have now done justice to my new learnings about Reiki through my romantic relationship with a Reiki Master. At this point I must honestly say that I do not know how my relationship with Bobbi will turn out. I do know that I must be my real self in order for our relationship to flourish, and being my real self means speaking my mind about Reiki. If Bobbi is able to accept this and I am able to read this essay to others while we are romantically involved with each other, then it means that Reiki is becoming increasingly more real and more important to me. For I would somehow see it that both Bobbi and Reiki are intimately connected to my own spiritual path in life. But this will not be easy for Bobbi to accept. It runs counter to her notions of privacy, and it runs counter to her perspective that receiving Reiki is well worth the money she is spending for it. But if we are able to both accept and acknowledge each other's different perspectives on Reiki and are willing to discuss this openly in our spiritual exploration group, then it is possible that some kind of Reiki magic can indeed take place for me. And this is about the most I can say at this time. You know—I do believe that I may eventually be writing a third essay on Reiki.

SURVIVED INTERNATIONAL REIKI CONFERENCE

(12/2/02)

It's hard to believe that only a little over four months have passed since I wrote my second Reiki essay—at the Starwood Pagan festival. I am psyching myself up to finally read this essay to Bobbi this weekend. As you might have guessed from the title of this third Reiki essay, I accompanied Bobbi to the International Reiki Conference in Toronto in September, as I stayed for the Introductory weekend part of the conference. And I must say—it is quite amazing to me that Bobbi and I are still involved in a romantic relationship after all the turmoil that we went through from my being at this conference. But we are still involved with each other, and seem to be gradually working our way back to the good feelings we have for each other. The personal details of what we suffered through are not relevant here, but my developing thoughts and personal insights about Reiki are what is significant in regard to sharing my knowledge of Reiki with others. So what can I add about Reiki to what I have already written?

Like anything else, there are sincere spiritual aspirants who follow Reiki and there are egotistical shallow "wannabees" (in Bobbi's language) who follow Reiki as well. For another comparison, there are ethical, natural, high level spiritual Reiki Masters and there are guru type Reiki Masters who are forming cult-like followings with many dogmatic rules and restrictions. At the Toronto International Reiki Conference, I must say that I did feel that the Japanese Reiki Masters leading the conference were of the first type: i.e. ethical, natural, high level spiritual people. One of these Reiki Masters was also a Buddhist monk (with the physique of a strong muscular weightlifter), and I did feel my own sense of personal spiritual impact when in his presence. Can I justify the fact that these Japanese Reiki Masters likely made around fifteen or twenty thousand dollars for these few days of work? Well, when one thinks about the horrible inequities in our modern capitalistic society: baseball stars, movie stars, rock & roll stars, etc., it hardly seems justified to put blame on Reiki Masters for making this kind of money from Reiki. To the best of my perceptions, these Japanese Reiki Masters were not phony or manipulative. And neither did I think were the Canadian and American Reiki Masters who organized the conference. I enjoyed meeting all the Reiki Masters who appeared to me to be at the highest levels at the conference, and I must say that I did feel some kind of elevation of spirit when in their presence. But the bulk of the approximately one hundred people who attended the conference were a disappointment to me, most especially America's most popular Reiki Master: William Rand, but this in itself is not necessarily a criticism of Reiki as much as it is of our modern American capitalistic technological society.

164 Modern Religions: An Experiential Analysis And Exposé

The problems that Bobbi and I ran into at the conference were something completely unexpected, as Bobbi and I essentially had the same feelings about most of the people attending the conference. I can actually remember feeling sad that I had to return to Maine at the end of the weekend, as I felt the higher levels of wanting to experience the Reiki energy further at the conference. It is so difficult for me to separate the feelings I had about Reiki at the conference from the personal difficulties that Bobbi and I experienced from the conference. But I can see that speaking my mind and letting my thoughts go where they may, is the necessary process for both my openness to Reiki to develop as well as for my relationship with Bobbi to develop. Lets see now—to stop my mind and to meditate and let the universal energy enter me. Is this not the substance of receiving Reiki? Well it is for me at least. Are there many other spiritual disciplines that I can say the same for? No doubt there are—again at least for me. But I am still involved with a Reiki Master, and this is the spiritual discipline that for whatever reason is continuously part of my life. It is like riding the wave that is in front of me. I went to the Reiki conference with Bobbi because I wanted to experience and share with her the part of her world which was tremendously important to her. Did it backfire? I still haven't exactly figured that one out. I feel terrible that Bobbi's high state was brought so drastically down by what we went through after she returned from the conference. But perhaps what is most important here is that Bobbi did receive the spiritual high that she was seeking from being at the conference and receiving her attunement directly from one of the Japanese Reiki Masters. This will always be inside of her, and I am very glad that she was able to experience this. And my own feelings about the highest level Reiki Masters who I met at the conference are positive ones. It does take quite the act of will to decide to focus upon the positives here and let the negatives dissolve the way they are best dissolving. But it is also the truth. The Reiki energy did reach me—in spite of the turmoil. So what does all this mean? Well, I suppose it means that there is a strong likelihood that some day I will write a fourth essay on Reiki.

MY DEVELOPING THOUGHTS ON REIKI

(1/4/04)

What more can I say about Reiki? It has been fifteen months since the International Reiki conference that I attended in Toronto, and Bobbi and I are still together. We have certainly had our share of personal challenges and ups and downs in the two and a half years that we have been with each other. But we are still together. We have stayed there for each other—with all our problems and turmoil and near break-ups. Reiki is still the central core of Bobbi's being—and I believe it always will be. I have not changed in my own perspective of Reiki; i.e. I am open to deeper higher levels of spiritual awareness, and I see Reiki as a form of meditation that allows one to tap into these deeper levels of awareness. I do not have any reality on the supposed universal Reiki energy that is so real for Bobbi, other than the deeper feelings of self that I have described in my first Reiki essay: *On Reiki Healing.*

When Bobbi is meditating and feeling like she is connecting with a universal energy that she refers to as Reiki, she is at her most real and deepest self. And this is the level I want to be able to share with Bobbi. I don't understand all the intricacies and details of chakras and auras and meridians and attunements and subtle bodies (see Cyndi Dale's books in [94] in Chapter One Notes), and I am quite skeptical about whether any of these things even exist. But I do understand the deeper, richer, and more real vibrations that I feel and sense from Bobbi when she is in a meditative Reiki state. And when my inner psyche is ready to join with hers, there is something that impacts me very deeply as I allow myself to soften and open myself up to the deep bond of connection that we share with each other. What exactly is this connection? Is it the connection of universal Reiki energy? Or is it simply the connection of being in love? Does it really matter? Perhaps it is all one and the same. Perhaps the universal Reiki energy for me is the experience of being in love with Bobbi; i.e. allowing my deepest self to open up to her deepest self. For I do realize that our deepest selves may very well become our no-selves; i.e. our oneness with the universe in the form of some kind of universal energy [63]. And I suppose there is no reason to not refer to this universal energy as Reiki, in respect for Usui when he originally experienced this universal energy in Japan in 1922.

166 Modern Religions: An Experiential Analysis And Exposé

Is there anything different about this kind of universal energy referred to as Reiki that sets it apart from what many other authentic highest level spiritual teachers have experienced throughout the ages—such as Buddha, Jesus, Rumi, Krishnamurti, Thich Nhat Hanh, the Dali Lama, Meister Eckhart, Mother Teresa, etc.? I dare say there is not. Ken Wilber elegantly described the higher levels of consciousness from psychic to subtle to causal to non-dual (see [2] in Introduction Notes). But Ken Wilber also emphasized the necessity of having a disciplined spiritual practice in order to truly experience these higher levels of consciousness (see [6] in Introduction Notes). For Wilber, his own disciplined spiritual practice is yoga, but he conveyed to me personally that he does consider the true authentic form of Reiki to be a legitimate disciplined spiritual path [64]). And what more can I say? I have no doubt that Ken Wilber would affirm that Bobbi's way of practicing Reiki is of this true authentic form, as it is a direct connection with the original pure Japanese way of experiencing Reiki, as opposed to all our inauthentic and crass modern Western technological versions of Reiki, from becoming a Reiki Master over a weekend to becoming a Reiki Master over the internet. Ken Wilber is considered by a number of people to be one of the most brilliant philosophical minds alive today and he has disclosed to me personally, during a two hour private meeting in his Denver apartment, that Reiki may be a legitimate disciplined spiritual path to travel on. And these are my developing thoughts on Reiki at this time.

REIKI: MEDITATION WITH TOUCH

(11/25/04)

And now I am no longer in a romantic relationship with a Reiki Master. It has been nearly a year since I wrote my last Reiki essay: *My Developing Thoughts on Reiki*, and Bobbi and I ended our relationship two months ago. So how do I now view Reiki? As the title of this essays says, I view Reiki as "meditation with touch."

I have seen Bobbi gather a group of interested and impressed Reiki aspirants around her as she gave her Reiki talk at a health fair, followed by giving individual Reiki healing sessions to interested participants. I have observed how Bobbi's Reiki article in a well-known new age magazine in Maine was very well received and generated respect and interest from Reiki Masters all around the country. I have learned that Bobbi continues to receive very positive feedback from her Reiki students who are taking her twelve week adult education Reiki class. But does any of this give any more credence to the validity of the claims Bobbi makes about the universal Reiki energy that was supposedly "re-discovered" by Japanese founder Mikao Usui in the early 1920s and has been transferred or "channeled" from Reiki Master to Reiki Master over the years in a lineage that Bobbi is so very proud of? I daresay that as far as I'm concerned, the answer is a resounding NO to this question. I wish Bobbi all the best in her Reiki practice, both for personal reasons and because I do not think that Reiki has any serious cult dangers attached to it (see [57] in Chapter Two Notes). Certainly the vast majority of people in this country and in the world practice forms of religion that I believe are essentially nothing more than indoctrinated fantasy and superstition. Of course I do not know for certain that Reiki—or any other religious system, is not based upon complete truth, but everything inside me tells me that this is not the case. Then why is it that I generally feel so very peaceful and relaxed when receiving a Reiki healing session from others?

First of all the question must be asked: does Reiki even exist? The phenomenology of what is actually going on in a Reiki session [65] consists of a person going into a quiet meditative state that may be accompanied by contemplation, and is generally accompanied by light touch, though it is also possible that a Reiki master will not actually touch the person but rather place her/his hands in the person's "energy fields" (see Cyndi Dale's books in [94] in Chapter One Notes). Each of these ingredients in themselves is enough to put a person into an altered state of consciousness based upon the timing, setting, and sensitivity of the person doing the healing or initiation [66]. As far as I'm concerned, there is absolutely no need to utilize all the esoteric explanations of Reiki that Bobbi so very much believes in, to explain the beneficial effects of a Reiki treatment. And of course there is the extra added ingredient of "expectations," or more formally known as the "self-fulfilling prophesy" in psychology [67]. Chakras, Reiki "showers" (this is an energy shower—no water), Reiki attunements and symbols, hand positions, combing out the negative energies, distant healing, etc. all sound quite exotic and intriguing. But what is it that I actually do know from my own experience? It is merely that I am entering a peaceful relaxed state of being, with deep insights about my life soon to follow. I have no doubt that in my own case this is stimulated by the meditative state and light touch of the person who refers to her/himself as a Reiki Master, and who is guiding and touching me, especially if this person happens to be an attractive female. If we define Reiki as entering a deep meditative state accompanied by the laying on of hands while in this state, or by placing one's hands in a person's "energy fields," or even by thinking of a person psychically who is not physically in the same place, I would not have a problem with viewing Reiki as a legitimate spiritual practice. Indeed this is the state of mind I have been in the past year when listening to Bobbi talk on and on about her beliefs in the universal energy that gets transmitted from Reiki Masters through attunements and healings.

As I have discussed in my earlier Reiki essays, I have a problem with people paying large amounts of money to receive this universal energy that I do not believe actually exists—at least not in the formalized descriptions in which Reiki practitioners have learned to use. Lets go back to the Perennial Philosophy and its extensive reformulations as given by Ken Wilber (see [2] in Introduction Notes). I do believe in successive realms of consciousness as Wilber describes it in many of his books (see [2] in Introduction Notes). It also makes sense to me that Reiki, using my own rather simplistic definition as "meditation with touch," may very well enhance a person to experience an altered state of consciousness, resulting in a temporary exposure to a higher realm of consciousness. But I wish to leave things here with Reiki, and not go through any more mind stretching contortions to translate all the esoteric Reiki beliefs that Bobbi and other Reiki practitioners use, to my own phenomenological and more simple definition. In short, one could say that I OD'd on Reiki—for three years. No—it is not my fate to spend the rest of my life in a romantic relationship with a Reiki Master. It is time for me to assimilate all that I have experienced of Reiki with Bobbi into my own self-understanding and awareness. For this is most certainly my experience of living in a natural dimension, still alive and prompting me in my mid-fifties—to live based upon my own very real experiences in life, without the need of crutches to fall back upon. I feared the loneliness of ending my relationship with Bobbi, and now that I am alone I do not know what the end result of Natural Dimension will be. But I do know that remembering my own freedom of mind is at its basis. So Reiki is meditation with touch. And I shall move onwards in my life from Reiki to more interesting, rewarding, and fulfilling involvements.

ON NEOPAGANISM

(8/23/01)

This is an essay I have wanted to write for four years, ever since I went to my first pagan festival summer of 1997 at Starwood in western New York State. Summer of 1997 was a time of great exploration for me, as I began to explore, in addition to Neopaganism: Avatar, Reiki Healing, Self-Realization Fellowship, A Course in Miracles, and Conversations with God (see [32] in Chapter Two Notes). There had been nearly a twenty year break from my "new age spirituality" (as I now call what I formerly referred to as "modern religions") explorations of the 1970s. Somehow in my late forties I found myself immersed in spiritual exploration once again—in a somewhat similar way to my late twenties. Now that I am in my early fifties, I finally feel ready to put it all together and truly assimilate everything into my own philosophy of life—which I refer to as Natural Dimension (see [15] in Introduction Notes). But Natural Dimension is a whole other book, and I'll stay with Neopaganism (which I will define to be people in modern times who consider themselves to be practicing Paganism with present day adaptations) for this essay.

When someone asks me if I have any particular religious affiliation, I say that I was brought up Jewish, but that I do not really identify myself with being Jewish. For me, finding value and meaning from rituals necessitates understanding and believing in what these rituals were originally based upon. I do not believe in or relate to the bible—Old Testament or New Testament. Thus I am not comfortable with Jewish rituals or holidays, and I am even more uncomfortable with Christian rituals and holidays, as I do feel some ingrained Jewish cultural connections, especially after the horrors of the Holocaust. When I found myself at the Starwood Pagan festival in 1997, to my surprise I actually felt comfortable with the opening circle rituals. Paying respect and reciting simple acknowledgements to water, earth, fire, and sky did not feel like anything I could not believe in. Rather, it felt like a beautiful way to acknowledge my own love of nature, which is evidenced by the name I have chosen for my philosophy of life: Natural Dimension. The people surrounding me at this opening circle did look rather weird to me at first; some of them were skyclad (naked) and many of them had tattoos and/or painted bodies with body piercings in various places that I think I will leave for your imagination. This festival seemed to be the most uncanny combination of bikers and hippies and ex-hippies. A number of the men wore robes and colorful material that looked like skirts to me (they were "sarongs"). Then there was the priest and priestess leading the circle—and I liked them. They seemed very sincere about this whole ritual, and they did not appear to be egocentric about it, but rather appeared to be truly sharing this experience with the two hundred people at opening circle. After the rituals, the priest and priestess led people through the "spiral dance," and this was quite an interesting and fun experience for me. Everyone was holding hands and being quickly pulled in and out of various spirals of people; I found myself coming face to face with all the strange looking people, and staring right into the naked bodies and eyes of these people who were now all smiling and laughing, and I was doing the same. I have always loved to dance (see the section *A Natural Dimension of Dance* in [15] in Introduction Notes) though I used to feel somewhat inhibited about dancing in groups of people. But somehow at this point my inhibitions seemed to be disappearing as I found myself dancing along with the other people. The drum rhythms were going right through me, and my body was moving in a free and cathartic way. And thus I had my first experience at a Pagan festival.

Starwood is a five day festival and over a thousand people attended the festival. It was a gradual process for me over the next five days, but I slowly realized that I was actually becoming a Neopagan. There were five workshops every day, including topics from magic, witchcraft, massage, psychedelics, movement, yoga, acting, drumming, Paganism, and batik. This was truly an intellectually interesting and stimulating festival; the balance of mind, body, and spirit was designed in an exceptionally harmonious way. I found myself camping out in the midst of throngs of people, getting used to using the one rather funky bathroom for all the people at the festival (there were separate bathrooms for men and women), and gradually getting to know some people through my workshops. In the evenings (and during lunch hour as well) there were various bands performing in the main stage area, and most of the bands had a strong rhythmic drumming element to them. The first night, after my experience at opening circle, I was amazed to find myself dancing right near the stage in the midst of the dancing enthusiasts, most of whom were at least twenty years younger than me. Was I really a forty-seven-year old mathematics professor? Somehow I felt ageless at Starwood; it was almost like being in a fountain of youth for me—some strange but delightful whole other planet. And when the dancing experience to the first evening's band finally ended—near midnight, many of the people were walking past the various vendors/crafts booths to the sounds of whole other drumming rhythms; and lo and behold I found myself following the people and discovering the nightly drumming bonfires. It took me a while to fully participate, but it became my nightly ritual to go to these bonfires until around 3:00 A.M. (they lasted all night), and I eventually became one of the dancers going around the bonfires. Many people danced skyclad, though I stopped short of the full skyclad experience myself—well at the bonfires, anyway.

I could go on and on with describing the fascinating environment at this Pagan festival, but I do not want to stray too far from the context of the significance of Neopaganism as a new age spirituality. However, I do want to at least mention something about the family context of this festival. I gradually realized that there were a number of families who attended this festival every summer (the festival began in 1980), and I occasionally would see teenagers going around together in small groups. My son Jeremy was nearly sixteen at the time, and toward the end of the festival I had a conversation over dinner with a mother and daughter who described to me how wonderful it was to share the Starwood experience with your children. I somehow knew that I wanted to bring my own son to Starwood the next summer. Suffice it to say that I have now been to four Starwood festivals, and my son Jeremy has been to three of them with me. It has truly become a father/son tradition for us, and we both have a special and rejuvenating experience being there.

And I thus come to a stable base for my new age spirituality explorations. At this year's Starwood festival I engaged in some very interesting intellectual discussions about the relationship of Judaism and Paganism, and my interest in new age spirituality, with some of the foremost Pagan leaders—such as Isaac Bonewits, Oberon Zell, and Phyllis Curot ([68], and see [83] and [85] in Chapter One Notes). It occurred to me that the founder of Judaism, namely Abraham, was originally a Pagan. But of course the founder of Christianity, Jesus, was originally Jewish, and the founder of Islam, Ishmael, was the grandson of Abraham. For me, all these religions are truly interconnected and it is so tragic that there are such bitter and violent animosities between them. I have become comfortable considering myself to be a Neopagan, as I see no conflicts with either Judaism or my exploration of new age spirituality. Freedom is an essential ingredient in Neopaganism, and it is my experience that Neopagans practice what they preach, at least at the Starwood festival. I cannot speak for other Neopagan groups, but I am primarily interested in conveying my own experience. I have found no gurus, financial pressures, oppressive authority structures, emphasis on bringing in other people, or any of the other traps that are so prevalent in many of the other new age spiritual organizations that I have written about. Yes—I have experienced that considering myself to be a Neopagan is quite consistent with living in a natural dimension in my 52nd year of life.

NOTE: Since writing this essay, I have been to two more Starwood festivals, in 2002 and 2003, and in 2004 I attended both the Rites of Spring Pagan festival and the Twilight Covening Pagan workshop in western Massachusetts; I attended the above Pagan festivals with my son Jeremy. For an extension of this essay that includes a more up-to-date (as of 2011) illustration of my Neopagan experiences, see Appendix: Part IV: *Neopagan Rituals: An Experiential Account* (see [82] in Chapter One Notes for the publication reference for this article).

CHAPTER TWO NOTES

1) See my Scientology essays in Chapter 4.

2) See in particular my essay *On Scientology* in Chapter 4.

3) See the Scientology section and *Summary of Results and Concluding Statement* section in Chapter 1, as well as my Scientology essays in Chapter 4, in particular *The Misunderstood Word*.

4) See my Reiki essays in Chapter 2.

5) See my Scientology essays in Chapter 4, and the section *Excerpts from "The Maturation of Watler Goldman"* in Chapter 4.

6) For more in-depth information about Scientology, see Chapter 4: *Encounters with Scientology*.

7) See Hermann Hesse (1971), *Siddhartha*; New York: Bantam Books (original work published 1951).

8) See my essays about these groups in Chapters 2, 3, and 4.

9) See Paul Twitchell, Eckankar: *The Key to Secret Worlds* (see [46] of Chapter One Notes for reference).

10) See my Reiki essays in Chapter 2.

11) See the Eckankar section and *Summary of Results and Concluding Statement* section in Chapter 1.

12) See my Divine Light Mission and Unification Church essays in Chapter 3.

13) See the *Summary of Results and Concluding Statement* section in Chapter 1.

14) See David Lane, *The Making of a Spiritual Movement: The Untold Story of Paul Twitchell and Eckankar* (see [47] in Chapter One Notes for reference) and the Eckankar section in Chapter 1 in regard to Paul Twitchell's alleged plagiarism and questionable formulation of the long line of Eck masters.

15) As of May, 2011, Harold Klemp is still the living Eck Master.

16) See my Avatar and A Course in Miracles essays in Chapter 2, as well as the related sections and the *Summary of Results and Concluding Statement* section in Chapter 1.

17) See James Redfield (1993), *The Celestine Prophesy*; New York: Warner Books; and Larry Dossey (1989), *The Recovery of the Soul*; New York: Bantam Books.

18) See the related sections and the *Summary of Results and Concluding Statement section* in Chapter 1, which shows that I subsequently placed Conversations with God in Neutral territory regarding cult dangers.

19) See my Scientology essays in Chapter 3, my Avatar essays in Chapter 2, and the related sections for Scientology and Avatar in Chapter 1.

20) See the Tikkun section in Chapter 1 and my essay *Current Spiritual Involvement: 2004/2005* in Chapter 5.

21) See Barbara Marx Hubbard (2001), *Emergence: The Shift from Ego to Essence*; Charlottesville, VA: Hampton Roads Publishing Co.

22) From the Tikkun section and the *Summary of Results and Concluding Statement* section in Chapter 1, it can be seen that I subsequently placed Tikkun in Neutral territory as opposed to Favorable, primarily because of the lack of an authentic spiritual focus in the experiential component of Tikkun, based upon my experiences at Tikkun workshops.

23) See Barbara Marx Hubbard's book *Emergence* in [21] above, and Duane Elgin (1993), *Voluntary Simplicity*; New York: William Morrow & Co.

24) See my essay *On Self-Realization Fellowship* in Chapter 2, and the related sections in Chapter 1.

25) I have subsequently become aware of cult danger concerns related to Ilchi Lee and his Dahn Yoga organization, and I frequently receive e-mail notices from this organization (www.dahnyoga.com).

26) See Mary Morrisey (1996), *Building Your Field of Dreams*; New York: Bantam Books; and Daphne Rose Kingma (1998), *The Future of Love*; New York: Broadway Books.

27) For book information for Marianne Williamson, Michael Lerner, and Cornell West, see [54], [87], [88], and [90] of Chapter One Notes; see also Deepak Chopra (2000), *How to Know God*; New York: Harmony Books; and Jim Wallis (2000), *Faith Works:*

Lessons from the Life of an Activist Preacher; New York: Random House.

28) See my essay *Assistant Avatar Master* in Chapter 2.

29) See my est essays in Chapter 3; in particular *est: Part 1: The Human Zoo* and *est: Part 2: The Message of the East*.

30) In a subsequent development this book publication idea was eliminated due to irreconcilable differences between the prospective publisher and the Conversations with God Foundation.

31) As it turned out, Walsch never did respond to my offer to send him copies of my Conversation with God essays soon after the Conversations with God conference ended.

32) See my respective essays in Chapter 2 and related material in Chapter 1.

33) See the related material on Omega Institute for Holistic Studies in Chapter 1.

34) To be completely honest here, I must mention that perhaps much of what I experienced as "beneficial" that was going on for me at the Course in Miracles groups I attended at this time was related to a woman I met at these groups with whom I subsequently became involved in a romantic relationship that lasted for a few months.

35) See the Course in Miracles related sections in Chapter 1, where I gave it a Neutral rating, in-between cult dangers and favorable modern religions.

36) See my Divine Light Mission essays in Chapter 3 and the Divine Light Mission section in Chapter 1.

37) I participated in a few Self-Realization Fellowship worship sessions in Portland, Maine at the home of a woman who I met through my ballroom dancing activities.

38) Sri Daya Mata died December 1, 2010.

39) See my Avatar essays in Chapter 2 and the Avatar section in Chapter 1.

40) See my Self-Realization Fellowship material in Chapter 1.

41) See my est essays in Chapter 3 and the est section in Chapter 1.

42) See my Scientology essays in Chapter 4 and the Scientology section in Chapter 1.

43) See the related Conversations with God and Course in Miracles material in Chapter 1 and Chapter 2; see also Rhonda Byrne (2006), *The Secret*; New York: Atria Books; and Wayne Dyer (1997), *Manifest Your Destiny*; New York: HarperCollins.

44) See the Avatar section and Summary of Results and Concluding Statement section in Chapter 1, where I gave Avatar a Moderate Cult Danger classification; note that Avatar has the third highest score on the Bonewits Cult Danger scale for the seventeen modern religions that I have experientially analyzed.

45) Numberama refers to my mathematics enrichment book: *Numberama: Recreational Number Theory in the School System* (Swanville, Maine: Natural Dimension Publications, 1993).

46) See my Scientology essays in Chapter 4, in particular my essay *The Misunderstood Word*.

47) See my Scientology essays in Chapter 4, in particular my essay *Sample Dianetic Auditing Process and Concluding Statement*.

48) See my essay *On Eckankar* in Chapter 2.

49) For a thorough description of transpersonal psychology, see Scotton, Chinen, & Battista (Editors) (1996), *Textbook of Transpersonal Psychiatry and Psychology*; New York: Basic Books; and Roger Walsh & Frances Vaughan (Editors) (1993), *Paths Beyond Ego: The Transpersonal Vision*; New York: Penguin Putnam.

50) See Roberto Assagioli (1965), *Psychosynthesis: A Manual of Principles and Techniques*; New York: Viking Press.

51) See Chloe Wordsworth (1998), *Scientific Principles of Holographic Repatterning* (unpublished manuscript, excerpt available at www.repatterning.com/chloe-wordsworth.htm).

52) See my Scientology essays in Chapter 4, in particular my essay *The Engram and the Dream*.

53) See my Scientology essay *The E-Meter* in Chapter 4.

54) See Julian P. Johnson (1985), *The Path of the Masters*; Springfield, MA: Nataraj Books (original work published 1939).

55) See *Excerpts from "The Maturation of Walter Goldman"* in Chapter 4.

56) This has evolved into a relatively recent field of study known as "psychoimmunology"; see for example Jeanne Achterberg (1985), *Imagery in Healing: Shamanism and Modern Medicine*; Boston: Shambhala.

57) See the Reiki material in Chapter 1, where I have given Reiki a Neutral classification, in-between mild cult dangers and favorable modern religions.

58) See my essay *Scientology in the 21st Century* in Chapter 2.

59) See these respective essays in Chapters 1, 2, 3, and 4; see also Huston Smith (1991), *The World's Religions*; New York: HarperCollins.

60) See Hiroshi Doi, *Modern Reiki Method for Healing* (see [71] of Chapter One Notes for reference).

61) See for example the books listed in [103] in Chapter One Notes, as well as Jeanne Millay (1999), *Multidimensional Mind: Remote Viewing in Hyperspace*; Berkeley, CA: North Atlantic Books; Jeanne Millay (Editor) (2009), *Radiant Minds: Scientists Explore the Dimensions of Consciousness*; Washington DC: Library of Congress; and Elliot Benjamin (2010), *License Plate Synchronicity: An Experiential Account and Analysis*; The Ground of Faith Journal, December (http://thegroundoffiath.net/issues/2010-12/); this article is also available on the Integral World website (www.integralworld.net) and the paranthropology website (paranthropology.weebly.com/elliot-benjamin.html).

62) See for example Ian Stevenson (1987), *Children Who Remember Previous Lives: A Question of Reincarnation*; Charlottesville, VA: University Press of Virginia; and Brian Weiss 1988), *Many Lives, Many Masters*; New York: Simon & Schuster.

63) See Ken Wilber's books listed in [2] of Introduction Notes, and Huston Smith's book: *The World's Religions* (see [59] above for reference).

64) See my essay *On Ken Wilber's Integral Institute: An Experiential Analysis* (see [20] in Introduction Notes for the references; or see my article as Appendix: Part 1 in this book).

65) For a description of phenomenology, which essentially means the study of experience, see Giorgi, A. (1970*), Psychology as a Human Science*; New York: Basic Books; and Moustakas, C. (1994), *Phenomenological Research Methods*; Thousand Oaks,

CA: Sage. For a philosophical precursor to American phenomenology, see William James (1976), *Essays in Radical Empiricism*; Cambridge, MA: Harvard University Press (original work published 1912).

66) See the books listed in [103] in Chapter One Notes, Jeanne Millay's books in [61] above, and also Charles Tart (1969), *Altered States of Consciousness: A Book of Readings*; New York: John Wiley & Sons.

67) See N. P. Spanos (1986). *Hypnotic Behavior: A Social-Psychological Interpretation of Amnesia, Analgesia, and "Trance Logic"*; The Behavioral and Brain Sciences, 9(3), 449-467; and George Hansen (2001), *The Trickster and the Paranormal*; Philadelphia: Xlibris.

68) Note that the Bonewits Cult Danger Scale, which I have used extensively in Chapter 1 and the Appendix to experientially evaluate the cult dangers of twenty-two modern religions/new age spiritual organizations, is the creation of Isaac Bonewits, who died in 2010. The Church of All Worlds, which includes polyamory as a stable basis for its social and sexual network, and pays tribute to Robert Heinlein's science fiction book *Stranger in a Strange La*nd, was co-founded by Oberon Zell (see [82] and [85] in Chapter One Notes, and Appendix: Part 4: *Neopagan Rituals: An Experiential Account*).

CHAPTER 3

ENCOUNTERS WITH SOME MODERN RELIGIONS IN THE 1970s

est: PART I: THE HUMAN ZOO

[1] (April, 1977)

I need to record something of my experiences of the first weekend of the est training here in New York City, before I go into my second weekend. To begin with, I must say that the bulk of the three hundred people taking part in this training are quite naive and suggestible—psychologically speaking. These are everyday-ordinary people; many are middle-aged, successful family type people, who are dissatisfied with their lives and curious to engage in something of the new spirituality. And est does indeed smack of the new spirituality for these people. est is a remarkable combination of Scientology, Existentialism, Gestalt Therapy, and Zen. I pay high tribute to Werner Erhard for his creativity and originality in putting together the many diverse philosophical movements around him, especially that of Scientology, from which he has gathered many terms and processes. But est possesses a far more influential mechanism than its mere philosophical brilliance. And this is the mechanism of group—or rather "mass"—influence. The est trainer, at least in the person of Stuart Esposito, although he seems to be quite a "real" human being [2], in my opinion is also very much an articulate demagogue. Esposito has an uncanny ability to speak right through a person and to instantaneously make a person see him/herself in her/his most genuine and authentic self. For many people this was quite a disaster. One must remember that we are dealing with people who are not very much used to introspection and searching for awareness. So for these people, it naturally seemed like magic to all of a sudden be shattered of their defenses which they are so used to carrying in all manners of their lives: work, marriage, friendship, etc. I could not help both admiring and applauding the artistic and really phenomenal ability which

Esposito repeatedly demonstrated on one person after another—breaking down the person's image of him/herself and bringing the person to almost total exposure in front of three hundred relative strangers. But Esposito also demonstrated some human decency and caring, and a truly incredible amount of patience.

For the most part, these people do not know what has happened to them. They found themselves howling on the floor, screaming at the top of their lungs, agreeing with the est trainers that they were indeed "ass-holes," and feeling self-indulged pain in their ascetic-weekend bodies, as food breaks and bathroom breaks were intentionally few and far between. I can well understand how 300 (or rather 299) est followers have already been produced from merely the first weekend of the training. Perhaps it is a good thing for our formerly "normal" American, for many of these people would never join an encounter group, and are too conservative and tied to their daily patterns of living to ever truly explore their own depths of personal possibilities. So perhaps est is truly the best thing around for them. However, I personally do not like est. For me, est is little more than a mass of crowded strangers, each one in a desperate phase of his/her life, seeking the answers that will make her/his life meaningful. I am not in that position at all. These people, of course with some exceptions, are the "straights" of society, the bourgeoisie of Hermann Hesse's *Steppenwolf* and the "child people" of Hermann Hesse's *Siddhartha* [3]. What is amazing to me is that these people have allowed themselves to undergo such heavy doses of the new psychology, although it is of course in the only form they would ever swallow: herd conformity.

But I must try to transcend my bitterness at the conventional social tea-party these people displayed at their mid-training meeting; for they had truly been through a rough time this past weekend. They enjoyed immensely the experience of seeing each other dressed up in their business suits, comparing notes on their day-to-day successes at work, and listening to the dulled and lulling excuse for an est leader, Sam, take them on some pretty straightforward Gestalt fantasy trips. But this mid-training seminar was just as much part of the est training as was the first weekend. During the first weekend, we all started out equal, including myself. By now, personalities have come to the front, cliques have emerged, salesmanship and groupishness have begun to take shape, and the sociological conditions have been artistically webbed for the full impact of the est training in the second weekend.

I already have many images in my head of the various people and the interesting effects that they have gone through. However, this est experience has had emotional impact for me also, and I am not yet able to fully record my sense impressions to any real degree. I came out of the est weekend feeling that est was "internal" to me [4]. I spoke a few times at the microphone and I felt I was able to be myself and still be accepted. I felt that Esposito was truly "real," and this is all that I ask for in life. So I stuck around and did my best to take part personally in the training, keeping all agreements and attempting to follow the instructions of the processes. I especially appreciated the opportunity to do some TRs from Scientology, as Erhard has put in a whole section of "being-there" exercises which are essentially straight out of Scientology [5]. However, the use of these estian TRs are designed to totally demolish the facade of these society people and send them whimpering and trembling into their real selves. This purpose was successfully accomplished in many cases, and was one of the most significant memories of the training for many people. I was quite affected by the howling and bitter cries of suffering emanating from hundreds of people surrounding me on the floor. It was both frightening and somewhat exhilarating. This is when the term "human zoo" came to my mind, as the only words I could conjure up to describe my experience. I was truly appalled by the enormous suffering in that room, only representative of the deep-down locked up turmoil that our whole country is in.

This was the real meaning of est for me, at least so far. Unlike the bulk of these unfortunate people, I have not compromised my life and I have no intentions of ever doing so. Therefore I do not need est, Scientology, or any other spiritual organization. What I do need is a continuation of "real" experiences and relationships together with the opportunity and environment where I can develop my own creativity, independence, and philosophy. I am getting all of this, and even more. Therefore I feel the ability and even the calling to study est, like I studied Scientology. I believe the impact of est will be more powerful, far-reaching, and long-lasting than that of Scientology [6], and so I shall learn what I can from est and Erhard, incorporating it into my ever-growing philosophy of life. For learning about est is acquiring knowledge, and I am, always was, and always will be a seeker of knowledge. Let us leave it at that for now.

est: PART 2: THE MESSAGE OF THE EAST

(April, 1977)

I am now an est graduate. I have successfully completed the est training. This was quite an arduous task, but it was well worth it. I feel altogether differently about est now than I did after the first weekend. I now have basically good feelings about est, and much respect and admiration for Werner Erhard. est is unmistakably a religious philosophy, in many ways similar to that of Scientology. But from what I can see so far, there are much less tricks and questionable ethical procedures than in Scientology. The financial costs are also phenomenally cheaper and more reasonable. I feel somewhat reluctant to give away any of the est secrets, something that I did not feel in Scientology and did not feel after the first est weekend. Perhaps the title of this essay expresses all that is really important about est. est gives you the message of the East, but in Western terms. est is truly a beautiful mixture of Eastern and Western philosophy, designed skillfully by Erhard to lure, trap, and confound the mind, and then to supersede the mind with the spirit. The key word in est, and one that I can relate to, is "experience." A key phrase in est, and also one that I can relate to, is "be here now." I do not feel that I have learned all that I want to from est, as I feel about Scientology. Unlike Scientology, est is not paranoid about other mental disciplines, such as psychology,and I do not feel very much conflict between est and my interests in psychology. est stresses full acceptance of the individual as he or she is, and I believe they are truly sincere in this. I do not wish to invalidate the est training for others by prematurely revealing the hidden techniques and meanings of the estian interpretation of precisely what the message of the East it. I feel that my first essay on est, *est: Part 1: The Human Zoo*, is legitimate, as it expresses purely my experience of the first est weekend, before any real secrets were revealed. I am indeed surprised that est: Part II is turning out the way it is, but what can I say? est is internal to me. It is now part of my personal system of life. Whether or not this will endure, I do not yet know; but I intend to find out eventually, in San Francisco. For now, I see est as being quite consistent with my own philosophy of life, i.e. with living in a natural dimension.

est: PART 3: RELIGION AND BIG BUSINESS (OR ON BRINGING GUESTS)

(July, 1977)

est is truly disgusting; I really don't know how much more of it I can stomach. It is such a degrading and crafty organization. In addition, it is an exceedingly dangerous organization. It is dealing with the mass phenomenon, and it specializes in demagoguery. In comparison to est, I would have to call Scientology "honest." And if you have read my essays on Scientology (see Chapter 4), you can imagine what it takes for me to say this. To begin with-- philosophically, psychologically, and theologically, in my opinion est is little more than second-rate Scientology. It seems to me that Erhard has stolen from Hubbard like a master thief. Nearly all parts of Scientology can be found in est: engrams, beings-at-cause, the tone scale, the "misunderstood word," auditing processes, Eastern spirituality, etc. Everybody thinks Erhard invented all this; but from my perspective the truth is that Erhard basically incorporated Hubbard's entire philosophy, with bits of Existentialism and odds and ends from India and China, and covered it all up with such a remarkable feat of expert salesmanship and business technology that Hubbard himself would blush at the sight! But I confess—like I have described Hubbard, I must say that Erhard is a genius, although of a different type than Hubbard. Erhard's genius involves his mastery of the mass phenomenon. Hubbard's main fault (which I consider to be one of his more decent characteristics) from a pragmatic business point of view, is actually his respect and dignity for the individual person. I never thought I would be saying this, but when I think back to the one-to-one relationship of pre-clear to auditor, the auditing sessions that last for hours non-stop until the pre-clear shows unmistakable signs of happiness (although of course the pre-clear is paying for this happiness quite steeply by the hour), and the massive files of all auditing processes for each and every individual pre-clear, one truly must give Hubbard some credit [7]. I am not forgetting that the pre-clear pays up to his/her ears for all this concern and respect, but I do believe that Hubbard at least began with some kind of altruistic concern and caring for the human being as an individual. On the other hand, for Erhard the individual human being seems to be nothing more than a member of a herd of cattle. The comparative ratio of auditor to pre-clear is not one-to-one, but three hundred to one. And this is why financially speaking, est is extremely well off—and this is why I call Werner Erhard a genius in his own right.

I am now in San Francisco and have been through three sessions of the Be Here Now seminar, which is the first est graduate seminar, plus a twelve hundred person guest lecture by Werner Erhard. The graduate seminar leader wears the most plastic fixed smile that I have seen in years. She turns off and on her smile at her own discretion--to create effects. She is one of Erhard's closest disciples, and has been with him from nearly the beginning. She doesn't look like much, and what's more—she isn't much. This is quite obvious to me, and I even think it is becoming obvious to a few members of the audience. It appears that the main focus of this Be Here Now seminar is to enable the est organization to survive and grow, through inducing, pressuring, and nearly coercing the est audience to bring "guests" to the seminar. Each week our leader posts our statistics on the screen—number of guests present, and makes an agreed upon (as long as it is to her agreement) number to shoot for the next week. Her reasoning that she presents is that through playing the game of "bringing guests" we are preparing to play the game of "life," and that she doesn't care whether we bring guests or not. This is how Erhard handled her, and this is how he told her to handle us. The guest numbers have so far gone up from 8 to 23, and session #4 is supposed to have 110 guests. She has also hinted that she will be treating us with less politeness and indulgence, and more the way Erhard himself treats people; i.e. talking to who people really are. Basically, I believe she means to work on the strength of our intentions in relation to bringing guests. If it is difficult for you to believe that three hundred mature and and intelligent adults actually put up with this, don't feel bad—it is difficult for me to believe too.

One person, after experiencing Werner Erhard himself give a day-long seminar on completing your relationships with your parents, had the insightful realization after Erhard's third standing ovation from two thousand people, that Erhard's power is both remarkable and dangerous, as she thought of the power that Hitler himself utilized in mass hypnosis. Werner Erhard has gotten people eating out of his hands. Over 110,000 people have done the est training. Erhard now is doing six day special family courses, where the cost is $650 per individual family member. I wouldn't care if there was anything to all this—even if it were merely neutral regarding one's mental health. But speaking as a counselor and future psychologist—I believe that est is truly dangerous to one's mental health [8]. est does not induce people to place responsibility and dependence on themselves—as it professes to do. Rather, est craftily and secretly teaches people to place responsibility and dependence on the est organization—in effect on Werner Erhard himself. First it cruelly and inhumanly persuades you to minimize the importance of all your meaningful relationships, by constantly barraging you with the dictum that nobody and nothing in life really matters. This is not just the growth psychology beliefs in self-realization, but something altogether twisted and sick. When people constantly stand up and speak into a microphone in front of three hundred relative strangers their deepest innermost hang-ups, and the leader wears her fixed smile while they are sobbing away, and they continue to sob when they are sitting while everybody present politely ignores them, I call this both sick and dangerous. These people are so deluded; est is slowly replacing all significant others in their lives. These people are so less independent and "at cause" than when they first came into est. And to think—all this just to make Werner Erhard rich! How disgusting and humiliating to mankind. How insulting and degrading to the individual human being. As est says, life is a game that one plays and the est seminars are where one learns what specific games in life to play. est is especially for the successful male businessman—the person so used to giving orders that he is just longing for someone to give orders to him. Or for the middle-aged housewife and mother who never did anything of distinction before. est is so sick; I actually feel a commitment to stay in est for as long as I can and expose to the public as much of it as I am able to. For this is my "experience." I only hope that if I ever get through this Be Here Now seminar, the remainder of my encounters with est will involve more of psychology, philosophy, and religion, and less of big business and cheap, manipulative, underhanded con jobs.

est: On Pseudo-Realness

(August, 1977)

I have now been through seven sessions of the Be Here Now seminar series, and I have decided that I've had my share of est—for a while, anyway. In my previous essays on est, I realize that I have been quite emotional—which I am not in the least defending or apologizing for, but I would like to supplement these essays with a more level-headed critique. I've thought of the term "pseudo-realness," and I think this is a good name for what goes on in est. Nobody knows me in est; not in the least. I do not work well in masses. I do not like to speak into microphones, and I do not like to share personal secrets with a mass of strangers. I felt this way four months ago, when I first took the est training, and I have not changed my feelings. It really seems crazy to me. Is it intimacy or not? I contend that it is "pseudo-intimacy," not real intimacy. Intimacy—at least to me, requires the presence of one other human being who cares for me and knows me well. For me, intimacy is related to privacy and freedom. It is such a beautiful thing. It cannot be demanded or artificially produced. I have seen in est many cases that look very much like something intimate is happening between a person and the est mass, but I contend that it is false intimacy—or pseudo-intimacy. This has been my experience repeatedly when in est.

People come to their weekly est meetings directly from work. They are "on," and can be manipulated as easily as children. They lack any real depth of self, and therefore lick up the est processes of self-absorption like a thirsty dog licks up water. For this is one of their rare experiences of being alone with their selves; of course safely in a room full of crowded strangers. How existential; how pitiful and how sad. est contends that life is a game; and this certainly is true to est form, for est repeatedly stresses that it is not better to be happy than sad, nor even alive than dead. You are perfect as you are, no matter how you are. I remember how after I completed the training, this kind of est motto really touched base with me, as can be seen from my second essay on est: *The Message of the East*. But a true test of realness can only be made over time, where relationships have a chance to be formed, and people can be seen more clearly for who they really are. Yes—I must admit that I was quite enthusiastic about est when I finished the training, and if the training were all that existed, it would have been quite difficult for me to discover how shallow the training actually was. Just like the old weekend marathon encounter group so popular in the late 1960s was found to be quite shallow as far as long-term change and formation of friendships and relationships are concerned [9], similarly but many times more so, est is shallow. It seems like the harder and more dramatically we are hit, the more intense and severe is the immediate reaction, but the less "real" the whole thing is over an extended period of time.

What does this mean in regard to the many dedicated "estians" who have been with Wener Erhard since the beginning—1971? It means, at least from my own experience of them, that they are pseudo-real followers of a super-charismatic personality; people who are afraid and by this point incapable of living life according to their own precious personal ideas, whatever they once might have been. It is possible to totally reveal yourself to others, to completely unravel your heart, to burst out in tears and screams, and at the same time to be unknown in your deepest self to these same others. I am convinced that this phenomenon exists and I am labeling it "pseudo-realness." It will require much further study and investigation on my part to get any kind of a handle on this phenomenon, and for now I will need much time away from est and my other toy religions to become quite clear on what exactly "realness" is, in order to accentuate and develop my concept of pseudo-realness.

ON WERNER ERHARD

(July 8, 1978)

I now feel like I have completed all that I want to get out of est. I have just left in the middle of Werner Erhard's course on Celebrating Your Relationships. The course was held at the Oakland Coliseum and was attended by nearly nine thousand people. That's 9,000 times $50 a head, making a total of nearly half a million dollars. Erhard is beyond doubt an immense, powerful, awesome figure. And he did say some very beautiful things. He began the day by reading us selections from his favorite poetry, mostly that of E. E. Cummings. He tried to convey to us the experience of pure love. I wish to remember him in this light, and this is one of the reasons I left when I did, as he was getting more and more "esty." He said some very profound things about jealousy, which touched a deep part of me. I believe I understood the poems Werner Erhard was reading as well as anyone in the Coliseum, including Erhard himself. But then he overdid it. He started throwing around terms like "ecstasy" and "magnificence" as if they were readily accessible to everyone by the mere fact of one's existence. I have once been in ecstasy and I have once experienced magnificence, and I do not believe that these states are available to everyone by the mere fact of one's existence. I believe they are available only to those who aspire to them so longingly that they are willing to sacrifice their own lives in order to achieve them. And once achieved, to maintain any sort of connection with these very special states takes a tremendous amount of work, courage, persistence, idealism, and most of all—love.

The pseudo-realness of the nine thousand person est mass was quite sickening to me. They all need Werner Erhard; he is their guru. He is selling them ecstasy and magnificence, and they are buying. He is also selling them freedom, and they have already bought that at the est training. So now we are going past "experience," to the deepest context in which our lives are lived, that of ecstasy—getting totally blown away by the relationship. If only it were that easy. Ecstasy at 11:00 and hot dogs at 12:00. Real life is just not a carnival. It is a series of tears and joys, of strengths and weaknesses, of profundity and mediocrity. And most of all, real life is a series of personal relationships you have with other human beings. I don't consider any ordinary person in that nine thousand person est mass to be having a personal relationship with Werner Erhard, as Erhard claims. People are using Erhard the way I believe people have always used Jesus, and Erhard is encouraging this big time. I guess people will always need to do something like this. But I am thankful I have not had to, and I hope the children I bring into this world never have to either. Enough of est; enough of Werner Erhard.

NOTE: est was dissolved in the 1980s due to legal pressures and Werner Erhard disappeared from the scene, but a number of est offshoots have arisen to take its place and have survived as of May, 2011.

ON THE UNIFICATION CHURCH

(1977)

I seem to have a propensity for following attractive young women and thereby discovering new religions. This is how I discovered Scientology and this is how I discovered The Unification Church. In November of 1975 I "blew" (Scientology term meaning unauthorized leave) from my Dianetic Internship of Scientology and was away for one week when I decided to go back to Scientology. On my way to Beacon Street (Boston) and the Church of Scientology a bright and cheerful young lady walked towards me with a lovely smile on her face and said hello to me. As this was not a usual event for me, I decided to follow her and find out exactly what was going on here. I said to her that she must be into something or other in order to smile at strangers, and she said that she was only into life. Still suspicious, I rode with her to Kenmore Square and found myself face to face with the Unification Church of Boston, as this young lady was Julie—one of their main lecturers. Somehow my following mini-involvement with the Unification Church resulted in me not going back to Scientology for another eight months, after I spent a most interesting week experiencing the religion of Reverend Moon.

The tactics of The Unification Church have some similarity to those of est. They lecture at you for hours upon end, until your mind has lost any remaining capacity to think original thoughts and you yield to the dogma of what is being presented to you. And what is being presented to you is indeed quite interesting and ingenious. In a serious of seven or eight lectures, the history of religion from the time of Adam & Eve until present time is presented, but in a very unique interpretative scheme. The focus is on a series of central figures, including Adam, Abraham, Isaac, Jacob, Moses, Jesus, and Charlemagne. It is shown how each of these figures was a vehicle of God and had the power to bring everlasting peace to the world, and how each of these figures failed at his mission. Precise mathematical schemes are made use of, such as a parallelism of temporal events between the two thousand years from Abraham to Jesus, and then the two thousand years from Jesus to today. Some very convincing and interesting arguments are used to show how significant events in history are being repeated, as we supposedly are on the path towards the coming of the 2nd messiah. Jesus was the 1st Messiah, but Jesus has failed in his mission. Judaism was originally God's highest expression, Christianity was a higher expression of God than Judaism, and by Moon's mathematical calculations the 2nd Messiah is walking the earth today.

Up to this point I was quite impressed with this whole schema, and found it very stimulating and challenging for my atheistic-Jewish mentality. But then the dice became loaded. Upon reading some of Moon's literature, specifically the holy bible of The Unification Church: *Divine Principle* (see [24] in Chapter One Notes), I learned that Moon goes further in his mathematical dexterity and "proves" that this 2nd Messiah can come from only one place—and this of course is Moon's own homeland: Korea. Moon sees himself as a prophet, supposedly not the messiah [10], but he is quite convinced that it is his mission in life to gather the people of the world together for the coming of the 2nd Messiah, who will be coming forth any day now—from the only country in the world that has kept enough faith and honor to bring forth a messiah: Korea.

Looking back at the people of The Unification Church, I have basically good feelings. At the time, I was so affected by the crafty manipulations of Scientologists that The Unification Church was almost a pleasant respite for me. The people in The Unification Church were quite sincere and real in their beliefs, and fairly straightforward. There was little manipulation and authoritative pressure—in comparison to Scientology anyway. The Unification Church indeed seems to be practicing a relatively pure form of love and prayer and song, and in the figure of Reverend Moon has brought an authentic Eastern light to Christianity. I do not believe that Moon is any kind of heavenly prophet—nor that there is any 2nd Messiah on his way, but I do respect the calmness and sincerity of these followers of Reverend Moon whom I have met. I realize that the "Moonies" have gotten a lot of bad publicity the past few years, but from my own experience with them (which I admit is fairly limited) I am not yet willing to join the bandwagon of anti-Moonie sentiment. Reverend Moon has written a series of ten essays which are undoubtedly some of the most beautiful pieces of religious literature I have ever read [11]. The Korean version of "heart" is truly a magnificent concept of what it means to be human. Reverend Moon believes wholeheartedly in the importance of being willing to risk your life in order to achieve a spiritual state, and he also believes that the only way to personal happiness is to put others before oneself. Unlike the followers of Guru Maharajji [12], the followers of Reverend Moon are not, at least not as of yet, worshipping any human figure as an incarnation of God, and perhaps this is why I put the Unification Church on a level one step ahead of Divine Light Mission.

However, in addition to the specific Biblical references of The Unification Church, which I have much trouble relating to, I cannot buy the coincidence that the 2nd Messiah must come from Moon's homeland—Korea. But aside from this territorial stipulation of Moon's, I believe The Unification Church has some modern and intelligent interpretations of Biblical passages, and uses interpretative schemes that are quite consistent with today's scientific version of reality. The Unification Church has sponsored world get-togethers of prominent scientists, and is truly attempting to create an authentic merger of science and religion. The Unification Church has also begun programs designed to combat the use of communism, as they feel that communism destroys the religious freedom of the individual and his/her expression of God. All in all, I would like to someday take another and further look at The Unification Church, and see more clearly what happens as one progresses in their religious organization. But for now, I feel rather calm when I think back upon my experiences with the religion of Reverend Moon, and I shall leave it at that—for today.

THE MOONIES

(1978)

It's about time that I said a few more words about The Unification Church of Reverend Moon. I've been living in Berkeley, California the past six months, and have certainly gotten my stomach-full of "Moonies." I know in my previous essay *On the Unification Church*, I presented a relatively positive and respectful picture of Reverend Moon's new religion. Looking back upon this essay, right now I feel a bit foolish. However, I did admit that I was naive as to Moon's organizational methods and that I intended to do further investigation and exploration regarding The Unification Church. It has been nearly two years since I attended my week of lectures in Boston, and I have not made any other investigations, aside from what I've been reading in the San Francisco papers regarding the Moonies, which is quite a lot. The anti-Moonie sentiment and publicity is truly staggering. There are many ex-Moonies who have openly described their experiences inside Moon's organization, and there seems to be little about the Unification Church that is not already known. I had been playing around with the idea of spending a weekend with Creative Communities, one of Moon's satellite organizations, but I really don't think there is much that I could add to what is already known about the Moonies. Personally I cannot help being turned off to the Moonies—both from my personal experiences when being approached by them in the San Francisco area, and from all that I have learned about them from reading the papers. I feel like I know them very well, and I do not feel any more desire or curiosity to study them further. I know that I should always remember the relatively pleasant week I spent with them in Boston and not let myself get caught up in the massive public anti-Moonie sentiment here in San Francisco, but this is quite difficult to do while living in Berkeley. This is one of the reasons I was thinking of spending a weekend with them in order to come to my own conclusions regarding the Moonies, given that I began studying them quite seriously and spontaneously two years ago. But for now, I'll leave this short essay as a sort of epilogue to my essay *On The Unification Church.*

A FURTHER LOOK AT
THE UNIFICATION CHURCH

(May, 1978)

I am glad that I finally have something substantial to add to my previous two essays on The Unification Church. I'm presently teaching my course Psychology, Religion, & Human Values for the third time at the Berkeley Adult School, and in many ways this third time has been the most rewarding one for me. One of my students has been very taken up with The Unification Church, as her sister had been with The Unification Church for three weeks and then was surreptitiously removed from the Church by her family and went through intensive "deprogramming" (see [22] and [23] in Chapter One Notes). I have been in conflict about the Moonies all through the course, as I have met this student's other sister (who conducted the deprogramming) and her mother, both of whom have sat in on my course. They are all very nice and very intelligent, and have certainly given me a lot of information regarding some of the more devious and authoritarian tactics that The Unification Church employs. However, something inside of me could not yet become a firm anti-Moonie, at least not until I explored them further—by myself.

As chance would have it, one evening I was taking a walk on campus (U.C. Berkeley) and saw a sign posting a lecture about communism going on at that very moment. Somebody had written on the sign that the organization sponsoring this lecture was the newest Moonie front, and my appetite became whetted. I attended the lecture, and found myself to be the only non-Moonie present. The memories began to come back to me, as the lecturer went through the same traditional and dogmatic method of explaining the doctrines of the Church, which I had gotten such an earful of—two and a half years ago in Boston. The Moonies attending the lecture were a very respectful and attentive audience, although they all had a dulled and unchallenging look about them, ready to accept whatever this lecturer was saying as the only possible truth in the world. I knew right away that they were all Moonies—just by looking at them. After the lecture was over, one of them asked me how I liked the talk, at which point I answered authentically and got them to admit that they were all with The Unification Church. At this point, I proceeded to tell them about my current interests and my course, and I immediately noted a few pens taking down my name and every word out of my mouth. When I started to express that I felt very uncomfortable about them writing down what I was saying, I got a hearty good-natured laugh from all of them, a strange manipulative kind of laugh, designed to make me feel at ease, as if there was certainly nothing underhanded in their dealings with me. A number of times I felt like a few of them were just laughing along with a comment one of them would say, somehow or other intending to make me feel like part of their group—like I had an instant family if I wanted it. We ended up by me reluctantly inviting one of them to sit in on my course the following Monday, while they invited me to a big lecture to be given by the president of The Unification Church, Neil Salonon, the Tuesday following my course. Well today is Tuesday and I have just gotten back from that lecture. Due to a mix-up because of a holiday, The Unification Church member who was supposed to sit in on my course did not do so, but as two of my students were going to the lecture tonight, I decided to meet them there.

And what is the result of my evening? The result is that lo and behold I once again feel better disposed toward The Unification Church. I still cannot relate at all to their biblical references and spiritual beliefs, but there is definitely something inspirational about the quality of their personal experiences. In many ways they remind me of my boyhood friend Richie, who is the source of my essays on Guru Maharajji [13]. It seems that Reverend Moon is nearly everything to his Unification Church devotees that Guru Maharajji is to Richie (see [13] in Chapter 3 Notes). They really did seem like relatively harmless children tonight, quite naive to the depth of mature human relationships, but certainly sincere and idealistic in their quest to make a better world. And I was very impressed with the degree of openness they displayed, as they had much of their most sacred literature on exhibit and sale, showed a film describing their mass eighteen hundred couple wedding ceremony in Korea, invited all kinds of questions from the audience, and seemed to desire to have a real relationship with all people, whether or not they believed in Reverend Moon. Their president, Neil Salonon, gave quite a beautiful talk, as he described very personally his own experience of joining The Unification Church; in many ways his talk reminded me of the sharing done at an est seminar [14]. A five year veteran of The Unification Church set herself up behind me and my students, and fielded all our comments and criticisms regarding the Church. To my surprise, this veteran seemed to be truly open to much of our complaints, especially some of the manipulative and privacy-destroying techniques employed by Unification Church members. She claimed that these tactics were not condoned by Reverend Moon, but rather were examples of misuse and misunderstanding of what The Unification Church was supposed to stand for.

I did not expect to come away feeling encouraged about the humanistic possibilities of Reverend Moon's Unification Church, but this is how I am feeling. If I think back to my initial experiences with The Unification Church two and a half years ago in Boston, I feel a direct continuity with the good feelings I started to have about them then. I know that this will not be my final essay on The Unification Church, as I will eventually determine if these feelings I am having are valid as far as revealing any more truth about The Unification Church. But I do wish to leave my present state of knowledge of The Unification Church one step higher than the level on which I wrote my previous essay *The Moonies.*

AN EX-MOONIE SPEAKS

(December 31, 1978)

A few weeks ago, my friend Debbie Bell, an ex-Moonie, came to talk about her experiences with Reverend Moon's Unification Church to my high school psychology class. Debbie was eighteen years old when she joined up, and did not even know they were the Moonies for three months. She believed wholeheartedly that Reverend Moon was the 2nd Messiah, and to this day she is still confused about whether Reverend Moon really is the 2nd Messiah. Debbie was on the streets eighteen hours a day selling flowers, and eventually became an Introductory Lecturer of the religious philosophy contained in *Divine Principle* (see [24] in Chapter One Notes). Debbie has an extraordinary amount of energy, and I can just picture her proselytizing Reverend Moon and *Divine Principle* to others. She said that she brought in many people to The Unification Church, and brought the Church a lot of money through her selling of flowers. Debbie has described to me all kinds of weird trips the Unification Church laid on her, things like exorcising the devil out of her because of a sexual experience she had had with her boyfriend. Debbie became convinced that Satan the devil was truly inside of her, and she reached a point where she totally lost her own identity and did not know who she was anymore. She was allowed absolutely no privacy at all, as she was constantly surrounded by smiling protective Moonies, from sleeping to eating to making telephone calls to going to the bathroom. Debbie described their artificial friendliness as "love-bombing," whereby a veteran Moonie is assigned to the newcomer as soon as he or she enters the Church, and the newcomer is immediately made to feel like he or she belongs to a close-knit family. Eventually Debbie was assigned the high honor of cleaning Reverend Moon's room, and she even met and interacted a little with both Reverend Moon and his wife. Debbie does not have very much to say of Reverent Moon personally; it seems that his mystique was all she really encountered. She finally ran away from The Unification Church, borrowing money from them for a phony reason, and she fled with her boyfriend back to "reality."

Hearing Debbie describe her experiences with The Unification Church is quite scary. It certainly does echo the various statements made by other ex-Moonies that have reached public disclosure in the daily newspapers. Debbie is a highly spiritual person, and it is very important to her to know and understand God. She is still trying to integrate her experiences with the Moonies into her self-identity, just as I spent a long time integrating my experiences with the Church of Scientology into my own self-identity [15]. Talking to my high school psychology class was excellent therapy for her, just as my own teaching of Scientology to my religion classes at the Berkeley Adult School had been excellent therapy for me. Debbie and I joked about setting up a joint public lecture where I would talk about Scientology and she would talk about The Unification Church. Well, after the recent episodes with Synanon and The People's Church, this idea does not sound very enticing to either of us. In fact, the horror story of the nine hundred person mass suicide and murder in the People's Temple in Guiana plus the authoritarian practices of Synanon and Scientology, and the cold-blooded murders of Mayor Musconi and Supervisor Milk in their San Francisco offices, was enough for me to seriously consider changing the name of my book from *Modern Religions: An Experiential Analysis and Exposé* to *Natural Dimension* [16]. Yes I have much to say, but I want to live to say it. As I wrote in *Scientology and Fear* [17], I am no martyr—and success as a writer is not by any means my highest priority in life [18].

At any rate, after learning about Debbie's firsthand experiences with The Unification Church, my stomach is rather full right now. I don't think I can digest anything more that has to do with Reverend Moon and his Moonies. Ugh! Good Riddance, Reverend Moon.

NOTE: Although Reverend Moon and The Unification Church are both very much still here as of May, 2011, I have learned from the ICSA conferences I attended that the great majority of second generation Unification Church members are choosing to not remain in The Unification Church as they get older.

ON GURU MAHARAJJI (DIVINE LIGHT MISSION)

(1977)

I have been somewhat familiar with Guru Maharajji and Divine Light Mission for about six years now. It all began when my boyhood friend Richie and his wife Linda became devotees of Guru Maharajji, back in the summer of 1971. At that time Maharajji was fourteen years old and was proclaimed throughout India as a living perfect master, and moreover—one who was destined to bring peace to the world, in his own lifetime. Thus Maharajji came to America, and brought forth a new religion to many confused and disenchanted young Americans. At the time, Maharajji was quite a comical figure to our population at large, as to me he looked like nothing more than a plump, egocentric fat boy who had barely started to shave. This was the lord and master of the human race? A direct incarnation of God? The only thing that kept me from totally discounting this new religious fad was the respect I have always had for my friend Richie, whom I have known since I was eleven years old. I was sure that Guru Maharajji was just another phase that Richie was going through, and would soon pass over. Well this phase has lasted for six years so far, and if anything it appears to be stronger than it ever was. As I have kept up my friendship with Richie, I have had no choice but to take Guru Maharajji more and more seriously, until I now feel that he deserves a proper place in my book on modern religions, right after Scientology, est, and The Unification Church. Maharajji is now a young man of nineteen, a husband and a father, and an outcast from his family because of his marriage to an American girl. Guru Maharajji is still somewhat on the plump side, but Divine Light mission has thousands of ardent followers all over the world, and is growing stronger every day.

A devotee of Guru Maharajji is called a "Premi," and to a Premi—Guru Maharajji is everything that Christ was to his followers, two thousand years ago. Premis proclaim that Guru Maharajji is in a class with Buddha, Moses, and Christ, and that Maharajji is here to complete the job that these other perfect masters before him began. This claim is very similar to that made by the followers of Reverend Moon, founder of The Unification Church, except for the fact that the Unification Church does not always specifically name who this living perfect master is (though see [10] of Chapter Three Notes). I have been to an ashram (the spiritual place of worship for Premis) twice, and attended Millenium, the vastly publicized Guru Maharajji festival in Houston's astrodome in November, 1973, while I was living in Houston, Texas. So what have I to say about all this? Well, to me—Guru Maharajji is still little more than a plump, egocentric, fat boy, but one who is growing up fast. I have no way of knowing whether Maharajji is truly a living perfect master, or if a perfect master has ever existed. But for what my opinion is worth, I do not believe that Maharajji is any more or less human than you or I or anyone else in the world. Maharajji is from India, a country that believes wholeheartedly in reincarnation, gurus, and transpersonal beings. I think that Maharajji himself believes that he is all that he is proclaimed to be, for he has heard nothing else for his entire life here on Earth.

At first glance it might seem totally remarkable that hundreds of young men and women in a New York ashram can bow down on the floor to a picture of Guru Maharajji and wholeheartedly proclaim that he is the Lord of the Universe. But if you stop and think about it, is this really any more or less silly than the advent of Christ—or of any other religious figure who is said to be something more than a mere human being? What is important is that all these people really do believe that Maharajji is Lord of the Universe, and they find peace, comfort, and even salvation in this belief. They have given their lives to Guru Maharajji, just as their ancestors have given their lives to Christ. It is tough to live a life without some sort of supernatural religious belief, and it gets tougher as one gets older [19]. I myself have changed from a confirmed atheist to a confused agnostic. What is attractive about Maharajji is exactly what makes him appear so unlikely to be a true perfect master—his age, his fatness, and his richness. His followers defy all logic and all intellectual use of the mind, and what better way is there to stress the unimportance of the mind than to accept that which appears wholly non-rational, unreasonable, and contrary to everything the mind has always thought?

Accepting Guru Maharajji is wholly an act of faith; there is nothing logical about it, nothing whatsoever [20]. There is Sat-Sang—a nightly get-together where Premis take turns in opening up their hearts about all that Guru Maharajji has done for them in their lives. There is Meditation—a special kind of meditation which is taught by the "Initiators" in a seven hour experience called "Receiving Knowledge," whereby one is fully initiated into Divine Light Mission and promises to accept Guru Maharajji as one's savior for the duration of the universe. And there is Service—the job of every Premi in his/her continued efforts to spread the presence of Maharajji to others and to do his/her share in bringing peace to the world. The message of Guru Maharajji is pretty straightforward Eastern Buddhism; one must get rid of one's individual personality and join with the universal and everlasting. What is different about Guru Maharajji is the physical presence of Maharajji himself, which supposedly makes it actually possible to achieve or at least move close to this state.

I have grown, over the years, somewhat fond and tolerant of Guru Maharajji. I like the Premis I have met, and I definitely feel a lot of love, warmth, and good will in the ashrams that I have attended. I suspect that this religious ardor and warmth is very much lacking in many of our more traditional places of worship that exist in Judaism and Christianity. I believe that Maharajji will appear as a much more legitimate figure to prospective followers when he is in his twenties compared to when he was fifteen, and there is really no telling how far

Divine Light Mission will spread. A follower of Guru Maharajji, aside from the inner peace of mind he/she gains, becomes part of an extended family that gets together every evening for Sat-Sang. There is much joy and happiness in an ashram; peace and love certainly do reign throughout. It seems to be a very human quality to need a transpersonal human figure to put one's faith in, and perhaps we are today witnessing a rebirth of authentic religious feeling in this country.

But for the record—in my opinion Guru Maharajji is a pleasant trap. A trap to give up on life—to give up prematurely. There is no more self-imposed growth once one accepts Guru Maharajji, for there is no more self. It is tempting, but luckily not tempting enough for me. I believe there is a better way. A way in which all of our potential mental abilities can be respected and utilized, but a way in which our spiritual centers do transcend our minds. This way rejects any one human figure as being the representation of God. This way stresses that the path is where it always was—within the individual, and then across to other individuals. This way explores anything and everything in life that is worth exploring, and calls it knowledge and experience. This way in not new—it is as old as Socrates and it persists in some of us die-hards, some of us who love life too much to ever give in to the conventions of repressive society or to the dogmas and mind-destroyers of proselytizing religions, whether they be modern or traditional. I am by no means saying anything unique when I talk about this way, for I am merely following in the line of a rich cultural heritage, but I do wish to stress that my life will be lived to indeed do my share to see that this line does continue [21]. Natural Dimension has no need of a name when one is in the woods, doing theoretical mathematics, playing the guitar, or watching a bird [22]. However, Natural Dimension does have need of a name when one is sitting in a mind-molding classroom, working at a mind-lulling job, and witnessing a mind-shattering religion. And so I have decided that more—much more—of my philosophy of Natural Dimension will be making its way from my own personal self to the selves of others—as an alternative, an alternative to everything "un-natural" that is around you.

LETTER FROM RICHIE

(1978)

What more can I say about Guru Maharajji? I didn't intend to write a second essay on Guru Maharajji but I have just received a letter from my aforementioned friend Richie, in which there contains such a beautiful illustration of the experience of being a Premi, that I wish to share it with everybody who is interested in learning more about Guru Maharajji and Divine Light Mission. I know that Richie will not be offended by my inclusion of parts of his personal letter to me in my book, and to give any sort of an authentic account of what it means to be a devotee of Guru Maharajji the message must come straight out of the horse's mouth, so here it is:

"Dear Elliot,

Well it seems to be about that time again; it's never an easy thing to write to you because I can't just scribble off a "How are you, I am fine" letter. But since I've started I'm sure the momentum will carry this through....Linda and I just got back 3 days ago from Rome, Italy. We had a 5 day festival there with Guru Maharajji. 15,000 people from 50 different countries, and simultaneous translating headphones in 15 different languages. So much love—such concentration on one person. 15,000 hearts meeting just to see him smile. Love is all there is and love is infinite. God is love. I'm learning that in my relationship with Linda I only glimpse the possibilities of love; but with Guru Maharajji I can't even comprehend the magnitude. I see him totally transforming so many souls that for me to not call him Lord or Master would be a gross ingratitude. And I warn you, Elliot, if you dare write anything about Guru Maharajji without first receiving knowledge, all you'll be doing is drawing a paint by numbers picture without the colors. It's like looking into the wrong side of binoculars; all you'll be defining is something that's too far away for you to grasp. The further I dive into Maharajji the less I understand and the more I realize that the key to God Realization is to experience it and not to intellectualize about it. You can read all the books you want about love but that will never give you the feeling you get when you look into Diane's eyes. And the feeling I have with Linda is nothing compared to the love Maharajji has in store for me. I'm learning that the more I love him and open myself up to him—the more I feel that love inside of me. The more love I "feel" the more love I can "share"....I haven't written a song for months; in fact, this is the first time I've taken pen in hand for this length of time. But I feel totally satisfied—Maharajji must be filling me up—he "is" filling me up....love to Diane—write.

tell me everything soon,

Richie"

Well—that's Richie. This is the kind of thing I've been hearing from Richie for the past six years. In regard to the possibility of me ever "Receiving Knowledge," the last time I saw Richie—about seven months ago in New York, I told him that I would be curious to experience Receiving Knowledge. His response was that before I would be able to Receive Knowledge I would have to be ready to accept Guru Maharajji as Lord of the Universe. In other words, Receiving Knowledge only works if you already have utmost faith in Guru Maharajji. Thus, I cannot see how I will ever be able to experience Receiving Knowledge. But it is true what Richie says about my not Receiving Knowledge being a severe detriment for me to convey an authentic picture of Guru Maharajji and Divine Light Mission. This is much of the reason why I am including this excerpt from Richie's letter and writing this follow-up essay to *On Guru Maharajji*. I hope that Richie has added significantly to your understanding of what it is like to be a devotee of Guru Maharajji.

NOTE: For a fictional portrayal of the experience of becoming a devotee of Guru Maharajji, see *Excerpts from "The Maturation of Walter Goldman,"* particularly the excerpt entitled *Alienation*, in Chapter 4 of this book, where the main character Walter is modeled after myself, and Walter's friend Zachary is modeled after my friend Richie.

MOONIES AND PREMIES

(1979)

It's been six months since I wrote *Letter from Richie*. I've written Richie three letters in that time period, after having sent him copies of my previous two essays about Guru Maharajji. Although Richie sent me a card stating that our friendship will always be maintained, I have not received any more letters from him. In a certain way it is unfortunate that the prime source of one of the five religions I am writing about happens to be one of my closest friends, but I feel that I must pursue this process of writing about Guru Mahrajji, using Richie as a central source of my experience. I'll probably see Richie in another three months and perhaps I'll have more to say about Divine Light Mission at that time. But until then I would like to express some common bonds that I feel exists very deeply between Reverend Moon's Unification Church and Guru Maharajji's Divine Light Mission.

I see The Unification Church and Divine Light Mission as being very distinct from the other three modern religions that I am writing about: Scientology, est, and Gurdjieff. When I am in contact with people from these latter three modern religions, I feel much more on guard and hardened than I do when I am with followers of Reverend Moon and Guru Maharajji, whom I shall hereupon refer to as Moonies and Premies respectively. It is as if Moonies and Premies have a pure kind of religious love in their hearts, appealing to me emotionally through their simplicity. Whereas Scientology, est, and Gurdjieff are all super-aware and psychologically sophisticated (relatively speaking) [23], Moonies and Premies are almost naive in their knowledge of modern-day mankind and our intellectual/philosophical preoccupations. I think back to my statement in *On Guru Maharajji*: "there is much joy and happiness in an ashram; peace and love certainly do reign throughout." When I was in the ashrams of Divine Light Mission, a part of me wished so much that I too could bow down on the floor to the figure of Guru Maharajji and proclaim him to be the Master of the Universe and the guiding force of my life. Then I would be able to merge my self with all the beautiful people surrounding me, and give up my ghastly preoccupation with discovering truth all by myself. Similarly, it would be so nice to be able to accept Reverend Moon as the heavenly prophet proclaiming the coming of the 2nd Messiah from Korea, thereby transcending all the materialistic preoccupations that I seem to be falling into. The inner contentment and glorious smile of a Moonie is so inviting and seductive to me; it truly reaches the simple me behind all my outer complexity. Reverend Moon has even issued a statement supporting Jews and Israel, seeing the three nations of Israel, U.S., and Korea as the nations which are holiest in the eyes of God. And it is precisely this notion of God that unites The Unification Church and Divine Light Mission.

Both religions make tremendous use of a very direct kind of God, one whom you can unite yourself with by giving up your selfish ego and putting your life under the care and leadership of either Reverend Moon or Guru Maharajji. How different this is from the thousands of hours of auditing and working-on-yourself in Scientology and Gurdjieff respectively, and from the existentialist core of "nothingness" that you get from est (see [23] in Chapter 3 Notes). I am not by any means saying that anything is automatic for Moonies and Premies, as they must constantly be either praying to God through Reverend Moon or meditating upon themselves through the God form of Guru Maharajji. But once they truly join these religions, they do become like little children in the lost paradise, and their task is to maintain the spiritual experiences they have gone through by either Receiving Knowledge or revelation through prayer, rather than shoot for a long-range future specific goal such as going "Clear" in Scientology or achieving the state of "No. 4 Man" in Gurdjieff (see [23] in Chapter Three Notes). In a certain sense, est also works by immediate realization that must be maintained over time, but the immediate realization one gets after the est training is actually the opposite of a loving and infinite God; it is the absence of any meaning in the universe other than you are "it" and there is nothing to look for (see [23] in Chapter Three Notes). By an intellectual stretch of the imagination perhaps we could call the "it" and the "nothing" another version of the God of eastern philosophy, but whatever we do, the astounding complexity of est can never match the beautiful simplicity and authentic childishness of Moonies and Premies.

To make this comparison even more interesting, we find that The Unification Church and Divine Light Mission have both become eager and relatively successful capitalistic enterprises, having built up many small and some not so small businesses (which certainly is also very true of Scientology). Both religions believe in uniting spiritualism and materialism, and both Reverend Moon and Guru Maharajji live quite wealthily and have been the source of much attack from the American press and public because of this [24]. They also both want to bring everlasting peace to the world in our own lifetimes, and the more I think about them the more enticed I am to include them in my own humanistic vision of humankind. I am in the process of becoming quite materialistic, or at least "monetarialistic," and as I know that I will always keep my own spiritual essence, which I refer to in name as Natural Dimension (see [15] in Introduction Notes), perhaps I should not too easily put blame on Reverend Moon or Guru Maharajji for their own materialistic ventures [25]. I need to believe that materialistic endeavors do not necessarily preclude spiritual experience, or else I myself will never transcend the materialistic world that I must partake of. Of course I can never see myself believing in the biblical proclamations of Reverend Moon or the God incarnation of Guru Maharajji, but then again there is much in humanistic psychology and the human potential movement that I can accept but not have any reality about to believe in (I view myself as a spiritual agnostic), including astrology, reincarnation, past lives, seances with spirits, etc. [26]. Are the spiritual beliefs of Moonies and Premies really any more unreasonable than so many existing beliefs and values in the human potential movement? I dare say they are not; what they are missing is a true openness to the philosophies and ways of life of others, a true humility that theirs is not the only right path. However, I see a trend in both Divine Light Mission and The Unification Church which indicates that Moonies and Premies are starting to become more open to these philosophies and spiritualities of others, and if this can truly emerge into being, perhaps we can all join together in our fight against the repressive forces of society, wherever they may be. At any rate, I will let this essay stand as my offer to unite Moonies, Premies and the human potential movement in the endeavor to bring everlasting peace to the world (see [25] in Chapter Three Notes).

DIANE GETS SAT-SANG

(September 22, 1978)

Well I have finally seen Richie again, as myself, Diane, Richie, and his wife Linda got together for an interesting evening in New York a few nights ago. Guru Maharajji is now going on twenty-one and has two kids. Richie and Linda were wearing Guru Maharajji teashirts when we greeted them, with pictures of Guru Maharraji all over their bedroom and living room. If anything, their devotion seems to he growing stronger over time. They want to follow Guru Maharajji all over Europe and then follow him around the U.S. on his periodic Divine Light Mission festivals. They no longer talk about making it in music and they no longer talk about having kids and a family. Linda seems so spaced out on Guru Maharajji that she is not able to be interested in or relate to anything that Diane and I say about our own lives. She indeed seems to be falling into the trap that I wrote about in *Moonies and Premies*, i.e. not being able to see anyone else's path as valid. Of course this might be an inaccurate projection I am making, but this was my experience. Richie was made Food Service Coordinator for Divine Light Mission in New York, and he considers this to be a divine privilege and honor. However, I am happy to say that my friendship with Richie is still intact, as he was able to be quite open to both myself and Diane.

But what was most interesting for me during this evening was to see Diane's experience of receiving Sat-Sang from Richie. Diane listened very attentively to everything Richie said. In fact, she listened so attentively that Richie ended up saying how beautiful it was to finally be able to relate his blissful experiences of Guru Maharajji to a non-Premi who truly gave him space to share himself, and that he was now willing to give us credit for having something special and maybe he could learn something from us. Believe me, coming from my old friend Richie this was truly an incredible statement to hear. For so many years, I have been trying to convey to Richie that I too know something, and he finally has given me the space to live and breathe on my own terms.

Richie realizes that the Premies in Divine Light Mission have much to learn about love, as their own personal relationships leave much to be desired, from Richie's experience. Richie says that Premies are only human, and he has many objections to much that goes on in the Premi community. Richie feels that his relationship with Linda is his way of learning how to love Guru Maharajji, and he believes that marriage should be a sacred path for all people to learn how to love. He says that marriage gives you a direct mirror into your own self. Yes—much of what Richie says is very true to me, as I have expressed so many similar ideas in my own philosophy. But then Richie goes on and talks about the necessity of having a Master in order to find out who you are in your deepest self. The Master knows where you want to go and sets up the conditions for you to go in exactly that direction. Diane retorts that she has no need or desire to have a Master, as she and I learn from each other. Finally, Richie accepts that perhaps it is our fate in life to walk a spiritual path without a Master, and a dangerous impasse gets resolved. Diane says she is able to understand everything that Richie has been saying, in a way that not many people would be able to understand. Richie says that he knows this and appreciates this greatly.

What did "I" do this whole evening? Well, I played the piano a little bit (my old piano which I had given to Richie and Linda as a wedding present), and I listened a whole lot. Richie and Linda were totally flabbergasted at my silence after their opening of their hearts about Guru Maharajji. They expected me to argue and debate like I always used to. No—I no longer have anything to argue with them about. That's them—and this is me. If we can all accept each other, there does not have to be any one right or wrong way for everybody. Only time will tell what is really "real," and I think a few more years will be necessary before we are able to formulate any definite conclusions about Richie and Linda and Guru Maharajji.

ELLIOT GETS SAT-SANG

(March 17, 1979)

About five weeks ago I had a telephone conversation with Richie. I must tell you a little bit about my circumstances in order for you to fully appreciate the impact that this conversation had upon me. Diane and I had just celebrated the ninth anniversary of our falling in love, and as an anniversary present I gave Diane enough money to go for a long weekend personal retreat to Mendocino, California (we were living in the Berkeley, California area at the time). This was a very significant few days for us, and marked the beginning of a whole new era in our relationship. However, it was a long few days for me, and it felt pretty weird being in our five room house all by myself. I went through many deep insights about my life and our relationship, and soon before Diane was expected home I decided to call my friend Richie in New York. To really appreciate the meaning of my calling

Richie, you should realize that I have a general aversion to the telephone and that I virtually always write letters rather than call friends. Well, the phone call has cost me $20, so I figure I at least better try to get another essay on Guru Maharajji out of it, so here goes.

I didn't tell Richie the details of what was going on between Diane and me, but I did tell him that we were still in process, and have not attained nirvana yet. This was all Richie needed. For the next half hour I got Sat-Sang. Of course Richie and Linda were the same, were living in total bliss and harmony, were like little children with each other, etc., etc. We went through our old guru-no guru controversy, and I totally made up for having played the piano during our last Richie & Linda get-together. I once again succumbed to Richie's exhortations and proselytizing excitement. It made me realize how long it had been since I had actively searched for God. I told him that I still believed in Natural Dimension; i.e. in Mutual-Internalness (see [4] in Chapter Three Notes) between me and Diane. I told him that Diane and I were almost "there." Richie has been in on our journey from nearly the beginning, and he understandably took my reassurance with somewhat of a grain of salt. He stressed the importance of sharing your self with a community of other people, and I stressed the importance of making Diane into a happy human being. I told him that this was my life work, and if I could achieve this aim then I would also become a happy human being. I asked him if he could accept that he had his way and I had mine, and perhaps they were both O.K. His reply was remarkably brilliant. He said that when I tell him that I am living in love and bliss, then he would affirm my existence. I had nothing left to say. I could not say that I was living in love and bliss, and I could not say that I did not want to be living in love and bliss. I said that it was "Internal" for me and Diane to have children soon, and he minimized the importance of this to me, saying that nothing in external circumstances was necessary to be happy. I disagreed with him in this respect, and we said good-bye in a very distant place.

So what have I learned from my spiritual telephone conversation with my friend Richie? I learned that I am still vulnerable to authentic spirituality. It is still something that is very much a part of me. I am still on a search, although I spend much less time actively searching than I used to. But it just takes a few real words from a real friend to remind me of who I am. I need to conquer materialism first; this is the only reason I have taken a rest in my search for truth and for God. But

I foresee that I will be moving again shortly, as the quest for authentic spirituality is as valid in my life now as it ever was. Thank you Richie for giving me Sat-Sang.

RICHIE GETS SAT-SANG

(April 15, 1979)

I'm now at a small private public beach in the town of Mendocino, California, which I have just made into a nudist beach. Natural Dimension is alive and well, as Diane and I are recapturing who we truly are; God is Mutual-Internalness (see [4] in Chapter 3 Notes). Do you hear that—Richie? Last weekend I wrote you a letter which I don't expect you to answer, for you are too wrapped up in your Guru Maharajji to really see me for who I am. But in my letter I said that although I love you both, you and Linda are two of the most closed-minded people I know. I said some stuff about truly being open and susceptible to what life has in store. This is Natural Dimension, Richie. Sometimes I'm uptight, and sometimes I'm uninhibited. I seem to work in extremes. But put me in nature with Diane for a few days, and I inevitably find out who I am. If I believed in past lives, I would say I'm Albert Einstein reincarnated. Am I happy? I'm on the road to being happy. I'm almost content, and that is a nice place for me to be in. And whatever I have achieved and will achieve in life, I have done it directly to life itself. You my friend have cheated; although you think you know all the answers, you know absolutely nothing. For I know that I know nothing, and therefore I know far more than you. You'll say you know nothing, nothing except that Guru Maharajji is Lord of the Universe. What kind of weakness is it that needs a guru—the way you and Linda need Guru Maharajji? Why is true love not enough for a human being? It is enough for me—more than enough, and I am thankful to be alive. The challenge, the mystery, and the ecstasy are all experiences in life that I feel privileged to have had. I could not have experienced one without the other. So now my friend—I am giving "you" Sat-Sang. I don't expect you to ever listen, and that is why this is going down as an essay for my book—instead of as a letter to you. I know you don't care, but I am sorry that I feel you aren't there anymore. I'm no guru; I'm only a human being. But it's good to be alive.

GURU MAHARAJJI GETS SAT-SANG

(May 31, 1982)

I truly do believe that this will be my last essay on Guru Maharajji. I had lost touch with Richie for over three years, when one night I came home from my Men's group meeting and who do you think was on the phone with Diane? It turned out that Richie was still very interested in us and was not able to locate us the past few years, but finally managed to find us through a mutual friend. He had heard that we had a baby, and he seemed to be genuinely interested in us all getting re-acquainted. And so we all got together in New York for an evening last Thanksgiving, and then Richie and Linda visited us at our home in Easthampton, Massachusetts for three days—just a few days ago.

Well I would have to say that Richie and Linda will always be our friends, but with serous limitations. Richie and I go back a long time, and neither of us wants to throw that away, but there is virtually no change in their effervescence over Guru Maharajji. But to do justice to their faith, I must say that there have been some interesting and positive developments in the Premi community. It turns out that Divine Light Mission no longer exists as the organizational structure of the religion, and that the term "Guru" has been dropped; he's now referred to simply as Maharajji. It seems that Maharajji honestly does not want any more of the circus antics and fanfare that overrided all the festivals in their old days. The whole thing seems to be simplified to such an extent that it is nearly impossible for anyone to locate Premies on their own, without knowing someone first. I welcome these changes very much, and I am nearly tempted to stop calling Maharajji a cult. However, when I look at the intrinsics of what is really going on, I nearly want to vomit.

To backtrack a little, when we got together with Richie and Linda in New York last Thanksgiving, I was very affected by the beauty and happiness that Richie and Linda had preserved in their ten year marriage. Diane and I have been through so many struggles, and we have preserved the special ingredient of our love, but we by no means live day-to-day life in the honeymoon stage, which is how Richie and Linda seem to live every day. I've had a long-standing jealousy of their relationship, but it always was that Diane and I were on the path of reaching our potential.

Well this time it didn't seem like we were on too much of a path. I was having tremendous difficulties in supporting my new family, my in-law problems were intense, and we were not at all happy. Richie and Linda were truly caring and helpful. I will always appreciate their sincere interest and wisdom in regard to what I needed to do to get back on the track. But the personal details are not relevant right now; the point is that I felt a very real bond with Richie and Linda; a couple bond. This couple bond was the motivation that led me to acquire more learning experiences with Maharajji. Richie had changed his tune about Receiving Knowledge over Thanksgiving. He said that the Initiators were giving out Knowledge much more easily now, and that you did not first have to believe that Maharajji was Lord of the Universe in order to Receive Knowledge. Soon after our New York visit I wrote to Richie that I would like to experience Receiving Knowledge—this summer in Boston. After a few tumultuous months of bad communication about this matter, Richie and Linda came to visit us, and Richie and I talked and talked and talked. It was very draining on me—both mentally and physically, and I knew that if I was going to keep some kind of a friendship with them, I had to put a stop to Richie's unceasing unwanted advice that he would continuously give me. And so it was left that I was going to check out Maharajji for myself.

And now I have checked it out enough to satisfy any lingering curiosity that can possibly still be in me. Receiving Knowledge is just as it always was—you have to first open your heart to Maharajji, as a child to the Lord. This is the only way in which the meditation techniques of Receiving Knowledge have the effect they are noted for (see [33] in Chapter One Notes). I verified this quite personally, having spent a few intensive hours with an Initiator in one-to-one dialogue, both in the Hartford, Conneticut ashram and in the car ride from Hartford to New York, and there is no way that I could ever Receive Knowledge. It is so very obvious to me how Maharajji fills the hearts of those who are at their dead-end; those who do not have the courage to face life on their own. I had a very sad firsthand experience of this while spending the night in the apartment of a very pitiful Premi. Enough! I can stand it no longer. I saw continuous pictures of Maharajji in the slide show at the Hartford ashram—a fat egocentric young man. I feel a repulsion towards him—and I always will. Yes his followers are sincere, including Richie and Linda. They believe that they have found God, and there is no changing that.

But for me, I choose to meditate on my own special form of God—the gift of my family, i.e. me, Diane, and Jeremy. I have my own mission in life, and it is to be worthy of the gift I have received, and to make all the potential beauty inside my gift come out. To hell with everything else. I am now content, and I foresee the day when I will be happy. If God is not in me, then there is no God. For I have preserved the ultimate meaning of religion: LOVE [27].

AFTERWORD #1: Nine years later I visited Richie and Linda in Montreal, Canada with my then ten year old son Jeremy in 1991, and it was evident that Guru Maharajji continued to be the ultimate source of spiritual meaning and happiness in both of their lives, as they were still living in total bliss and harmony. As of 2005, Divine Light Mission is alive and well.

AFTERWORD #2: Seventeen years after my 1991 get-together with him, I received a surprise phone call from Richie in April, 2008, after not having heard from him in all these years. Within a few minutes it was the same old story—Richie urging me to check out Maharajji and Receive Knowledge that is now available through the guru's CDs that can be done at home, etc. Maharajji and Divine Light Mission both have new names (check out Prem Pal Rawat and Elan Vital at www.elanvital.org) but the more things change the more they seem to stay the same. As of May, 2011 I have had no further contact with Richie or Divine Light Mission/Elan Vital.

OCCULT SCHOOL

(1977)

Well this time I really hit it. I have found my most interesting religion since Scientology. I'm referring to none other than George Gurdjieff, as expounded by P.D. Ouspensky in his popular book *In Search of the Miraculous* (see [40] in Chapter One Notes). The lucrative San Francisco front for this occult school is a theatre group called The Theatre of All Possibilities. The actors put on a religious play about love, and then get together with their audience, whom they personally sold tickets to from mostly off the streets (in my case an attractive actress/occult school member approached me while I was riding a bus), for some wine and conversation, and anyone in the audience who shows promise is invited to the Open House on Monday evening, at which time the philosophy of the school is somewhat explained. From Monday night until Tuesday night the people who have gotten this far have twenty-four hours to get up $100 for a month's tuition at the Gurdjieff school. It is understood that this is an experiment for a month only, for to continue as a student after this time a full commitment is required, and a fee of $200 a month.

I have been to three sessions in my first month as a Gurdjieff student, and I have spent about twenty hours at their school. I do believe that I have experienced all that I am willing to experience at this school, although I never do know what I will end up doing about something. It has been quite heavy for me, as they got to me where I am most vulnerable, and perhaps in my only vulnerable places left: "love" and Hermann Hesse [28]. For God's sake—they claim that Hermann Hesse was actually a student at their school! I honestly do not know what to do.

Their philosophy of work depresses me so much that I cannot even yet write about it. For the moment lets just say that in their book I'm an official "tramp." Their philosophy of marriage is quite conventional and conservative—actually closer to reactionary. But it just so happens that where I am at in my present state of affairs, I am temporarily trying to push myself into a more conservative frame of being—in both work and marriage. I know that this is only a phase I am going through, and one that does seem at this time necessary for my present survival as a human in society, but I do intend to come out of it in not too long a period of time. But the question that I am struggling with is: if I join up with this Gurdjieff school, will I ever come out of it?

It is so tempting. Leaving the school so abruptly is quite a challenge to my self-discipline. And how can I not follow upon the path that my beloved Hermann Hesse allegedly traveled upon? Well Hesse says "do your own thing." The beauty of Hesse is that he is not a guru; a true Hessian can not follow Hesse, but only him/herself. So that part of the problem is solved (see [28] of Chapter Three Notes).

Hey folks—guess what? Some overweight spiritual woman named Sharon Korn wants to be my guru. Sharon and Alex are the stars of the play Journey to Jerusalem, playing Adam and Eve, and they are the married co-founders of this San Francisco branch of the Gurdjieff school. Everybody in the school pays homage to Sharon and Alex, for they are the "teachers." Gurdjieff claims that it is not possible for a mere human to be free, and it is only a matter of what influence an individual will fall under. Gurdjieff set himself up as a "teacher" and quite paternally exercised his will upon his subjects, one of the brightest of whom was P.D. Ouspensky (see [40] of Chapter One Notes). Ouspensky adopted Gurdjieff's philosophy and eventually rejected Gurdjieff. The philosophy and the school survived and spread, and so it reached San Francisco where Sharon and Alex Korn have founded their own Gurdjieff school, and where Elliot Benjamin is presently one of their students. I feel so terrible that I can't find out more underground information about this school for you. But if you are interested, read *In Search of The Miraculous* and stand out on a San Francisco street corner, and soon you too shall know the truth. But my life goes on, and I'm afraid that the Theatre of All Possibilities, as enticing as it is to me, is one step too dangerous for my present psyche.

THE GURDJIEFF SCHOOL: A RECOLLECTION

(1978)

I am finally able to write about Gurdjieff again, nearly six months after my initial experience with The Theatre of All Possibilities.. The account I have given in *Occult School* is one of a naive and inexperienced aspirant in Gurdjieff and Occult philosophy. I have since become aware of the substantial literature on Gurdjieff, both by Gurdjieff himself and by others who had been connected to him (see [40] of Chapter One Notes). However, I am very glad that my first experience with Gurdjieff was as it was, for it gave me the flavor of the Gurdjieff Work—in its full impact. Kathleen Riordan Speeth described the philosophy and psychology of Gurdjieff both comprehensively and succinctly in *The Gurdjieff Work* (see [40] of Chapter One Notes). I have no wish to duplicate what she has already made available. Neither can I add anything to her vivid descriptions of what goes on in the actual Gurdjieff groups. However, what I can do is describe my personal experience of spending twenty hours in the Occult School of George Gurdjieff, from the perspective of my own philosophy of Natural Dimension.

It seems to me that Gurdjieff has much in common with L. Ron Hubbard, founder of Scientology [29]. Like Hubbard, Gurdjieff is an authoritarian philosopher, dogmatic and rigid, and is brilliant and a creative genius. Like Hubbard, Gurdjieff is a proselytizer, wishing to spread his ideas to others and form a following of loyal disciples to his own personal system of life. This is where I must part company with Gurdjieff. Gurdjieff is interesting for me to integrate into my own philosophy. He spurs me to connect myself more to nature and the heavens, to place more stock in astrology than I have previously allowed myself to do. I also respect Gurdjieff immensely for all that he has integrated from such diverse and ancient cultures throughout the world. Gurdjieff has the same resentments and hostilities toward the "machine-like normal person" of society that I do. Gurdjieff is obviously a super-aware individual; an authentic "teacher" figure if there ever was one.

But I do not believe that self development need be as harsh and rigid as it is in a Gurdieff group. I felt an intense excitement in the group as a captivating charm pervaded the whole atmosphere. There we all were, sitting on hard chairs in a large circle—about twenty five of us, waiting for the "teacher" to join us. The "teacher" was one of the actors in the play Journey to Jerusalem. He has been in the School for eight years, and is striving to become a "Number 4 man," i.e. an integrated individual who has surpassed the previous isolated states of humankind dealing with the preoccupation of the mind, emotions, and intellect (see [40] in Chapter One Notes). He is strong and intense, seemingly a tower of strength and super-human awareness, until his own "teacher," the co-star of Journey to Jerusalem and co-founder of the School (who is also his wife), Sharon Korn, joins us. Then he becomes like a little boy, totally under her power and her auspices. Sharon proceeds to gently interrogate all the newcomers to the School, including myself. "What is your goal in life? Why are you here? What do you seek to gain?", etc. Sharon has the uncanny ability to look through a person and instantaneously bring out the person's inner core, in many ways similar to the est trainers I had earlier come into contact with [30]; but Sharon does it in a much more personal and intimate setting. My turn comes, and I find myself blurting out my long held secret desire and aim in life: to achieve a "perfect marriage." Yes I was real—and Sharon smiles; she likes that. She and her husband, who is the co-star of the play and the co-founder of the School, Alex Korn, are also seeking to form a "perfect marriage." This is what their whole play Journey to Jerusalem is all about. I like Sharon, and feel myself dissolving in her power, picturing myself becoming a disciple of her, Alex, and Gurdjieff.

But then I remember Diane, and I realize that it is not "internal" (see [4] of Chapter Three Notes) for her to stay up until 3:00 in the morning—two days a week, in bitter severe seven hour encounters with twenty five aspiring dogmatic, ferocious, reactionary cultists. No—this is not Diane's way of development. And neither is it mine. Like Scientology, it is virtually impossible for only one member of a couple to be doing the Gurdjieff Work. The Gurdjieff School was such a strange temptation for me. The spiritual confrontations, the opportunity to do bodywork on the acting stage, the intensity of spiritual quest, the newly formed potential relationships and friendships; all these and more nearly got me hooked again, for the first time since Scientology. Unlike my experiences with The Unification Church and Divine Light Mission, I cannot say that I feel my connection with Gurdjieff has been fully satisfied and terminated. I am still interested in reading Gurdjieff's philosophical texts, and I somehow have a wish to some day meet with the students of the Theatre of All Possibilities again. However, I am not willing to pay $200 a month for spiritual enlightenment; in fact, I am not willing to pay one cent for spiritual enlightenment. I firmly believe that God is free. To me, economics and religion are two separate disciplines, and shall always remain so. Gurdjieff is a relatively minor figure—at least to me. He is only major because he has tried so hard to make himself major. And this was his main fault. The true guru will not "try." But Gurdjieff was certainly an interesting fellow, and deserves to be studied and understood. At least this is how it appears to me, in my own natural dimension. For this reason, perhaps in the future I shall write yet another essay on the philosophy of George Gurdjieff

MORE ON GURDJIEFF

(1978)

My wife and personal editor, Diane Benjamin [31], claims that my previous two essays on Gurdjieff leave my readers rather confused as to what Gurdjieff is actually about. As I take her suggestions quite seriously, I wish to attempt to somehow amend this situation, but I am still at a loss as to how to accomplish this task. I have read Gurdjieff's autobiographical book *Meetings with Remarkable Men* (see [40] in Chapter One Notes), and I certainly have gained an appreciation of the kind of person Gurdjieff was, and the sources from which he gathered his unique philosophy of life. I realize that to fully comprehend Gurdjieff's philosophy I must plumb through the twelve hundred pages of his book *Beezlebub's Tales to his Grandson* (see [40] in Chapter One Notes). This will be a torturous process for me, and I have no intention of doing this for quite a while. Perhaps for the moment it will suffice if I give some impressions that I have gotten of the man George Gurdjieff—from what I have learned through my experiences with The Theatre of All Possibilites and my reading of Gurdjieff's autobiographical book *Meetings with Remarkable Men*.

George Gurdjieff is in many ways a model and inspiration for a part of what I would like to accomplish in life. He is brilliantly sharp and crafty when it comes to making money, and he has totally allowed all his natural creative thought processes to take shape in staggering intensity and complexity. I would have to say that in my way of thinking, Gurdfieff lived in a natural dimension (see [15] of Chapter One Notes). He is the authentic freelancer; the most independent individualist I have ever been made aware of. Gurdjieff had a love of life and of real wisdom. He used his multi-varied talents, skills, and mental acrobatics to procure enough income for himself to pursue his diverse spiritual aspirations and adventures. I am still fascinated and deeply stirred by the possibility of Hermann Hesse being connected with Gurdjieff. In reading about Gurdjieff's descriptions of his exclusive band of spiritual travelers, The Seekers of the Truth, who traveled throughout ancient holylands in Asia in search of primordial truth, I am struck by images from Hermann Hesse's book *The Journey to the East* [32], where he described a league of journeyers who swore to secrecy and traveled all over the world in pursuit of authentic wisdom from the past. In both Hesse's and Gurdjieff's descriptions, each individual member of the group had his own personal reasons for joining the group, but also felt a sense of being part of a special secret society that would search after precious remnants of ancient civilizations to throw light upon the meaning of humankind's existence as spiritual beings.

This is also the opening captivating theme expressed in Ouspensky's popular book *In Search of the Miraculous* (see [40] in Chapter One Notes), which led to his eventual meeting with Gurdjieff. Thus Gurdjieff is still very much gnawing inside of me, and through learning more about him I believe that I will perhaps uncover some very special events in the life of Hermann Hesse, which may not be publicly known. But I am still quite frustrated as to my ability to inform you of any more of the specifics of Gurdjieff's philosophy. My mind is all used up right now, and I just do not have the mental energy nor the inclination to think back any more to my actual experiences in the Gurdjieff group. For it really was not all that important to me, and at this point it seems very much in the past. I consider it to be another example of what I refer to as "pseudo-realness" [33], in relation to what I wrote about est. No matter how much I might admire and respect Gurdjieff as a self-educated and aware person, I still cannot condone the intentional manipulative efforts he has made to set himself up as a guru. I'm going to leave Gurdjieff now for a long time, as I have other more important books to read: Nietzche, Hesse, Jung, Ayn Rand, etc. When I am good and ready, I'll return to Gurdjieff, and when I am really good and ready I'll consider returning to the Theatre of All Possibilities. Perhaps I'll return to learn more about Hermann Hesse. Once I find out whatever it is I seek to learn from this whole Gurdjieff phase that I seem to be in, I will then write what I hope will be a final essay on Gurdjieff. So once again I must leave my essays on Gurdjieff as unfinished business.

EDEN WEST

(July 30, 1978)

I'm afraid that I must try your patience with me, for this is another essay on Gurdjieff and yet this may not be my final essay on Gurdjieff. I have not read *Beezlebub's Tales to his Grandson* nor have I returned to The Theatre of All Possibilities, but I have had a significant learning experience in regard to increasing my knowledge of the Gurdjieff network.

I have come into contact with another branch of the Gurdjieff school; this branch is called Eden West, and is under the tutelage of Mya Martin. I learned about them through seeing a notice about a performance in "sacred dances," collected by Gurdjieff, in a public theatre in Berkeley, California. Sure enough, the performance was a demonstration of the "work" being done by a Gurdjieff group that calls themselves a Gurdjieff community. The movements that were performed reminded me very much of the types of dances and rituals that Gurdjieff and Ouspensky talked about in their books *Meetings with Remarkable Man* and *In Search of the Miraculous* (see [40] in

Chapter One Notes). They also reminded me of some of the dances in the play Journey to Jerusalem put on by The Theatre of All Possibilities. The movements were rigidly exact, performed as a repetitive structure of movements that apparently give the sensation of transcending your mind, similar to a state of yoga and meditation [34]. They are all done collectively, sometimes in unison and sometimes in an interesting counterpart between sections of the group, often with different functions for the men and the women. Similar to the Gurdjieff group I had participated in via The Theatre of All Possibilities, Eden West stresses an extremely rigid role segmentation between men and women. This is exceedingly obvious in a few of their dances, the men being tough and war-like while the women portray the gentle delicate waltz. I remember how Gurdjieff claimed that true art must leave the exact same response in every viewer, as there is an exact specific meaning in the work of art that must be conveyed to everyone in perfect duplication [35].

This was certainly the attempt that was made last night. These dances reached me in the sense of a primitive awareness; a sort of Jungian archetype of man and woman [36]. A large part of me was resisting the "macho" message, but I still could not help but accept as a part of me the intensely energetic primordial creature that was being stirred up in my Jungian collective unconscious. Yes—I too wished to get up on the stage and grunt and prowl and make like a Gurdjieff Tarzan. Once again I felt the temptation of yielding my free mind and spirit to a charismatic and authoritarian teacher. When Mya Martin would say "sit" and the class of thirty would automatically obey, she could have been addressing a pack of dogs. The fanatical obedience of the class was the same fanatical awe that I observed in the responses of the members of the Theatre of All Possibilities to the presence of Sharon Korn. Make no mistake about it—Mya Martin is a Gurdjieff guru; a 3rd generation Gurdjieff teacher—from Gurdjieff to Bennet to Martin. She was tall and slender, claimed to have had a baby at age forty-six, and of course had a magestically powerful look in her eyes.

However, I must concede to Mya Martin one crucial benefit of the doubt; one that may motivate me to learn more about Eden West and to write yet another essay about Gurdjieff. And this benefit of the doubt is that Mya Martin claimed that Eden West is totally free (i.e. it cost no money). I was very surprised by her statement, as I remembered all the conflict that I had gone through because of the $200 a month fee of the previous Gurdieff school I had come into contact with (see my previous Gurdjieff essays). Thus I approached Mya Martin after the performance and told her about my financial experience with the Theatre of All Possibilities, and I asked her to confirm her statement that Eden West was free. She replied as she had done at the performance, saying that "they couldn't afford to charge money for the work," meaning exactly what I always have said—spiritual enlightenment should be free of money. She also said that she had been involved with the Theatre of All Possibilities and thoroughly disagreed with their practice of charging money. This interested me greatly, for the practice of charging money was one of the main tenets of Gurdjieff's philosophy. Could it be possible that I have finally found an authentic modern religious group that has totally separated themselves from business? If so, Eden West might prove to be a bright final religion for me to write about.

NOTE: As of May, 2011, Gurdjieff groups are still quite popular for new age spiritual seekers and aspirants to occult studies.

BESHARA

(March 22, 1979)

And the path goes on. From Scientology to est to the Moonies to Guru Maharajji to Gurdjieff—and now to Beshara.

Last night Diane and I were looking through the Berkeley Monthly for evening activities, and I happened to come across a lecture called The Unity of Existence by the Beshara Foundation. Diane was tired so I went by myself—and I have found the old me once again, smack in the middle of another modern religion. What stands out in my mind are their "courses." Specifically I am focusing upon their "peak course": an eight month intensive introspective experience course given in a farmhouse in England, costing $3,000. The speaker was very quick to point out that this money included room and board, and that with inflation nowadays this was a very reasonable price for eight months of survival. Although he was fairly defensive about the money, I must admit that this was certainly quite a legitimate fee for eight months of living expenses, and that I might have a rather biased outlook in regard to religion and money from all that I experienced with Scientology, est, and Gurdjieff. They also offer one day courses for $200, and this is certainly a reasonable price, in comparison to all the courses and conferences that fall under the heading of humanistic psychology and the new age personal growth movement. From the little that I know about them at this time, I must say that Beshara does not appear to deserve any censure for shady business practices.

What I get so far is that in order to achieve the state of "perfect man," which is their goal in life, you need to take one of their courses—which will eventually lead you to their eight month course in England. They steadfastly claim that they have no guru, but they do have some sort of an "advisor." They began in 1971, the same year that est began, but they cannot pinpoint their beginnings to any one person. They say that Beshara just sort of evolved [37]. I've been to two sessions at their house, and I'm starting to feel like I am making a pest of myself with all my mundane questions about their organization. But I'm also beginning to somewhat trust them, and I do not give trust to any modern religion very easily.

Their spiritual beliefs are that God is working through "you," and they play down the importance of any kind of method or technique. They have a weekly session called "Zihur" (or "self-remembering") which I have experienced tonight and consists of first doing an "Abluet," which means purifying yourself through washing your face, neck, and feet, and then sitting in Japanese style and chanting some holy words in Arabic, rhythmically moving back and forth while holding hands and gathering momentum and force as the energy intensifies [38]. I allowed myself to pretty much join in with this communal experience, even though they said that it was O.K. if I did not want to sit in the circle; some people did choose to sit off on the side by themselves. It reminded me somewhat of a dance class that I had taken at the East Bay Socialist School. It seemed to be a cathartic experience for those who participated (including me in a minimal kind of way), but it was also far more than this for the Beshara members. For in their experience it was God speaking through them; it was the outflow of their real selves.

At any rate, I won't be going to England in the immediate future. Not that a part of me doesn't want to go. But I have taken on the responsibilities of adulthood, and I do believe that this is part of my own path of spiritual elevation. For the immediate future I cannot even foresee being able to take the time off from work to do their ten day course. Thus I do not know how much longer I can meaningfully interact with the people I have met from Beshara. What they mean by "self experience" and what I mean by "self experience" do not seem to be all that different, but I do not expect them to recognize that my path is as valid as their own. What is important though is that I am back; my exploration of modern religions has by no means ended. I have more to learn of Beshara, and I am thankful that I have been able to regain my open state of experiential exploration—which has enabled me to accumulate all the learnings on modern religions that I have so far accumulated.

CHAPTER THREE NOTES

1) In this essay and all the essays in Chapters 3 and 4 as well as most of the essays in Chapter 5, which comprise about a third of this book, my writing style reflects my younger years of having written these essays primarily in my late twenties. My writing style also reflects the idealistic and turbulent times of the 1970s in which most of these essays were written (see [9] below). I believe that the inclusion of these essays in my "younger" writing style is an interesting balance with my combined academic/experiential writing style in Chapter 2 and Appendix: Part 4, and especially with my experiential analysis writing style in Chapter 1 and in the first three parts of the Appendix.

2) I am using the term "real" to mean genuine, authentic, and transparent, in the sense that was described by Carl Rogers in *On Becoming a Person* (Boston: Houghton Mifflin, 1961), a book that was instrumental in developing the field of humanistic psychology.

3) See Hermann Hesse (1977), *Steppenwolf* (New York: Bantam Books; original work published 1929); and Hermann Hesse (1971), *Siddhartha* (New York: Bantam Books; original work published 1951). The German novelist Hermann Hesse served as an inspirational literary mentor to me when I was in my twenties; see my essay *A Hessian Model of Why People See Out Modern Religions* in Chapter 5.

4) My own personal meaning of "internal" is described in my essay *On Internal* in my self-published book *Natural Dimension* (Swanville, Maine: Natural Dimension Publications, 2012). Essentially I use the term "internal" to describe my inner experience of natural creativity and flow with the universe, in the context that has been described in distinctive ways by Carl Rogers and Hermann Hesse (see [2] and [3] above, and Hermann Hesse's book *Demian* (New York: Bantam Books, 1965; original work published 1925).

5) See my Scientology essay *TRs* in Chapter 4.

6) As it turned out, I was quite mistaken about this prediction, as est dissolved in the 1980s and Scientology has maintained its overwhelming presence in the world, as of May, 2011.

7) See my Scientology essays in Chapter 4, in particular *Sample Dianetic Auditing Process and Concluding Statement*, and also the excerpts from my semi-autobiographical novel, entitled *Excerpts from "The Maturation of Walter Goldman"* in Chapter 4.

8) See the related est material in Chapter 1, where I have placed est in the Mild Cult Danger classification.

9) See Eugene Taylor (1999), *Shadow Culture: Psychology and Spirituality in America*; Washington DC: Counterpoint.

10) As one progresses in the Unification Church organization, it is indeed made quite clear that Reverend Moon is the 2nd Messiah. See any of the book references in [23] of Chapter One Notes.

11) For information about Reverend Moon's various speeches and writings, see the Sun Myung Moon and the Unification Church in Their Own Words website (www.Tparents.org).

12) See my Divine Light Mission essays in Chapter 3 and the Divine Light Mission section in Chapter 1.

13) See my Divine Light Mission essays in Chapter 3, in particular *Letter from Richie*.

14) See my est essays in Chapter 3.

15) See my Scientology essays in Chapter 4, and my essay *A Comparison of Scientology and Judaism* in Chapter 5

16) I subsequently decided to keep these as two separate books, and I obviously have kept the name of my book *Modern Religions*.

17) See my essay *Scientology and Fear* in Chapter 4.

18) From my perspective of over thirty-four years later, as I am now sixty-two years old, I must say that experiencing success as a writer means to me that I feel successful as a philosopher, and this, along with continuing to maintain and develop my eight year harmonious love relationship with Dorothy, are indeed my highest priorities in life.

19) See my essays in Chapter 5: *The Phenomenon of Religion*.

20) See my Divine Light Mission material in Chapter 1, where I gave Divine Light Mission a Moderate Cult Danger classification and placed it on the "pre-rational" level of consciousness in Wilber's consciousness level continuum (with my own "pseudo-rational" extension).

21) Promoting my philosophy of extended science and experiential analysis is my current (2011) way of promoting my original philosophy of Natural Dimension (see [1] in Chapter Three Notes).

22) See my essay *My Conception of Integral* (see [15] in Introduction Notes for reference) for a description of my philosophy of Natural Dimension.

23) See my est and Gurdjieff essays in Chapter 3, Scientology essays in Chapter 4, and respective related material in Chapter 1.

24) See the related material in Chapter 1, where from my experiential analysis we see that both Scientology and The Unification Church received from me the highest rating of "10" both in the categories of Wealth and Front Groups on the Bonewits Cult Danger Scale. Divine Light Mission, although not nearly as extreme as Scientology and The Unification Church, did receive higher combined scores from me in the Wealth and Front Groups categories than that of est and Gurdjieff.

25) From my more seasoned perspective over thirty years later, I now view this essay as an example of the somewhat naive idealism and optimism of my youth, but it legitimately expresses my idealized outlook at the time (see [1] in Chapter Three Notes). Of course there are grave dangers involved in the guru authoritarian role, especially in the case of Reverend Moon (see my Unification Church and Divine Light Mission material in Chapter 1).

26) Transpersonal Psychology is currently (2011) the field that represents these more esoteric or "spiritual" components of the human potential movement of the 1960s and 1970s. For information about Transpersonal Psychology see the books listed in [94], [96], and [103] in Chapter One Notes, and [17], [21], [27], [50], [54], [56], [61], [62], and [67] of Chapter Two Notes.

27) The nature of God being within the individual as well as in the world is very much a part of various modern and new age spiritual interpretations of God, including Neopaganism, Avatar, and Conversations with God. See my related Chapter 2 essays and Chapter 1 material, and Huston Smith's book *The World's Religions* (see [59] of Chapter Two Notes for reference).

28) See my essay *A Hessian Model of Why People Seek Out Modern Religions* in Chapter 5, and my essay *On Transcendence of Hermann Hesse* in my book *Natural Dimension* (see [4] in Chapter Three Notes for reference).

29) See my Scientology essays in Chapter 4 and the Scientology section in Chapter 1, and the books in [1] in Chapter One Notes.

30) See my est essays in Chapter 2 and the est section in Chapter 1.

31) My ex-wife Diane took her maiden name when we got divorced in 1985. However, to protect her anonymity I will not use her legal middle or last names in this book.

32) See Hermann Hesse (1961), *The Journey to the East*; New York: Bantam Books.

33) See my est essay *On Pseudo-Realness* in Chapter 3.

34) See the books listed in [94] and [103] in Chapter One Notes, and [49] and [67] in Chapter Two Notes.

35) I do not agree with Gurdjieff in this respect; the individualized interpretation of art is at the heart of the qualitative disciplines of phenomenology and hermeneutics, and of a number of philosophical perspectives on art and creativity. See for example Julia Cameron's book *The Artists Way* (see [94] in Chapter One Notes for reference), my article *My Conception of Integral* (see [15] in Introduction Notes for reference), my article *Art and Mental Disturbance* (Journal of Humanistic Psychology, 2008, Vol. 48, No. 1, 61-88); see also the books listed in [66] in Chapter Two Notes for a description of phenomenology, and Bentz, V. M., & Shapiro, J. J. (1998), *Mindful Inquiry in Social Research*; London: Sage, for a description of hermeneutics.

36) See Jung, C. (1961), *Memories, Dreams, Reflections*; New York: Vintage; and Jung, C. (1936), *Modern Man in Search of a Soul*; New York: Harcourt Brace.

37) For more information on Beshara see the Beshara Publications website at www.beshara.org/pages/books.html

38) These practices of Beshara appear to have much in common with Islamic Sufi practices; see for example descriptions of practices related to this in Huston Smith's *The World's Religions* (see [59] in Chapter Two Notes for reference). From the little that I have encountered of Beshara, It appears to me that this modern religion is an offshoot of Islam.

CHAPTER 4

ENCOUNTERS WITH SCIENTOLOGY

ON SCIENTOLOGY

[1]

On this day, January 11, 1977, after two years of most interesting experience with the recent world religion of Scientology, founded by L. Ron Hubbard in 1950 (the year of my birth) with the advent of Dianetics, I shall write. I want to convey something of my experience with Scientology. As of now, I am on official "pastoral counselor" (auditor) of Scientology, and am nearly an ordained minister of their church. The one thing I am though, that they do no know about, is a TRAITOR. To me, Scientology is little more than phenomenological experience. I believe that anything in this world has the right to be studied by the human mind and soul (freely), and Scientology is no exception. If there is any one piece of external data that I can point to which shows a unique contribution I have made to the world, it is my singular—I believe—simultaneous progression in both Scientology and psychology. I hear stories of practicing psychiatrists who turn towards Dianetics (a sub-study of Scientology), but to simultaneously advance in both Scientology and psychology (I am crossing my fingers that I really did get my Master's in counseling from Boston State College) is an achievement that I am quite proud of. In my experience, L. Ron Hubbard makes Sigmund Freud look modest. The sad to me, thing though, that I must begrudgingly admit to Hubbard, is that I do not believe that L. Ron Hubbard, in his psychological, philosophical, and theological works, is any less great than Freud. I pay this tribute to Hubbard, fully realizing that he would probably laugh at my even comparing him to the "bumbling idiot" that he considers Freud to be

230 Modern Religions: An Experiential Analysis And Exposé

(although he does give Freud a bit of credit for one or two things). But what can I say? *Dianetics: The Modern Science of Mental Health* (see [1] in Chapter One Notes) is a great book. It is Hubbard's first main non-science fiction book, and I believe he has written about twenty Scientology related books since then. His writings should indeed be publicly known and acclaimed, and he should go down as one of the greatest psychologists/philosophers/theologians in the history of our time. Perhaps, you are wondering, if I am so enthralled with L. Ron Hubbard, why do I call myself a traitor to Scientology? I shall try to explain.

You must remember that I, Elliot Benjamin, live in a natural dimension. That comes first. "Realness" is important to me. I got interested in Scientology because at the time it was "real" to me. Indeed, Scientology is quite alluring when one is trapped in our materialistic, self-shattering society. A Scientologist is a spiritually oriented person—make no doubt about it; and human beings have been attracted to spiritualists for thousands of years. But Scientology is a very unusual kind of spiritualism. It successfully combines the technology of the West with the mysticism of the East, and is so expansive and all-encompassing, but it has one major flaw and lack: FREEDOM! Yes—that's it. A Scientologist is a slave. A slave to the ideas of Mr. Hubbard. Hubbard's ideas are remarkably brilliant, but the price is a bit too high for me—and I am not just talking about the financial price. You literally must sell your soul to Scientology in order to become a Scientologist. I believe that Hubbard has made some ideological mistakes, has overdone some of his ideas, and in short—has committed the human fallibility of being imperfect. Another way of saying this is that Hubbard is not God. Perhaps some day I shall write a psychological/philosophical analysis of Dianetics and Scientology. I cannot fight the temptation to manipulate Scientologists. They manipulate others, and so they deserve to be manipulated in turn. If they can catch me, fine. So far, they haven't. As I continue to survive in their church, I take the attitude that if they let me stay with them, with all that is in my mind—as finally evidenced a little by what I have so far written, it is their own shortcomings, and they must pay for it. For they let me stay with them only because they believe I am one of them. No way. I am studying them. The price is costly to me—both in finances and in emotional stress, but I love it!

THE ENGRAM AND THE DREAM

It is taboo, according to Scientology, to mix Scientology with other mental practices. I want very much to get over this barrier, and really explore what L. Ron Hubbard has contributed to mankind [2]. According to Hubbard, an "engram" is a mental image picture containing a moment of pain and unconsciousness. It is recorded in the "reactive mind," which is the stimulus-response, animalistic, lower level mind that is responsible for the irrational behavior of human beings. The engram is locked deep inside the person and is the root of all of his/her emotional stress and most of her/his physical stress. This concept of the engram seems to have some close relationships with the "traumatic experiences" of Freud and psychoanalysis. A child gets bitten by a dog; in psychoanalysis this may be a traumatic experience, and in Dianetics this is an engram. In both schools of thought, the experiences of childhood and of infancy are extremely crucial to the later development of the human being. In psychoanalysis the childhood trauma goes into the unconscious mind, where it is repressed and is allowed expression in dreams. However, this trauma may be responsible for much of a person's neurotic behavior, as a person may scream at the sight of a dog and never know why. Similarly, in Dianetics this engram is forgotten and is stored in the reactive mind, but it can be "keyed in" (activated to express its impact on the organism) by what is called "secondaries," such as the bark of a dog, or even "locks," such as the mere sight of a dog in later life. Thus there seem to be some direct parallels in the psychologies of psychoanalysis and Dianetics. Both schools rely very heavily on the memories from the past. A major difference though is in the use and respective importance of the dream.

For Freud the dream was the major source of all the unconscious material that needed direct expression. While both Freud and Hubbard agree on the primacy of "reliving" the traumatic experience or engram and in catharting, Hubbard places absolutely no importance on dreams whatsoever. Hubbard developed a therapeutic technique called "auditing" where the pre-clear (i.e. patient or client, literally one who has not reached the state of "Clear"—a happy and healthy human being who can transcend his/her body and is no longer bothered by anything from her/his past, and who has exceptional analytical powers as a human being) relives the actual engram that is in his/her reactive mind, over and over again until it no longer has any force upon the pre-clear who is doing the reliving. Whereas psychoanalysis is free-flowing and sort of poetic in its giving expression to wherever the patient goes in his/her free association, Dianetics is quite rigorous and scientific, directing the pre-clear (often referred to as the "p.c.") with firm and standard questions, proceeding upon ultra-logical and systematic lines. In a certain sense Dianetics has taken the basic material of psychoanalysis, has added material, deleted material, changed material to new forms, and has created a much more scientific—in the sense that whenever auditor does "A" the pre-clear will do "B"—psychology, complete with nearly two hundred axioms as a basis. But although Dianetics has been described as another version of psychoanalysis, I can testify that it is far more than this. Dianetics deserves to be studied in its own right, as a separate psychology. Hubbard did not steal Freud's ideas, but rather he has built upon them. I urge all people who are interested in psychology and more specifically in psychoanalysis, to read Hubbard's first book: *Dianetics: The Modern Science of Mental Health* and find out for yourself what exactly is going on here [3].

THE MISUNDERSTOOD WORD

On the first page of every Scientology book that has been written by L. Ron Hubbard is a brief passage that I will paraphrase as follows:

It is essential when studying Dianetics and Scientology to never go past a word or phrase that you do not understand. The only reason anyone gives up studying something or becomes confused or unable to learn is that the person has gone past a word or phrase that was not understood. If you are having trouble grasping the material or it becomes confusing, then there must be a word in the material that you did not understand. Your job is to not go any further, but to go back BEFORE you got into trouble, find the misunderstood word (M.U.), and get it defined.

This seemingly innocuous and wise statement has been the source of much agony and frustration for me in Scientology. Ever since I was a kid, I have always read books with a dictionary by my side and conscientiously looked up almost every word I would come across that I did not understand. I saw myself though as being pretty unique and peculiar in this regard, going along with a requirement for detail that I seemed to possess. When I discovered the professional dedication and extreme place of importance that Scientologists put upon getting all your misunderstood words defined, I was completely enthralled and very impressed. Here was a whole society that thought it of the utmost importance to look up words in the dictionary! I really did feel my calling. I enjoyed immensely the experience of looking up words in a dictionary and feeling like I was doing the right thing, instead of feeling like an over-meticulous freak. However, although two years later I still read with a dictionary by my side and look up "almost" every word I come across that I do not understand, the mere thought of the professional "word-clearers" of Scientology nearly makes me sick.

When you take a course in Scientology you are surrounded and constantly watched by well-intentioned, professionally trained Scientology word-clearers whose sole job is to watch the students and intervene when a student looks dull or confused. The intervention has totally rigid and assigned patterns, as set forth by Hubbard in the training materials for word-clearers. There are nine different types of word-clearing, called method-one, method-two...to method-nine. Some of these types of word-clearing are done on the E-meter (Hubbard Electrometer: a type of lie-detector that is used extensively in auditing and word-clearing [4] which will be discussed in my E-meter essay in this chapter). It has been my experience that about 70 percent of the time the word-clearers are indeed enabling the student to find a misunderstood word that is the source of his/her difficulty in study. The problem is the other 30 percent. Hubbard says 100 percent of the time—if a student is bored, he/she has an M.U., and any word-clearer worth his/her post will persevere and not quit until he/she gets the student to find that M.U. That 30 percent for me has been a somewhat humorous form of psychological torture. Until you spend two hours battling a word-clearer on an E-meter to prove that you don't have an M.U. but you just are not interested in what Hubbard is talking about, you haven't lived. When you do read something interesting and you want to stop and think about it for a while, you got a problem—and an M.U. And heaven forbid if you ever get so brazen as to question the 100% technology of the "misunderstood word"—this means you got an M.U.! In short, you can't win.

When you finally concede you do have an M.U. (in order to get rid of the word-clearer), if you're unlucky you will have picked a word like "an" or "put." What you must do is learn every single damn definition of the word, even if there are twenty definitions, and put the word in a sentence in each one of the ways it is used in its respective definition. If you come across a word in the definition you do not understand, then you must go through this same process until you get that word defined—also in all definitions and all sentences. What is the result? The result is that when I am in a course in Scientology, I do not have M.U.s. When I come across a word that I do not understand, if the word-clearer is in sight, I just go right on in my reading as if this had never occurred. Later, when I come home, I might look up the word in a dictionary—in my own way and my own time. A word-clearer is like a robot, not directed by a mind of his/her own, but trained like an automaton by L. Ron Hubbard. When you start questioning a word-clearer on philosophy and he/she keeps on saying that same stupid statement: "But just before that—was there a word you didn't understand?" you begin to realize this. So, in conclusion like so many other parts of Scientology, L.Ron Hubbard has taken a basically good idea, has gone to extremes with it, has made it into a rigid authoritarian decree, and has built up a formidable machine-like technology. If only we were intellectual robots, I would have no quarrel with the mis-understood word technology or with anything else in Scientology. But Mr. Hubbard has put in 100 percent where 70 percent should be. This is his great flaw, and this is why I'm afraid I must write the way I am writing.

TRs

One of the most interesting facets of Scientology that I have found are the "training drills," better known as TRs (training routines). When a beginning student comes on a Scientology course, he/she very quickly gets introduced to about six or seven of these training drills, knows as O.T. (Operating Thetan) [5]:TR Zero, TR Zero Bullbait (see below and [6]), TR 1, TR 2, TR 3, and TR 4. These beginning training drills are practiced over and over again, from the new arrivals on an introductory Scientology course to the veteran experienced Scientology auditors. The main purpose of these drills is to enable the student or auditor to really "be there." The most popular and widely used of Hubbard's training drills is TR Zero, which is called "Confronting Pre-clear." I will paraphrase Hubbard's description of TR Zero as follows:

The student auditor and coach are instructed to sit facing each other a comfortable distance apart—about three feet. The idea is to get the student to confront a pre-clear with only auditing, i.e. to get the student able to simply be with the pre-clear, not to do anything else but BE there.

In order to accomplish this, the student auditor and coach are instructed to sit facing each other, neither making any conversation or effort to be interesting. They are told to sit and look at each other and say and do nothing for some hours. They must not speak, blink, fidget, giggle or be embarrassed or anaten (weakening of analytical awareness), as they must not confront WITH a body part, but rather they must just confront and BE there. It is explained that confronting with a body part can cause somatics (body sensation, illness or pain or discomfort) in that body part being used to confront. It is stated that L. Ron Hubbard developed this technique in Washington D.C. in March 1957 to train students to confront pre-clears without using social tricks or conversations and to overcome obsessive compulsions to be "interesting."

I have spent many an hour doing TR Zero with other Scientologists, and I am still fascinated with this most interesting spiritual drill. I do not believe that TR Zero is a facade or sham maneuver put out by Hubbard. After doing TR Zero for half an hour, I indeed would feel that I was really experiencing "being there." It is quite difficult to look right into the eyes of a relative stranger for half an hour or more, but in doing so I always felt a special kind of closeness and mutuality with my TR Zero partner. There both of us were, in the early morning hours, doing TRs—while the cars and people on the street went whizzing by, on their way to the rush-rush everyday world of work. It certainly was as if I was experiencing what it meant to just sit there and do nothing, to really be there, to really "be." The TR Zero experience probably has similarities to the experience one has while meditating. But the focus on TR Zero is the "twoness" of the drill. One is not alone as in meditating, but one is nonverbally interacting with another human being. There is a subtle energy flow that is being exchanged between these two human beings, both of whom are seeking spiritual elevation, and the result is almost always a rise and heightening of some kind of spiritual power—or more simply the attaining of the ability to "be there."

This training drill and the other beginning training drills are the basis of a Scientologist's "power." When you meet a Scientologist on the street and you see this Scientologist looking so deeply and wide-eyed into your eyes with his/her dilated pupils, you can bet that this Scientologist has just done TR Zero in the nearby church. He/she has gained an ability to "be there," and this "being there" is exactly what has attracted so many people to the church, and is the secret behind the marked success of the "body-routers" (whom I will talk more about in the next essay). Should everybody do TRs? I really don't know. I always enjoyed doing TR Zero with a stranger, as I found it an excellent way to get to know somebody, without any need of polite conversation. However, after one or two TR encounters with the same person, I found it rather boring and superfluous to do TRs with this same person again, unless a substantial portion of time had passed, or unless I were doing TR Zero Bullbait, where the coach would purposely try to push the student auditor's buttons, voicing quite often explicitly gross and/or sexual remarks to test the student auditor's discipline and concentration (see [6] in Chapter Four Notes). Of course my perspective on doing TRs might just be my own quirk of individuality, but I certainly don't see any other Scientologists willing to write openly about Scientology [7]. I believe, in my own developing theory of psychology, that I would use Hubbard's TRs, but in conjunction with perhaps some principles from Gestalt and Rogerian psychology. Of course this would be ultra-taboo to Hubbard and Scientology, and I would be branded as a "squirrel" (one who alters Scientology and does off-beat practices). In conclusion, I hope that I have at least given some insight into L. Ron Hubbard's quite ingenious and rigorous method of training Scientologists to become auditors and enabling Scientologists to learn what it means to "be there" [8].

BODY-ROUTERS & BODY-REGERS

Today I wish to write about one of the most controversial and successful aspects of Scientology: body-routing and body-reging. First off it must be realized that in L. Ron Hubbard's philosophy, there are three main parts to human beings: body, mind, and spirit. The name for the spirit is "thetan," and the mind is divided into the "reactive mind" and "analytical mind" (the higher functioning mind). The thetan controls both the mind and the body, using the mind as an intermediary device to make the body do what it desires [9]. Consequently the term "body-routing," to a Scientologist, literally means for the thetan to guide bodies on a carefully planned out route. This carefully planned out route has a number of terminals, but the main focus is to take bodies off the street and put them in a Church of Scientology. Once a body is in a Church of Scientology, the body-router has completed his/her job and the body-reger takes over. The job of the body-reger is to registrate a person on either a Scientology course or a contract to receive auditing.

Intermediate between the body-router and the body-reger are the receptionist, the bookstore officer, and the personality test administrator, all of whom are very carefully trained to set up this newly arrived body for the sales pitch of the body-reger. And I must say that the sales pitch of the body-reger is a truly remarkable piece of craftsmanship, especially if the body-reger has completed L. Ron Hubbard's professional salesmanship course.

To begin to explain how a Scientologist has such amazing impact upon the naïve newcomer to Scientology, the concept of ARC (Affinity, Reality, Communication) must be understood (see [8] in Chapter Four Notes). According to Hubbard, relationships between people can be totally understood by the level of affinity (degree of liking), level of reality (agreement and mutual experience), and level of communication (basically "real" communication—not very different from the communication that takes place in the encounter groups of humanistic psychology) that exist between two people at a given time. Hubbard has described ARC as a triangle where an increase in any one part of the triangle increases the levels of the other two parts. Thus if a couple has a misunderstanding, a good communication will enhance their degree of liking for each other and also their agreement about what is real. Hubbard develops this concept much more extensively, but for our purposes here it merely needs to be understood that ARC is the language of Scientology—in its everyday use amongst Scientologists (for more information about ARC, see *A Personal Exercise in ARC* in Scientology Appendix 2 in this chapter). Thus, you might hear "there was a lot of ARC in this area," meaning that the resultant measure of affinity, reality, and communication was very high. So the body-reger is trained to "like" the Scientologist-to-be, to make him/her feel totally understood through a feeling of "mutuality" with the body-reger, and to receive every bit of communication from this newcomer with a perfect acknowledgement. On top of all this, the body-reger has just done a nice set of TRs and is "all there," with a beautiful intensity in her/his eyes that seem to go right through your being. As the body-reger couples ARC, TRs, and professional salesmanship techniques with a truly genuine belief that getting this newcomer signed up on a Scientology course is helping to save the planet, the naïve newcomer has quite the time resisting the sales pitch of the body-reger. To make matters even more stimulating, the body-reger is often an extremely attractive young woman, and the naïve male newcomer may be captivated with her charm and the look in her eyes, which seem far more fruitful to him than his mundane everyday life.

Getting back to the body-routers, to understand how they manage to so routinely bring bodies into the Church to begin with, the concept of the "tone scale" needs to be looked at. Hubbard has developed a mathematical scale of personality, from death to total awareness. On this scale, each tone level of personality has a number assigned to it. For instance, apathy = .5, covert hostility = 1.1, fear = 1.3, anger = 1.5, boredom = 2.0, conservatism = 3.0, enthusiasm = 4.0, etc. Thus the job of the body-router is to bring the person up-tone, either from fear to anger, from boredom to conservatism, from apathy to covert hostility, etc. How? By maintaining excellent TRs and using a lot of ARC, put together with a sales pitch to get a free personality test (which happens to be designed to demonstrate severe personality defects in the person; see my own Scientology personality test in Scientology Appendix 1 in this chapter). The trick is to put on a tone level that is slightly higher than the tone level of the person you are trying to capture. Thus if someone is in "apathy" you don't come on with "enthusiasm" as this will not reach the person; perhaps "anger" will have a more advantageous effect. Through "obnosis" (a Scientology term meaning "observing the obvious") a Scientologist is very thoroughly trained to know the tone-level a person is on by merely looking at this person, and the Scientologist is extensively drilled to bring up his/her tone-level (for more information about the tone-scale, see *A Personal Exercise in the Tone Scale* in Scientology Appendix 3 in this chapter). Thus the person walking down the street, bored and feeling quite alone and inconspicuous, all of a sudden meets somebody who seems to truly understand how he/she feels, and has something interesting to offer: a free personality test. So why not follow this interesting stranger down the street a few blocks to the Church of Scientology? And then the body-router has completed his/her job, the receptionist, bookstore officer, and personality test administrator take over, and the pathway is opened up for the sales pitch of the body-reger: Q.E.D. (meaning "end of proof" in mathematical language) [10].

THE E-METER

Much publicity has been given to the Hubbard Electrometer—or E-Meter. Technically speaking, the E-Meter is a specially developed

"Wheatstone Bridge" that is well known to electrically minded people as an electronic device to measure the amount of resistance in a flow of electricity (see [4] in Chapter Four Notes). The E-Meter has been designed by L. Ron Hubbard, who claimed to have been an engineer [11], to measure the large and minute changes in the electrical resistance of a human body. The widespread use of the E-Meter in Scientology is based upon the principle that an individual's emotional state, his/her thoughts, etc., instantly raise or lower the electrical resistance of the body (see [4] in Chapter One Notes and [4] in Chapter Four Notes). Many people are skeptical as to how accurately the E-Meter can do what it claims to do, but I must confess that in my experience, and I have audited over sixty hours with an E-Meter, the E-Meter is indeed quite an effective tool in giving a physiological measure of a person's thoughts and emotions. There are basically ten different needle manifestations that may occur—as set forth by L. Ron Hubbard in *The Book of E-Meter Drills* (see [4] in Chapter Four Notes), and from my experience these needle manifestations do seem to have a high degree of accuracy, especially the "Floating Needle" and the "Fall."

The Floating Needle is a needle that moves back and forth in a lazy, relaxed, even fashion—uninfluenced by anything the auditor says or does. This needle manifestation indicates to the auditor that the p.c. (pre-clear) is approaching the end of the process being run, and should soon be getting a cognition (new state of awareness), an erasure (removal of the engram that was troubling him/her) and should be V.G.I.'s (Very Good Indicators—laughing, smiling etc.). These four states: Floating Needle (F/N), Cognition, Erasure, and VGIs are known as "End Phenomenon" of a process being run on Dianetic Auditing. On the other hand, the "Fall," which is a sharp movement of the needle to the right, indicates that there is tension or a thought in some area. When a "Fall" occurs, the auditor knows to pay special attention to the question he/she has just asked the p.c. The Fall is the main device that is used to decide upon what items to run on a process. For example, if a p.c. is having a "drug-rundown," the auditor will ask the p.c. to name the different drugs he/she has used during his/her lifetime, and the auditor will run a dianetic process on any drug that produces a "Fall" as the p.c. says it. After a session is over, the p.c. is taken to the Examiner and is put on an E-Meter; it is expected that her/his needle will float. If his/her needle does float, the auditing session has been considered basically successful, but if her/his needle does not float, then the p.c. is taken back into session and special "review auditing" may be done on the session [12].

In the auditing that I myself received, I found the E-Meter to be quite accurate in perceiving when I was feeling tense, when I was trying to hide something from Scientology, and when I was feeling relaxed. I still possess an E-Meter and I intend to give serious thought to how I may someday be able to put the E-Meter to use in my practice as a psychotherapist (although this may very well prove to be legally not feasible to do, based upon Scientology's legal threats [13]). The main gripe I have against the E-Meter as used in Scientology is the same concern that I discussed in my essay *The Misunderstood Word*. And this is the unswerving totality with which L. Ron Hubbard forces upon every word that he speaks and writes, and every idea that he thinks of. No I do not believe that the E-Meter is infallible. There were times I was auditing when the E-Meter would tell me something, and my own personal sensitivity as a therapist would tell me something else. I believed my own sensitivity and consequently got into much trouble with Scientology Ethics (to be discussed in the next essay: *Ethics*) which lead to my eventual leaving of Scientology. A Dianetics and Scientology auditor is chained to do whatever the E-Meter and L. Ron Hubbard say to do, and this I cannot accept. I cannot deny that L. Ron Hubbard is a smart man, and that the E-Meter may be a helpful therapeutic device; but both can make mistakes, and in my experience both have made mistake—often. L. Ron Hubbard has given us a very useful and ingenious therapeutic device in the E-Meter, and I would like to see this tool being used in as widespread and effective a manner as possible. I would welcome any and all electrically minded therapists to read through and practice the content and instructions in the booklets *Introducing the E-Meter*, *The Book of E-Meter Drills*, and *E-Meter Essentials* (though obtaining copies of these booklets as well as an E-Meter may necessitate going undercover as a Scientology student; see [4] in Chapter 4 Notes), and then go out and see to what use you can put an E-Meter, or similar type of device, in your own practice of psychotherapy (but do be careful about the legal ramifications with Scientology). In conclusion, I consider the E-Meter to be potentially a very useful therapeutic device, although one that needs careful and long-lasting study by various occupational experts who are not connected with Scientology, in the hands of a truly competent and humanistic psychotherapist. However, I am afraid that although a Scientology auditor is quite competent in observing all of L. Ron Hubbard's rigidities, I do not consider a Scientology auditor to be either competent or humanistic as a psychotherapist.

ETHICS

Our own judicial proceedings can learn something from the ethics system of Scientology. All Scientologists are continuously assigned an ethics condition, based upon their product output, as evidenced by their weekly statistics, or total number of points according to their specific criteria of judgment. For a student, his/her statistic is "student points," for an auditor it is "well done auditing hours," etc. (the student point system is more fully explained in my next essay: *The Educational System of Scientology*). This organizational set-up is very behavioral and very efficient, as all Scientologists are continuously on the go, seeking to raise their stats and thereby raise their ethics condition. The eleven ethics conditions are: Power, Power Change, Affluence, Normal Operation, Emergency, Danger, Non-Existence, Liability, Doubt, Enemy, and Treason. There is an Ethics Officer who is in charge of enforcing all of L. Ron Hubbard's directions on ethics proceedings, and in assigning ethics conditions to Scientologists. The Ethics Officer is also responsible for detecting Scientologists who come with fraudulent purposes or who are influenced by people antagonistic to Scientology. The goal of the Ethics Officer is to raise the ethics condition of the entire Church, and to get as many Scientologists into "Normal Operation" as possible. Once a Scientologist falls into "Liability" he/she is taken off post, and in order to move back up into "Non-Existence" this Scientologist needs to get the signatures of a majority of staff members on a special petition that he/she has made up for this purpose. I myself have gone this route after I blew (unauthorized leave) from a Dianetic internship and later sought to regain admission into the Church.

All in all, I would say that Scientology Ethics is basically a good thing (for Scientology), as it certainly does keep a check on undesirables to Scientology, and puts just about the right amount of fear into Scientologists to keep them working smoothly and efficiently. Given the continuous and enormous pressures which every Scientology staff member is faced with, some kind of Ethics handling is most definitely needed. The Ethics Officer is usually held in high regard by Scientologists, and is looked upon as a friend to help them get back on the track when they falter. All complaints on a course or on a post are also handled by the Ethics Officer, as Scientologists are constantly urged to voice their opinions, as long as it is through the correct channels. The Ethics Officer uses the E-Meter in his/her questioning of Scientologists to determine if any laws of Scientology have been violated. In my own ethics file, I was listed as having committed a "high crime" by mixing Scientology with other mental practices—specifically that of Gestalt therapy. As a punishment, I was put into the Ethics condition of "Treason" and had all my Scientology materials, certificates, and E-Meter confiscated. I managed to work myself back up to "Non-Existence" after having done fifteen hours of amends (filing, collating, etc.), getting the necessary number of signatures on my petition, buying the $500 Dianetics course over again in order to do a "re-train" on Dianetics, and signing a document stating that I would never again do anything to harm Scientology. As I said in my opening essay: *On Scientology*, I am a traitor to Scientology and I am fully admitting it right now. This book is quite harmful to Scientology as it is exposing to the public eye many things that L. Ron Hubbard has worked very hard to keep private to Scientology. But this is a decision I have made, and I am going by my own set of ethics—which tell me to write all I know about Scientology—and so I shall continue.

THE EDUCATIONAL SYSTEM OF SCIENTOLOGY

One of the things that initially attracted me to the Church of Scientology was their educational system. Hubbard has indeed instituted some very modern educational procedures for students on a course. First off, the educational system is totally competency-based. Each student, upon entering a Scientology course, receives a checksheet which contains a series of ordered steps—readings, tapes, clay demonstrations, drills, etc., which must be done in a particular sequence. The student then proceeds at his/her own pace, although there is quite an emphasis upon working efficiently but as rapidly as possible. The student is given a certain number of points for each educational task he/she completes. For instance, the student receive three points for every page she/he reads, two points for every word he/she looks up in a dictionary, twenty-five points for a successfully completed clay demonstration, seventy-five points for a major drill, etc. At the end of the day the student adds up all the points he/she has made, and posts this number on a graph that is hung on a wall, along with the graphs of the other students on the course. Each day this is done, and while the student is on course anybody can come into the course-room and see how the student is progressing by merely taking a glance at the curve of her/his graph. This is the system that is used to determine the Ethics condition of all Scientologists, as each Scientologist has a graph according to what his/her product statistic is determined to be [14].

While at first I somewhat rejected this system as being far too behavioral and rigid, I have since come to appreciate this system as an extremely effective and pretty accurate means of both evaluating the entire educational and organizational system of Scientology, and promoting the maximum amount of progress on courses and on staff. Scientologists have come to accept their "statistic" as a symbol of their identity, and to be in "Power" indeed has a powerful effect throughout the Church. At times the pressure is so great to increase one's stats that it is not uncommon for Scientologists to falsify their statistics. When this is found out it becomes a pretty serious Ethics matter. Because of the extreme emphasis upon one's statistics, Scientologists are super-motivated to "produce." There is a very positive and seductive kind of energy that flows throughout the Church, with all Scientologists rapidly and cheerfully going about their business—trying to increase their stats and thereby increase their reputation and fringe benefits. And of course the most sought after fringe benefit for a Scientology staff member is the receipt of free auditing, which is given to those Scientologists who are at the top of their posts. In order to get a promotion to a higher office on staff, there actually is very little favoritism, as an individual is considered to be as good as his/her statistics show, and is judged accordingly. Thus to a Scientologist, the more he/she produces, whether for example it is a course supervisor who gets a student to complete a course or a body-reger who gets a p.c. signed up for a twelve and a half hour auditing intensive, the Scientologist is that much closer to receiving auditing her/himself, and this is really the Scientologists's major goal in life. For to receive auditing is to go up the bridge and to eventually go "Clear" and "O.T." (O.T. is an abbreviation for Operating Thetan—a state higher than Clear; see [1] in Chapter One Notes). A Scientologist will literally do almost anything to go up the bridge, including do away with all of his/her savings, reject her/his family, divorce his/her spouse, etc. For the Scientologist believes that he/she is seeking spiritual salvation, and indeed this Scientologist is seeking spiritual salvation. If one can believe wholeheartedly that L. Ron Hubbard and his system of auditing is infallible, then it becomes a fairly logical argument that you are indeed giving "pennies for pearls" (a frequently used Scientology motivational phrase). Of course, this is exactly where I part company with Scientology, as I see L. Ron Hubbard and his system of auditing as having far too many rigidities and limitations to ever allow myself to seek spiritual elevation through Scientology.

Getting back to the educational system developed by Hubbard, there are basically three things that are emphasized to a new student on course. One is the proper relationship between "significance" and "mass." This is accounted for by the student being required to do many clay demonstrations and also to frequently demonstrate with small physical objects a concept that he/she is studying. The second thing emphasized is the importance of proceeding upon a "gradient," which is the central idea behind the entire competency-based method of the checksheet. Lastly, there is the doctrine that behind every confusion there lies a "misunderstood word," and I have already said enough about M.U.s previously. There are two special "Study Courses" where a student learns extensively the entire Study Technology developed by Hubbard and then receives a form of auditing where the student goes through, on an E-Meter, everything that she/he has ever studied before in his/her life and clears up all M.U.s that have been accumulated. The student listens to eight study tapes put out by Hubbard, and in doing so becomes fanatically convinced of the 100 percent doctrine of the Misunderstood Word. As a student is proceeding on course, the course supervisor will frequently give the student a "target" in order to motivate the student to achieve the maximum output that he/she is capable of. It is much to the advantage of the course supervisor that his/her students proceed both rapidly and effectively on course, since the course supervisor's own statistic is the total number of points earned in her/his course-room. But there really is a basically friendly and relaxed sort of efficient rapidity that you see when you walk into a Scientology course-room, and I must compliment L. Ron Hubbard in devising a most ingenious and successful educational system for Scientology.

SCIENTOLOGY AND SPIRITUALISM

Scientology is officially a religion and is most certainly a spiritual philosophy. There is a concept in Scientology known as the "eight dynamics." The first dynamic is the individual self, the second dynamic is the individual's family and sexual relations, the third dynamic is the social group, the fourth dynamic is all mankind, the fifth dynamic is all animal and plant life, the sixth dynamic is the entire physical universe—or "MEST" (matter-energy-space-time), the seventh dynamic is thetans—or spirits, and the eighth dynamic is the infinite being—or God. According to Hubbard, the eighth dynamic can be known only after all the other seven dynamics are completely known, and each individual must find the eighth dynamic—or God, for him/herself. However, Hubbard has laid down some pretty significant spiritual laws, one of the most interesting of which is reincarnation. Scientology pays much tribute to some of the ancient religions of the East, such as Hinduism and especially Buddhism.

Scientology believes wholeheartedly in the phenomenon of life after death, and in reincarnation. In fact, it has become routine practice in Dianetic Auditing for the p.c. to eventually become directly aware of his/her past lives, a phenomenon known as "back-tracking" [15]. Thus, when auditing someone, I would be asking for incidents going earlier and earlier in a person's life, and would eventually ask for a date and get a reply such as 1834. Whether this is indeed an authentic recollection of a past life or rather an imaginative speculation is a matter of conjecture [16]. At any rate, it is very natural and commonplace for a Scientologist to talk about his/her past existences and to believe that certain problems she/he is having in this lifetime are directly related to experiences that he/she has had in some of his/her earlier lifetimes. According to Hubbard, children choose their parents; i.e. after a thetan leaves his/her body, he/she joins up with a body just being ready to come into the world and takes on the identity of this new physical organism. Hubbard says that the child has been through much trauma in her/his former lifetime, and therefore must learn things all over again and that this is why the child appears as helpless and incapable. Hubbard believes that children are terribly messed up and hindered, as they have numerous engrams piled up in them from their previous fatal accidents and deaths. Hubbard has instituted Child Scientology, where it is now possible for a child to receive Dianetic Auditing, in just the same manner as an adult.

When reading Hubbard's first Scientology book: *Dianetics: The Modern Science of Mental Health* (see [1] in Chapter One notes), you will find no mention of anything spiritual, as the radical concept in that book is the claim that a human being under Dianetic Auditing could remember back to his/her birth and to her/his pre-natal experiences [17]. These ideas are now considered old hat and super-standard in Scientology, and the exciting current emphasis is upon remembering one's past lives. I have audited someone who supposedly re-lived his birth in the auditing process, and I am still not convinced that this person really did remember his actual birth, much less his pre-natal experiences. But then again, I tend to be quite conservative in spiritual matters, and as I myself cannot remember back to any incidents before the age of three, the accuracy of such long-term memory is at this point in time not "real" to me. But I am quite open to seeking to explore the depths of my own memory, through either psychedelic drugs, a quasi-Scientology type of auditing, or whatever means is developed by psychology and/or religion in the future. But as of now, I must say that through my own experiences as both a Scientologist and a Dianetic Auditor, I am not any more convinced of the existence of life after death and reincarnation than I was before I went into Scientology.

DIANETIC AUDITING PROCESS AND CONCLUDING STATEMENT

In the concluding essay of this section, I would like to give an illustration of the standard questions asked in a typical Dianetic Auditing process. The following is a paraphrasing of the Dianetic Auditing process on the flow of "what others did to you," on the emotion of anger:

There is an initial series of eight auditing instructions/questions, which guide the p.c. to recall and state a particular incident of another causing him/her anger, to determine when the incident took place, to say where the incident took place, to visualize the incident happening, to determine the time duration of the incident, to focus upon the beginning of the incident (with eyes closed), to tell the auditor what she/he sees, to move through the incident to a particular later time as determined by incident duration, while the auditor gives a mild acknowledgement such as "umm-hmm" or "continue" if the p.c. says anything, and finally to tell the auditor what happened. After this initial series of auditing instructions/questions are completed, the auditor gives a second series of four auditing instructions, which instruct the p.c. to once again focus upon the beginning of the incident, to tell the auditor when he/she is visualizing the incident, to move through the incident until the end, and to tell the auditor what happened. Then the auditor asks the p.c. an extremely important question which determines whether the previous series of four instructions will be repeated or an earlier incident of another causing the p.c. anger will be asked for, repeating the original series of eight instructions/questions. The question asked is whether the incident is erasing or going more solid. If the p.c. answers that the incident is erasing, then the second series of four instructions is repeated, with the erasing/more solid question asked again at the end of the instructions. If the p.c. says that the incident is going more solid, then the original series of eight instructions/questions is asked, but with the substitution in the very first instruction of asking the p.c. to locate an "earlier" incident of another causing him/her anger. If the p.c. cannot think of an earlier incident of another causing him/her anger, then the next question asked is whether the process currently run starts earlier. If the p.c. says it does not start earlier, then the auditor repeats the second series of four instructions, asking the p.c. to focus upon the beginning of the incident, etc. If the p.c. says that it does start earlier, then the auditor asks the p.c. to focus upon the new beginning of the incident, and continues with the remaining three instructions in the second series of four auditing instructions. This process is continued for as long as necessary until the End Phenomenon is reached, which consists of the Floating Needle, Cognition, Erasure, and VGIs (VGIs meanVery Good Indicators; see my earler essay in this chapter: *The E-Meter*). It is not uncommon for this kind of auditing process on a single flow of an incident to last three hours or more, where the p.c. is going back earlier and earlier to past lives, by use of an affirmative answer to the related auditing question after the second series of four auditing instructions.

This then is the essential format (in my own paraphrasing) of the standard Dianetic Auditing procedure, and there is virtually no variation permitted on this procedure. There are a number of safety measures that may be taken if the process gets bogged down and does not seem to be getting anywhere, and some of these safety measures can only be done by Class IV auditors—which is a much higher level of auditor training than the Dianetic auditor. While the auditor is asking the p.c. standard auditing questions and noting the p.c.'s responses, the auditor is also maintaining excellent TRs and ARC, is operating his/her E-Meter, and is even recording on worksheets what is going on in the session. Thus an auditor keeps an ongoing written record of the entire auditing session, and in addition to this has a number of things which he/she must write up after the session is over. All those written reports, together with the after-session report from the Examiner, go into the "p.c. Folder." Every p.c. has a folder which contains all written records of all the auditing the p.c. has ever received.

The auditing arrangement in Scientology is indeed quite scientific and ordered, and I must yield that we in psychotherapy can learn much from some of the safety precautions and scientific carefulness with which the pre-clears of Scientology are treated. However, I feel an obligation to also let it be known that the fee for Scientology auditing is (as of 1977) about $70 per hour and is presently going up 5 per cent each month. The focus of the Scientology body-regers is on selling twelve and a half hour intensives, where all the auditing is done over a single weekend. The body-regers will go to virtually any means to get their prospective pre-clears to sign up for auditing, including have the prospective p.c. begging for and borrowing the money from relatives and friends. A common slogan that Scientologists often utilize is "pennies for pearls." It is not uncommon for young people in college to drop out of school and give their college savings over for auditing. It is not uncommon for people in their sixties to take out their bank accounts and hand over $15,000 for a few months of auditing. After all this auditing is received, the p.c. is sent right back to the body-reger and is made aware of all the further possibilities to gain even higher powers as a spiritual being—of course still at $70+ per hour. In Scientology there is what is known as the "bridge," where one reaches higher and higher levels of spiritual development, through receiving more and more Scientology auditing. A way of obtaining this Scientology auditing for free is to join the staff of Scientology by signing a two and a half year or five year contract. The salary you get is minimal but "if" your stats are high, you have the opportunity to receive auditing for free. Another way of obtaining auditing at no cost is to train to become an auditor yourself and to do what is known as "co-auditing" with another auditor trainee. This is the path that I chose, but unfortunately I did not receive nearly as much auditing as I would have liked, and it is obviously now too late for me to receive any official auditing in a Church of Scientology, something which I do regret [18].

When a student comes on a Scientology course, this student is exposed to an extremely rigid and disciplined schedule, where he/she is either studying from 9:00 a.m. to 6:00 p.m. Monday to Friday days, or from 7:00 p.m. to 10:30 p.m. Monday to Friday evenings, plus from 9:00 a.m. to 10:30 p.m. both Saturday and Sunday [19]. The result is that a student in Scientology gradually becomes more and more part of the Scientology group and less and less part of the outside world. There is a term that Hubbard has coined for non-Scientologists, known as WOG—meaning "wise old gentleman." This is a derogatory term used to show how a non-Scientologist thinks he/she knows something but actually knows nothing. The in-group sentiment and total exclusion of non-Scientologists is truly phenomenal [20]. There are large pictures of L. Ron Hubbard all over the Church, and the newcomer is literally deluged with the books and writings of Hubbard, without having time to really think for him/herself about what she/he is learning (this not thinking for oneself is effectively reinforced by the highly trained word-clearers). The newcomer finds that he/she must stick to his/her agreed upon schedule and is not allowed to take any time off to think things over when things get invariably intense. All the TR's, ARC, and salesmanship of the body-regers are then pitted against the resistances of the newcomer as soon as this newcomer completes his/her first Scientology course, with the intention of getting her/him on a higher level Scientology course—or signed up for some auditing (see [19] in Chapter Four Notes).

When somebody joins a Scientology course, he/she is considered to have joined up for the "duration of the universe," and everybody in the Church will do their part to try to make this new person into one of them. The message is "Go Clear," and it does not matter how much it costs or what must be sacrificed in order to do so. And the amazing thing is that so many newcomers in a few months become veterans, bringing in other newcomers to the Church. Luckily for me, my wife had the good sense to reject Scientology—not because of its ideas but because of its manipulation, super-strict schedules, and high costs. It is virtually impossible for a couple to stay together when one member is a Scientologist and the other member is not, and when I saw that I could not convince my wife to become a Scientologist, I decided to take a long and hard look at the totality of Scientology and L. Ron Hubbard, and I managed to rise above Hubbard's teachings and the Scientologists's pressures. I somehow was able to take in the theory of Scientology, without really becoming an authentic Scientologist. I simultaneously progressed in both Scientology and psychology, neither field knowing I was doing the other [21]. The only things that enabled me to keep my sanity through all this, much less my ability to remain clear-headed enough to have kept in mind everything that I have written, is the communications about Scientology that I would continuously have with my wife Diane, whom I am very thankful to for her good common sense and willingness to stay in communication with me during this extremely dangerous and confusing time period in my life.

And thus I conclude my essays on Scientology.

SCIENTOLOGY APPENDIX 1: LETTERS, PERSONALITY TEST, AND CERTIFICATES

July 23, 1975

Dear Diane,

I've been asked to write to a friend about a win that I've had in Scientology. You certainly are my friend, so I figured I would write to you.

Last night—well back-tracking a little, Tuesday morning—remember how I didn't get that drill done because I had to coach somebody else? Well Tuesday night the supervisor wanted me to coach that same person. I protested and spoke to the Director of Training—"real big," and he agreed with me and really worked to help me progress on my course. Tonight I had a heavy day at work and I really did not feel like doing heavy drills. So I got the agreement from this same "big guy" and did some lighter clay demos, worked with some mass, and gradually felt calmer and more relaxed.

So Scientology is still real to me. I take each day as it comes, and do what I must to get what I need—and so far it works!

see you tomorrow,
Elliot

November 5, 1975

Dear Diane,

Whew! "Hermann" [22] got to me just in time. My heaviness Sunday night led to something very internal and very right (and also very economical). I've decided to leave the Church of Scientology. I blew—Monday morning—E-Meter and all (it's up in the top of your closet). So take your $1,100 and put it right back in your bank—before I go crazy again—Hurry! My conscience really did bother me, and they found out about my trickiness, individualistic methods, and falsification of worksheets. My Gestalt group was very good...

love,
Elliot

NOTE: Although I do have my human limitations, I am including the following personality test not as a revelation of my schizophrenic tendencies, but as an example of the very common phenomenon which occurs for most newcomers to Scientology when they take this specially designed personality test. That is, the pattern of my personality curve is very similar to nearly all other patterns of personality curves of non-Scientologists (see descriptions of this in a number of the books listed in [1] of Chapter One Notes) and is one of the main tactics of the body-regers that enables them to sign people up for Scientology courses and especially for Scientology auditing.

SCIENTOLOGY PERSONALITY TEST:
ELLIOT BENJAMIN, 1975

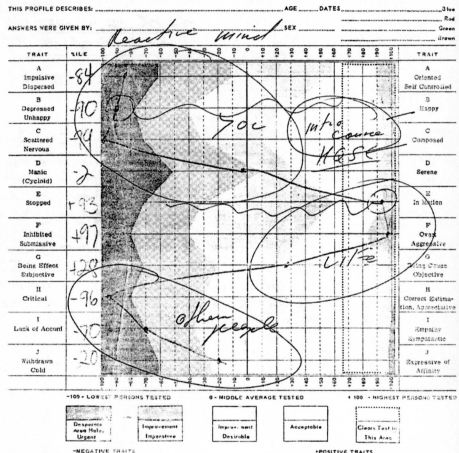

AMERICAN PERSONALITY ANALYSIS
PROFILE REVISION OF DECEMBER 1960

THIS PROFILE DESCRIBES: .... AGE .... DATES ....
ANSWERS WERE GIVEN BY: .... SEX ....

−100 - LOWEST PERSONS TESTED   0 - MIDDLE AVERAGE TESTED   + 100 - HIGHEST PERSONS TESTED

| Desperate Area Halo, Urgent | Improvement Imperative | Improvement Desirable | Acceptable | Clears Test in This Area |

−NEGATIVE TRAITS

IMPULSIVE—Scattered, dispersed, not following directions
Depressed—Unhappy, sad too much of the time
Nervous—Scattered, fidgeting, tensions, tics, restlessness
Manic—Cycloid emotions, irresponsible, changeable without reason
Stopped—Quiet, unable to work or play, reserved
Inhibited—Submissive, easily dominated, propitiative, covert
Being Effect—Subjective, prejudiced, illogical actions, introverted
Critical—Invalidative, making nothing of people and things
Lack of Accord—Hard boiled, un-understanding of others' realities
Withdrawn, Cold, out of communication

+POSITIVE TRAITS

Oriented—Self mastery, determinism, planning, control
Happy—Feeling of well being, cheerfulness, satisfactions
Composed—Good muscular control, steady
Serene—Responsible, not easily upset, even temperament
In Motion—Energetic, lively, outgoing, active
Aggressive—Dominating, pushing ahead, overt
Being Cause—Objective, out going, overt, creative
Correct Estimation—Pleasant, appreciative, good judgement
Empathy—Feeling with others and acting accordingly, affinity
Expressive of Affinity—Cordial, expressively warm-hearted

QUALIFIED SCIENTOLOGIST CERTIFICATE:
ELLIOT BENJAMIN, 1975

PRACTICING DIANETICIST CERTIFICATE:
ELLIOT BENJAMIN, 1976

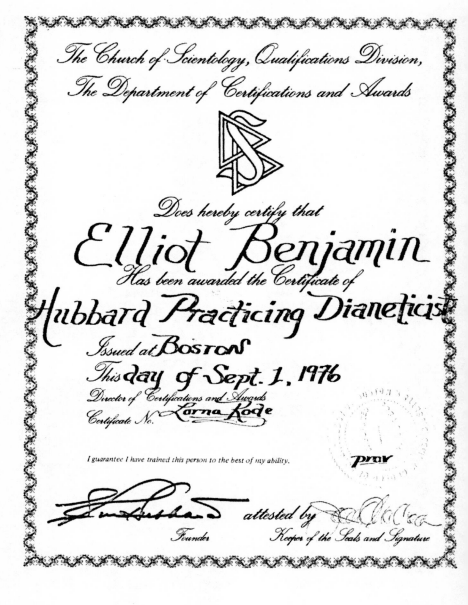

SCIENTOLOGY APPENDIX 2:
A PERSONAL EXERCISE IN ARC

(February, 1975)

1) I'm missing my wife—being separated. My affinity is high, but our communication is nil and my reality (that she really does exist) is diminishing. By writing a letter expressing interest and good feelings, she will become more real to me, and I will get a response—bringing forth communication and enhancing the reality. Result—I won't be missing my wife as much.

2) I desire to learn more about camping and nature. My affinity towards nature is high, but my reality that it really exists gets foggy by spending too much time in society. Just spending some time in nature will increase its reality for me. By reading books on camping, talking to people, and experiencing aspects of the woods I will increase my communication with nature—and will thereby learn more about it.

3) I desire to overcome my jealousy of my wife's relationships with others. One problem might be that I have a low affinity for other people my wife deals with. My interacting with them—even superficially, they'll become more real to me, and by talking meaningfully to them I will experience communication with them and this will increase my affinity for them and hopefully cure my jealousy of my wife's relating to them.

4) I feel attracted to another worker at my job. My affinity is high, and our communication is pretty good, but there's no reality that we have any commonly admitted attraction for one another. By casually remarking that I'm going to the same place that she is, we start to meet at a place other than work, and admit more openly that we do have feelings of attraction for one another—thereby allowing a relationship to develop.

5) I desire to learn how to ride a motor-bike. In this case my reality is high since I see motorbikes everywhere and know they exist. But my affinity is moderate—smudged by fear, and my communication is nil. By sitting on the bike and starting it up a few times, I communicate with it—and gradually reduce my fear,

increasing my affinity, and enabling me to learn how to ride the bike.

6) I asked somebody for directions to the canteen. He said to follow him. This was a communication—and we exchanged a short look into each other's eyes—establishing a small degree of affinity and some reality that we are both here—part of the Church of Scientology.

7) AFTER CLASS PRACTICAL (paraphrased): I am instructed to use the ARC Triangle data on someone I know in order to increase the ARC between this person and me, to write up what I did and observed, and to get it checked out by my supervisor.

SCIENTOLOGY APPENDIX 3:
A PERSONAL EXERCISE IN THE TONE SCALE

(February, 1975)

H-7: (the below-zero parts of the tone scale)

- 0.2: Being Other Bodies: a time in the past when I was too insecure to be myself, and would take on the personalities of those around me.
- 1.0: Punishing Other Bodies: the rapist who savagely rapes and tortures women.
- 1.3: Responsibility As Blame: the above rapist who later on confesses his crime—expressing disgust at himself for his acts.
- 1.5: Controlling Bodies: the army drill sergeant who drills basic-training units in a condescending manner.
- 2.2: Protecting Bodies: the over-protective mother who prevents her children from experiencing anything in life that is dangerous.
- 3.0: Owning Bodies: the executive administrator of a large impersonal corporation.
- 3.5: Approval From Bodies: the child who needs the smile and pat on the head from his/her teacher instead of her/his own self-motivation in order to do an activity.
- 4.0: Needing Bodies: the child who won't stay in school unless his/her mother stays with her/him.

- 8.0: Hiding: the child who fakes being ill and stays in bed all day to escape going to school—which he/she is very afraid of.

M-10:   Observations at restaurant last evening:
wife: "enthusiastically" relating teaching experience.
brother-in-law: "conservatively" listening.
one waitress: feeling "antagonism" towards some other customers.
other waitress: feeling "bored," waiting for us to leave.
people near us: "enthusiastically" engaged in conversation.
person at other table: "conservatively" eating—thinking about something.
another person at table: "bored"—just eating his meal.

H-13:

- My brother-in-law was approaching us, feeling somewhat ill-at-ease but high tone-scale; tone scale of conservatism. I immediately said some personal recollection of his life enthusiastically to him, and he really got into it—and reached the level of enthusiasm.

- I first saw my wife's friend, who was in "covert hostility" toward Scientology, not wanting to talk about it with me. I expressed "antagonism" toward Scientology regarding their time consumption of my day-to-day life, and brought her up to "anger"—freely expressing herself to me. If I had acted "enthusiastically" about Scientology, she would have probably regressed to "fear."

- My wife's neighbor was in the state of "boredom"—at which point I expressed "conservatively" the possibility of her starting a crafts store and brought her up to "conservatism" on the idea. As the talk continued, I became "enthusiastic" about the idea and brought her up the tone scale from conservatism—approaching enthusiasm.

SCIENTOLOGY POSTSCRIPT 1:
SCIENTOLOGY AND FEAR

(August 14, 1978)

It is now one and a half years since I wrote all these essays on Scientology. In this time span I have extended my material on Scientology to the rest of the essays in this book and have put together quite an interesting little piece of work on modern religions, if I do say so myself. I have sent my manuscript to one publisher so far, and got it sent back un-read but with a list of two other suggested publishers to send it to. Now comes the fear. The publicity about Scientology is beginning to become a big news item, as Scientology is being indicted for stealing thousands of government documents. On the other hand, Scientology is conducting lawsuits against various individuals who have written and spoken out against them. The lawsuits are minor compared to some other maneuvers that Scientology has been accused of, such as alleged fires to an individual's personal belongings, continuous harassment with the intent of driving an individual to a mental hospital, spreading false rumors to destroy an individual's reputation, and threats on an individual's life. So what am I to do? I never expected Scientology to embrace my book, but their near Gestapo tactics have exceeded even my own expectations of their reactions to other ex-Scientologists' exposés about their church. Yes—I am afraid. I am afraid for my own life and the lives of my family. I am no martyr. I do not see myself as a statue of stone like Joan of Arc. I rather see myself in my own back yard—pondering the trees and doing theoretical mathematics.

But I also do have my pride and dignity. This book has become such a living part of me. I wish I were able to get back into communication with Scientology and have them accept my book—I would even agree to take out Section 9: *Quotes from L Ron Hubbard*, and the other direct quotes I have used from Hubbard's writings [23]. I really do not like the idea that publishing my book now must become a measure of not only my determination, but my courage. There was a time when I wanted fame and glory, but that time is over with. I realize that I am a writer, and I must be true to my own self. This is why I will proceed with my plans to publish this book—for this reason and none other. Whatever comes from the publishing is superfluous—money, fame, whatever. I always did like a challenge, and I indeed have met my share of personal challenges in my own lifetime. I hope that the challenge of publishing this book will be one that both myself, my family, and my future publisher can successfully meet. It is interesting that for one year, while every week I was teaching my course Psychology, Religion, and Human Values at the Berkeley Adult School—reading most of the essays in this book including all my essays on Scientology [24], I was living one block away from the Berkeley Church of Scientology. I would continuously pass by the church and fight a vague temptation to go in. Eventually I'll be moving back to Boston—which is where I had the bulk of my experiences with Scientology. I know the intensity of these Boston Scientologists when there is something they want. So I shall be prepared for what I will have to deal with when this book will be finally published. But notice I say "when"—not "if."

I initially taught my class at the Berkeley Adult School mainly in order to put Scientology fully into my own phenomenological experience (see the books listed in [66] of Chapter Two Notes for a description of phenomenology) and out of my warped sense of having done something unethical. After having taught this class three times, I have certainly succeeded in my goal. Week after week, I would have stimulating open discussions with my handful of students—about Scientology and all my other religious involvements. Gradually Scientology became part of my own life experience which I finally did incorporate into my self concept. No—I cannot see myself going back to the Boston Church of Scientology to communicate with them. I think that I am past that point. I will probably proceed with my attempts to find a publisher, and then wait for them to strike. All I can say is that when I hear from them I'll be ready: lawyers, police, and even doctors, if necessary. Could you imagine if all the religions that I have written about made a pact to join together to "get" me? Luckily for me, I think they are each too egocentric with their own greatness and uniqueness to ever join together for anything, especially for a communal pact to do away with one small obscure writer. So—do read on and learn about my encounters with some other modern religions as you think critically about both the benefits and the dangers of the modern religions that I have encountered.

Elliot Benjamin: traitor to Scientology

SCIENTOLOGY POSTSCRIPT 2:
SCIENTOLOGY ON TRIAL

(September 23, 1979)

It is now two and a half years since I wrote these essays on Scientology. In the past year I sent these essays to another publisher, and I got back a vehemently destructive critique of my writing style [25]. My determination to publish this book has not been diminished, but I believe that my fear of Scientology has been. The Bay Guardian newspaper of San Francisco has recently put Scientology on their front page—reporting on a courtroom trial in Oregon. It turns out that an ex-Scientologist has sued Scientology for deceitful techniques and unethical behavior and she has won her suit—the court billing Scientology for over two million dollars, and classifying them as a counterfeit religion. The article goes on to describe many of the ideas and practices of Scientology that I have described in my essays, but includes some interesting tidbits about L Ron Hubbard that I did not know about. It turns out that Hubbard has falsified his credentials, and never did graduate from the colleges that he claimed to have graduated from. The article makes it sound like Hubbard is unquestionably nothing more than a super con-artist. The article also says that Scientology is probably doomed, as many more ex-Scientologists will undoubtedly try their own luck in suing Scientology for personal damages, based upon the success of this case in Oregon. All in all, it seems that in ten years the essays that I have written about Scientology will be nothing more than historical data on an extinct modern religion (see the Note below for a description of how incorrect my prediction was). But the question still remains: what positive things can we learn from Hubbard and Scientology? Is it all evil and destructive to human possibilities, or should we carefully bother to extract the wheat from the chaff? As my fear of Scientology is now greatly diminished, I feel much freer in regard to thinking further about the psychological/philosophical analysis of Scientology that I talked about in my essay *The Engram and the Dream* in Chapter 4 above. I wonder if it is perhaps not entirely unfeasible for me to get back into communication with the Boston Church and try to get their cooperation in my venture. What?! No, that would be rather far-fetched. I'm sure that Scientology has not yet admitted defeat. Scientology is an amazingly resourceful animal, and they are not yet ready to beg for mercy. But at any rate, I can no longer say that I am afraid to publish these essays on Scientology. Whether or not I ever develop the interest and ability to extend my material on the concrete ideas of Scientology is an open question right now. But as far as publishing these essays are concerned, I can no longer use fear as an excuse.

NOTE: See my essay *Scientology in the 21st Century* in Chapter 2 for a glimpse of how Scientology has survived and thrived a quarter of a century later. I consider my tri-perspective experiential analysis in Chapter 1 to be a replacement for the philosophical analysis that I had indicated I wanted to write about Scientology. In regard to my determination to publish this book, I am still determined but I have been a bit slow at doing this, as it is now (as of May, 2011) almost thirty three years since I wrote *Postscript 1: Scientology and Fear* and I am finally getting my act together and am formally self-publishing this book and hopefully will have it available on Amazon in a month or two. Oh well, as they say—better late than never!

EXCERPTS FROM
THE MATURATION OF WALTER GOLDMAN

(1980)

CHAPTER 7: THE CHURCH OF SPIRITUAL MECHANICS

Walter's 19th birthday happened to fall on his day off—a Thursday....Who was the real Walter Goldman? For now Walter brought himself through the past three months and saw how stable and normal he had become—successfully holding down a job, and what was more, a meaningful job....Yes—our friend felt like he was definitely growing up, and he felt pretty good about himself. But surely he must not forget those who had helped him on his way, and just as this thought came to him Walter found himself walking over to the commune to pay a visit on Zachary and Linda.

But I'm afraid our story must take another turn right now, for Walter Goldman never got to the commune that day. For on the way over, an attractive young lady came up to him and asked him if he would like to take a free personality test—the lady looking deeply into his eyes. Walter felt his self-control slipping away from him, as he followed the attractive lady two short blocks past University Avenue—into an old building that had a sign saying: Church of Spiritual Mechanics. Walter thought to himself: "Oh no—what am I getting myself into?" But the smile of this attractive young lady was so reassuring, and Walter followed her inside the building. Once inside, Walter was greeted by a super-friendly receptionist, a woman in her early twenties who was not quite as attractive as the lady who had brought Walter in to this church, but was just as captivating in her own way. She sad that Walter should sit down in the room on the left and someone would be with him in a moment. Walter obeyed the order, and found himself sitting in a little room with a long table with chairs around it, staring at this weird picture of a man who looked like a sea captain. The man seemed to be in his late fifties and had a bright twinkle in his eyes. His picture was blown up to take up one whole wall. Walter found the man to not look exceptionally stimulating, as he had sort of a fat face and blubbery cheeks.

When the personality test administrator came in, Walter asked him who the man in the picture was, and his tester replied proudly: "That's Lawrence Hobart—the founder of The Church of Spiritual Mechanics." Walter laughed to himself—"What a dumb looking founder of a church—this spirtual mechanics stuff must be a real joke." But he found himself spending the next hour absorbed in answering some highly sophisticated psychologically probing questions about his personality, his interests, his fears, his desires, etc. Walter had to respect the personality test as being very ingenious and scientific, and he was anxious to get his results. He didn't have to wait long, as another attractive young lady soon came back to him with his test—scored and tabulated. She proceeded to explain to Walter how he had some very severe personality defects—as he was withdrawn and afraid of people and was a generally depressed person. Walter felt struck by these results, as these were things he knew used to be true about himself but he thought that he had made so much progress in changing his personality since he had been in California. But then the attractive young lady looked very very deeply into his eyes and said: "Walter—I would like to help you—and I don't want you to think I'm just a salesperson. A year ago I came into the Church just like you and took a personality test and got very similar results to yours. I was told that I could totally improve my personality by taking a few courses that the Church offers—and I decided to give it a try, as the costs were reasonable enough and what did I have to lose? Within three months I felt like a brand new person—I felt so much more alive and part of the world, so much less shy and more sure of myself. And my personality test gave me real scientific evidence that I was a changed person. It would make me so happy if I could share this miracle with you—if you would try to help yourself the way I did."

All the time this woman was speaking to him, Walter again felt himself drifting into the look in a woman's eyes. There was something so captivating in the way all these people looked at you—something that made you just want to give up all your earthly desires and follow them to outer space. Walter found himself replying: "How much would it cost me?" And the lady smiled brightly and replied: "I'll tell you what. We have a special two week Introductory Course for newcomers who don't know anything about our Church—and right now we have a special half-price rate if you sign up today—which makes it just twenty-five dollars. There's no obligation to do anything after that, and I think you'll learn enough about Spiritual Mechanics through this course to answer all the questions you now have about us. How does that sound to you?" Walter replied: "Hmm. I must say—that sounds quite reasonable. When does your course meet?" The woman answered: "Well—we have two schedules—one is a full-time day schedule—from 9:00 a.m. to 5:00 p.m.—Monday to Friday, and the other is an evening and weekend schedule—Monday to Friday evenings from 6:00 p.m. to 10:00 p.m. plus Saturday and Sunday from 10:00 a.m. to 8:00 p.m." Walter right away exclaimed: "Oh—there's no way I could manage either one of those schedules as I have a nighttime job at Napa State Psychiatric Hospital and I work from 11:00 p.m.. until 7:00 a.m. and I have to sleep until 2:00 p.m. to get enough sleep—and my days off are Wednesday and Thursday." The woman thought a minute and said she would be right back. Sure enough, she came back within a minute, saying: "Walter—I have great news for you. I just spoke to my supervisor, and he said that he's willing to make an exception in your case and you can take the Introductory Course on a part-time schedule over three weeks." Walter thought out loud: "Lets see—if I get up by 3:00, eat lunch and relax a little, I can be here by 5:00—and if I leave by 9:00 I can eat supper and be ready to leave for my job by 10:00. I think I can be here from 5:00 until 9:00 every day except Thursday—which I would like to just hang around my apartment and not do much of anything. Would that be O.K.?" The woman replied: "Well—that would make a total of twenty four hours a week—and seventy-two hours over three weeks. The course is an eighty hour course over two weeks—so how about if we say that last Thursday you come in from 9:00 to 5:00—and we'll call it a compromise?" Walter thought a minute, and felt like he was already getting a special privilege from the Church by getting the course half-price and being able to take it part-time, and that it really wouldn't kill him to spend just one of his days off doing something different—and so he said: "Sure—that sounds fair enough. Can I pay you tomorrow night?" The woman replied: "That will be fine. Would you mind signing an enrollment card so the instructor will be expecting you tomorrow?"

And Walter signed his name and address, still not having a phone out of his own choice, on the blank enrollment card that said: Church of Spiritual Mechanics—Introductory Course. The woman squeezed Walter's arm as she said she'll be looking forward to seeing him tomorrow night, and she focused her dilated eyeballs onto those of Walter. Walter left the Church in quite a stupor of bewilderment and confusion. What had he just done? Twenty-five dollars was no piddling sum of money—even if it was only half-price for their course. Had he been taken for a ride by a few beautiful girls? But then he thought to himself: "Oh well—twenty-five dollars isn't the end of the world either—and I could use a change of pace from Napa State Hospital, and besides—it's my birthday!" So Walter called it a birthday present to himself and decided to go to the Berkeley library and get out a book about the Church of Spiritual Mechanics so he would know what he was getting himself into. But to Walter's disappointment there were no books listed under Church of Spiritual Mechanics in the library, and by this time he was no longer in the mood to visit Zachary and Linda, and so he walked back to his apartment, made himself a supper of hamburgers and spaghetti, and spent the evening watching a western comedy on television.

The next day Walter reported to the Church of Spiritual Mechanics at his agreed upon time of 5:00 p.m. He did not see his personality test administrator, but he was greeted by the same super-friendly receptionist—who gave him a yellow name tag to wear and guided him up the stairs that led to the Introductory Course-room. As Walter walked down the corridor he noticed a long table covered with books about the Church of Spiritual Mechanics—all the books written by Lawrence Hobart. Walter decided to buy one of the books in order to find out more about the Church; the book cost two dollars and came along with a dictionary of Spiritual Mechanics terms that was another dollar. Once upstairs, Walter was greeted by another receptionist who took his twenty-five dollars and gave him a receipt for the Introductory Course, and then brought him over to the Director of Training. The Director of Training was also an attractive young woman, but she struck Walter as possessing a wisdom beyond anything he had observed in a person before. She seemed to know the answer to all questions that he could think of, and she gave this impression to him without trying. For on another level she seemed young and modest, and Walter almost felt like asking her out for a date. The Director of Training introduced herself to Walter as Joanne, and she asked him to sit down opposite her as she wanted to ask him some questions on the Hobart Electrometer—or E-meter. She said the E-meter was a sort of complicated lie-detector machine which recorded a person's thoughts and feelings through sending a harmless stream of electricity through the body. Walter felt right away squeamish but obeyed Joanne as she hooked her eyeballs into his eyes and told him to hold two tin cans that were attached to the E-meter. Then she adjusted some dials on the machine and asked Walter a few straightforward questions, never taking her controlling gaze away from him. She asked: "How did you learn about the Church of Spiritual Mechanics?" "What do you want to gain from the Introductory Course?" "Are you associating with anybody who is antagonistic to the Church of Spiritual Mechanics?" "Have you come to the Church of Spiritual Mechanics with a purpose other than what you have already stated?"

After each question Joanne said "Thank you" very respectfully to Walter's simple earnest answer, and when all her questions were answered she seemed quite satisfied with him, broke her fixed stare and took him into the course-room, introducing him to the course supervisor—a young man in his late twenties. By this time Walter was getting used to the Spiritual Mechanics "stare," as he found the same kind of look in the course supervisor's eyes that he found in the eyes of the receptionist, the personality test administrator, the Director of Training, and the original extremely attractive woman who approached him in the street with the offer of taking a free personality test. The course supervisor proceeded to give him a series of checksheets which had a sequential order of activities—inclusive of readings, writings, demonstrations with clay, etc., that Walter was supposed to go through. He told Walter to find a seat and begin working as rapidly and efficiently as he could, and that if he came upon any words that he didn't understand, he should look them up right away in a dictionary. Walter took a seat beside a group of students who seemed very absorbed in what they were studying, and he began reading his first assignment, which happened to be from the book he already had bought in the downstairs bookstore: *Spiritual Mechanics: Modern Science of Mental Health.*

Walter spent the next four hours reading about the ideas of Lawrence Hobart, and he had to admit that he was very impressed. Hobart talked about the concept of the "engram"—which was a mental image picture of moments of unconsciousness that were stored in the "reactive mind"—an animalistic non-logical mind that was supposedly the cause of all of our later problems in life. Walter found some similarities with the books he had read by Sigmund Freud on psychoanalysis, but he found Hobart's conception of the engram to be far easier to understand and to make more common sense. Walter had to force himself to leave the course-room at 9:00 p.m., for he was really getting into the book he was reading, and he did not want to stop. But he left the Church, and got home at 9:10, made some franks and beans and soup, and got ready to be picked up by Paul Gimsky at 10:00 p.m. Walter was assigned to G-1 West that night, and rather than do any mathematics or psychology, he spent his full three hours of free time continuing to read Lawrence Hobart's book: *Spiritual Mechanics: Modern Science of Mental Health.* By the time Walter came back to the Church the next day, he had finished his first reading assignment and was ready to do his first clay demonstration.

Walter had hardly ever worked with clay before, as he had been a squeamish child who liked to think much more than anything else. But Walter read through Hobart's rationale for clay demonstrations, and it made a lot of sense to him. Hobart said that people needed the proper relationship of mass to significance, and that after thinking about abstract matters for a long time one needed to do something with them in a "solid" form. So Walter was told to make clay sculptures of a real life situation that he saw as an engram. And Walter thought about his own life, and remembered back to being made fun of by other children when he was trying to climb the monkey bars in nursery school. Walter was very struck by this childhood memory, as he never did climb the monkey bars that day, but got down and ran home crying. Could this be an engram? Could this be the source of much of his present day shyness and social withdrawal? Walter spent the next hour making a sculpture in clay of the whole situation, and then he called over the course supervisor who was supposed to see if he could tell what the clay demonstration was by looking at it. The course supervisor looked it over carefully and then said: "This looks to me like a boy being made fun of by other children—and he gets an engram." Walter turned over his slip of paper that described his nursery school experience of an engram; the course supervisor smiled, said "That's a pass," and checked off Walter's checksheet, telling him to move on to the next readings. At the end of the night, Walter was given a sheet of graph paper with his name on it, and a description of a point system which he was supposed to use every evening: three points for every page he read, two points for every word he looked up in a dictionary, twenty-five points for every clay demonstration he did, etc. Walter was supposed to graph his points every night, as that way he, the course supervisor, and anyone who came into the course-room could immediately see the progress of all the students in the course, whose graphs were taped to the walls of the course-room.

Walter found the educational system of the Church of Spiritual Mechanics to be stimulating, exciting, logical, and fun. Walter was making rapid progress, as could be evidenced by the sharp upward curve of his graph, which he was very proud of. By the fourth night, Walter began the section of the checksheet called TRs. Walter had been greatly looking forward to doing this section ever since he started the course, as he was very curious to experience what he saw the other students doing—which was sitting opposite one another and staring into each other's eyes—for ten or fifteen minutes. Walter had never done anything like this before, and although he was afraid of the idea of looking so closely at somebody for so long without saying anything, he felt all tingly at the prospect of being paired up with one of the pretty girls in the course-room.   TRs stood for "Training Routines"—or Training Drills, and were designed as an exercise to help a Spiritual Mechanic "be there." Walter's turn finally came as he was paired up with a middle-aged man who had been in the course a few days longer than him. Walter felt his Adams' apple go into a song and dance, as he had to make some kind of physical adjustment for keeping the rest of his body so rigid, and he was told to try to not even blink his eyes. Walter at first felt embarrassed and silly looking so closely at this man, staring into his eyes. But after a while the embarrassment began to disappear, and even his Adams' apple began to quiet down. For Walter actually found himself relaxing, and being fascinated by the man's eyes—not like he felt with the staff members of the Church, for this man did not have that kind of glued eyeball appeal. But Walter just saw a microcosm of the world in the man's eyes, and soon it was as if he was looking at the man—and not looking at the man at the same time. Walter was experiencing "being there"—and after fifteen minutes the course supervisor came by, checked off Walter's checksheet, and told him to proceed right along.

From then on Walter was told to pair off with somebody as soon as he came into the course-room and do at least fifteen minutes of TRs every night. This soon became Walter's favorite part of the course, especially when he was able to pair himself off with one of the pretty girls in the course-room. For Walter felt some kind of continuity with his intimate experience of love-making with Barbara in the Rocky Mountains. With a girl he was attracted to his imagination took over and he was making love to the girl as he was "being there." Walter had an idea that this was not what he was supposed to be doing when doing TRs, but he decided to let it be his own little secret, and as far as anyone knew—Walter Goldman was a model student in the Introductory Course of the Church of Spiritual Mechanics. Walter absorbed Lawrence Hobart's writings easily and thoughtfully, as he was well used to reading complicated books on philosophy and psychology, and he found Hobart's writings to be so clear, simple, and yet brilliant in its creative explanations of how mankind and the world became as they are. Walter learned about the "tone scale"—which was a mathematical system of discovering the personality of a human being by observing a human being's outer appearance, mannerisms, and gestures. He learned about the "dynamics"—a concentric series of circles which represents self, family, society, etc., in ever wider enclosures. He learned about the "analytical mind"—the perfect machine-like structure that a human being's mind could be when it was discharged of engrams. And he learned that the goal of the Church of Spiritual Mechanics was to relieve the whole planet of all of its engrams, and for everybody to attain the state of "Clear"—a happy and healthy super-human being who no longer has a "reactive mind," and is functioning with a 100 percent accurate analytical mind. Walter learned that the term "Spiritual Mechanic" meant that the process of "clearing" a human being was just a matter of mechanically discharging all the engrams in the reactive mind—in a very scientific and mathematical manner. Walter thought how wonderful it would be if he too could attain the state of "Clear," and he no longer did mathematics and/or psychology or philosophy in his free time at the hospital, as all he was now interested in was progressing in his course at the Church of Spiritual Mechanics and reading more and more of Lawrence Hobart's writings.

Walter finished his course exactly one week early, as he came into the Church on his day off on Thursday to do his last clay demonstration. The course supervisor congratulated him and the whole class applauded as Walter was given his official certificate from the Church of Spiritual Mechanics for completing the Introductory Course. Then he was congratulated by Joanne—the Director of Training, who said she was very impressed with Walter's graph, and that she would love to have him train to be an "auditor"—who were the special Spiritual Mechanics trained to relieve people of their engrams and help a person become Clear—in a scientifically programmed therapeutic process called "auditing." Walter felt quite honored and thanked Joanne, and was led to a small room where he was introduced to another receptionist, but this one having a power in her eyes that was greater than even that of Joanne's—the Director of Training. By this time Walter understood that the controlling dilated pupil stare of a Spiritual Mechanic was achieved through the daily practice of TRs, and that he himself was gaining some of this eyeball control through his TR practice in the Introductory Course. The "heavy TR" receptionist said she would get right to the point. She said that relatively few graduates from the Introductory Course were asked to train to become auditors. She said that the real testing ground was yet to come though, as there was another course from where the cream of the crop were picked for the auditor training course. She said this other course was called the Hobart Qualified Spiritual Mechanic Course, or HQSM. In the same breath she said this course was $175.00, with a 5% discount for full payment in advance. She said this was like asking for "pennies for pearls," for when you are chosen to be an auditor you are promised free auditing in return, and thereby would be able to go "up the bridge, to the state of Clear" for the price of a television set. While she was saying this her TR stare was so penetrating that Walter actually saw himself walking up a bridge, and saw a cheap television set being thrown into the water. And Walter signed the enrollment card for the HQSM course, promising to bring a check for $166.25 (5% discount for full payment in advance) to the Church of Spiritual Mechanics the next evening.

All night at work and all day at home Walter could think only of the state of Clear. Imagine the chance that he, Walter Goldman, had to really become a superior being, transcending the everyday concerns and rat race that he had always hated so much. Walter considered the money he was spending to be a mere trifle for what he would be getting in return, and he withdrew the money from the bank without any conflict—well perhaps he had a slight twitch at his money for the University being reduced a little—but he still had enough for his tuition and this investment was obviously well worth it. Walter only hoped that he would be good enough to pass the HQSM course, as he was scheduled to be in the course for two months, and he agreed to come in on his days off also.

Walter was given a blue name tag this time, and he was treated with a look of mutual respect and understanding from the receptionist, book store officer, and personality test administrator as he made his way to the adjoining course-room with the sign on the door that said "HQSM," and met his course supervisor—a serious looking middle-aged man who immediately gave Walter his checksheet and graph and told him to begin working. The readings for the course were now mostly private writings by Lawrence Hobart that were intended only for Spiritual Mechanics who were studying to eventually become auditors. Walter felt very proud to be amongst this class of twelve students, all of whom had an intelligence and intensity that he fit into very well. For everybody was there to become an auditor, and Walter knew that the competition would be intense and perhaps half of them would make it.

And so Walter Goldman became a bona fide Spiritual Mechanic. He learned how to do "Hard-TRs"—or "Bull-baiting." This consisted of one person staring fixedly into the eyes of another for half an hour, while the other person did everything in his or her power to embarrass and/or make the first person laugh. This was called "pressing someone's buttons," and when someone would move a muscle the partner would say "flunk" and the drill would start all over. This drill was supposed to teach a Spiritual Mechanic to be a super-strong human being who would not flinch at anything. Walter enjoyed these TRs to his very core, as he was easy for co-students to make laugh, as he found himself very relaxed and off-guard with these fine other people. But in a few days the course supervisor came up to him and said that he was not satisfied with Walter's progress in TRs, as this was not a game but was very serious and if he expected to ever graduate from this course and become an auditor he had better start improving real soon. This had a strong effect upon Walter, and our friend soon became very rigid and nearly impossible to be made to flinch no matter what was said to him.

Much bull-baiting was done around the topic of sex. At first Walter was shocked at how often the words "fuck" and "cunt" were used by both men and women, but he soon became immune to even these words, and even gained the ability to be bull-baited by one of the most attractive women in the course and not even move his Adams' apple. Yes—Walter was becoming a superior human being—well at least this is what he was thinking. He was reading some very abstruse writings by Lawrence Hobart, all about spirituality and life after death, and going back to pre-natal experience in the process of auditing and going Clear. At times Walter found himself stopping to think a little about some of these way-out ideas that were becoming increasingly more difficult for him to accept. But then a Spiritual Mechanic staff member would invariably come over and ask him to come over to the E-meter and bring a dictionary along with him. This staff-member, Walter soon learned, was a professional Scientology "word-clearer" and was instructed to find out what his source of confusion was by discovering his "misunderstood word" through a series of questions on the E-meter. At first Walter tried to protest that there were no misunderstood words, and that he only was not totally convinced about some of the spiritual things Lawrence Hobart was talking about. But the word-clearer only matter-of-factly replied: "Thank you for telling me that" and asked Walter: "But just before that—was there a word you didn't understand?" Walter soon found himself picking a word just to get away from the word-clearer and E-meter, and then he had to define the word in all its meanings and use it in a sentence in each one of its meanings; even words like 'but" and "with." By this point Walter started to have his first real doubts about the Church of Spiritual Mechanics, but he had spent nearly $200 already, and he was determined to pass the course and become eligible to train to become an auditor and thereby be eligible to receive auditing himself.

Walter was so determined to finish this course that he continued to read after-hours at work, stopped thinking about what he was reading, proceeded extremely rapidly, became an unflinching expert in his TRs, and successfully graduated from the HQSM course in a record time of five and a half weeks. The same procedure followed this course as followed the Introductory Course; Walter was congratulated by the course supervisor and Director of Training, was given his Hobart Qualified Spiritual Mechanic certificate, got his round of applause from the other students, and was once again taken to the "heavy TR" receptionist. But this time Walter stared right back at the receptionist as she said: "Walter—I'm happy to tell you that your completion of the HQSM course in under six weeks entitles you to a special rate in the Auditor Training Course. You can take the Auditor Training Course for only $500 instead of the ordinary $1,000." Walter broke his stare, and exclaimed: "What!? Five hundred dollars!? Are you crazy? That's over half the money I've saved up for school. There's no way I can give you that money." At which point the "heavy TR" receptionist said sharply: "Walter—you've just broken your TRs. I thought you graduated from HQSM with honors. Nothing should make you flinch—especially not a meager sum of money. We don't want to stop you from going to school—we only want to give you the most precious gift that Lawrence Hobart has given to mankind. I assure you that if you become an auditor your capacity for making money will be increased so much that $500 will seem like what $50 seems like to you now. And don't forget—if you hadn't proven yourself to be such an exceptional student the rate would have been the usual $1,000. What I want you to do is take your time and think it over—and come back to see me when you make up your mind."

Walter apologized to the "heavy TR" receptionist for breaking his TRs and left the church, feeling all twisted up and confused inside. He knew that he should talk to somebody about his dilemma, but he also knew that he was too deeply involved in the Church of Spiritual Mechanics to not train to become an auditor, and that nobody who was not involved in the Church could understand this. When Walter took out $475 (5% off for full payment in advance) from his bank account, he did not have the same essentially non-conflicting feeling he had when he had taken out the money for the HQSM course. For Walter realized that he was now putting off going to the University for another six months. But what choice did he really have? He no longer studied mathematics—nor psychology—nor philosophy. He studied the writings of only one man—Lawrence Hobart, founder of the Church of Spiritual Mechanics. And the next day Walter handed a check for $475 over to the "heavy TR" receptionist, and he proceeded to enter the third course-room, the sign on the front door saying: "Auditor Training Room."

And Walter learned to dilate his pupils wider and wider—as he progressed through the Auditor Training Course. TRs were extended to one hour every evening—always done with bull-baiting, and Walter began to come to the Church at 4:00 instead of 5:00. He learned how to use the Hobart Electrometer, as he had to go through a series of challenging E-meter drills, practicing very thoroughly with other students. By the third week of this course to train auditors, he began to learn the nitty-gritty of what auditing was all about, and he practiced asking precise questions as part of his TR drills; silly questions such as "Do Birds Fly?", "Do Fish Swim?", etc. Walter felt more and more that he was becoming immersed in a strange and bizarre world that was very cut off from the rest of society. He began reading writings by Hobart that stressed how evil and damaging the rest of the world is; i.e. everybody who was not a Spiritual Mechanic and working to achieve the super-human state of Clear. By the end of the third week, Walter was given a sample list of an auditing process—this was known as AP- 1: Auditing Process 1. It consisted of a pre-determined sequence of questions to ask, such as: 1) Locate an incident of another causing you (some emotion). 2) When was it? 3) Move through the incident. 4) What was the duration of the incident? 5) Close your eyes. 6) What do you see?....etc. After each question Walter was supposed to wait for an answer, keep his TRs "in"—meaning "be there" with the person, and then give the person a firm acknowledgement, such as "thank you," or "good," etc. Walter had to simultaneously be working the E-meter with his left hand and taking down notes with his right hand. The person receiving auditing was called a "pre-clear"—or PC, and Walter also got his chance to experience what it is like to receive auditing.

It happened one day when one of the more advanced students on the Auditor Training Course needed a PC to practice on, and since Walter was making satisfactory progress on his course, the course supervisor asked him if he'd like to be a PC. Walter was excited and enthusiastic, and right away said "Yes." The supervisor made out a folder for him, gave it to the student auditor, and then took him to the Auditing Center of the Church. Walter was led into a little cubicle of a room, that consisted of a small table, chairs opposite one another, a wooden divider in the middle, and an E-meter on one side. Soon the student auditor came in, said hello to Walter, sat down on the chair by the E-meter, and then said: "This is the session." He had his TRs in very nicely, as he looked at Walter in the way that Walter now understood so well. Then he said: "We are going to run process AP-1 on 'fear.' The first question is: Locate an incident of another causing you fear." Walter thought about his life, and came up with the incident of climbing the monkey bars as a kid, the other children around him making fun of him; it was the same incident for which he had made a clay demonstration of for an engram in his Introductory Course. The auditor saw that Walter had an incident, and he said "good." The auditor went through the set out series of auditing questions that he was supposed to ask, and Walter found himself reliving, in his mind, the whole experience on the monkey bars as a child. When he was asked to tell what happened, Walter went through the entire incident, and then, all of a sudden, he found himself exclaiming: "Oh God-Wow!" The auditor nearly broke his TRs, but disciplined himself and calmly asked: "What's going on?" And Walter could not speak or communicate at all for another minute, as he traveled with his mind, seeing where he would end up—and then he smiled broadly and said: "I just got this amazing memory—it was the first time I ever smoked marijuana and got stoned—and I went to a children's park and had virtually the same experience I just told you about; except this time no-one made fun of me and I even went down the sliding pond. Now I understand how connected all these things are—drugs, auditing, spiritual mechanics, life, everything." The auditor looked at Walter with a trace of a twinkle in his eye, and said: "Thank you. This is the end of the session."

Walter was bewildered, but he couldn't stop himself from laughing, as it seemed so funny to all of a sudden remember back to getting stoned with Zachary, and before he knew it the auditor was leading him into a room with a sign on the door saying "Auditing Examiner," and Walter was told to sit opposite a woman who was going to check out his auditing session on the E-meter. She smiled in a very friendly way to Walter, asked him to hold the two tin cans, observed his E-meter, and then said: "Your needle is floating." Walter knew that this meant his auditing session was considered to be successful, and he was guided back to his course-room, where he got back to work and read more of Lawrence Hobart's writings that were meant only for auditors in training.

As Walter learned and understood more of what auditing was all about, he realized that he had gotten a major "Cognition" in his auditing process; i.e. a new awareness of life. This was the goal of every auditing session, and a session was run until this end goal was achieved—even if it took five hours for it to work. Walter's session lasted only twenty-five minutes, but with a good auditor this was not at all unusual. Soon Walter was chosen repeatedly to be a PC for a student auditor, as he gained a good reputation of being an easy PC to work with. Walter enjoyed all his auditing sessions, as he found it to be an experience that resembled getting stoned. He always left his auditing session gaining a new realization about his life—"blasting away an engram"—in Spiritual Mechanics language. And he always left feeling light-hearted and silly—like a big burden had been relieved from his life, although he would have preferred to have some time after his session to really take in his new awareness of life, instead of having to always go right back to work in his Spiritual Mechanics studies. And when it was Walter's turn to practice auditing on another PC, he did the best job he could, and his PCs always got a floating needle and left the session feeling like they learned new things about themselves. And so our friend found that he had a real talent in life—that it was perhaps his fate to become an auditor in the Church of Spiritual Mechanics.

However, in all our excitement about the Church of Spiritual Mechanics, we neglected to look at the other main part of Walter's life—his work at Napa State Psychiatric Hospital. Walter was progressing in exemplary fashion in the hierarchy of the Church of Spiritual Mechanics, but little by little his co-workers at Napa State Hospital began to see a real change take place in him. It began by Paul Gimsky noticing that Walter never seemed to do mathematics anymore. All Walter did in his spare time was read books by some guy with a funny sounding name. At first Paul didn't think that much about it, but when the patients who couldn't sleep at 3:00 a.m. and were used to coming over to Walter to rap, stopped coming over to him, Paul began to worry a little. He noticed that Walter seemed to be losing his interest with the patients at the hospital....

CHAPTER 8: ALIENATION

Walter Goldman was becoming more and more confused with each passing day. He progressed in his Auditor Training Course at the Church of Spiritual Mechanics, put in his night's work at Napa State Hospital, got about five or six hours sleep a night, and began his day anew. His days off were now all being spent at the Church, as he was under a lot of pressure to advance in his course, as he was now in the "elite" class of Spiritual Mechanics, and he felt a grave responsibility to work as hard as he possibly could to achieve his goal of becoming an auditor. But Walter was no longer living his own life; every minute of his waking day was spent absorbed in the world of Lawrence Hobart and Spiritual Mechanics, as his time at the hospital he now looked upon as only extended study time for his progression on the Auditor Training Course. Walter no longer even stayed in bed when he awoke to leisurely take in his dreams, as he looked upon this as an indulgent waste of time, when he could use this precious time to get to the Church earlier to progress on his course. And this was even more apparent to him since Lawrence Hobart looked upon dreams as mere idiocy—not worth a second of one's waking time. And so—bit by bit our precious young friend became little more than a spiritual robot, or more precisely—a "Spiritual Mechanic.".…

Walter proceeded to tell his old friend Zachary all about Lawrence Hobart and the Church of Spiritual Mechanics; how he had originally felt the need to elevate himself spiritually, how he was training to become an auditor—to help "clear" the planet, how he was in the process of becoming a super-human being, etc. Zachary listened patiently and calmly to Walter's whole story—which took close to three quarters of an hour, and then quietly said: "Walter—I can see you haven't been wasting your time these past four months. Once again, I'm proud of you—and now I think you're ready to listen to my own story. For fate has prepared you very nicely for what I'm going to say to you. For I—my friend—have been shown the light. I have seen the primal colors, with my third eye. I have tasted of the golden nectar, I have heard the sounds that vibrate above human perception. I have found a direct incarnation of God, and he is inside me this very minute. His name is Guru Mabasanda—and he is a fourteen year old perfect master who has come to this country from India in order to purify all those who will listen to him. I thought I was content with Linda and my music, but only now do I see how shallow my life has been. I have a new family—Walter; a brand new family of devotees of Guru Mabasanda, and once again—just as I opened up your eyes and brought you out to California and to new levels of awareness—I want to give you the gift that I have found. Come with me to the ashram this evening, and let me introduce you to my new family."

Walter was nearly in a state of shock. He saw Zachary and then he didn't see Zachary. There were certain resemblances to the old Zachary—the good-natured laugh and smile—but inside there appeared to Walter to be a heaviness and urgency that he had never seen in his friend before. Zachary had always been so fun-loving and free, such a joy to be with—so full of life and mischief. Walter was scared, and felt his head spinning all across the room. But he managed to reply to his friend: "Wow Zack—that's really something. Right now

I'm already late at my own church, but I'll certainly keep your offer in mind, and I'll come over to talk to you the next chance I get."

And Zachary looked at Walter sweetly—not like a Spiritual Mechanic doing TRs, but rather like a little lamb about to be slaughtered, and he said: "Yes my friend—I will be awaiting your visit and my being able to share the gift of my Guru Mabasanda with you." And then he left.

Walter never did get to the Church that day. For after Zachary left, he had the headache of his life. It was all he could do to get himself back to bed, and he fell into a deep sleep for the next five hours. He awoke with a flood of dreams in his head—for the first time in months. In his dreams he saw this fat fourteen year old Indian kid sitting in a yoga position in a white robe—with swarms of people bowing down to him, Zachary being one of them. Then he saw—on the other side of the Indian kid—Lawrence Hobart sitting on a chair—with his sailor's cap on, saluting to a multitude of people who were bowing down to him, and Walter was one of this crowd. Then he saw Lawrence Hobart and the Indian kid turn around, look at each other, and laugh. But nobody else saw it. Not Zachary, nor one of the followers of the Indian kid nor Lawrence Hobart. Only Walter saw it—and he realized that the whole guru thing was a big sham—whether it was Lawrence Hobart or Guru Mabasanda or anyone else. He started shouting to both crowds to look up and see their two heroes laughing to each other about how they were duping everybody. But Walter was invisible and nobody could hear him either. Everyone just kept their heads bowed down, worshipping their respective idols. And Walter began to cry. He cried for himself, for Zachary, and for the whole human race. At this point, he woke up. The day had gone by, and for the first time in two and a half months Walter had not rushed into the Church of Spiritual Mechanics. He felt unusually relaxed—and he gradually recollected his immense dream, and made himself some franks and beans as he awaited Paul Gimsky's knock on the door to take him to work....

"Ethics" was the part of the Church in which Walter heard many horror stories about and dreaded, but had never experienced before. Ethics was where a Spiritual Mechanic was scrutinized on the E-meter by a trained Ethics Officer, to discover if he or she were harboring any resentment and/or wrong-doings toward the Church. If this were found to be the case, the Spiritual Mechanic was required to make amends through either menial office work, a stiff fine, confiscation of course materials, or if conduct had been especially severe, suspension from the Church for a period of time. Suspension from the Church to one who believes that the Church is his or her only means of spiritual survival is a grave punishment that has sent more than a few Spiritual Mechanics into the confines of a mental hospital. In Walter's case, the Ethics Officer concentrated on why he had missed his study time the day before without bothering to communicate to them, and when Walter described his visit to Zachary and his falling asleep (he made sure to not disclose his dream about Guru Masabanda and Lawrence Hobart) the Ethics Officer decided that Walter was not really a Spiritual Mechanic criminal and he ordered a relatively light sentence: fifteen hours of amends in the filing room. And so Walter spent the next three days at the Church doing filing and collating—giving his mind a much needed rest, and gradually giving himself the time and space he so desperately needed to think objectively about his life. Of course he was still in a very regimented environment, but he began to remember back to what he was like when he first started working at Napa State Hospital; how he had taken such an interest in teaching arithmetic to Bertha, how he put his job on the line for her, how he would rap with patients in the middle of the night, how he organized a ping-pong tournament for G-1 West patients, etc. Then he remembered how he so diligently would study mathematics every night and read various books on psychology and philosophy—the last one being by Carl Jung: *Modern Man in Search of a Soul.* Yes—our friend was beginning to come back to himself, and....

The confusion surrounding his Brooklyn identity vs. his California experiences only added to Walter's already massive state of alienation from all his immediate surroundings. He tried to be more empathic to the patients in his care at Napa State Hospital, but Walter knew that his heart was no longer in it; he was just going through the motions. He continued to progress on his Auditor Training Course at the Church of Spiritual Mechanics and continued to do well and was now nearing completion of the course, but it meant less and less to him as he approached the coveted state of "auditor." In short, our friend was immersed in the crisis of manhood, the crisis of taking on the role of adulthood in our society of challenge as he experienced his 20th year of life on Earth. What is life without meaning? So one can support oneself—so one can progress in intellectual strivings—so one receives respect and admiration from others—is that enough to live for?

Perhaps for most people it is, but it was not enough for our friend Walter Goldman.

During this time of self-doubt and scrutiny a fruitful talk with Zacary would have been so beneficial, but Walter knew this option was no longer open to him. For Zachary belonged to another world now. Perhaps someday he would regain his old friend, but right now Walter knew that interacting with Zachary would be one-sided and dangerous, as Guru Mabasanda was one more headache he did not need. And so our friend was left to himself to figure out how he would get himself out of the mire he was drowning in. Mathematics was still something of the past for Walter, as his mind was so clouded up with his inner turmoil that it was all he could do to keep up enough concentration to finish up his Auditor Training Course at the Church. He no longer studied Spiritual Mechanics either during his free time at the hospital, as he had gotten into the habit of spending his nights watching late movies on television with the other attendants, and occasionally even dozed off—which was a severe violation of hospital rules. Walter was not proud of himself for his "ordinariness," and this only added to his depression. To make matters worse, one day Paul invited Walter to accompany him to a nearby bar before they went to work, and since Paul was now Walter's closest tie to sanity, he agreed. Thus our friend began to rekindle his fondness for beer, as this seemed to be the one thing that could make him forget about his problems, confusions, and anxieties. And so Walter got into the habit of drinking down one or two cans of beer every night when he got home from the Church—before Paul would come to pick him up. How different was Walter's life now from what it had been just a few months ago! Beer, television, naps, adding up to the sum total of "ordinariness."

Each day grew worse for him, as Walter was approaching the last few days of his Auditor Training Course. He had done all the required readings, clay demonstrations, TR drills, and was finishing up his actual auditing requirements. He had audited successfully for over sixty hours, and had one last PC to finish up on. This PC was going through a heavy process on the emotion of "depression," and Walter was trying to give the PC his Cognition. The sessions were difficult and time-consuming, and Walter barely escaped each session with his PC's "floating needle." Walter had to run processes of "When others caused you to be depressed," "When you caused others to be depressed," "When others caused others to be depressed," and "When you caused yourself to be depressed." Each process affected Walter personally, even though he was supposed to be completely objective and uninfluenced by anything a PC says. But "depression" was overtaking Walter like a thunderstorm, and it did not help any to every day have to listen to three or four hours of somebody else's somber stories of depression.

Finally the day came when Walter's PC got his Cognition; Walter's PC got an insight that he had always caused his own depression and that he had the power to change his life in such a way that he would no longer be depressed. Ironically, his PC's Cognition likewise was a Cognition for Walter. It was true—just like his PC, he was causing his own depression by the very situation he had put himself in, and he had the power to change his life in such a way that he would no longer be depressed. But where should he start? What was the first thing to do? Walter did not have long to think about this, as the PC Examiner happily told Walter that his PC had completed the process of "depression" and that Walter had completed his Auditor Training Course. The by now quite familiar and expected process took place; the certificate, the student applause, the congratulations by the course supervisor and the Director of Training, and the visit with the "heavy TR" receptionist. But now—for the first time in a long while--Walter's mind was working rapidly and creatively. He already decided what he would do, and he mustered up all the TRs that were within him, as he prepared himself for his confrontation with the "heavy TR" receptionist. He went into her office, exchanged a ferocious look of silence with her, and began the conversation....

CHAPTER FOUR NOTES

1) Unless otherwise indicated, all the Scientology essays in this chapter were written in January or February of 1977. See my article *Scientology in the 1970s from Various Perspectives in Time* on the Rick Ross website: rickross.com; 2008. This article includes excerpts from some of the Scientology material in this book, inclusive of this first Chapter 4 essay: *On Scientology*.

2) Although I have edited and updated much of my book to reflect current politically correct language, I have decided to leave the bulk of my word usage in Chapter 3 and this chapter on Scientology intact (including my rather liberal use of the word "really"), as it reflects my phenomenological experience of Scientology, est, The Unification Church, Divine Light Mission, and Gurdjieff groups in the 1970s (see the books listed in [66] in Chapter Two Notes for a description of phenomenology); therefore I am keeping the common term "mankind" instead of replacing it with "humankind" as I generally do in my current (2011) writings.

3) I recommend reading both Hubbard's and Freud's seminal books Hubbard, L. R. (1950), *Dianetics: The Modern Science of Modern Health* (see [1] in Chapter One Notes for reference); and Freud, S. (1970), *The Interpretation of Dreams*: New York: Avon Books (original work published 1900).

4) See L. Ron Hubbard (1961), *E-meter Essentials*; Los Angeles: Bridge Publications.

5) Thetan means "spirit" in Scientology language, and Operating Thetan (O.T.) is a Scientology state of consciousness considered to be higher than "Clear."

6) TR Zero Bullbait is an exercise in which Scientologists purposely try to push a fellow Scientologist's "buttons" while coaching TRs in order to help strengthen a Scientologist's intention and resolve, using all kinds of humor, vulnerabilities, and sexual innuendos to do so; see the section in Chapter 4 entitled *Excerpts from "The Maturation of Walter Goldman"* for a vivid account of TR Zero Bullbait taken from my semi-autobiographical novel.

7) There were a few books written by ex-Scientologists exposing Scientology in the early 1970s that I was not aware of at the time; see the books listed in [1] of Chapter One Notes. In more recent times there have been a number of personal accounts written by ex-Scientologists, some of which can be found in the Scientology Personal stories section of the Rick Ross website (www.rickross.com), including my own portrayal (see [1] above).

8) For a semi-autobiographical fictional account of the TR experience, see the section *Excerpts from "The Maturation of Walter Goldman"* in Chapter 4.

9) See any of L. Ron Hubbard's Scientology books, in particular *Scientology: The Fundamentals of Thought* (see [1] of Chapter One Notes for reference).

10) See *Excerpts from "The Maturation of Walter Goldman"* in Chapter 4 for a semi-autobiographical fictional account of the whole experience of getting caught up in Scientology, where the main character Walter Goldman succumbs to the temptations of the body-routers and body-regers in the fictional Church of Scientology that I referred to as The Church of Spiritual Mechanics.

11) A number of L. Ron Hubbard's claimed life achievements have subsequently been determined to be false claims; see the books listed in [1] of Chapter One Notes—in particular Joe Atack's book: *A Piece of Blue Sky: Scientology, Dianetics, and L. Ron Hubbard Exposed* (see [1] in Chapter One Notes for reference).

12) For more information about Dianetic Auditing, see *Dianetic Auditing Process and Concluding Statement* and *Excerpts from "The Maturation Of Walter Goldman"* in Chapter 4.

13) I no longer possess an E-meter, which is probably a good thing in terms of avoiding a Scientology lawsuit.

14) For further descriptions of both Ethics and The Educational System of Scientology, see *Excerpts from "The Maturation of Walter Goldman"* in Chapter 4.

15) See Robert Kaufman's book *Inside Scientology* and Joe Atack's book *A Piece of Blue Sky: Scientology, Dianetics, and L. Ron Hubbard Exposed* (book information in [1] of Chapter One Notes) for illustrations of the incredible science fiction type of imagery of some of these past-life recollections. However, it is

also true that Scientology "backtracking" is quite similar to the practice of past-life therapy, which is currently (2011) accepted in a number of transpersonal psychology circles; see in particular Brain Weiss' popular book *Many Lives, Many Masters* (see [96] in Chapter One Notes for reference).

16) For another popular new age transpersonal psychology version of these ideas, see Stanislav Grof (1985), *Beyond the Brain: Birth, Death, and Transcendence in Psychotherapy*; Albany: State University of New York Press.

17) See Stanislav Grof's book listed in [16] above for a perspective that is quite similar to that of Hubbard and Scientology in regard to a person being able to remember back to his/her birth and prenatal experiences.

18) For a semi-autobiographical fictional account of my experience of both giving and receiving auditing, see *Excerpts from "The Maturation of Walter Goldman"* in Chapter 4.

19) See my essay *Scientology in the 21st Century* in Chapter 2 for a description of some of the more recent flexible course scheduling arrangements that it is possible to make in a Scientology mission (small church) in Maine, from my brief 2002 Scientology excursions.

20) See my essay *A Comparison of Scientology and Judaism* in Chapter 5 for an illustration of some of the similarities of exclusive group sentiment and practices in Scientology and Judaism.

21) See my first Scientology essay in Chapter 4: *On Scientology.*

22) "Hermann" refers to my inspirational literary and philosophical mentor Hermann Hesse; see [3] in Chapter 3 Notes.

23) The referred section of quotes of L. Ron Hubbard have not been included in my book for obvious legal survival reasons.

24) At the time I was teaching my course Psychology, Religion, and Human Values at the Berkeley Adult School, my book consisted essentially of Chapters 3, 4, and 5.

25) See *Letter from a Prospective Publisher* in *Natural Dimension* (see [4] in Chapter Three Notes for reference).

CHAPTER 5

THE PHENOMENON OF RELIGION

A HESSIAN MODEL OF WHY PEOPLE SEEK OUT MODERN RELIGIONS

(12/2/79; updated 5/8/04 and 12/15/10)

Now that I have described my own personal experiences over the past thirty-five years in nineteen modern religions and new age spiritual organizations, it remains to be shown why it is that people flock to these massive organizational spiritual structures in such large numbers. My own basis for understanding other people stems from my ability to understand myself. And my ability to understand myself has been significantly shaped by the writings of the early 20th Century German novelist and poet Hermann Hesse (see [3]. [4], and [32] in Chapter Three Notes). I realize that all that I have gotten out of Hesse's novels is rather unique to myself; i.e. I cannot expect anybody else to be affected in quite the same way that I was affected when I first read one of Hesse's most acclaimed novels, *Demian*, back in 1972 when I was twenty-two years old (see [4] in Chapter Three Notes). But for approximately six years after I read *Demian*, I actually traced my own spiritual development to a sequenced course of twelve Hesse novels which I assigned myself to, each novel corresponding to a unique phase of development which I was going through. The twelve Hesse novels I had read in that six year period were (in the order of my own reading) *Demian, Sidhartha, Steppenwolf, Narcissus and Goldmund, The Glass Bead Game, Rosshalde, The Journey to the East, Peter Camenzund, Beneath the Wheel, Knulp, Gertrude,* and *Strange News from Another Star* [1]. I read all these books sparingly, at very special times. I subsequently read *Klingsor's Last Summer*, and various collections of Hesse's poetry, essays, short stories, and autobiographical writings (see [1] in Chapter Five Notes). Hesse's writings form the core of my own philosophy of Natural Dimension, and are the cornerstone from which I am able to freely and fully experience, understand, and assimilate into my own self-concept all the modern religions/new age spiritual organizations that I have written about in the first four chapters of this book.

Hermann Hesse was a poet searching for beauty in life. His search took him right back into his own self; into his dreams and fantasies, into a striving to merge his unconscious with his conscious, through the forms of art, love, and poetry, in quite a mystical and romantic way. My understanding of Hermann Hesse actually began before I had ever heard of him, with my falling in love at age nineteen with my ex-wife Diane. If it were not for my initial falling in love experience I indeed would have had virtually no understanding whatsoever of Hermann Hesse, and I may have labeled him as merely a second-rate adolescent dreamer, as many mature, sophisticated, successful people have done. But whenever I read Hesse, it truly touched a deeper part of my self. It touched the part of me that had once experienced pure love. This experience transcended my intellectual mind; a mind that was exceedingly analytical and well-developed, overly developed to the point where I could never stop thinking and just relax and "be." After my initial love experience in which I do believe that I had experienced some kind of transcendental form of being, I soon came back down to the level upon which my society was at, which I refer to as "reality" [2]. I subsequently understood my falling in love mystical experience in the context of a "peak experience" as described by Abraham Maslow in books such as *Toward a Psychology of Being* and *The Farther Reaches of Human Nature*, and more recently in the context of the higher levels of consciousness as described by Ken Wilber in books such as *Sex, Ecology, Spirituality*, and *Integral Psychology*, and *One Taste* [3].

In November 2003 I had the privilege of spending five hours with Ken Wilber and others in his Denver, Colorado apartment, including a private incredibly stimulating two hour conversation with him. The way in which I managed to get this special invitation was primarily based upon my work as a mathematician and my mathematics enrichment writings, including my book: *Numberama: Recreational Number Theory in the School System* and my essay *A Group Theoretical Model of Shifts into Higher Levels of Consciousness in Ken Wilber's Integral Theory*, which was inspired by Wilber's own preliminary mathematical ideas of consciousness [4]. However, once all the other people had left and Ken Wilber made it clear that he wanted to dialogue with me in private, it was truly my own initial falling in love experience of over forty years ago that enabled me to hold my own and gain the respect of one of the world's greatest philosophers. For I was able to truly understand Ken Wilber as we mutually agreed upon the importance of fully utilizing and appreciating the joys of thinking, and then transcending thinking in higher realms of experience and consciousness. For Ken Wilber his medium of attaining these higher realms of experience and consciousness has largely been through his yoga practice. I did not go into personal detail about my own initial falling in love experience, but I instead described my rather unique meditative practice of the past twenty-five years, which consists of my spending a few early mornings a week in bed doing pure mathematics for two or threee hours, followed by playing my classical piano repertoire between twenty and forty five minutes [5]. Ken Wilber thoroughly appreciated my mathematics/piano meditative discipline as a valid and authentic meditative practice, and I do believe that this was the most satisfying compliment I have ever received in my life.

However, getting back to my initial higher level consciousness experience of falling in love at age nineteen, something stayed with me as I came back down to the level of reality and society. What stayed with me was a constant reminder that there was more to life than met the eye; more to life than what my family and friends were striving for, more to life than the status symbols that society had always held up before my eyes. And so when two years after my initial love experience I discovered Hermann Hesse through reading *Demian* (which by the way was strongly recommended to me by none other than my boyhood friend Richie—the source of my Divine Light Mission/Guru Maharajji essays in Chapter 3 and the real life Zachary in the excerpts from my semi-autobiographical novel *The Maturation of Walter Goldman* included in Chapter 4), I was brought back to the deep subjective experience of "self" that I had had, and my own path in life was thus found and formed. However, I go into all this in more depth in my book *Natural Dimension* (see [4] in Chapter Three Notes), so let me now attempt to show how all that I have learned from Hermann Hesse can serve to explain why people seek out modern religions and new age spiritual organizations. For the sake of simplicity I will from now on use the term "modern religions" to include both the modern religions I have written about in the 1970s as well as the new age spiritual organizations I have written about in the

1990s and 2000s, as they are representing one and the same thing—just by different names.

I believe that people who seek out modern religions are initially people who are still searching for value and meaning in life (see [9] in Chapter Three Notes). This search has taken them away from the religious indoctrination they were given as children, and has brought them to a new state of readiness and awareness. This new state of readiness and awareness is easy prey for the proselytizing modern religious organizations that have been springing up all around us [6]. We are indeed living in a confused and conflicted and even tormented era—as pointed out by virtually everyone who writes a book about psychology and/or philosophy these days. We are living in a post-existentialist era, or "postmodern" era in Ken Wilber's philosophy [7], where people are returning to what can be described as "God," but in a totally new way. A prime example of this can be seen in more recent times from both Avatar and Conversations with God [8]. The newness of the way fits the time that we are living in, for people wish to break out of long held traditions that no longer serve them as meaningful, and find new ways of being and relating and searching for God. Thus we get our mass dosages of TM (Transcendental Meditation), "Be Here Now," Eastern gurus, chanting, etc. Of course there are still plenty of people who are quite content with following the religions they were brought up on, or in maintaining the scientific-atheistic-evolutionary framework on which they were educated. This is described in colorful fashion by Clare Graves, Christopher Cowan, and Don Beck in their Spiral Dynamics language as being respectively on the blue meme and orange meme of the first tier (see also Ken Wilber's book *A Theory of Everything* and his novel *Boomeritis* for an extensive description of Spiral Dynamics [9]). However, these are not the people I have been writing about, nor are they the people who have fascinated and enticed me so much to experience all that I have in both the 1970s as well as the past decade.

I believe that the people of the modern religions are the potentially more poetic and artistic of our population-at-large, the people who are not satisfied with the archaic dogmas of life and not afraid to venture out on their own in search of something new and stimulating [10]. Every hard-core Scientologist was once a confused and disenchanted renegade from what he or she had previously digested from family, friends, religion, and psychology—all of his/her life. Every est graduate adopted a new hero and a new language and rejected all the faith that he/she had in the past put in others and all the ways in which he/she was previously instructed to find salvation. The followers of Reverend Moon's Unification Church have undergone a very frightening transformation from traditional Christian beliefs to a modern interpretative scheme of the bible mixed with a coming Korean messiah and a label of being an "anti-Christ." The Premis of Guru Maharajji's Divine Light Mission rejected all forms of Judaism, Christianity, Atheism, etc. and pledged themselves to an adolescent perfect master from India who proclaimed to bring everlasting peace to the world in their own lifetimes. The followers of George Gurdjieff's occult school have come from all kinds of philosophies and religions and have adopted an intricately complex philosophy of life which forms the remainder of their own lives as one of constant self-work and struggle where the number one source of knowledge is received from the "teachers" of the Gurdjieff school. And in a very similar way, the followers of Eckankar, Avatar, Conversations with God, A Course in Miracles, Self-Realization Fellowship, and the other modern religions I have written about have all put their faith in their leaders, gurus, channelers, etc. who proclaim new ways of experiencing the higher levels of consciousness to transcend the mind and find source, soul, higher self, God, etc.

As seemingly diverse and separate as all these paths to spiritual salvation appear to be, they hold for me some common unifying threads and patterns. They are all breaking away from the old and helping to form the new. They are all in the process of establishing alternative religious institutions, new religious hierarchies for the 20th & 21th Centuries, which with the exceptions of Gurdjieff, Self-Realization Fellowship, and Reiki, all began in the latter half of the 20th Century (these three exceptions began in the first half of the 20th century). They all have one common originator (i.e. one for each modern religion) who either controls the religious organization directly or else continues to exercise control of his/her followers through his/her own writings and disciples—even after his/her death [11]. Our twelve modern religion originators are L. Ron Hubbard, Werner Erhard, Reverend Moon, Guru Maharajji, George Gurdjieff, Paul Twitchell, Chloe Wordsworth, Neale Donald Walsch, Helen Schucman, Pamarahansa Yogananda, Harry Palmer, and Mikao Usui [12].

What do these twelve ultra-human beings have in common? They all believe that they have the way out for the ordinary human being—the way out from the sleep state that human beings indulge in, and the path to a new land of happiness and bliss, where authentic spirituality will once again reign and humankind will see with new vision. In the most severe guru/disciple modern religions that I have written about, the motto is pretty much "Follow the master and find yourself." I can especially appreciate the strength of this kind of heavyweight invitation, for I myself have gone through my own form of master/disciple relationship with my uniquely personal experience of Hermann Hesse [13]. But luckily for me, there were some keynote differences in my own experiential development under the tutelage of a sacred spiritual and philosophical guide. These difference were the absence of any kind of organizational institution, any rigid set of rules and restrictions and techniques, and any exposure to the powerful effects of mass psychology. These differences were the crucial variables that have enabled me to not fall into the dangerous patterns that I have described in this book. For the invasive presence of the organizational hierarchies, rigid laws, and mass psychology influence that are so prevalent and prominent in many of the modern religions founded by the above modern religions originators are exactly what has the subtle contradictory effects of simultaneously both freeing and enslaving the individual. Nowhere is this more obvious than in the case of the poor Scientologist who after years of struggling has finally gone "Clear," thereby supposedly achieving a state of super-human powers and total freedom, but who now owes thousands of dollars to friends and banks, has a few years left on a contract to work in a Church of Scientology for $30 to $40 a week (in the 1970s), has permanently broken relations with all of his/her previous friends and acquaintances years ago, and has severed his/her ties so abruptly with all of society's non-Scientologist institutions that he/she is no longer capable of existing in any day-to-day life other than that of Scientology [14]. A similar case of what is essentially enslavement can be made for The Unification Church [15], and to a lesser extent most of the other modern religions that I have written about have similar diametrically opposed subtleties as to what they promise the neophyte aspirant and to what actually develops over a few months or years in the organization [16].

The dangers of human beings in masses has always been with us and probably always will be. Whether it is the nine thousand person guest lectures of est guru Werner Erhard or the fifteen thousand person Divine Light Mission festivals of Guru Maharajji or the one thousand person Humanity's Team conferences of God channeler Neale Donald Walsch or the one thousand person thirteen day Wizard festivals of Avatar originator Harry Palmer, there is the very real danger of the individual losing his/her selfhood and allowing him/herself to be swept along in the mass of public feeling. The few people who do not get swept along are too often the Hubbards and Erhards and Walsches and Palmers, branching out and forming their own new massive organizations to sweep thousands of ardent followers along their own paths. It seems almost impossible to break this dangerous pattern. Exceptional human being breeds mass of followers who thereby breeds one non-conformist individualist who thereby breeds another mass of followers...ad infinitum. However, one possibility for a break in this disgustingly boring and dangerous pattern is to skip out on the organization; i.e. to make available to the individual all the newness and vitality that modern religions hold for people—minus the pledge to dissolve one's life in a barrage of herd conformity and new ways of treading through technical bureaucracy and organizational hierarchy. This for me is the beauty which Hermann Hesse presents [17]. Hesse's message is essentially not all that different from the message one gets from the est training, Avatar, or Conversations with God; i.e. "you" are where it's at, all knowledge comes from within, and experience is the key to life. But the only way one can authentically put this vital message into actual practice, from the perspective of Hermann Hesse, is to learn this message as a "free" individual, not spiritually tied to any authority figure nor to any organizational hierarchy. Hesse's message is a call to life, a quest for freedom, and a test of courage. Do not confuse Hermann Hesse's message with the message of the modern religions that I have written about. They may appear similar at first glance, but they are dangerously and deceptively different; as different as night and day, as different as slavery and freedom, and as different as death and life. This then is my Hessian model of why people seek out modern religions.

WHY DO PEOPLE TURN TO RELIGION TO BEGIN WITH? (1979) (WITH 2004 AND 2010 AFTERWORDS)

After examination of why people seek out modern religions, the question still remains as to why people seek out any kind of religion at all. This is a question that anthropologists, psychologists, sociologists, and philosophers have been attempting to answer for many years. Primitive societies have had their shamans and sorcerers and soothsayers, and likewise we have and currently still have our rabbis, priests, ministers, gurus, est trainers, etc. I do not see much difference in the actual phenomenon of people believing in mystical things, be it ancient or modern civilizations. This was all convincingly emphasized by Carl Jung nearly seventy years ago (see [36] in Chapter Three Notes). Jung does not place any more stock in the technology and organized religion of modern society than he does in the primitive rituals and magical explorations for strange occurrences in primitive society (see [36] in Chapter Three Notes). It all brings us back to the basic point that a human being is quite an unusual animal. Humans want something more of life than to merely survive. Humans want to understand what they are all about, why there is an earth and a sun, why they are alive, why they die, etc. These are questions which do not allow for any kind of concrete and certain formulas, but only titillate the imagination of the youthful and the grown-ups who refuse to give up their youthfulness.

I always wondered, as a kid, about if there really were a God and if we had souls that lived on after our bodies died. I am now nearly thirty years old and I still find myself wondering about these very same things, having no more certainty on these matters than I did twenty years ago. But the important point is that I still continue to wonder about these things. I just cannot seem to stop. I do not see what in life is more important than to achieve wisdom as to the true intrinsic nature of life itself. The fact that I do not seem to be getting anywhere does not deter me. I have gotten used to the process. It is this noble process of contemplation that we have inherited from the wisest of our ancestors who have developed their brains sufficiently to bring about the formation of the creature "human being." And it is this same archetypal contemplation and wonderment that has given birth to mankind's need for religion [18]. And of course there is always the possibility that our own biblical God actually did exist and has instructed mankind to worship him/her/it in all of the many diverse religious patterns that have unfolded. Whatever the true explanation is, if indeed there is one at all, it remains that mankind has always needed something more than just bread. Human beings want so badly to find some kind of supernatural explanation for their seemingly absurd existential condition. I know in myself that I have always needed a real Cause that gives my life meaning. This is why I am so infatuated with religion to begin with, from Judaism to Scientology. And how ironic it is that the closest I can come to any kind of real Cause brings me right back to myself—right back to where I started from. This is the message I have gotten from Hermann Hesse, who has successfully refused to be any kind of a guru or to tell anybody else what to think or how to live. Hesse's message is only that the path to wisdom lies within you—somehow or other, and that if there is a God you can only find him/her/it by delving inside yourself and not outside of yourself to any kind of organized religion—be it modern or traditional. With this, Hesse wishes you a "bon voyage," and I second his greetings. We never should stop searching, for this is the essence of being human. I have found my own path of day-to-day life, and I can only hope that this path may some day shed a little more light on the strivings toward ultimate understanding which I myself have longingly undertaken.

2004 AFTERWORD

A quarter of a century later, and virtually nothing more for me to add to this essay. I am now going on fifty-five and am still searching, still retaining my youthfulness to explore the meaning of life. With all my explorations and accumulated knowledge of modern religions, new age spiritual organizations, etc., I once again return to my own self for ultimate knowledge. I search for my own calling, my own true path, and I come up with the deepest me—the philosopher in search of spiritual wisdom. My current mentor is Ken Wilber, who is considered to be one of the world's greatest philosophers (see [13] in Chapter Five Notes). Mind in service of spirit; this to me is Ken Wilber's philosophy in a nutshell. And I do believe that it is my calling to follow in these same footsteps, utilizing my own mind—in all its mathematical dexterity, in service of my own spirit, which is intimately connected to the universal spirit. What is this universal spirit? Prana, Chi, Tao, Reiki energy, Source, a Conversation with God? Perhaps the answer is a resounding "Yes" to all of the above, and much more. Perhaps it all comes back to the Hessian inner voyage that I know so well through my own deepest feelings and inner experiences (see my previous essay *A Hessian Model of Why People Seek Out Modern Religions*). Perhaps this is the most I can say about what spirituality means to me at this time in my life, and consequently why people turn to religion to begin with.

2010 AFTERWORD (12/15/10)

How time flies, as it is now six years later and I am sixty years old. Can I add anything of substance to my 1979 essay to explain why people turn to religion to begin with? Lets see—in the past six years I have managed to publish over fifty articles in psychology and philosophy, and I am currently working on my Ph.D. dissertation which focuses upon an exploration of the possibility of life after death. This exploration is certainly consistent with the gist of what I wrote about over thirty years ago in my preliminary essay, and many of my published articles have reinforced and developed what I have written about in this essay as well as my previous essay: *A Hessian Model of Why People Seek Out Modern Religions*. I'm now actively involved in teaching transpersonal psychology, giving transpersonal talks at conferences, and I do believe I will finally succeed at getting this book formally self-published and available on Amazon. I am continuing to seek the answers to the spiritual questions I have had all my life, and I have maintained my wonderful romantic relationship with my "significant other" Dorothy for the past six years, a true blessing in my life. I have used my mathematical and intellectual abilities to publicly promote and debate, through some of my articles, the merging of spirituality with science, and the validity of psychic and paranormal experiences [19]. But do I actually "know" anything more about these spiritual questions than I did thirty years ago? Well yes and no. I believe I know some things "experientially," but not in a way that I can yet put into words. Perhaps my License Plate Synchronicity articles [20] is the most I can say about all this. At any rate, I am content that I have been true to my deepest self calling to be a genuine philosopher [21], and I have made my peace with the universe by following my calling. And at this point this is about the most I can say.

A COMPARISON OF
SCIENTOLOGY AND JUDAISM

(1980)

Now that I have described my experiences in the 1970s with the Church of Scientology, I feel that it would be interesting for me to look at the similarities and differences that exist in the two religions which have had the most impact upon me in my life—Scientology representing the modern religions, and Judaism representing the traditional religions. In comparing Scientology with Judaism, I feel that I really am making a comparison between what I conceptualize as a generalized form of traditional religions and modern religions. Judaism is a religion that is over four thousand years old, while Scientology is a religion that is at this point thirty years old. What do such seemingly diverse spiritual structures as Judaism and Scientology share together? These questions I will now make an attempt to tackle and make some kind of opening experiential analysis for.

As a boy, I went to an orthodox Jewish school known as a yeshiva. There I studied both Hebrew and English, both American History and Jewish history, and was instructed quite completely in all the rules, regulations, and commandments of my religion. I was taught to both love God and fear God, for God was almighty and always present, watching you every moment of your life. I used to obey certain rituals such as wearing little prayer caps (yamulkahs) on my head, going to shul (synagogue; Jewish temple) on Saturdays, attempting to not ride buses and not turn on lights on the Sabbath, never have milk and meat together, etc. As a boy I did not question any of these commandments, but I felt quite guilty and frightened when I would inevitably break these obligatory rituals. I did not realize that these were only rituals, and that the true God was far more interested in my own private undeveloped thoughts, fantasies, and feelings than in anything I did or did not do in the external world. But I succumbed to the exhortations of my teachers, and I was a good Jewish boy, adept at reading Hebrew and at reciting the designated prayers at the Sabbath service. Then I went to college away from home, and began to think for myself. I studied anthropology and questioned anything and everything that I was taught about the bible. I could not resolve the mounting discrepancies that I was discovering between Judaism and anthropology, and so I gradually stopped keeping the rituals, stopped going to shul, and I soon became a declared atheist.

I imagine that this little story is quite common amongst many young people today, but it was still a tremendously difficult decision for me to make, and one that has had much impact in shaping the remainder of my life. But what is the point of bringing this up now? The point is that after I so bitterly rejected all the dogmas and rituals of the traditional religion which I had been brought up on—like so many other young people have likewise done (see [9] in Chapter Three Notes), I soon found myself getting swept away in just as much rigid dogma and ritual, but this time in a sugar-coated modern religion that was very different on the outside but quite the same on the inside to the traditional religion which I had so emphatically left behind. I find it to be very interesting that so much of the things we are breaking away from in traditional religions are with us just as much or even more so in modern religions. Scientology promised to enable me to achieve total freedom, but bit by bit I discovered that in order to be a Scientologist I had to obey a great many commandments and rituals. I had to keep to a rigid and burdensome daily schedule of courses; I had to promise to not reveal any "inside" information about Scientology to non-Scientologists; I had to agree to go out and try to sell L. Ron Hubbard's literature and bring in people to the Church of Scientology; I had to applaud enthusiastically after each person in Scientology spoke—no matter how I felt about what the person said (a mass psychology technique that has also been adopted by Werner Erhard in est; see my est essays in Chapter 2); I had to submit to regular ethics checking on the E-Meter; I had to write weekly letters of report to "Ron" (L. Ron Hubbard), etc.

In short, I soon found a whole new set of expectations and requirements that left me more enslaved to Scientology than I ever was to Judaism. Whereas Judaism had a connotatively derogatory term they used for non-Jews: "Goy," Scientology had a connotatively derogatory term for non-Scientologists: "Wog" [22]. Just what is it that traps people into leaving something distasteful behind and then going out and discovering this same distasteful thing again—but this time accepting it because it has a new color? Anthropological studies of religion show that themes of heaven and hell, rituals, and sacred practices are very different from culture to culture, depending on such diverse factors as time period, geography, climate, size of population, etc. [23]. Thus this barrage of modern religions that we are witnessing today is actually just another theory of heaven and hell, ritual, and sacred practice. For a Scientologist, heaven means to go Clear and hell means to remain being a Wog. For an est graduate, heaven means to "get it" and hell means to still think there's something to get (see my est essays in Chapter 2). For someone engaged in the Gurdjieff work, heaven means to achieve the states of Number 4 and Number 5 man, while hell means to remain in the ordinary sleep-state characteristic of being a machine-like human being (see my Gurdjieff essays in Chapter 2, and [4] in Chapter One Notes). Just as concepts of heaven and hell are very different in Alaska and Africa, they may be quite different from one religion to another—be it modern or traditional. But the generalized theme of searching for everlasting happiness and avoiding a cursed meaningless existence still remain with the people of the modern religions. The people of the modern religions generally view heaven as not a place in the sky that one goes to after one dies, but as something inside yourself that you strive for your whole life, giving up a lot of freedom along the way. It is this striving that structures their whole lives, as they, like their comrades of the traditional religions, find themselves worshipping a leader outside of their selves and attributing tremendous wisdom and power to this leader, feeling both love and fear for him or her (the leader has generally been male; see [12] in Chapter 5 Notes), as I did for my own Jewish God as a boy.

As far as rituals and sacred practices are concerned, we once again have just made a trade-off of one kind of ritual for another. Instead of reciting the "Shama Yisrael" in shul on Saturday morning—as orthodox Jewish people do, we attend est seminars and "go into our space" and conduct Scientology auditing sessions with the much adored statement: "Your Needle is Floating." These two statements: "Go Into Your Space" and "Your Needle is Floating" have become the ritualized sacred practices of est and Scientology. They have all the meaning to est graduates and Scientologists that the Shama Yisrael has to the Jew and "The Lord is My Savior" has to the Christian. It takes a while to really see the analogues and patterns of similarity and identity that exist between traditional religions and modern religions, but once found these patterns become quite intriguing. For it helps us to understand what our own forefathers went through, thousands of years ago, in adopting the then "modern religion" and its code of ethics, rituals, and commandments. I honestly contend that the current modern religious leaders such as L. Ron Hubbard, Werner Erhard, Reverend Moon, and Guru Maharajji are very similar in nature to the ancient religious leaders such as Bhudda, Jesus, Moses, and Mohammed (see Chapters 3 and 4 for experiential accounts of Scientology, est, Divine Light Mission, and The Unification Church). However, there are also some differences between these ancient and modern religious leaders, as I have described some of the modern manipulative and unethical procedures of certain modern religious leaders in the previous chapters [24]. But much of the difference is only in the passage of time and the eventual evolutionary determination of which religion will survive and which religion will fade. Thus the terms "modern" and "traditional" become much more blurry upon closer examination, and we find that Judaism and Scientology are in basic substance not very much different at all. For me, I have gone through my own evolutionary forms of being both a Jew and a Scientologist, and I am left only with a greater and wider appreciation of the interconnections of all religions in all times.

THE ALTERNATIVE SEDER

(April 14, 1979)

If one does not believe in God, can one still be considered religious? If one does not believe in God, can one still be considered Jewish? These are questions that Diane and I are trying with great effort to answer, for we want to know how to bring up our future children in regard to religion in general and Judaism in particular.

One week out of the year Jews observe the holiday of Passover, which commemorates the victory of the Jews over their enslavement by the Egyptians, thousands of years ago. There are many rituals that are performed during this holiday, such as the eating of matzoh (unleavened bread), bitter herbs, eggs dipped in salt water, the telling of the story of the struggle and miracle of the freeing of the Jews, etc. There is a sequenced order of structured activities that is called a "seder," and there are books called "hagadas" which describe explicitly everything in detail that should be done during a seder, which usually lasts a few hours. I have been going to seders ever since I was a kid, and I used to look forward to them and have a lot of fun, as the children love all the wine, the symbolic food, the telling of the story, and especially the hiding of the "aphikomen" (some matzoh that is wrapped up and hidden somewhere in the house). So Passover certainly seems to be a pleasant Jewish holiday for both children and adults alike. Then why do I have a problem with it?

I guess it's my nearly pathologically intense need for total truth and honesty in life. The Passover Seder attributes the victory of the Jews over the Egyptians totally to God. God is portrayed in a traditional patriarchal fashion, with the pronoun "he" ascribed to God. Is this nothing more than just a harmless little representation of biblical poetry—as my friend Isaac seems to think? I have a hunch that the effect of this personification of God on children is neither little nor harmless. I have only to look at my own Jewish upbringing as a child, which I have described somewhat in my previous essay: *A Comparison of Scientology and Judaism*. From my present vantage point I grew up warped, as I believed in many things that I now consider nonsense. And these were not just harmless childish fairy tales that I believed in. These were things like a powerful and awesome God who knew everything I was thinking, had total control of my life, could send me to heaven or hell, etc. [25]. I was burdened by many commandments and compulsions which left me with much guilt and sin whenever I inevitably broke them. Is this how I want my own child to grow up? No, it is not. I do not reject my Jewish ancestry; I am proud of it. The Jews as a people are where I came from, and rejecting them is rejecting a part of myself. This point is especially important to stress after the unspeakable tragedy of Hitler's massacre of six million Jews. So I have no intention of ever rejecting the culture and history of Judaism that is ingrained in me. What then am I rejecting? I am rejecting Judaism as a religion. Why? Because I do not believe in God—at least not the kind of God that is portrayed in the Old Testament and the Passover Seder.

Perhaps it is time that I get to the title of this essay: *The Alternative Seder*. My conflicts about religion and Judaism have been with me for over fifteen years. But it is only actually within the last year or two that I have actively been trying to resolve them, for this is when the prospect of being a father has become real to me. About two years ago I started going to a "Habarrah" group—which is a Jewish group of young people who get together weekly to explore their feelings about Judaism and discuss various points about Judaism that are of concern to them. I participated for about five or six weeks, and then I left the group. The reason I left the group is that the points about Judaism that were of concern to me were not of concern to the others. What was of concern to me was how could one call oneself Jewish if one did not believe in God? I tried to generate discussions on this point, but it just did not go anywhere, as the favorite topics were the plight of the Israeli Jews, the observance and non-observance of rituals, the celebrating of Hanukkah as opposed to Christmas, etc. All these things, to my mind, should have come after the primary point was dealt with; and the primary point is: what is Judaism to begin with? All this was especially frustrating to me as I was currently teaching my course Psychology, Religion, and HumanValues at the Berkeley Adult School, and I was used to deep, open-ended, exploratory discussions about religion for two and a half hours every week. I wanted so badly to have this same kind of experience with my own Jewish people. But it didn't work. And neither did our alternative seder work the night before last.

Diane and I invited our closest Jewish friends in California to our house for a "different" kind of seder—Mike and Paula, Isaac, Debbie, Tina, and a few others. I read my previous essay *Why Do People Turn to Religion to Begin With?* and I hoped it would spark the kind of discussion my essays used to spark at the Berkeley Adult School. From the very start, everybody seemed to feel nervous and awkward, including myself. People were in a hurry to start eating and begin the ceremony and rituals that they came for. One friend termed my proposed discussions as "after-dinner conversation." I left for a little while to take home an elderly person from my old senior citizen psychology class at the Senior Center of Berkeley who I invited to our seder at the last minute, and when I came back (about 10:45 p.m.) the only people who were left were Mike and Paula, and Isaac—who was on his way out. This was especially significant to me, as the night before, Diane and I were at a traditional seder with friends of Mike and Paula that lasted until 1:00 in the morning. Our alternative seder was a real bomb, and I felt embarrassed, disappointed, and depressed. Diane and I did appreciate the interest that Mike and Paula showed in our attempt, but it was still quite a failure to us.

I feel like I am trying to move a dead horse. Perhaps I am playing in a ballpark that is just too small for me. I want open-ended discussions about religion and about God, and I want my children to grow up with this around them. If I cannot find this in Judaism then I shall reject Judaism as a religion. There is a line from the song If I Were a Rich Man from the Jewish musical play Fiddler on the Roof that says "If I were rich I'd have the time that I lack to discuss the holy books with the rabbis seven hours every day." All I am asking for is one hour a year. My form of holy books is our own selves, but the meaning is essentially the same. Judaism used to be a pure and beautiful religion where people lived their beliefs in God. If this were still the case, I believe there would be much fewer modern religions and cults around us today [26]. I feel an emotional bond whenever I listen to Fiddler on the Roof, and it is more than just the culture and the people that are having an impact upon me. It is the sincerity of the people's belief in God. I originally rejected Judaism back when I was still in my teens, largely because I felt that people who prayed to God in shul were not deep-down sincere in their praying. They said the designated passages, performed the rituals, but I saw them as lacking the personal depth and total self-involvement that I believe my ancestral Jews in Europe had, and which I must admit that the followers of the modern religions of the Divine Light Mission, The Unification Church, and even Scientology do have. But I have not yet given up on Judaism as a religion. I have been thrown back for a loss, but this is something in life that I have grown very used to. I almost look forward to the challenge. But this year's alternative seder was very disappointing to me. The next big Jewish holiday coming up is Hanukkah. If at first you don't succeed, try again. If then you don't succeed, try again... [27].

THE ALTERNATIVE BRISS

(September 5, 1981; written a week before my son was born, in preparation for my speech at his circumcision)

I would like to take this opportunity to express my feelings in regard to the inauguration of my son: Jeremy Richard Benjamin, into the religion of Judaism. In a few minutes he shall be circumcised—and thereby take his place in the honorable tradition of being a Jewish male. And yet sadly I must confess that the Jewish authorities who guard my religion do not consider that my son Jeremy is truly having a briss (circumcision). Why is this? Because he is not being circumcised on the eighth day of his life, as the bible dictates, but he is being circumcised a few days after that. So let me try to explain my reasons for this blasphemous action on the part of the boy's father.

You see, I, Elliot Benjamin, live in a natural dimension. Few people who know me know what this really means. But my son shall know this well. It means that I live according to my authentic feelings, i.e. according to what feels right to me. When it comes to a decision that Diane and I must come to together, we go into our space and don't come out of it until we are in agreement about what the right thing to do is. So far we have always come out of our space with a united decision. And when it came to deciding upon what to do in regard to a briss, my sense of what felt right and wrong for me deep inside told me that I needed to experience being a father, just with Diane and Jeremy, before opening up our world to others (this strong feeling had much to do with the fact that Diane needed to spend nearly a week in the hospital after her difficult Caesarian birth). Who can understand this? Certainly not the Jewish authorities who one-by-one informed us that this was making the briss totally meaningless as far as the Jewish religion was concerned. But I was firm and unyielding—and Diane decided to find out if any "moile" (authorized Jewish circumciser) would indeed perform a briss after the eighth day. To our relief we have found a moile who agrees to do this—and he is highly recommended to us from a well-known reformed rabbi in Boston.

So we have made the necessary arrangements—and here we all are, awaiting this emotionally charged coming event. For me, the fact that I have experienced the time that I needed to have alone with Diane and Jeremy, has given me the strength and readiness to feel like what will now take place is indeed a religious experience. For me, it is verily Jeremy's inauguration into Judaism, whereas if I had submitted to the Jewish authorities and had it done on the eighth day as they demanded, then it would have been a meaningless ritual to me. Diane and I both feel strongly that we want Jeremy to have Jewish roots, and this is something very significant to us. We feel that by making a few personal changes to meet our human needs we are more able to fully embrace the Jewish religion. And now we are happy that you are all here—sharing our joy and pride of being new parents with us. To those who don't understand us, I pray that in the future you will at least be willing to accept us—for we now have the well-being of a third one to consider.

We'll never change—we're too religious. Let's have the briss.

AN EXISTENTIALIST VIEW OF RELIGION

(1979)

After I gave up my orthodox Jewish beliefs plus my faith and security in God while in college, I was left hanging in mid-air. There I was, nineteen years old, all the religious beliefs that had been so important to me all of my life were gone, and I actually saw no reason why I should live—or even why anyone else should live, for that matter. My approach to this gloomy state of mind was purely philosophical. I felt that without some kind of logical explanation for why I was alive and why there was a universe, life was utterly meaningless. And so I became acquainted with existentialist literature and I at least found some comradeship and support in this depressing and difficult revelation that I was coming to. For some reason or other, I felt a lift whenever I would read an existentialist passage about the absurdity of life, being authentic and real, anxiety and dread, preoccupation with death, etc. My own father had died before I was two years old, and I had grown up with both an intrigue and a fear towards death. I was always conscious of having only one parent, and so it felt good to me hearing other people talk openly about death in the middle of the day.

But it was more than just these things that attracted me to existentialists. Here I was, in my 19th year of life, already practically an old man, with virtually no experience whatsoever in the work-a-day world of reality/society. I desperately needed some stable adults whom I could respect and model myself after. I did not find them in any of my teachers or family. But when reading existentialist literature, there I found grown-up adults who were voicing the same inner torments that I myself was living through. I gradually became familiar with the names of Sartre, Heidegger, Marcel, Kierkegaard, Nietzsche, etc. I learned that there was religious existentialism and atheistic existentialism, and also depressing existentialism and optimistic existentialism. I eventually resolved to choose the path of atheistic optimistic existentialism, and I did a major paper for a Utopias course in which I formed a plan for the perfect society, a blending of existentialism, pure love (based upon Eric Fromm's *The Art of Loving*) and utopian socialism (based upon the work of Martin Buber) [28]. I enjoyed doing this paper immensely, as by this time I had fallen in love with Diane, and I was told by my Utopias course professor that it was one of the best papers he had ever received. And so I escaped from the dangerous predicament that I had found myself in, and instead of getting drowned in the mire of existentialism, I made use of existentialism to embark on a new road of life, where I would eventually once again find myself in the throngs of the forces of religion.

But just what is the existentialist view of religion? As there are many different existentialist viewpoints, I prefer to give my own existential analysis of religion, so here goes:

Human beings are animals—thrown into this universe by utter chance, having no rhyme nor reason nor logical explanation for their existence. There is no such thing as God. God in only a term that scared people have made up because they lacked the courage to face up to the absurdity and meaninglessness of life. They also made up the concepts of a soul and life after death. It is so obvious, from a study of anthropology and evolution, that mankind's heritage is from the ape only. There is no mystical basis for morality and ethics, and therefore the one thing which a human being does possess is freedom. All we can say about human beings is that they exist. Existence precedes essence—and a human being is free to form whatever he or she will become; free to live—or not to live. There is no inherent reason to do either, and there is no God to judge us after we die. Life is just something to do—or not to do. Real life consists of authentic realizations of the nothingness of life, and comes about within infrequent episodes of intense anxiety and dread. People engage in social conversation in order to pass the time of day and put veils over their faces. They are afraid to really look at one another and to admit the sad and terrible truth. That there is nothing—there always was nothing—and there always will be nothing. Religion is nothing more than mankind's invention. Religion is an extension of primitive human beings' preoccupation with magic to explain things they could not understand. "Real" human beings have no need of religion. They are capable and willing to face life without any crutches and to look right into the eye of the void in which they live. Let me be real, and let me be free. Let me live, and let me die—all at my own choosing.

This then is my own existential analysis of religion. However, although at one time in my life I held to this view completely, the picture is far too complex for me now to limit myself to any one viewpoint of religion. There is a place for the Jewish part of me, the Existentialist part of me, and even the Scientologist part of me. May they all learn to live with one another in harmony and peace—and to aid one another in their constant quest for unity.

UNITARIANISM

(December 2, 1979)

As I approach my 30th birthday, I know that deep down inside I am still groping for the answers that will shed light on the riddle of life for me. I hardly ever have the time to think deeply and ponder about the nature of life the way I did during the few years when I experienced the modern religions I have written about in the previous chapters of this book. But yet I have retained the essential core of my being—spirituality. Whenever I would earn the right to a free moment, I once again would regain my child's consciousness of complete ignorance as to the nature and meaning of the world and life. Sure, I believe that I know as much as any human being alive about the nature and meaning of the world and life, but as far as absolute and real knowledge is concerned, I am completely ignorant. At least I realize it, and I therefore am comfortable in calling myself an agnostic. But how shall I bring up my children? Do I want them to have a life without religion, i.e. without what I consider to be the true meaning of what religion essentially is? [29]. Certainly not. In the face of society's immorality and machination of life and destruction of human freedom and dignity, I want my children to have a fellowship that will help them grow into real live human beings, fully able to enjoy life and all the happiness that life has to offer [30]. I feel that I have been especially lucky and fortunate to have risen above my destructive education and socialization process, but I do not want to take this chance on my children. I want them to have the help and support that I feel a child deserves to have in growing up in a community of caring human beings. Therefore I have decided to become a member of the Unitarian-Universalist Church of the World. I have finally found a religion where I can be myself, where I can continue to explore and search for the meaning of life—without any dogmas and doctrines, where I can relate to the people in my congregation, and where my children will learn what I believe the real meaning of religion is all about. I thank Arnold Westwood—minister of the Amherst, Massachusetts Unitarian-Universalist Church, and Nancy Foster, the president of the Church, for opening my eyes that there is indeed a place for me in the world of organized religion. If you are interested in finding out more about Unitarianism, I highly recommend the book: *Challenge of a Liberal Faith* by George Marshall [31].

Even though I know it is my inner path to become a Unitarian, it is still not at all an easy step for me to take. I feel much conflict and guilt over officially rejecting Judaism. But I know that this process has long been under way and this is only my official stamp of leave-taking (see my previous Chapter 5 essays: *The Alternative Seder* and *The Alternative Briss*). The problem is that for me, Judaism is no longer a religion; it is a culture. Since I do not believe in God (I do not disbelieve either) and I do not take the bible seriously, and I do not believe that there is a chosen people, I can no longer say that my religion is Judaism—no matter how sugar-coated and attractive the reform and liberal Jews try to make Judaism look [32]. My quest for pure religion and truth is as strong as it ever was—and I need people who are truly open and searching themselves. I have found this for the first time of my life in the Unitarian Meetinghouse in Amherst, Massachusetts. There, all of me is accepted and actually treasured—the authentic spiritual searcher, the philosopher, the humanist, the social activist, the intellectual, the musician, and the romanticist [33]. Just as Natural Dimension Teaching Agency is my way of making peace with the world of work [34], Unitarian-Universalism is my way of making peace with the world of religion.

NOTE: My son Jeremy had a naming ceremony in the Unitarian-Universalist church I belonged to in 1981, around the same time that he had his Jewish briss, and during his ceremony I read this essay on Unitarianism. When I moved to the Boston area and subsequently to Maine in 1985, I tried going to my local Unitarian churches, but the feeling was not the same for me and I soon ended my personal religious association with Unitarianism. For more information about how this process occurred for me, see my next essay: *More Recent Spiritual Organization Involvement: 2004/2005 (with 2008 and 2010 Afterwords)*.

MORE RECENT SPIRITUAL ORGANIZATION INVOLVEMENT: 2004/2005 (WITH 2008 AND 2010 AFTERWORDS)

As it is now nearly a quarter of a century since I wrote my previous essay *Unitarianism*, I would like to briefly describe my current perspective in finding spiritual organizations where I feel emotionally safe and comfortable, intellectually stimulated, and spiritually nourished. As I described in the Note at the end of my previous essay *Unitarianism*, when my son Jeremy was born in 1981 we actually had both a Jewish briss for him (see my earlier Chapter 5 essay *The Alternative Briss*) as well as a naming ceremony in the Unitarian-Universalist meetinghouse in Amherst. At this naming ceremony I read my essay *Unitarianism*, and my son is in actuality both a Jew and a Unitarian. For the next two years I continued to find fellowship and support in our Unitarian community; however once we moved away from Amherst and closer to Boston this kind of Unitarian fellowship did not continue for me. The Unitarian Church I visited closer to Boston did not have this same feeling of comfort and belonging for me, and I had a similar experience when I visited my local Unitarian church in Maine in 1985. Consequently I soon stopped identifying myself as a Unitarian. There was no particular upset or red flag about Unitarianism for me; it just became apparent to me that Unitarianism was not the religion that could continue to satisfy my needs.

For the next thirteen years of my life I had very little involvement in any kind of religion at all, modern or traditional. When Jeremy was bar-mitzvahed in the Jewish religion at age thirteen in 1994, I read the last essay in Chapter 5 of this book: *Life Without Religion?* to my son in front of our congregation in Maine, as my father to son blessing. This essay describes my spiritual agnostic perspective on religion, and the essence of my spiritual viewpoint of always continuing to wonder and search for the meaning of life and the universe. A year later, in 1995, I encountered the modern religion of Eckankar, and my second stage of modern religions exploration was initiated, which I called "new age spiritual explorations," as described in Chapter 2. In 1997 I discovered Neopaganism through attending the five day Starwood festival in New York State, and I brought my sixteen year old son Jeremy with me to Starwood in 1998, which is described in my essay *On Neopaganism* in Chapter 2. I have now been to six Starwood festivals and my son Jeremy has been to five Starwood festivals with me. We both do indeed consider ourselves to be Neopagans, and in two weeks we will be at the Rites of Spring Pagan festival in Massachusetts, as the timing of Starwood does not work for Jeremy this summer [35].

As far as Judaism is concerned, in 2002 a spiritual friend of mine recommended Michael Lerner's book *Spirit Matters* (see [87] in Chapter One Notes) to me, and I was intrigued by the open-minded, exploring, spiritual, idealistic, questioning nature of Michael Lerner's view of Judaism, as established in his Tikkun organization. I immediately joined Tikkun, and in 2002 I attended a one day Tikkun conference in Boston, which was led by Michael Lerner and intellectual Black leader Cornell West, who was the co-chair of Tikkun, along with Michael Lerner [36]. The conference took place at a Methodist church, and it was truly an enlightening exposure to me that Judaism could indeed have a deeper authentic spiritual perspective to it than what I had previously encountered in my interactions with Jewish people, which I have written about in my earlier essay in this chapter: *The Alternative Seder*. In the summer of 2003 I participated in the political/spiritual five day Tikkun conference in Washington D.C., at which I actually was part of a handful of Mainers who spoke to our congressmen and senators concerning a peaceful resolution of the Israeli/ Palestinian conflict. But for me, I had reached my limit of how much political involvement I was comfortable with [37], and also how much Jewish concentration I was comfortable with as well (although it should be noted that approximately 25% of Tikkun members are not Jewish). However, I am still left with a much greater appreciation of how I can identify myself with being Jewish while still retaining the essential qualities of who I am.

Retaining the essential qualities of who I am in relation to an idealistic organization is no easy task, and I suspect that what is appropriate is for me to have at least two or three organizations that I am able to comfortably relate to for this purpose. Neopaganism definitely continues to play an important role in my life, but there is not much room there for the intensely philosophical part of me that wrote this book. The Tikkun version of Judaism does enable me to retain the parts of me that strongly identify with my Jewish upbringing—while searching for authentic spirituality, but the strongly Jewish political focus of Tikkun is not who I am in my deepest feeling of self. Who am I in my deepest feeling of self? Well anyone who has read this book knows quite well that in my deepest feeling of self I am a "philosopher." I'm a "Natural Dimension" philosopher, but without going into the actual essays in my book *Natural Dimension* (see [4] in Chapter Three Notes), I will simply say that for me, philosophy is the use of the mind in service of the spirit. In all my readings and exposures in life, nowhere have I encountered this mind in service of spirit in a more extraordinarily brilliant and authentic and comprehensive manner than in the writings of Ken Wilber [38]. I feel this sense of being mentored by Ken Wilber in a similar way that I felt my calling to be mentored by Hermann Hesse in my twenties (see [38] in Chapter Five Notes). However, there are two very significant differences here, aside from the fact that I am no longer in my twenties, but in my fifties. The differences are that Ken Wilber is very much alive, and Ken Wilber has formed an idealistic organization to fully put his philosophy into practice; this organization is called Integral Institute (see [1] in Chapter One Notes).

I think at this point I will hold off on saying any more about Ken Wilber and Integral Institute, for I have no doubt that I will be writing essays in the near future about my current involvement with Ken Wilber and Integral Institute that will be included in my book *Natural Dimension* (see [13] in Chapter Five Notes). Actually I have already written two essays regarding my proposal to form an Integral Mathematics component of Integral Institute, which Ken Wilber was quite receptive to as a future possibility, in my private two hour meeting with him in his Denver apartment in November 2003 [39]. I am considering attending the five day Integral Consciousness seminar in Colorado this summer in which Ken Wilber will be leading a number of the sessions, and I am visiting the Dean of Students of Integral University, Lynne Feldman, in a few weeks at her home in New Jersey [40]. My involvement with Ken Wilber and Integral Institute is just beginning, but I have optimistic high hopes for finding a true community of like-minded people where I will be able to actualize the deepest me—i.e. the natural dimension philosopher me who uses his mind in service of spirit (see [13] in Chapter Five Notes).

I will briefly mention my current involvement in the International Cultic Studies Association (ICSA), a cults awareness organization founded in 1979, which changed its name from American Family & Friends in 2005 (see the section on ICSA in Chapter 1). I am extremely impressed with the intellectual leaders of this organization as well as with the courage and sincerity of the people who are moving beyond their involvements in cultish spiritual organizations. Having recently attended their annual summer conference in Edmonton, Canada in 2004, I have become familiar with and/or met some of the cults awareness originators and current well-known authors and leaders, including Robert Jay Lifton, Margaret Singer, Janja Lalich, Michael Langone, Steve Kent, Nori Muster, Steve Hassan, etc. [41]. I am optimistic that condensed versions of my *Conversations with God* and *Avatar* essays in Chapter 1 of this book will be eventually published in ICSA's Cultic Studies Review journal [42]. I am seriously considering offering a post-cult involvement spiritual practice workshop at a future ICSA conference, and I have even discussed this prospect as part of a panel with Steve Hassan and Nori Muster [43]. It has been wonderful for me to finally "come out" as an ex-Scientologist at this conference, although it has also been challenging for me to witness the Scientologists attending this conference, possibly in order to gain information to use against anyone who voices criticisms of Scientology [44]. But at this point in time, it appears that I have found a rich source of support and stimulation and interest in my exploration of modern religions in the context of my philosophy of Natural Dimension, and I look forward to continuing and extending my involvement with this remarkable cults awareness organization [45].

Finally, I would like to very briefly mention that I am in the midst of a current new age spiritual organization exploration, and this is the Human Awareness Institute, abbreviated as HAI. Primarily HAI is a "sensitivity, touch, and spirituality" kind of organization, where the bottom line is extending "love" between people in sensual ways. I attended my first HAI workshop two months ago, and I have been to a few HAI get-togethers and joined some HAI internet correspondence lists. I feel from HAI a sense of community and support and challenge to extend my personal boundaries in growing ways, but it is much too soon for me to make any definitive statements about HAI at this time [46].

2008 AFTERWORD

My involvement in the International Cultic Studies Association has productively continued, as I did give my post-cult spirituality workshop at the 2006 ICSA conference in Denver, and I will be giving a talk on the boundaries between cultic and benign in spiritual groups at the upcoming 2008 ICSA conference in Philadelphia (see [45] in Chapter Five Notes). I currently have three articles published in the ICSA E-Newsletter, on Conversations With God, Avatar, and Integral Institute (see Appendix: Part 1 for my article on Integral Institute). My involvement in Tikkun has not continued, although I had an interesting personal correspondence with Michael Lerner which involved him condescendingly criticizing an article I had submitted to Tikkun on the topic of war and madness, which subsequently got published in two Peace magazines [47]. I expressed to Michael Lerner my disappointment at his harsh tone and lack of humanistic sensitivity to me, and he actually apologized to me and asked for my forgiveness.

My involvement in Ken Wilber's Integral Institute has not continued, though I did get my *Integral Mathematics* article published in the AQAL journal of Integral Institute (see [39] in Chapter Five Notes), and I now have fourteen articles published on Frank Visser's

Integral World website [48] (see my Integral Institute article in Appendix: Part 1 for more information about my current experiential perspective on Ken Wilber and Integral Institute). I have described my involvement in the Human Awareness Institute (HAI) as well as my recent involvements with Acceptance and Commitment Therapy (ACT) and The Center For Creative Consciousness (CCC) in my article on the boundaries between cultic, benign, and beneficial in spiritual groups (see Appendix: Part 2 (see [45] in Chapter Five Notes). But in regard to my current involvement in any kind of spiritual organization, I have gone full circle with humanistic psychology as I have recently re-entered the Ph.D. Psychology program at Saybrook Graduate School and Research Center, which is the former Humanistic Psychology Institute that I was a doctoral student at thirty one years ago. I am doing a concentration in Consciousness and Spirituality, and I have a prospective doctoral dissertation committee consisting of worldwide experts in the fields of parapsychology and dreams, creativity and mental health/disturbance, and clinical hypnosis; respectively Stanley Krippner, Ruth Richards, and Claire Frederick. My tentative dissertation topic is an experiential study of the phenomenon of life after death, primarily through my experiences via personal sessions with mediums at a Spiritualist summer camp in Maine which is part of the Church of Spiritualism (see Appendix: Part 3, and [45] in Chapter Five Notes), which I believe is a most fitting culmination of my study of modern religions.

2010 AFTERWORD (12/16/10)

As 2010 soon comes to its close and I think about what I can say about anything new in my involvement with spiritual organizations since my 2008 Afterword, the dominant organization that comes to my mind is Saybrook, which has recently once again changed its name, this time to Saybrook University. I am currently a doctoral candidate at Saybrook and working on my Ph.D.dissertation, whose title is now *An Experiential Exploration of the Possibility of Life after Death Through the Ostensible Communications of Mediums with Deceased Persons*. I have been through many trials and tribulations at Saybrook, but also a great deal of personal growth and extremely stimulating mentoring, most especially from well-known parapsychologist Stanley Krippner (see [103] in Chapter One Notes for a book reference for Stanley Krippner), who I am greatly indebted to and is still serving on my dissertation committee. After a great deal of personal challenge to retain the essence of my researcher-based experiential research approach for my Saybrook dissertation, an approach which I have described extensively in this book, I believe that I will now be successful in this endeavor. The chairperson of my dissertation committee is now Jeanne Achterberg, well known for her innovative work in transpersonal imagery and healing (see [56] in Chapter Two Notes). The third person on my committee is now Bob McAndrews, who was my research instructor in four courses at Saybrook, and who introduced me to autoethnography, an experiential research method that is at the crux of how I have researched all the modern religions in this book (see [21] in Introduction Notes). I have also greatly benefited from the involvement of my dissertation consultant Genie Palmer from the Institute for Transpersonal Psychology, for her wonderful support and stimulation to focus upon Rosemary Anderson's transpersonal research method of Intuitive Inquiry [49]. Through these research methods of autoethnography and intuitive inquiry I have able to finally justify my researcher-based experiential research approach in my dissertation proposal to my dissertation committee's satisfaction [50].

Saybrook is a graduate school and it is a bit of a stretch to consider it as a spiritual organization, although it can be argued there is a bona fide spiritual component to Saybrook in its strong focus upon transpersonal studies. But perhaps the most relevant new spiritual organization that I have recently become involved with is the Association for Spirituality and Paranormal Studies (ASPSI) (recommended to me by Stanley Krippner). I attended the four day ASPSI workshop in Pennsylvania in 2010, and I will be returning to give a talk in June, 2011 related to my dissertation, and to take part on a panel to discuss the relationship of "psychic phenomena to the afterlife." This is a new involvement for me and it is premature for me to say much about ASPSI at this point, but I have every reason to believe that my involvement with ASPSI will become a very fruitful venture for me, both personally and professionally.

In regard to my involvements with ICSA and Tikkun, they are both continuing. I am planning on submitting an article about my work with mediums at a Spiritualist camp to the ICSA E-Newsletter, and submitting a proposal to give a talk about this at an ICSA conference (see [45] in Chapter 5 Notes). I have had further dialogue with Rabbi Michael Lerner of Tikkun, regarding his posting my article *Integrated Politics: Libertarians and Liberals Against the War in Afghanistan* on the Tikkun blog. At this point in time I am still waiting to find out if Michael Lerner decides to post my article, which will be the determining factor on whether or not I continue my involvement with Tikkun and its related organization: The Network of Spiritual Progressives, although it appears that this is not going to happen [51]. I have been to two more weekend workshops at Kripalu, one with Julia Cameron and one with Cyndi Dale (see [94] in Chapter One Notes). I continue to have good feelings about Kripalu, and I still believe that Kripalu is a beneficial spiritual organization without cult dangers (see Chapter 1; and see Endnote [6] in Appendix: Part 4 for a February, 2013 update on my current involvements).

LIFE WITHOUT RELIGION?

(1980)

Can human life have meaning without religion? It all depends upon how loosely we define religion to be. If we define religion to be the pursuit of wisdom about the universe in which we live, then I contend that it is indeed necessary for human life to have religion in order for there to be any real meaning to life (see [52] in Chapter Five Notes). But it is absolutely necessary that we do not mistake the term "wisdom" for scientific knowledge. Wisdom means knowledge plus experience, or the achievement of some kind of state of being or awareness where life is viewed from a viewpoint that is different from the more ordinary state of being. Who achieves wisdom? One who achieves wisdom knows it within him/herself and has no need to publicize it to others. Perhaps wisdom is merely the state of remaining in touch with your own essence as you grow older, while those around you lose themselves in the temptations—both materialistic and non-materialistic—around them. This does not necessarily mean to cut yourself off from the level of reality which exists in our society-at-large, but it does mean to have some kind of an alternative set of personal reality, which I would like to call "religion" (see [52] in Chapter Five Notes).

So now we are talking about two levels of reality—one in society and one that is entirely your own. It seems that as one reaches successive enlargements of one's own personal self through the socialization mechanisms of society, one becomes exposed to more and more ideas and ways of being. Sooner or later, you must face the crucial question of whether to become a follower or a leader. It seems likely that an in-between path does not really exist, except perhaps in our mental institutions (see [10] in Chapter Five Notes). Is it possible for us all to be leaders? To be first off, leaders of our own private selves, is what I see to be the only pure form of religion. It is so crucial to be a leader of your own private self and not a follower of someone else's private self. Given this definition of religion, it seems that too many of us are leading a life without religion while living under a pretense of being devout followers of some prestigious traditional or modern religious leader.

I believe that all people have the capabilities within themselves to find their own religious values and beliefs, and perhaps the only kind of justifiable leadership is that kind of leadership which encourages people to find their own values and beliefs—and thereby find their own personal religion. It is exactly this kind of leadership which I have found in Hermann Hesse, and which many other people have found through the humanistic psychology of Carl Rogers and Abraham Maslow [53]. God is just a name; a name that we give to that which we do not know about. It can equally well be called First Cause or Primal Energy or even Life. It doesn't matter what you call it but it does matter how you approach it. As philosopher and humanistic psychologist Sam Keen described in *To a Dancing God* and Ken Dytchwald described in *Bodymind* [54], we cannot ever expect to find God or First Cause or Primal Energy without developing our total selves—body, mind, and spiritual essence, for they are all in actuality one interconnecting mechanism. This integration of all our potentialities is fully necessary in order to truly lead a life with religion. It is not sufficient to put on your fine clothing and go to church on Sunday or synagogue on Saturday. Nor is it sufficient to shave your head and chant Hare Krishna or attend weekly est seminars.. We need a total organismic integration—an integration from within. I've already said enough about the dangers of organized religion and mass psychology to not reiterate on this point any longer, but I do want to emphasize that I believe that in spite of all the grave violations which have been committed in the name of religion, there is still a pure form of religion that exists, and life without this pure form of religion is indeed quite intolerable and meaningless—at least to me.

CHAPTER FIVE NOTES

1) See [3], [4], and [32] of Chapter Three Notes for references to *Steppenwolf, Siddhartha, Demian,* and *The Journey to the East.* For the rest of the Hermann Hesse books, see *Magister Ludi*; New York: Bantam, 1969 (also published as *The Glass Bead Game*); *Beneath the Wheel*; New York: Bantam, 1953; the following Hesse books were published by Farrar Straus and Giloux (New York): *Peter Camenzind,* 1969; *Klingsor's Last Summer,* 1971 (original work published 1920); *Gertrude,* 1955; *Rosshalde,* 1970 (original work published 1914); *Knulp,* 1976 (original work published 1915); *Strange News from Another Star,* 1975 (original work published 1919); *Stories of Five Decades,* 1954; *Reflections,* 1971; *Autobiographical Writings,* 1950; and *Crisis,* 1975 (original work published 1928).

2) My contextual meaning of "reality" is actually the opposite meaning of the term "reality" that Ken Wilber wrote about in his groundbreaking first book *The Spectrum of Consciousness*; Wheaton, Illinois: Quest Books, 1977, which he wrote at the age of twenty-three. For a description of my contextual meaning of "reality," see the section entitled *The Reality Argument* in my article: *Art and Mental Disturbance*; Journal of Humanistic Psychology, Vol. 48, No. 1, pp. 61-88.

3) See Abraham Maslow's books *Toward a Psychology of Being*; Princeton, NJ: Van Nostrand, 1962; and *The Farther Reaches of Human Nature*; New York: Penguin Books, 1971. See Ken Wilber's books in [2] of Introduction Notes, and his book *One Taste: The Journals of Ken Wilber*; Boston: Shambhala, 1994.

4) See [45] of Chapter Two Notes for my *Numberama* book reference; www.integralscience website for my Mathematical Group Theory and Consciousnes essay; www.integralinstitute for Ken Wilber's essay *A Calculus of Indigenous Perspectives*; and Ken Wilber (2006), *Integral Spirituality*; Boston: Shambhala.

5) For many years my classical piano repertoire lasted for forty-five minutes, but the past few years I have reduced my piano practice to twenty minutes; however, these twenty minutes has the same

meditative effect for me as my initially longer piano playing time frame.

6)   See any of the books listed in [13] of Introduction Notes for further developments along these lines.

7)   See any of Ken Wilber's books listed in [2] of Introduction Notes.

8)   See my Avatar and Conversations with God essays in Chapter 2 and related material in Chapter 1.

9)   See Don Beck & Chris Cowan (1996), *Spiral Dynamics: Managing Values, Leadership, and Change*; London: Blackwell; and Ken Wilber's books *A Theory of Everything* and *Boomeritis* (see [97] in Chapter One Notes).

10) This theme has similarities to the main theme in my articles *The Artistic Theory of Psychology* in Inner Tapestry Journal, August, 2006 and *An Artistic View of Mental Disturbance* on the Integral World website, 2006 (www.integralworld.net); this theme is more fully expressed in my article: *Art and Mental Disturbance* (see [2] in Chapter Five Notes for reference) and especially in my self-published book: *Art and Mental Disturbance*; Swanville, Maine: Natural Dimension Publications, 2006.

11) For our present purposes I am not including the additional five new age spiritual organizations that I listed in Chapter 1, all of which I have characterized as either "Favorable" or "Neutral" in regard to being beneficial or having cult dangers, with the exception of Twelve Step Support Groups, which I have characterized as having mild cult dangers.

12) Note that with two exceptions, Chloe Wordsworth, the originator of Holographic Repatterning, and Helen Schucman, the originator of A Course in Miracles, all the originators of the modern religions that I have written about are male.

13) See my essay *On Transcendence of Hermann Hesse* in my book *Natural Dimension* (see [4] in Chapter Three Notes for reference). See also my article *On Ken Wilber's Integral Institute: An Experiential Analysis* in Appendix: Part 1; this article was published in 2006 on the Integral World website (www.integralworld.net) and in 2007 in the ICSA E-Newsletter (Vol. 6, No. 2).

14) See any of the books and material critical of Scientology in [1] in Chapter One Notes; my Scientology material in Chapter 4 and in particular *Excerpts from "The Maturation of Walter Goldman"*; and my article *Scientology in the 1970s from Various Perspectives in Time* (see [1] in Chapter Four Notes for reference).

15) See the book listed in [23] in Chapter One Notes, and my Unification Church essays in Chapter 2.

16) For a more recent example of this see my Avatar essays in Chapter 2.

17) See Hesse's books listed in [3], [4], and [32] in Chapter Three Notes, and [1] in Chapter Five Notes.

18) See for example Huston Smith's (1991) book *The World's Religions* (see [59] in Chapter Two Notes for reference).

19) See my 2010 Integral World (www.integralworld.net) following articles: *Integrated Metaphysical Reflections*; *License Plate Synchronicity*; *Perhaps Science and Spirituality Can Go Together: A Response to the Lanes*; *Synchronicity and Mathematics: A Response to the Lanes; Agnosticism, Probability, and Apophenia*; *Open Minds, License Plates, and Respectful Communications*; see also my article: *An Experiential Analysis of Mediums and Life after Death* in The Ground of Faith Journal (http:// homepages.ihug.co.nz/~thegroundoffiath/issues)

20) See my articles *License Plate Synchronicity, Synchronicity and Mathematics, Agnosticism, Probability, and Apophenia*, and *Open Minds, License Plates, and Respectful Communications* (see [19] above for references).

21) See the section *A Natural Dimension of Philosophy* in my article *My Conception of Integral* (see [15] in Introduction Notes for reference).

22) "Wog" is an abbreviation for the condescending term "wise old gentleman." See the Scientology section in Chapter 1.

23) See for example R. F. Weir, (Editor) (1982), *The religious world: Communities of Faith*: New York: Macmillan; and Huston Smith (1991), *The World's Religions* (see [59] in Chapter Two Notes for reference.

24) See also Geoffrey Falk's book *Stripping the Gurus* (see [9] in Introduction Notes for reference).

25) See my previous Chapter 5 essay: *A Comparison of Scientology and Judaism.*

26) See my earlier Chapter 5 essay: *A Hessian Model of Why People Seek Out Modern Religions.*

27) As it turned out, I never did host another alternative seder, nor any kind of alternative celebration of a different Jewish holiday.

28) See Eric Fromm (1962), *The Art of Loving*; New York: Harper Colophon; and Martin Buber (1976), *I and Thou*; New York: Simon & Schuster.

29) See my last essay in this book: *Life Without Religion?*

30) See my essay that follows: *More Recent Spiritual Organization Involvement: 2004/2005 (with 2008 and 2010 Afterwords)*; my essay *On Neopaganism* in Chapter 2; and my article *Neopagan Rituals: An Experiential Account* (see [82] in Chapter One Notes for reference) for a description of how I have in actuality found a special kind of spiritual community that I have shared with my son Jeremy.

31) See George N. Marshall (1966), *Challenge of a Liberal Faith*; Boston: Church of the Larger Fellowship, Unitarian Universalist.

32) See my earlier Chapter 5 essays: *The Alternative Seder* and *The Alternative Briss*; see my Chapter 5 essay that follows: *More Recent Spiritual Organization Involvement: 2004/2005 (with 2008 and 2010 Afterwords)* for a brief description of my currently somewhat different perspective of Judaism based upon my experiences with Michael Lerner's Tikkun organization; see also the Tikkun section in Chapter 1.

33) See the Note at the end of my *Unitarianism* essay, and my essay that follows: *More Recent Spiritual Organization Involvement: 2004/2005 (with 2008 and 2010 Afterwords)* for brief descriptions of how my high hopes for Unitarianism did not work out, and of the more recent and current philosophical and spiritual organizations with which I feel my deepest bonds and sense of shared purpose.

34) Natural Dimension Teaching Agency was the original name of my non-profit corporation that I founded in 1980 in Massachusetts for the purpose of forming an alternative community mental health and learning center. My non-profit corporation is still legally in existence and now has the name

Natural Dimension Learning Center. Although as a business enterprise Natural Dimension has never been successful in the day-to-day world, I somehow enjoy keeping the corporation legally in existence, as it reflects a concrete version of my philosophical basis of Natural Dimension, as evidenced by the name I have given to publish this book: Natural Dimension Publications.

35) Rites of Spring in 2004 was the last Pagan festival that I attended with my son Jeremy, but in 2012 I returned to the Starwood Pagan festival with my "significant other" Dorothy (see Endnote [6] in Appendix; Part 4).

36) See [88], [90], and [91] in the Chapter 1 Notes, and the section on Tikkun in Chapter 1 for more information about Tikkun.

37) In the past few years I have become more involved in expressing my political views through a series of articles based upon my initial articles *Madness and War* and *Obama and the War in Afghanistan*, that have been published from 2007 through 2013 on the Integral World website (www.integralworld.net), the Peace and Justice Center of Easter Maine Newsletter (www.peacectr.org), La Voz de Esperanza (www. esperanzacenter.org), and Newpeople: Pittsburgh's Peace and Justice Center (www. thomasmertoncenter.org).

38) See the 2004 Afterword to my earlier Chapter 5 essay *Why Do People Turn to Religion to Begin With?* and see in particular my article *On Ken Wilber's Integral Institute: An Experiential Analysis* in Appendix: Part 1 (see [13] in Chapter Five Notes for references for this article) for my 2004 perspective on Wilber, which is essentially the same as my current (February, 2013) perspective.

39) See my essays *Integral Mathematics: An AQAL Approach* on the Integral World website, 2006 (www. integralworld.net) and in AQAL journal, 2007, Vol. 4, No. 1 (www.integralinstitute.org); and *A Mathematical Group Theoretical Model of Shifts into Higher Levels of Consciousness in Ken Wilber's Integral Theory* on the Integral Science website, 2005 (www.integralscience.org).

40) Although I did have a tremendously stimulating and interesting visit with Lynn Feldman, I decided to not attend the five day

Integral Institute seminar with Ken Wilber due to the extreme expense of the seminar.

41) See the books listed in [13] of Introduction Notes.

42) My condensed Conversations with God essay has been published in the 2004 ICSA E-Newsletter, and my condensed Avatar essay has been published in the 2005 ICSA E-Newsletter; see [61] and [67] in Chapter One Notes.

43) As it turned out, I facilitated a panel workshop entitled "Coming Back to Religion and Spirituality after Spiritual Abuse" at the 2006 ICSA conference in Denver, with fellow panelists Nori Muster and Nancy Michelon.

44) I published an article highly critical of Scientology in 2008 on the Rick Ross website (see [1] in Chapter Four Notes for reference) which is essentially a collection of some of my essays in Chapter 4 of this book, but thus far it appears that I am not well known enough as a Scientology critic to deserve censure or attack from Scientology.

45) I gave a talk at the 2008 ICSA workshop in Philadelphia which was the basis for my article *The Boundaries between Cultic, Benign, and Beneficial in Five Spiritual Groups* that is included in this book as Appendix: Part 2, and was published in the ICSA E-Newsletter, 2008, Vol. 7, No. 3. I have not been active in ICSA since that time, due primarily to my heavy involvement with my Ph.D. psychology program at Saybrook University, but I have kept up my ICSA membership, I still have good associations with ICSA, and I have submitted an article to ICSA based upon my experiential analysis of the cult dangers of Temple Heights Spiritualist Camp (see Appendix: Part 3), and I may submit a proposal to give a talk related to my article at an ICSA workshop in the near future.

46) I have continued my association with HAI for the past eight years, solely through my participation in the HAI Intimacy online network. This was initially both satisfying and meaningful to me, although I have had increasingly less interest in this network and I currently have virtually no more contact with HAI in any context; see the section on HAI in my article: *The Boundaries Between Cultic, Benign, and Beneficial in Five Spiritual Groups* in Appendix: Part 2 (see [45] above for the reference for this

article). As can be seen from my aforementioned article, I rated HAI in the "Favorable" category in my experiential analysis. Furthermore, I recommended to my transpersonal psychology student from Akamai University that she attend a HAI Introductory workshop, which she did and found to be extremely meaningful; she is considering following this up by attending a Level 1 HAI workshop. Although there may be some relatively minor cultish aspects to HAI, on the whole I believe there's much that is worthwhile and valuable in HAI, and worth pursuing.

47)   See [91] in Chapter One Notes and [37] in Chapter Five Notes.

48)   As of Febrary, 2013, I have forty-five articles published on Frank Visser's Integral World website (www.integralworld.net).

49)   See Rosemary Anderson (1998), *Intuitive Inquiry: A Transpersonal Approach*, in William Braud & Rosemary Anderson, *Transpersonal Research Methods for the Social Sciences: Honoring Human Experiences* (pp. 69-94); Thousand Oaks, CA: Sage; and Rosemary Anderson (2004). *Intuitive Inquiry: An Epistemology of the Heart for Scientific Inquiry*; The Humanistic Psychologist, Vol. 32, No. 4, pp. 307-341.

50)   My dissertation proposal is an "intersubjective" experiential research proposal that combines my own experiences in working with mediums, along with the "ostensible" communications of mediums with the deceased, as portrayed to me through my semi-structured interviews with mediums, for the purpose of exploring the possibility of life after death.

51)   See [91] in Chapter One Notes.

52)   I read this essay to my son Jeremy in 1994 during his bar mitzvah ceremony in Maine, in place of the traditional bar mitvah blessing Jewish fathers are supposed to say to their sons. See my Chapter Five essays *The Alternative Seder* and *The Alternative Briss* for an account of my earlier breaks with Jewish Tradition.

53)   See Carl Rogers (1961), *On Becoming a Person*; Boston: Houghton Mifflin; and Abraham Maslows's books listed in [3] of Chapter Five Notes.

54)   See Sam Keen (1991), *To a Dancing God*; San Francisco: Harper; and Ken Dytchwald (1986), *Bodymind*; Los Angeles: Tarcher; see also George Leonard & Michael Murphy, *The Life We are Given* (see [7] in Introduction Notes for reference).

APPENDIX

PART 1: ON KEN WILBER'S INTEGRAL INSTITUTE: AN EXPERIENTIAL ANALYSIS

(7/6/06)

NOTE: This article is essentially the same as the published versions of my article (see [13] in Chapter Five Notes), aside from some minor editorial revisions, and the correction of the mathematical error I had previously made in rounding off the Bonewits Cult Danger average scores to two decimal places instead of one decimal place.

There have been a number of people who have expressed serious concerns and misgivings regarding the cult dangers of philosopher Ken Wilber's Integral Institute [1]. These criticisms have generally focused upon Wilber's harsh comments regarding scholars who disagree with his philosophical opinions. This has become increasingly more evident with the development of the Integral Institute website and especially Wilber's private website (c.f. [1], [2]), although there was quite an uproar in academic circles in the aftermath of Wilber's aggressive and condescending remarks toward his critics in both his 1995 acclaimed book *Sex, Ecology, Spirituality* and his 2003 novel *Boomeritis* [3]. To Wilber's credit he did engage in highly constructive dialogue early on with his most prominent academic critics, as evidenced in the 1997 book *Ken Wilber in Dialogue* [4]. However, it appears that with the launching and development of Integral Institute over the past few years, there is now sufficient reason to examine both the asserted guru characteristics of Ken Wilber as well as cult dangers of Integral Institute. It is with this purpose in mind that I wish to apply the tri-perspective experiential analysis that I have described in my *Modern Religions* book [5] to Ken Wilber's Integral Institute.

Since my tri-perspective experiential analysis is based primarily upon my own experience, a crucial component for me is my private encounter with Ken Wilber in his Denver apartment in November, 2003. Having read a number of his books and having felt tremendous impact and inspiration from his writings [6], I decided to fly out to Denver to meet personally with Wilber, as my mathematical interests in applying my pure mathematical knowledge to his Integral theory of shifts in levels of consciousness (c.f. [7]) gained me this invitation. I spent five or six hours with Wilber in his Denver apartment, including two hours of private conversation. The openness, friendliness, graciousness, intellectual stimulation, and respect he showed me was totally amazing to me, especially since at that time I had not published any of my writings on spirituality and cults or anything for that matter aside from mathematics or mathematics education. I left my visit with Wilber feeling both privileged and "high," determined to develop myself as a philosopher in my own right, get my philosophical articles on spirituality and cults published, and to become involved with Integral Institute.

The main purpose of Integral Institute was to engage people in incorporating the "four quadrants" of individual (intrinsic), behavioral (extrinsic), cultural, and social in all academic endeavors: including psychology, sociology, religion, politics, education, medicine, law, philosophy, anthropology, etc. [8]. At that time there was also a strong interplay between Integral theory and Spiral Dynamics theory [9] to describe the levels of consciousness of both the individual and society, and an emphasis upon people becoming "second tier" thinkers, which essentially means to be able to take the viewpoints of all different levels of consciousness. Although recently Wilber has become much more detached from Spiral Dynamics as a comprehensive descriptive Integral theory model [10], at the time of my meeting Wilber I was aware (deep down) of a kind of Us vs. Them dichotomy regarding the "highest" levels of consciousness of the "truly Integral" thinkers. However, I must admit that I was so taken with all the Ken Wilber books I had read and my meeting with Wilber himself, that I did not pay much conscious attention to this preliminary note to me of personal warning.

Soon after my meeting with Wilber, I visited with one of the higher-ups in Integral Institute in New Jersey, and I became even more "high," as this person was extremely complimentary of my ideas and self-published books, and led me to believe that there was a place for me in the upper echelons of the Integral Institute organization. My Group Theory/Consciousness article got accepted in Allan Combs' Integral Consciousness domain of Integral Institute (c.f. [7]), and after a while I worked through the complications and challenges to have my Integral Mathematics article accepted in Integral Institute's prestigious AQAL (All Quadrants All Levels; the crux of Integral theory) internet journal. This process included a long phone editing conversation with Ken Wilber himself (and his close associates), and Ken even made arrangements to send me his Integral Spirituality manuscript (c.f. [10]) before it was officially published; needless to say I was quite honored.

However, while all this excitement and upward mobility and potential for me progressing in Integral Institute was happening, there were some simultaneous contradictory events going on that were starting to trouble me. For one, the costs of Wilber's seminars that began in 2004 were extremely expensive, even surpassing the costs of the Avatar workshops which I had written about with serious concerns regarding its cultish characteristics (c.f. [5], [11]). I had in fact made the initial agreement to attend this seminar in Colorado but changed my mind after taking stock of my realistic finances and discussing the matter with an old friend who had participated with me in an evening event in New York City to discuss the work of both Ken Wilber and controversial guru Andrew Cohen [12]. But even more troubling to me, I knew that Wilber had had some kind of disciple relationship with a far more controversial guru who I had no doubt was extremely dangerous to his followers. I am speaking of Adi Da, originally known as Free John amongst other names [13], [14], and I had broached discussing Wilber's involvement with him in our private meeting. Wilber explained to me that his involvement with Adi Da was minimal, and that he broke away when Adi Da became more bizarre and suspicious (c.f. [14]). However, I did not think that Wilber had a real understanding of the cult dangers of certain new age spiritual organizations, especially Scientology, both from my meeting with him as well as from his writings in the book *Spiritual Choices* [15], which he personally recommended that I read, and from his exuberant previous praise of Adi Da (c.f. [13], [14]).

But these were still relatively minor incidents to me, until I attended the 2004 ICSA (International Cultic Studies Association) [16] conference in Edmonton, Canada. At various times during this conference I found myself talking openly about the wonderful spiritual development possible in Integral Institute without any cult dangers, but some of the responses I got from people were less than enthusiastic and were actually rather disconcerting. In addition, as I found myself raving about Ken Wilber to my personal friends and acquaintances, I could see that people were taking me with a grain of salt, looking at me as if I were following a "guru." I was gradually becoming aware that there were strong viewpoints in both Ken Wilber and Integral Institute that I did not completely agree with, including Wilber's openness to gurus, appreciation of diverse and contradictory political stances, his condescending attack on the "new age" sensitivity people, rather viscously referred to by Wilber as the "Mean Green Meme" [17], as well as the extremely complicated and abstruse development of his four quadrants into eight "zones," where each quadrant has an inner and outer "perspective," as outlined in the *Integral Spirituality* manuscript that I had been privileged to read (c.f. [10]). Wilber also included more of his Integral Mathematics symbolism in this manuscript (c.f. [10], and although I managed to incorporate enough of this in my Integral Mathematics article to satisfy Wilber and his AQAL editors, I knew that my heart was not really in it, and his new theories seemed too abstract and contorted to me in regard to its potential of being applied effectively in practical situations.

But I was not yet ready to get off the Integral bandwagon. Philosopher/psychologist Allan Combs, a prominent author on consciousness in his own right [18] and a close colleague of Wilber as well as one of the leaders in Integral Institute, had submitted my article *Art and Mental Disturbance* [19] to the Journal of Humanistic Psychology, where it is presently being considered for publication (see [19] for the 2008 publication reference). Although Combs' Integral Consciousness domain in Integral Institute has not materialized and I was doubting if my Group Theory/ Consciousness article was ever going to appear on the Integral Institute website, I considered my positive association with Allan Combs to be an indication that Wilber and Integral Institute was still safe and legitimate for me. However, as my direct contacts with the higher-ups at Integral Institute became briefer and less and less frequent, my disillusionment began to increase. Approximately a year ago I was contacted by someone who read my article *Spirituality and Cults: An Experiential Analysis* on the Integral Science website [20] (separate from Integral Institute), and conveyed to me the serious concerns many people were having about the guru and cult dangers of Ken Wilber and Integral Institute, and suggested that I apply my experiential analysis to Integral Institute. I was not ready to do so at the time, but after being contacted by this same person a year later who now is conveying to me how these concerns have become increasingly escalated (c.f. [2]), the timing is right for me, based upon two recent experiences.

After having read Wilber's *Integral Spirituality* manuscript, I decided to try to assimilate his current ideas about his eight zones and perspectives into my *Spirituality and Cults* article (c.f. [20]) in order to progress from the Integral Institute approved designation of being

"Integrally Informed" to official acceptance in the AQAL journal, as my *Integral Mathematics* article had successfully gone this route. I must admit that not the least of my reasons for doing this was the prospect of having another phone conversation with Ken Wilber, as this was the last part of the editing process to have an article accepted in AQAL journal. I knew (deep down) that what I was trying to do was rather staged and artificial for me, as I did not truly believe in or appreciate the usefulness of Wilber's new ideas that I was trying to incorporate into my article. Sure enough, my article was not received well by the AQAL editor, and I was invited to rework the article for the purpose of making it "Integrally Informed," as it was explained to me that it was far removed from AQAL journal standards. Needless to say, I was not enthused by this invitation, and I responded in a rather lukewarm way, leaving it as a vague possibility in the distant future. I also asked when my Integral Mathematics article would be available to the public, and I have not heard back from this editor. This experience did remind me of the dictionary of Integral Institute terms that had been sent to me by the AQAL editor to prepare me for my phone conversation with Wilber to discuss my Integral Mathematics article six months ago. And how when I did talk to Wilber, he was not too happy about my lack of thorough understanding of the distinction between "quadrant" and "quadrivium" (c.f. [10]). Yes—I felt somewhat like I was "in school," trying to learn the "right way" and being the apprentice of the great philosopher. In my deepest self I knew that this was no longer right for me; it was not what I meant by the description I had given to my own philosophy of life: Natural Dimension (see [15] in Introduction Notes).

But the final break for me has occurred this past week as I returned to Denver, not to meet again with Wilber (my request to do so was not taken seriously by the higher ups in the organization), but to lead a panel workshop at the 2006 ICSA conference, entitled "Coming Back to Spirituality and Religion after Spiritual Abuse" (see [43] in Chapter Five Notes). I took the leap and finally decided to enter the public arena, promoting my *Modern Religions* book, talking openly about Scientology, and in the same breath I found myself quite naturally talking about my recent involvement with Ken Wilber and Integral Institute. Yes—I was starting to think about the possibility of there being cult dangers in the organization.

And finally this brings me to my tri-perspective experiential analysis of Integral Institute. I won't go through all three scales that I have used in detail, although the interested reader can find this in my related article and book (c.f. [5]). But to give a brief generic description of the first two scales, my first scale is the Anthony Typology (c.f. [15]), and there are three categories in this scale: multilevel/unilevel, technical/charismatic, and monistic/dualistic. Multilevel refers to authentic spiritual experience whereas unilevel refers to more mundane psychological or material gain. Technical refers to processes or techniques whereas charismatic refers to mystique and charisma of a guru figure. Monistic refers to non-judgmental openness to all people whereas dualistic refers to an Us vs. Them elitist dichotomy. Suffice it to say that although the Anthony Typology has been helpful to me in understanding the cult dangers (or beneficial qualities) of a number of what I have referred to as new age spiritual organizations (c.f. [5]), this is not tremendously helpful to me in evaluating Integral Institute. The reason is that it is difficult to pinpoint exactly what categories in the Anthony Typology in which to place Integral Institute. Wilber's writings are enormously complex and brilliant, full of ideas as well as recommended techniques and practices. But there is also the tremendously impactful and forceful presence and mystique of Ken Wilber himself, in his full 6' 6'' bald rather intimidating grand stature. Integral Institute is certainly open to all people who are interested, but there is most definitely the "right" way of being fully integral, second tier (or third tier), highest level of consciousness, etc. Perhaps the most I can say with confidence about Integral Institute in the Anthony Typology is that it is in the Multilevel category, in the context of representing an authentic potential of spiritual experience.

In regard to the second scale, which I have referred to as the Wilber Integral Model (c.f. [5]) I would place Integral Institute in-between the rational and trans-rational continuum, which I have described as a continuum from pre-rational to pseudo-rational to rational to trans-rational, along the lines of Wilber's previous writings (c.f. [5], [6], [8], [10]). However, one can start to see some alarms as there is little historical continuity with religious traditions, the emphasis being upon a modern assimilation of all spiritual and religious viewpoints. In addition, Integral Institute is most definitely run by Ken Wilber in what I consider to be a benevolent authoritarian manner, somewhat similar to the way in which Neale Donald Walsch runs his Conversations with God organization (c.f. [5], [20], [21]). I do not see any phasing out of Wilber's leadership during his lifetime. Thus, the lack of historical continuity and phasing out of leadership are red flags to me for Integral Institute in Ken Wilber's own Integral model.

But lastly and most critically, the fifteen item scale I have used and refer to as the Bonewits Cult Danger Scale (c.f. [5], [20], [22]) is what I generally place the most importance on. The following 15 items are what I utilize, averaging the ratings on a scale of 1 to 10, with 10 being the highest rating.

1. Internal Control: amount of internal political power exercised by leader(s) over members.

2. Wisdom Claimed: by leader(s), amount of infallibility declared about decisions.

3. Wisdom Credited: to leaders by members, amount of trust in the decisions made by leaders(s).

4. Dogma: rigidity of reality concepts taught, of amount of doctrinal inflexibility.

5. Recruiting: emphasis put on attracting new members, amount of proselytizing.

6. Front Groups: number of subsidiary groups using a different name from that of the main group.

7. Wealth: amount of money and/or property desired or obtained, emphasis on members' donations.

8. Political Power: amount of external political influence desired or obtained.

9. Sexual Manipulation: of members by leaders(s), amount of control over the lives of members.

10. Censorship: amount of control over members' access to outside opinion on group, its doctrines or leader(s).

11. Dropout Control: intensity of efforts directed at preventing or returning dropouts.

12. Endorsement of Violence: when used by or for the group or leaders(s).

13. Paranoia: amount of fear concerning real or imagined enemies, perceived power of opponents.

14. Grimness: amount of disapproval concerning jokes about the group, its doctrines or leader(s).

15. Surrender of Will: emphasis on members not having to be responsible for personal decisions.

For the above items, the number assigned to the item is based primarily upon my own experience with Ken Wilber and Integral Institute over the past two and a half years:

Internal Control	4
Wisdom Claimed	9
Wisdom Credited	6
Dogma	8
Recruiting	4
Front Groups	1
Wealth	5
Political Power	5
Sexual Manipulation	1
Censorship	5
Dropout Control	1
Endorsement of Violence	1
Paranoia	5
Grimness	3
Surrender of Will	1
AVERAGE SCORE:	3.9

This average score of 3.9 is comparable to the average scores of the six new age spiritual organizations which I have placed in Neutral territory, in-between Mild Cult Danger and Favorable Spiritual Benefits (c.f. [5]). Specifically these average scores on the Bonewits Cult Danger Scale are:

A Course in Miracles	3.5
International Cultic Studies Association	3.5
Conversations with God	3.7
Self-Realization Fellowship	3.7
Tikkun (new age primarily Jewish organization)	3.8
Reiki	4.1

Based upon some of my higher ratings in the Bonewits Cult Danger Scale, my ambiguous ratings in the Anthony Typology, and some of my red flags in the Wilber Integral Model, I would say that there are definitely things to be cautious and observant about in Integral Institute, not the least of which is Ken Wilber's strong ego and harsh criticisms of many of those who disagree with him (cf. [2], [14]). However, in a similar manner to the conclusions that I came to regarding both Conversations with God and Reiki (cf. [5]), I will give Wilber and Integral Institute the benefit of the doubt and place this organization in Neutral territory regarding cult dangers vs. beneficial spiritual characteristics. From my own experience, the new age spiritual organizations that I have described as having Mild cult dangers are est, Eckankar, Gurdjieff, and Twelve Step Support Groups (cf. [5]). I do feel confident that Ken Wilber and Integral Institute do not belong in this category, and certainly not in the Moderate cult danger classification in which I placed Avatar and Divine Light Mission, or in the High cult danger classification in which I placed Scientology and The Unification Church (cf. [5]). However, I most definitely do not think that Integral Institute belongs in the Favorable category in which I placed my experience with Neopaganism or the new age spiritual workshops I have done at Omega Institute for Holistic Studies or Kripalu Center for Yoga and Health (cf. [5]).

Perhaps a significant variable to determine if my Neutral placement of Integral Institute is justified or somewhat naive will be the response (if any) I receive from them based upon the exposure of this article. Given that I have decided to make all my writings on the cult dangers of new age spiritual organizations readily available to the public, I have little qualms about making this article available as well. It will be interesting to see if my Group Theory/Consciousness and Integral Mathematics articles will still appear on the Integral Institute website (assuming my articles would have eventually appeared there ordinarily), as I have certainly made some critical statements about both Wilber and Integral Institute. But make no mistake about it; for those people concerned about the possible cult dangers of Ken Wilber and Integral Institute, at this point I do not see anything serious enough to be very alarmed about. As far as my present knowledge can determine, if you do not like what you see at Integral Institute then you can disengage without repercussions. Big egos, strong ideas, and harsh criticism of opponents are not the same as cult dangers, and if I ever have anything to add to this appraisal I will not hesitate to do so in the future.

NOTES AND REFERENCES

1) See www.kenwilber.com

2) See www.integralinstitute.net

3) See Ken Wilber's books *Sex, Ecology, Spirituality* (Boston: Shambhala, 1995) and *Boomeritis* (Boston: Shambhala, 2003).

4) See Donald Rothberg and Sean Kelly (Editors), *Ken Wilber in Dialogue* (Wheaton, Illinois: Quest Books, 1998).

5) See Elliot Benjamin, *Modern Religions: An Experiential Analysis and Exposé* (Swanville, Maine: Natural Dimension Publications, 2013); available at www.lulu.com. My tri-perspective experiential analysis is also available as a long article on-line; see Elliot Benjamin, *Spirituality and the Cults: An Experiential Analysis* in The Ground of Faith Journal, 2005 (thegroundoffaith @hug.co.nz).

6) See Elliot Benjamin, *On the Philosophy of Ken Wilber* in Inner Tapestry Journal, Vol. 4, No. 2, 2005 (www.innertapestry.org).

7) See Elliot Benjamin, *A Mathematical Group Theoretical Model of Shifts into Higher Levels of Consciousness in Ken Wilber's Integral Theory*, at www.integralscience. org, 2004.

8) See Ken Wilber, *A Theory of Everything* (Boston: Shambhala, 2001).

9) See Don Beck & Chris Cowan, *Spiral Dynamics: Managing Values, Leadership and, Change* (London: Blackwell, 1996).

10) See Ken Wilber, *Integral Spirituality* (Boston: Shambhala, 2006).

11) See Elliot Benjamin, *On Avatar* in ICSA E-Newsletter, 2005 (http://cultinfobooks.com).

12) See Andrew Cohen, *Living Enlightenment* (Lenox, MA: Moksha Press, 2002).

13) See Adi Da's books *The Dawn Horse Testament* (San Rafael, CA: The Dawn Horse Press, 1985) and *Scientific Proof of the Existence of God will Soon be Announced by the White House!* (Middleton, CA: The Dawn Horse Press, 1980). Note that this last book includes a glowing forward by Ken Wilber.

14) See Geoffrey Falk, *Stripping the Gurus* (www.angelin.com/trek/ geoffreyfalk/blog/blog. html, 2005) for a particularly scathing

exposé on both Adi Da and Ken Wilber, in addition to many other gurus and spiritual leaders.

15) See Dick Anthony, Bruce Ecker, Ken Wilber (Editors), *Spiritual Choices* (New York: Paragon House, 1987).

16) Note that ICSA was originally called AFF (American Friends & Family), having changed its name to ICSA (International Cultic Studies Association) in March, 2005.

17) See Ken Wilber's books *Boomeritis* and *A Theory of Everything* (references in [3] and [8])

18) See Alan Combs, *The Radiance of Being* (New York: Omega Books, 1995).

19) See Elliot Benjamin, *Art and Mental Disturbance* (Journal of Humanistic Psychology, 2008, Vol. 48, No. 1, pp. 61-88).

20) See Elliot Benjamin, *Spirituality and Cults: An Experiential Analysis* (www.integralscience.org, 2005).

21) See Elliot Benjamin, *On Conversations with God* in ICSA E-Newsletter, 2004, Vol. 3, No. 2.

22) See the Cult Danger Evaluation Frame rating scale in Isaac Bonewits, *Real Magic* (York Beach, Maine: Samuel Weisner, 1971).

PART 2: THE BOUNDARIES BETWEEN CULTIC, BENIGN, AND BENEFICIAL IN FIVE SPIRITUAL GROUPS

(May, 2008)

NOTE: This article is essentially the same as the published version of my article (see [45] in Chapter Five Notes), aside from some minor editorial revisions.

In my previous ICSA (International Cultic Studies Association) essay on philosopher Ken Wilber's Integral Institute, I utilized a convenient numerical cult evaluation system based upon one's own experiences in a spiritual group, originated by Isaac Bonewits, which I referred to as the Bonewits Cult Danger Scale (Bonewits, 1971, Benjamin, 2007a). Based upon my experiences with this group, I came up with a cult danger score that contributed significantly to my conclusion that Ken Wilber and his Integral Institute did not possess significant cult dangers. Specifically, I placed Integral Institute in Neutral territory, in-between cult dangers and spiritual benefits, which may be referred to as "Benign." In this article I would like to extend my numerical experiential evaluation of cult dangers to five other groups, two of which have been the subject of other articles I have written for ICSA: Conversations with God, and Avatar (Benjamin, 2004a, 2005a). The three remaining groups I will evaluate are groups that I have experienced within the past few years: Human Awareness Institute (HAI) in November, 2004, Acceptance and Commitment Therapy (ACT) in August, 2007, and The Center for Creative Consciousness (CCC) in January, 2008. Based upon my own experiences as reflected in my numerical ratings on the Bonewits Cult Danger Scale, I will conclude that one of these spiritual groups (Avatar) has a moderate degree of cult dangers, two of these groups (Center for Creative Consciousness and Conversations with God) are in Neutral/Benign territory regarding cult dangers vs. spiritual benefits, and two of these groups (HAI and ACT) are in the favorable category in regard to offering authentic spiritual benefits.

I would like to begin by reproducing a summary of the Bonewits Cult Danger Scale from my previous Integral Institute article

(Benjamin, 2007a). The following 15 items are rated on a continuum scale from 1 to 10, with 10 being the highest, and the average for all 15 items is calculated. I would also like to stress that I utilize this scale in an experiential way, meaning that the ratings are primarily based upon my own experiences in the spiritual groups.

BONEWITS CULT DANGER SCALE

1.   Internal Control: amount of internal political power exercised by leader(s) over members.

2.   Wisdom Claimed: by leader(s), amount of infallibility declared about decisions.

3.   Wisdom Credited: to leader(s) by members, amount of trust in the decisions made by leader(s).

4.   Dogma: rigidity of reality concepts taught, of amount of doctrinal inflexibility.

5.   Recruiting: emphasis put on attracting new members, amount of proselytizing.

6.   Front Groups: number of subsidiary groups using a different name from that of the main group.

7.   Wealth: amount of money and/or property desired or obtained, emphasis on members' donations.

8.   Political Power: amount of external political influence desired or obtained.

9.   Sexual Manipulation: of members by leader(s), amount of control over the lives of members.

10.   Censorship: amount of control over members' access to outside opinion on group, its doctrines or leader(s).

11.   Dropout Control: intensity of efforts directed at preventing or returning dropouts.

12.   Endorsement of Violence: when used by or for the group or leader(s).

13.   Paranoia: amount of fear concerning real or imagined enemies, perceived power of opponents.

14.   Grimness: amount of disapproval concerning jokes about the group, its doctrines or leader(s).

15. Surrender of Will: emphasis on members not having to be responsible for personal decisions.

CONVERSATIONS WITH GOD

Conversations with God was originated by Neale Donald Walsch in the early 1990s as a popular new age book of the same title, followed within the next few years by a series of other "with God" books and the Conversations with God organization (Walsch, 1995, 1997, 1998, 1999, 2000, 2002, 2004). In my Conversations with God ICSA article (Benjamin, 2004a), I concluded that although Walsch certainly has an enormous ego and a tremendous charismatic theatrical presentation, Conversations with God does not present significant cult dangers, and I placed the organization in Neutral territory, in-between cult dangers and spiritual benefits. I will now give the numerical ratings I came up with on the Bonewits Cult Danger Scale for Conversations with God, as described in my book *Modern Religions: An Experiential Analysis And Exposé* (Benjamin, 2005b).

INTERNAL CONTROL	2
WISDOM CLAIMED	8
WISDOM CREDITED	7
DOGMA	8
RECRUITING	4
FRONT GROUPS	4
WEALTH	4
POLITICAL POWER	5
SEXUAL MANIPULATION	2
CENSORSHIP	2
DROPOUT CONTROL	2
ENDORSEMENT OF VIOLENCE	1
PARANOIA	3
GRIMNESS	1
SURRENDER OF WILL	3
TOTAL	56
AVERAGE	**3.7**

The average score of 3.7 which I came up with for Conversations with God on the Bonewits Cult Danger Scale is the same average score that I came up with for Self-Realization Fellowship, originated by Paramahansa Yogananda through the popularity of his book *Autobiography of a Yogi* in the 1940s (Yoganada, 1946), which I also gave a Neutral classification to (Benjamin, 2004a). We see that there are no ratings by me for Conversations with God greater than 8. My two ratings of 8 are for Wisdom Claimed and Dogma, representing the fact that although Walsch does have strong powerful beliefs in the validity of his ideas being told to him personally by God, he is also somewhat flexible in his interpretation of these ideas. The trust and admiration for him from his followers is quite high, but my 7 rating in Wisdom Credited shows that this trust and admiration does not go past reasonable limits in regard to listening to everything Walsch says without thinking for oneself. I gave a number of intermediate ratings of 4 for Front Groups, Recruiting, and Wealth, and 5 for Political Power, representing that there is a fair amount of emphasis in these categories, but does not reach inappropriate or excessive proportions. For example, there was a definite push when I was at the Conversations with God Humanity's Team Conference in 2002 for people to seriously consider signing up for the Leadership program, the "fast track" option being done in three months for a cost of $12,500. In my opinion this is an extremely large sum of money for three months of training, but there was not undo pressure put upon us to sign up for the Leadership training or any of the other Conversations with God workshops or retreats, which was in marked distinction from both Scientology and Avatar (Benjamin, 2005a, 2005b, 2005c, 2007b).

For all the remaining categories I gave relatively low ratings of 1, 2, or 3. Although much of the Conversations with God philosophy is based upon taking responsibility for your actions and for your life, there is also the aspect of surrendering yourself to your higher power or "God." Walsch is quite the theatrical comedian on stage, and my rating of 1 for Grimness reflects this lightness and humor which Walsch brings to his retreats as well as to his writings. There is no endorsement of violence whatsoever, and no obvious sexual manipulations, though the Walsch philosophy of complete individual freedom could have sexual overtones regarding being bi-sexual or even multi-sexual in romantic relationships. Walsch also displays some serious concerns about the dangers of traditional religions that do not share his views of non-hierarchy and openness. However, all things considered I believe we have a spiritual group here that is benign regarding being susceptible to significant cult dangers, although on the basis of my experiences with Conversations with God as reflected in my Bonewits Cult Danger Scale evaluation, I would not place this organization in the "favorable" spiritual benefits category. As I concluded in my previous Conversations with God essay (Benjamin, 2004a), Neale Donald Walsch does have a strong ego and charismatic personality, but Conversations with God is not a dangerous cult.

AVATAR

Avatar is an alternative spiritual organization founded in the late 1980s by Harry Palmer, an ex-Scientologist, and has a somewhat similar philosophy to Conversations with God in regard to a person being able to "choose" what he or she wants to experience in life (Palmer, 1994a, 1994b; Benjamin, 2005a). Avatar successfully markets itself by promising to enable people to learn how to actualize their dreams and gain a heightened experience of being alive (Palmer, 1994a, 1994b; Benjamin, 2005a). However, I concluded in my ICSA article on Avatar that unlike Conversations with God, Avatar does have significant cult dangers, and although there are some benefits from doing the Avatar course, the financial costs and organizational control are extremely high, and I do not recommend that one becomes involved with this organization (Benjamin, 2005a, 2005b). In examining the Bonewits Cult Danger Scale ratings I came up with for Avatar, as once again described in my *Modern Religions* book (Benjamin, 2005b), the higher level of cult danger for this organization as compared to that of Conversations with God will become evident in a quantitative way. My ratings on the Bonewits Cult Danger Scale for Avatar are based upon my involvement in Avatar from 1997 through 2001 (Benjamin, 2005b).

INTERNAL CONTROL	5
WISDOM CLAIMED	9
WISDOM CREDITED	9
DOGMA	10
RECRUITING	6

FRONT GROUPS	1
WEALTH	10
POLITICAL POWER	1
SEXUAL MANIPULATION	2
CENSORSHIP	5
DROPOUT CONTROL	5
ENDORSEMENT OF VIOLENCE	1
PARANOIA	7
GRIMNESS	5
SURRENDER OF WILL	5
TOTAL	81
AVERAGE	**5.4**

Avatar's score of 5.4 on the Bonewits Cult Danger Scale is the third highest score for all the groups that I have experientially analyzed in my *Modern Religions* book, only Scientology and The Unification Church having higher scores (although I gave both Scientology and The Unification Church significantly higher cult danger ratings than Avatar on the Bonewits Cult Danger Scale, with respective scores of 8.7 and 9.0 (Benjamin, 2005b, 2005c). On this basis it certainly does appear that Avatar presents a moderate degree of cult danger concerns, in a somewhat similar capacity to that of Divine Light Mission, founded by Guru Maharajji from India who came to the United States in the early 1970s as supposedly an enlightened fourteen-year-old perfect master (Divine Light Mission received an average score of 5.1 in my *Modern Religions* book (Benjamin, 2005b). I gave Avatar ratings of 10 in two categories: Dogma and Wealth, and ratings of 9 in two categories: Wisdom Claimed and Wisdom Credited. There is no deviating from the exact ways that Palmer set forth for his exercises to be done, and no differences of opinion tolerated regarding Palmer's philosophical views (Palmer, 1994a, 1994b; Benjamin, 2005a, 2005b). However, Palmer does not claim to be an all knowing "perfect master" and his followers do not see him in this totalistic way either; rather he is a more human guru, therefore deserving of ratings of 9 rather than 10 in the Wisdom Claimed and Wisdom Credited categories.

However, when it comes to Wealth there is no doubt that Avatar deserves the top score of 10. All roads lead eventually to the Avatar "Wizards" course in Florida, a thirteen day course that cost $7,500 plus all the extras for hotels, food, and transportation. And the expensive prices of the Avatar courses (the cheapest is the first 9 day course for $2,300 plus the above extras) is heavily marketed to anyone who shows preliminary interest in Avatar or who graduates from the initial Avatar training course or the Avatar Master's course (Benjamin, 2005a). I gave relatively high scores of 6 or 7 and intermediate scores of 5 in the categories of Internal Control, Recruiting, Censorship, Dropout Control, Paranoia, Grimness, and Surrender of Will. When you complete the Avatar Masters' course you are required to sign a lengthy contract stating, among other things, that you will not divulge any Avatar secrets. Avatar does take legal action against ex-members who make public their negative views of Avatar. Recruiting is a full-fledged business activity, and Palmer's book *The Masters' Handbook* (Palmer, 1997) is primarily a marketing tool for Avatar Masters who want to find their own paying Avatar students (Benjamin, 2005a). When one appears to drop out of the Avatar scene, both personalized mailings and phone calls are made to try to bring this person back to Avatar. Influence and control of Avatar members' lives is frequently done for the purpose of persuading Avatar members to sign up for their next level Avatar courses (each course has a course fee of at least a few thousand dollars plus the extras; see Benjamin, 2005a). Questioning of financial Avatar matters or disagreeing with particular Avatar exercises is looked upon with suspicion by Avatar leaders and is grounds for not granting a successful completion certificate of higher level Avatar courses (Benjamin, 2005a).

Even though taking personal responsibility for life is focused upon in Avatar, surrendering your will to "source" is considered to be of fundamental importance. Although on a major part of the Avatar drills there is much joking and laughter going on as part of the drill, this joking and laughter must stay in its proper place and not be addressed toward disagreeing with the Avatar structure or philosophical principles, in order to be successful on an Avatar course (Benjamin, 2005a). Avatar is run completely as a business, and Harry Palmer makes no pretenses about covering up his marketing strategies and course prices. I am not aware of any front groups in Avatar, endorsement of violence, or interest in political power (to all of which I gave ratings of 1). For Sexual Manipulation I gave a rating of 2, as the focus upon individual choice and freedom may have an effect upon decisions in regard to one's romantic and sexual involvements.

All things considered, we can see from my ratings on the Bonewits Cult Danger Scale that Avatar's cult dangers cannot be ignored. We have here a very expensive alternative spiritual organization with a highly organized and effective recruitment and marketing strategy. Although the leader/guru has not gone over the edge in terms of blatantly destructive practices for his followers, the dogma, recruitment focus, and high prices of Avatar courses are in themselves enough reason to be very much on-guard with this alternative spiritual organization. The philosophy of Avatar may be in some ways similar to that of Conversations with God, but the similarity ends there. Avatar has been described as "the new est," (est was a popular large group spiritual and personal growth organization founded by Werner Erhard in the 1970s; see Benjamin, 2005b) and there is truthfulness in this description. We see here another LGAT (Large Group Awareness Training Program) at work, as I have described in my essays on est (Benjamin, 2005b), and one that also focuses upon individual freedom and choice, but has no reservations about charging big bucks for their courses right away. What is alarming is how successful Avatar has been in getting people to pay these big bucks for their courses, myself included. However, it is also true that there is a world of difference between Avatar and Scientology or The Unification Church in terms of degree of cult dangers, as can be seen from a comparison of their respective Bonewits Cult Danger scores of 5.4, 8.7, and 9.0, and which quantitatively separates the moderate degree of cult dangers in Avatar from the high degree of cult dangers in Scientology and The Unification Church, based upon my own experiences. From the other end of the perspective, I have given minimal cult danger ratings to a number of spiritual groups, including est, Gurdjieff, Eckakar, and Twelve Step Support Groups, with respective Bonewits Cult Danger scores of 4.1, 4.3, 4.3, 4.4, and it appears that Avatar's score of 5.4 is in a different category of cult dangers from these groups as well (Benjamin, 2005b).

HUMAN AWARENESS INSTITUTE (HAI)

I first experienced HAI (Human Awareness Institute) in November, 2004, though I had heard about HAI frequently from my involvements with Neopaganism starting in 1997 (Benjamin, 2004b, 2005d). HAI was originated in the late 1960s by Stan Dale, and engages in intensive interpersonal intimacy and soul searching over a series of weekend retreats, in a developmental series of seven levels. The cost of the workshops is a few hundred dollars each, which is certainly reasonable for personal growth workshops. There are options for continued HAI involvements with frequent get-togethers, parties, and various internet exchanges. I have been to a few HAI get-togethers and parties since my Level 1 workshop (which was my only HAI workshop) and I am still connected to the HAI internet exchange entitled "HAI Intimacy" [1]. HAI has a reputation in pagan circles for being excessively sensual, including highly suggested (though still voluntary) group nudity. I did experience this HAI sensuality, and I must say that I was quite taken with HAI by the end of my weekend workshop. The sensuality is not encouraged to progress to sexuality during the HAI weekend, though there are few rules and restrictions to worry about in HAI. The HAI sensuality is involved with face stroking, "hand-over-heart" group exchanges, group massages, sensual mutual feeding, group showers, frequent nude hugging, free style dancing, opportunities for creative performance, and continuous intensive mutual intimate sharing. Yes—by the end of the weekend I felt quite youthful and like a fully sensual being, with a sexual attraction to a younger woman who was in my nude massage and shower group. Soon after my workshop ended I began an internet correspondence with a woman on my HAI Intimacy exchange group, and consequently made a fourteen hour drive to visit her for the weekend—not even having any idea of what she looked like. Without going into any more detail than this, I will say that I did get rather carried away with HAI, and made some foolish, immature, and unsafe decisions regarding my heightened sensual state of mind soon after my HAI workshop.

HAI refers to its workshop room as "The Room of Love" and invites everyone to come back to this Room of Love for new workshops in the level series or repeats of previous workshops. There is also the option to become an "assistant" at HAI workshops, and move up the ladder in the HAI network. I have encountered from others some concerns about HAI being a cult, but from my own experiences I have felt virtually none of the manipulative pressures to continue my involvement with HAI, and very little guru attributions to its founder, Stan Dale, who died recently. Rather, Stan Dale was looked up to with a great deal of respect and admiration, but not in the kind of way where one would give up one's self to follow a guru's pronouncements. Lets see what the Bonewits Cult Danger scale comes up with for me with HAI.

1. INTERNAL CONTROL	1
2. WISDOM CLAIMED	5
3. WISDOM CREDITED	5
4. DOGMATISM	5
5, RECRUITING	3
6. FRONT GROUPS	1
7. WEALTH	3
8. POLITICAL POWER:	1
9. SEXUAL MANIPULATION	3
10. CENSORSHIP	3
11. DROPOUT CONTROL	2
12. ENDORSEMENT OF VIOLENCE	1
13. PARANOIA	3
14. GRIMNESS:	1
15. SURRENDER OF WILL	1
TOTAL SCORE:	38
AVERAGE SCORE:	**2.5**

Well, the cult score I come up with for HAI speaks for itself. In comparison with the other spiritual groups I have experientially analyzed on the Bonewits Cult Danger scale in my *Modern Religions* book (Benjamin, 2005b], from my experience HAI is most definitely in the Favorable/Beneficial spiritual group category, surpassed only by my experiences of Neopaganism and Omega Institute for Holistic Studies (Benjamin, 2005b). This essentially feels consistent with my thoughts about HAI. There is an intensive and magical quality about HAI, but I must caution that there is also a provocative and extremely sensual quality that feels very good in the moment, but can easily lead one into chaotic and rather unsafe sexual involvements. Sometimes I do feel the impulse to do another HAI workshop or at least go to another HAI get-together, but this is not something my girlfriend/significant other and soulmate is comfortable with, and to be quite honest I would not feel comfortable with her going to HAI events either, having nude intimate exchanges with other men, etc. HAI served a transitory purpose in my life very soon after my previous romantic relationship of three years had ended. At this point in my life I choose to not continue an active involvement with HAI, although I do find some personal value from remaining in the HAI Intimacy internet exchange group (c.f. [1]). However, based upon my experience with the HAI organization for the past three years, I would not have a problem recommending HAI as a viable option for spiritual personal growth, as long as one's life circumstances comfortably allows for this kind of sensual environment to grow in.

ACCEPTANCE AND COMMITMENT THERAPY (ACT)

I experienced a five day ACT (Acceptance and Commitment Therapy) workshop in August, 2007 in Cape Cod, Massachusetts. After doing the ACT workshop I read a number of books on ACT (Hayes, Strosahl, & Wilson, 1999; Hayes & Strosahl, 2004), wrote an article about ACT (Benjamin, 2007c), have had some dialogue on the ACT internet forum, and have had a few supportive e-mail exchanges with ACT founder Steve Hayes. I was quite impressed with the amazing integrative perspective that ACT brings to psychotherapy, somehow combining ingredients from Humanistic, Existential, Transpersonal, Behavioral, and Cognitive psychology. Steve Hayes himself is a remarkable combination of personal qualities, being a recognized leader in Behavioristic psychology with nearly four hundred publications to his credit, but displaying a transcendental spiritual quality that somehow reminds me of Ken Wilber (Wilber, 1995; Benjamin, 2007a).

Hayes continually cites ACT research to scientifically back up his very strong contextual psychology ideas, which is based upon the premise that one needs to gracefully accept one's unmovable obstacles in life, while focusing upon one's deepest experience of self awareness and highest values (Hayes, Strosahl, & Wilson, 1999). There are many self processes and exercises to help a person accept his/her unmovable life obstacles, as well as high level meditations and visualizations to focus upon one's deepest experience of self and highest values. I went through some quite intensive exercises in my ACT workshop, and I left the workshop feeling extremely stimulated and refreshed. ACT seemed to me to be a wonderful way of uniting Humanistic and Behavioral psychology, and I was searching for a way to do something just like this in order to be myself in my new mental health job that is focused upon Behavioristic psychology treatments. Steve Hayes has been quite flexible and responsive to my own "idiosyncratic" (as quoted by Steve Hayes) portrayal of ACT, but he does not have a problem with how I have described ACT in my article (Benjamin, 2007c). However, there is undoubtedly a very strong claim to a set of core principles which govern ACT, inclusive of quantitative scientific research expectations, and there is a network of ACT practitioners with Steve Hayes as the acknowledged ACT chief. Lets see how ACT fares on the Bonewits Cult Danger Scale for me.

1. INTERNAL CONTROL	1
2. WISDOM CLAIMED	7
3. WISDOM CREDITED	7
4. DOGMA	9
5. RECRUITING	3
6. FRONT GROUPS	1
7. WEALTH	3
8. POLITICAL POWER	1
9. SEXUAL MANIPULATION	1
10. CENSORSHIP	1
11. DROPOUT CONTROL	1
12. ENDORSEMENT OF VIOLENCE	1
13: PARANOIA	3
14. GRIMNESS	1
15. SURRENDER OF WILL	1
TOTAL SCORE:	41
AVERAGE SCORE:	**2.7**

From ACT's score of 2.7 on the Bonewits Cult Danger Scale together with my experience of the ACT workshop, we once again have a Favorable spiritual group here, in the same league as my experience of Neopaganism, Omega Institute for Holistic Studies, Kripalu Center for Yoga and Health, and HAI (with respective scores of 2.1, 2.3, 2.5, and 2.6; see Benjamin, 2005b). The next closest score on the Bonewits Cult Danger Scale in the groups that I have experientially analyzed are my scores for my experience of ICSA

(International Cultic Studies Association) and A Course in Miracles, both of which I have scored as 3.5 and placed in Neutral territory in regard to cult dangers vs. favorable spirituality (Benjamin, 2005b, 2005c). Undoubtedly ACT has a strong belief system, as evidenced by my score of 9 for Dogma, and 7 for both Wisdom Claimed and Wisdom Credited, but all my other scores are no higher then 3, and I gave ACT more 1's than any of the other groups I have analyzed. Although Steve Hayes has graciously accepted my "idiosyncratic" view of ACT, which I characterize as an example of Humanistic Behaviorism (Benjamin, 2007c), it happens to be the case that I am essentially comfortable with ACT's basic philosophical framework, and this is why ACT is meaningful to me. If (and only if) one resonates with ACT's formulation of acceptance and commitment, then I do believe there is a spiritual path here, inherent within a scientific academic psychology framework that I personally find quite intriguing.

THE CENTER FOR CREATIVE CONSCIOUSNESS
(The Eagle and the Condor)

I have recently done my third workshop at Kripalu Center for Yoga and Health, and I must say that this Kripalu workshop left me with far more misgivings in regard to possible cult and guru dangers than my previous two Kripalu workshops (Benjamin, 2005b, 2005c). My workshop was entitled The Modern Mystic: Accelerating your Spirituality in Today's World, and the workshop presenter was Jonette Crowley, author of the book *The Eagle and the Condor* (Crowley, 2007). I read the book soon before doing my workshop, and I was somewhat prepared for the exceedingly bizarre and spiritual megalomaniacal presentation of Crowley. However, experiencing her in person in a relatively small group of workshop participants had more of an impact upon me than I had anticipated. It's not the actual beliefs of Crowley that disturb me; her beliefs appear farfetched in the extreme to me but this is something I encounter fairly frequently in my spiritual explorations. Reincarnation from both previous human lives as well as pre-human light energy forms, healing the universe through prayer and meditation at ancient power places throughout the world, uniting spirituality with her "twin flame" (beyond the concept of soulmate) shaman in Peru (inclusive of some physical cuddling), channeling her two major spirits of "White Eagle" and "Mark," etc.

are beliefs I could accept as foreign to me but not necessarily possessing cult dangers.

However, when Jonette Crowley writes and talks about how she is reincarnated from one of the highest beings who ever lived on the planet, that it is her mission to unite the eagle of North America and the condor of South America (symbolically by her masculine/feminine spiritual union with her "twin flame" shaman from Peru), and that she has initiated thousands of people via Himalaya Heart Activations and the Inca Codes from the Sun Discs of Peru, I start to get nervous. When she frequently encourages workshop participants to sign up for her trips to various ancient and esoteric power places throughout the world, along with promoting her future workshops and her book, I start to see a guru with followers. When I hear workshop participants tearfully express their spiritual realizations of how they wish to unite their masculine and feminine (the concrete version of uniting the eagle and the condor) and follow Crowley to Peru or the Himalayas, I know that I have another essay to write about the possible cult dangers of a modern religion.

Jonette Crowley is an extroverted woman with an extraordinary amount of charm and energy. She writes and describes how she is a channeler primarily of two spiritual entities: the calm gentle spiritual energy of the American Indian goddess White Eagle, and the powerful and cosmic philosophical teacher energy of the spirit Mark, although she has also channeled even deeper entities, such as White Buffalo Calf Woman and Kamara (Crowley, 2007). Crowley believes she is a reincarnation of these great spirits and that it is her mission to impart the gift of spiritual greatness to others, specifically through her Himalaya Heart Activation, Inca Code initiation, selling her book *The Eagle and the Condor*, and her various spiritually channeled CDs, and taking people on voyages to sacred sites throughout the world. She describes how she first experienced the presence of White Eagle almost twenty years ago when she was going through a personally very difficult time in her life.

As I listen to Jonette Crowley describe all the things she believes, I cannot help thinking that what she talks about is not any different from the talk of a psychotic person in a mental institution. Somehow Crowley has managed to overcome the downward spiral that many other people with her beliefs go through, and has emerged as a successful spiritual businesswoman (she happens to have an MBA in business administration) who is in constant demand to give spiritual workshops, take people on spiritual voyages, and who sells many CDs of her channeled lessons from her spirit guides. Crowley describes how her spirit guides have disclosed to her that there are seven dimensions of consciousness, inclusive of the higher dimensions of energy vibrations, genetic codes, magnetic communications, and God consciousness, with available CDs and courses channeled from her spirit guide Mark for each one of these higher dimensions.

But what is most significant for me at this point is to evaluate, based upon my limited experience with Jonnete Crowley and the Center for Creative Consciousness, which is the non-profit corporation Crowley has set up to promote her workshops, CDs, books, and sacred voyages [2], if there are significant cult dangers in this group. I must admit that in spite of Crowley's excessively absurd (in my opinion) proclamations and the corresponding cult concerns that I have mentioned, I have also received some benefits from participating in her workshop. Although I was not able to gain value from her spiritual/body exercises (which happened to include the same muscle-checking procedure that I previously wrote about in my essay on Holographic Repatterning (Benjamin, 2005b) or her heart activation or Inca Code initiation (the heart activation was quite similar to a ritual from the HAI (Human Awareness Institute) workshop I had attended, called the Hand Over Heart ritual), I did find value from the inner uniting of my masculine and feminine in one of the experiential voyages Crowley took us on.

I don't anticipate being bombarded by Jonette Crowley or anyone else from the Center for Creative Consciousness to sign up for her future workshops or go on any of her trips to remote parts of the world, though I am on her mailing list and expect to receive her informational mailings (I have received a number of promotional communications from Crowley and the Center for Creative Consciousness since I did her workshop, which was nearly four months ago). I would guess that my experience of Jonette Crowley and the Center for Creative Consciousness via her Modern Mystic workshop will leave me with a Neutral/Benign evaluation in regard to cult dangers vs. spiritual benefits, and it is now time for me to put some numerical ratings on my experience and see specifically how Crowley fares from my experiential analysis via the Bonewits Cult Danger Scale.

1. INTERNAL CONTROL   1
2. WISDOM CLAIMED   10
3. WISDOM CREDITED   6
4. DOGMA   10
5. RECRUITING   3
6. FRONT GROUPS   1
7. WEALTH   5
8. POLITICAL POWER   1
9. SEXUAL MANIPULATION   1
10. CENSORSHIP   1
11. DROPOUT CONTROL   1
12. ENDORSEMENT OF VIOLENCE   1
13. PARANOIA   3
14. GRIMNESS   1
16. SURRENDER OF WILL   9

TOTAL SCORE: 54

AVERAGE SCORE: 3.6

My average score of 3.6 on the Bonewits Cult Danger Scale certainly places the Center for Creative Consciousness in Neutral/Benign territory in regard to cult dangers vs. spiritual benefits, as this score is quite similar to my corresponding scores for a number of other spiritual groups that I have placed in Neutral territory, inclusive of A Course in Miracles, Self-Realization Fellowship, and Conversations with God (with respective scores of 3.5, 3.7, and 3.7; see Benjamin, 2005b, 2005c). My experiential ratings are certainly unusual for this group, with extremely high scores in the categories of Wisdom Claimed, Dogma, and Surrender of Will (10, 10, 9 respectively) but with a large number of very low scores, as the number of 1's (there are eight 1's) is one of the lowest of any of the spiritual groups that I have experientially analyzed (Benjamin, 2005b, 2005c). But when all is considered, from the perspectives of both my intuitive self-knowledge as well as my numerical experiential evaluation from the Bonewits Cult Danger Scale, I can comfortably state that Jonette Crowley and the Center for Creative Consciousness, although dogmatically promoting spiritual beliefs that I find personally preposterous, does not possess significant cult dangers.

CONCLUSION

In conclusion, we see that the experiential analysis one can do with a rating scale such as the Bonewits Cult Danger Scale can be extremely beneficial in gaining an experiential qualitative/quantitative comparative measurement that may indicate the degree of cult dangers one has experienced in a spiritual group. However, the Bonewits Cult Danger Scale is only one means of making these kinds of evaluations, and I have utilized other rating scales in my *Modern Religions* book to complement the Bonewits Cult Danger Scale, especially for the purpose of evaluating the category of Favorable/Beneficial spiritual groups (Benjamin, 2005b, 2005c). The account I have portrayed in this article is completely based upon my own experiences in the five groups I have described, but it has helped me gain clarity on the respective cult dangers of these five groups by utilizing the experiential qualitative/ quantitative measurement rating scale that I have discussed. We consequently emerge with experiential qualitative/quantitative boundaries that, in conjunction with other relevant means of evaluation, can be utilized to give us useful information to distinguish between the categories of Cultic, Benign, and Beneficial in spiritual groups that we have experienced.

NOTES

1)   More information about HAI can be found at www.hai.org; as of February, 2013 I have remained as an inactive member on the Hai-Intimacy internet exchange.

2)   More information about Jonette Crowley and the Center for Creative Consciousness can be found at www.JonetteCrowley.com; as of February, 2013 I continue to receive regular internet mailings from Jonette Crowley and CCC every week or two, but there have been no pressures to sign up for Crowley's workshops.

REFERENCES

Benjamin, E. (2004a). On Conversations with God. *ICSA E-Newsletter*, *3*(2). Retrieved May 4, 2008 from http://www.icsahome

Benjamin, E. (2004b). On Neopaganism. *PagaNet News*, Beltane, 2004, 12.

Benjamin, E. (2005a). On Avatar. *ICSA E-Newsletter*, *4*(2). Retrieved May 4, 2008 from http://www.icsahome

Benjamin, E. (2005b). *Modern religions: An experiential analysis and exposé*. Swanville, ME. Natural Dimension Publications (available at www.lulu.com, 2013).

Benjamin, E. (2005c). Spirituality and the cults: An experiential analysis. *The Ground of Faith Journal*. Retrieved May 4, 2008, from http://homepages.ihug.co.nz/-thegroundoffaith/issues/2005-04/index.htm#elliot

Benjamin, E. (2005d). Spirituality, cults, and Neopaganism: An experiential analysis. *PagaNet News*, Beltane, 2005, 24.

Benjamin, E. (2007a). On Ken Wilber's Integral Institute: An experiential analysis. *ICSA E-Newsletter*, *6*(2). Retrieved May 4, 2008, from http://www.icsahome.org

Benjamin, E. (2007b). Scientology in the 1970s from various perspectives in time. Retrieved May 4, 2008, from the *Rick Ross Website*: http://www.rickross.com

Benjamin, E. (2007c). An integrative/non-integral psychotherapy model. Retrieved May 4, 2008, from the *Integral World Website*: http/www.integralworld.net

Bonewits, I. (1971). *Real Magic*. York Beach, ME. Samuel Weisner.

Crowley, J (2007). *The eagle and the condor: A true story of an unexpected mystical journey*. Greenwood Village, CO. Stone Tree Publishing.

Hayes, S., Strosahl, K. & Wilson, K. (1999). *Acceptance and Commitment Therapy: An experiential approach to behavior change*. New York. Guildford Press.

Hayes, S. & Strosahl, K. (2004). *A practical guide to Acceptance and Commitment Therapy*. New York. Springer.

Palmer, H. (1994a). *Living deliberately*. Altamonte Springs, FL. Stars' Edge International.

Palmer, H. (1994b). *Resurfacing*. Altamonte Springs, FL. Stars' Edge International.

Palmer, H. (1997). *The Avatar Masters' handbook*. Altamonte Springs. FL. Starts' Edge International.

Walsch, N.D. (1995). *Conversations with God: An uncommon dialogu: Book 1*. New York. G.P. Putnam & Sons.

Walsch, N.D. (1997). *Conversations with God: An uncommon dialogue: Book 2*. Charlottesville, VA. Hampton Roads Publishing Company.

Walsch, N.D. (1998). *Conversations with God: An uncommon dialogue: Book 3*. Charlottesville, VA. Hampton Beach Publishing Company.

Walsch, N.D. (1999). *Friendship with God*. New York. Putnam & Sons.

Walsch, N.D. (2000). *Communion with God*. New York. Putnam & Sons.

Walsch, N.D. (2002). *The new revelations: A conversation with God*. New York. Atria Books.

Walsch, N.D. (2004). *Tomorrow's God: Our greatest challenge*. New York. Atria Books.

Wilber, K. (1995). *Sex, Ecology, Spirituality*. Boston. Shambhala.

Yogananda, P. (1946). *Autobiography of a yogi*. Los Angeles. Self-Realization Fellowship.

PART 3: AN EXPERIENTIAL ANALYSIS OF THE CULT DANGERS OF A SPIRITUALIST CAMP

(October, 2010)

NOTE: This article is an excerpt from a talk I will be giving at the Association of Spirituality and Paranormal Studies (ASPSI) in June, 2011, entitled *Extended Science, Experiential Analysis, and an Experiential Exploration of the Possibility of Life after Death through the Ostensible Communications of Mediums with the Deceased.* The full article will appear in the ASPSI 2011 Annual Conference Proceedings.

In my study of the cult dangers of various modern religious/spiritual groups (Benjamin, 2005, 2011), I have devised a means of conveying my inner experiences in a qualitative/quantitative concrete way, utilizing three different rating scales. The rating scale that I have found to be most useful is based upon assigning quantitative ratings from 1 to 10 in regard to the level of agreement with particular statements that describe various potential cult danger characteristics of modern religious/spiritual groups, where 1 is lowest and 10 is highest on a 15 item cult danger evaluation list, originally devised by Isaac Bonewits (1971/1989). For most of the groups that I have been involved with, my qualitative/quantitative ratings were given years after I experienced these groups and wrote experiential essays about them (Benjamin, 2005), giving me much time to assimilate and become "mindful" (Kabat-Zinn, 1994) of my initial experiences. Of course these are very much subjective ratings, but the main point is that I was able to share what I learned from being immersed in these groups in a deep way, which closed the information gap that always exists when trying to understand the experiences of others (James, 1902/1958; Sela-Smith, 2002).

The kind of experiential analysis I am suggesting may also be undertaken in conjunction with studying the experiences of others, as is done in phenomenological psychology (Giorgi, 1970), qualitative surveys, and sometimes experimental science studies, in order to understand the phenomenon one is studying in as comprehensible a way as possible. There are gains and losses in doing the kind of experiential analysis I am suggesting, but I don't think it should be a question of one or the other. This perspective is at the core of William James' (1912/1976) radical empiricism, and is also at the basis of Adrian van Kaam's (1966) conception of what he refers to as Anthropological Psychology. In the past few years I have applied my experiential analysis to examine the cult dangers of a number of currently active religious/spiritual and philosophical groups, including Scientology, The Unification Church, A Course in Miracles, Conversations with God, Avatar, Eckankar, Self-Realization Fellowship, Divine Light Mission, and Ken Wilber's Integral Institute (Benjamin, 2005, 2007, 2008, 2011). I will now utilize the Bonewits Cult Danger Scale in my experiential analysis of the cult dangers of a Spiritualist camp in Maine (see Table 1 and Table 2 below).

For the past three summers I have done experiential research with "mediums" at Temple Heights Spiritualist Camp in Northport, Maine. I conducted my research as a precursor to my Ph.D. psychology dissertation at Saybrook University on an experiential exploration of the possibility of life after death through the ostensible communications of mediums with deceased persons, and I have described a number of my personal experiences in various individual and group sessions with mediums who are involved with this Spiritualist camp (Benjamin, 2009a, 2009b, 2010). During this process of self immersion, I also gained experiences that enabled me to experientially analyze the question of whether there were significant cult dangers in this Spiritualist camp. In order to answer this question, I utilized the Bonewits Cult Danger Scale, and I assigned my qualitative/quantitative ratings based upon my experiences at this Spiritualist camp over the past three summers, revisiting my earlier related writings in the context of the assimilation, understanding, and interpretation ingredients of the field of study known as autoethnography (Ellis, 2009). A number of excerpts from these articles that pertain to my experiences regarding the cult danger characteristics on the Bonewits Cult Danger Scale are given below.

In order to effectively compare in a consistent way the cult dangers of this Spiritualist camp with the cult dangers of the other groups that I have experientially analyzed (Benjamin, 2005, 2011), I have not weighted the value of the ratings in each category. It is certainly true that some of the categories in the scale are more significant than others and ideally would warrant greater numerical weight assigned to them. However, my present purpose is to give an indication of a possible concrete experiential analysis methodology to comparatively explore the possible cult dangers of a Spiritualist camp, and it is understood that there are certainly a number of mathematical improvements that could be made in applying this scale to more accurately describe an experiential account of the cult dangers of a religious, spiritual, or philosophical group. The main point for this article is that I have been able to convey my experiential knowledge of the cult dangers of a Spiritualist camp in a concrete way that others can confirm or disconfirm through their own experiences, which is a primary ingredient in Ken Wilber's (1983/2001) formulation of valid data accumulation in scientific inquiry. It is a way of communicating my inner experiences as part of an extended science context (Braud & Anderson, 1998; Josephson & Rubik, 1992) in a combined qualitative/quantitative methodology, and it allows for meaningful "inter-subjective" (Wilber, 1983/2001) comparisons of the cult dangers of various modern religious, spiritual, and philosophical groups, in an interplay of mind and spirit. I believe that this kind of experiential analysis is at the heart of both the intra-subjective and inter-subjective extended science research that Adrian van Kaam (1966) has advocated for, and is also a good concrete illustration of the "radical empiricism" of William James (1912/1976). This kind of experiential analysis is also consistent with how a number of qualitative researchers have used alternative terms to those of positivist quantitative terminology, in order to describe the validity of qualitative research (Creswell, 2007). These alternative terms include trustworthiness, credibility, authenticity, transferability, dependability, and confirmability (Creswell, 2007, p. 202).

Experiential Descriptions of Potential Cult Dangers at a Spiritualist Camp

The following excerpts from my aforementioned articles describe some of the experiences I have had at Temple Heights Spiritualist Camp during the summers of 2008, 2009, and 2010, that my numerical cult danger ratings on the Bonewits Cult Danger Scale are based upon (see Table 1 below).

During this whole séance I must say that I was not very impressed. There were strong social expectations to express one's images and associations of other people in the circle, and view it as messages from the spirit world. The whole session seemed to me to be a textbook case of how belief in mediumship and the spirit world is highly correlated with environmental expectations, peer group influence, and hypnosis scales and measures of fantasy proneness. (Benjamin, 2009a, pp. 29-30).

But what had the most impact for me is the influence of the group consciousness of belief in soul survival upon the people who attend the various Spiritualist functions at this camp. Everyone who attends these Spiritualist functions, with the exception of myself, appears to be fully convinced of the reality of the spirit world and the ability of their loved ones to communicate with them. People at the Spiritualist camp frequently talk about their experiences of reincarnation, including my own workshop presenter who discussed some of his many past lives. He believes that this is his last incarnation, meaning that he will be attaining spiritual self fulfillment or Nirvana along the lines of Eastern religious and spiritual beliefs...I am by no means any more convinced of the reality of soul survival or reincarnation than I was before I started my experiential mediumship research activities a few months ago. But I believe that I have gained significantly in my understanding and appreciation of the sociocognitive perspective on medium channeling. (Benjamin, 2009a, pp. 32-33).

I found it interesting that the medium/lecturer did not feel comfortable with the notion of reincarnation, saying that he did not think there was any viable evidence to firmly establish the reality of reincarnation. His rationale for considering the evidence for life after death to be undeniable is not something I agreed with, but I knew this was the sacred cow of the Church of Spiritualism, and was not something I should be publicly questioning at this Spiritualist camp; certainly not if I have any hopes of getting the Spiritualist camp to approve me doing my eventual Ph.D. dissertation research studying them. (Benjamin, 2009a, p. 36).

Before the church service began, I had asked the administrator if she minded if I left some of my counseling brochures and business cards out with the other various advertisements, and she read through my brochure carefully and asked me about my study of cults. I was somewhat taken aback but explained to her how I did not view the Spiritualist camp as a cult, and I sincerely complimented the camp in its openness, non-manipulation, and genuineness. She seemed satisfied, and she approved me leaving my business cards and brochures in the camp....I felt this calm and relaxed feeling as we talked, and I honestly conveyed to her about my personal/professional research interests, which she seemed to take in stride....I honestly conveyed to the administrator how I was an agnostic and wanted to believe in life after death, but needed to experience this for myself. She was very understanding and non-judgmental. (Benjamin, 2009a, pp. 41-42).

I found myself frequently contributing to the group discussion, often interjecting my own perspectives and questions regarding how one can distinguish between a veritable life after death experience vs. a "super-psi" psychic parapsychological interpretation...I remembered back to the "sacred cow" of the Spiritualist church belief that they had "proof" of the certainty of life after death, and the guest medium frequently alluded to her church's beliefs in this regard. This medium was active in the National Spiritualist Church and frequently wrote articles in Spiritualist publications, but from my experience she had retained her modesty and genuineness. I realized that I needed to be careful to not overdo my questioning of her beliefs, as I did not want to come off as a skeptical academic researcher who was unable to appreciate an authentic spiritual experience. At one point the woman sitting next to me remarked that she did not understand how anyone could doubt the truth of an afterlife, based upon so many people's experiences. This stimulated me to again explain the variety of interpretations as alternatives to a bona fide experience of life after death. However, I also realized that I needed to discipline myself to go easy on how much intellectual knowledge I shared regarding all the research that I had learned about in this context. (Benjamin, 2009b, pp. 9-10).

We concluded in an amicable manner with the medium telling me that although there may be various interpretations of the afterlife experience, she hopes that there is life after death and she feels best to believe in this. I found myself spontaneously replying that I also hoped there is life after death, but that there is a strong part of me that has the need to continue questioning this and that I cannot easily believe. The medium smiled and we said goodbye as I thanked her for a wonderful workshop. (Benjamin, 2009b, p. 14).

But one of our prayer book recitations emphasized the "scientific proof of the fact of life after death." I remembered back to the interesting discussion and my disagreement with "the fact is proven" afterlife beliefs of the church at my medium workshop last week, but I felt able to express my disagreement at that medium workshop.

However, last night I felt like I was in a rigid doctrinaire church where people were enjoying the familiar and comforting church services from their childhoods. It seemed to me that these people were using the crutch of being able to relieve themselves of the existentia reality of their deaths by believing in the church dogma that claimed to prove the existence of an afterlife. (Benjamin, 2009b, p. 17).

And now the strangeness of the evening took its shape. The medium strongly encouraged us to talk continuously about whatever images we saw once the lights were turned off. He also advised us to sing and laugh and make merry, saying that silence was no conducive to seeing spirits materialize. This medium was very personable, good-looking, and had a charm that appeared to me to be an uncanny mixture of spiritual medium and used car salesman The lights were soon turned off, the medium sat in a chair in fron of us, the whole group (except for me) recited various Christiar prayers, and some of the people were continuously saying hello to their departed loved ones, as the medium responded to whatever form of deceased spirit they expected him to be. The medium had a mesmerizing way of bobbing his head back and forth, and speaking in a low hollow voice that sounded like some sort of communication from another realm. I don't know much about ligh mechanisms, but gradually we could see the features and outlines of the medium take shape, and then people were excitedly saying how they saw all kinds of visions of dead loved ones, old and young male and female. Me—I saw only the medium nearly the whole time. However, I must admit that for a brief period of time I did seem to visualize a much older person in white hair....The power of suggestion from the group was tremendously strong, and through al my consciousness studies readings I was well acquainted with how the power of suggestion could affect one's awareness of physical perception. (Benjamin, 2009b, p. 25).

The workshop leader/medium was personable and funny; one of her unforgettable remarks after describing the healing techniques we would momentarily be practicing of blowing healing breath energy into our co-participants' ailing body places, was that after her own intense experience of receiving this healing breath energy from twenty-two workshop co-participants, she had told her significant other that she had received a "psychic blow job." Yes—my workshop leader/medium was funny and charming (Benjamin, 2009b, pp. 30-31).

At any rate, I proceeded to enter the medium circle, to a group of thirteen women (including the elderly medium leading the session) loudly and vivaciously singing "Old McDonald Had A Farm." (Benjamin, 2009b, p. 33).

Medium #1 was certainly a character, as she identified herself in the context of being united in soul with Albert Einstein and the Islam founder Mohammed. She was also light and humorous, and her presentation and facilitation made the group atmosphere into an enjoyable and comfortable space, from my own experience and from what I perceived of the experiences of the other participants. (Benjamin, 2010, p. 38).

I was quite outspoken in my questioning of a long channeling the medium read to us that was related to the truth and value of faith....The medium, as well as some of the group participants, liked my interpretation and analysis, and the medium thanked me sincerely for bringing this to her attention. (Benjamin, 2010, p. 39).

I greatly appreciated Medium #3's personal realization and his impactful way of conveying to the audience of current mediums and future mediums that it was important to be truthful with yourself as mediums and not allow yourself to cater to your ego to impress your clients through fabricating material that you know deep down you are not truly sensing. Medium #3 spoke passionately about the lack of ethics of many mediums, and how important it was for mediums to offer their services in a sincerely devoted and honest spiritual context. (Benjamin, 2010, p. 41).

Experiential Cult Danger Ratings

Table 1 displays my experiential cult danger ratings for Temple Heights Spiritualist Camp, and Table 2 gives a comparison of these ratings with a number of selected modern religious, spiritual, and philosophical groups that I have previously experientially analyzed.

Table 1

The Bonewits Cult Danger Scale for Temple Heights Spiritualist Camp

Characteristic	Rating
Internal Control: amount of internal political power exercised by leaders(s) over members	1
Wisdom Claimed: by leader(s); amount of infallibility declared about decisions	10
Wisdom Credited: to leaders by members, amount of trust in decisions made by leader(s)	9
Dogma: rigidity of reality concepts taught; of amount of doctrinal inflexibility	9
Recruiting: emphasis put on attracting new members, amount of proselytizing	3
Front Groups: number of subsidiary groups using different name from that of main group	1
Wealth: amount of money and/or property desired or obtained; emphasis on members' donations	3
Political Power: amount of external political influence desired or obtained	1
Sexual Manipulation: of members by leader(s), amount of control over the lives of members	1
Censorship: amount of control over members' access to outside opinions on group; its doctrines or leader(s)	1
Dropout Control: intensity of efforts directed at preventing or returning dropouts	1
Endorsement of Violence: when used by or for the group or its leader(s)	1
Paranoia: amount of fear concerning real or imagined enemies; perceived power of opponents	2
Grimness: amount of disapproval concerning jokes about the group, its doctrines or leader(s)	2
Surrender of Will: emphasis on members not having to be responsible for personal decisions	5
Average Rating:	**3.3**

NOTE: The rating scale from 1 to 10 is from low to high, where 1 is the lowest and 10 is the highest; the average ratings are rounded off to one decimal place.

Table 2

Cult Danger Average Ratings for Selected Modern Religious, Spiritual, and Philosophical Groups

Group	Cult Danger Average Rating	Cult Danger Classification
Unification Church	9.0	High
Scientology	8.7	High
Avatar	5.4	Moderate
Divine Light Mission	5.1	Moderate
Twelve Step Support Groups	4.4	Minimal
Eckankar	4.3	Minimal
Integral Institute	3.9	Neutral
Conversations with God	3.7	Neutral
A Course in Miracles	3.5	Neutral
Temple Heights Spiritualist Camp	**3.3**	**Neutral**
Kripalu Center for Yoga & Health	2.6	Favorable
Human Awareness Institute	2.5	Favorable

NOTE: For information on my ratings in the individual categories in the above groups, see Benjamin, 2005, 2007, 2008, 2011. The Favorable classification implies that there are no significant cult dangers and that the group is beneficial in regard to one's personal growth and spiritual development, based upon my own personal experiences with the group.

As can be seen from the results in Table 1 and Table 2, based upon my own experiences I have concluded that there are not significant cult dangers at Temple Heights Spiritualist Camp. However, I did not experience enough bona fide personal growth and spiritual development at this Spiritualist camp to place this group in the Favorable classification. Rather, I have placed this group in the Neutral classification, along with such groups as A Course in Miracles, Conversations with God, and Integral Institute. From an examination of Table 1, it is obvious that I have given this group alarming ratings in a few of the individual categories; in particular my rating of 10 for Wisdom Claimed, and my ratings of 9 for Wisdom Credited and Dogma. However, there are no other individual ratings to cause concern, and I gave quite a few minimal ratings of 1 and 2. It is certainly true from my experiences that this Spiritualist camp is dogmatic, inflexible, and convinced of the absolute truth in regard to their beliefs in the veracity of life after death and the ability of their mediums to communicate with departed spirits. However, these qualities in themselves do not necessarily warrant the conclusion that a group possesses significant cult dangers. From my experiences, this Spiritualist camp puts little or no effort into such factors as recruiting new members, dropout control, sexual manipulation, or endorsement of violence, all of which are factors that are prevalent in the most notorious modern religious/spiritual groups (Langone, 1993; Muster, 1997; Singer & Lalich, 1996). But what is most important in regard to the main thrust of this article, is that I have been able to convey my firsthand experiences in regard to the cult dangers of a Spiritualist camp, through a qualitative/quantitative experiential analysis in the context of an extended science domain.

REFERENCES

Benjamin, E. (2005). Spirituality and the cults: An experiential analysis. *The Ground of Faith Journal*, April/May. Retrieved April 1, 2010, from http://homepages.ihug.co.nz/~thegroundoffiath/issues/2005-04/index.htm#elliot

Benjamin, E. (2007). On Ken Wilber's Integral Institute: An experiential analysis. *International Cultic Studies Association E-Newsletter*, 6(2). Retrieved April 1, 2010, from http:www.icsahome.com

Benjamin, E. (2008). The boundaries between cultic, benign, and beneficial in five spiritual groups. *International Cultic Studies Association E-Newsletter*, 7(3). Retrieved April 1, 2010, from http.www.icsahome.com

Benjamin, E. (2009a). An experiential analysis of mediums and life after death. *The Ground of Faith Journal.* Jan./Feb. Retrieved April 1, 2010, from http://homepages.ihug.co.nz/~thegroundoffaith/issues

Benjamin, E. (2009b). *An autoethnographic study in a Spiritualist camp for mediums.* Unpublished manuscript.

Benjamin, E. (2010). *An autoethnographic inquiry into the phenomenon of life after death.* Unpublished manuscript.

Benjamin, E. (2013). *Modern religions: An experiential analysis and exposé.* Swanville, ME: Natural Dimension Publications; available at www.lulu.com

Bonewits, I. (1989). *Real magic.* York Beach, Maine: Samuel Weisner (original work published 1971).

Braude, W., & Anderson, R. (1998). *Transpersonal research methods for the social sciences:Honoring human experiences.* London: Sage.

Creswell, J. W. (2007). *Qualitative inquiry & research design.* London: Sage.

Ellis, C. (2009). *Revision: Autoethnographic reflections of life and work (Writing Lives).*Walnut Creek, CA: Left Coast Press.

Giorgi, A. (1970). *Psychology as a human science.* New York: Basic Books.

James. W. (1958). *The varieties of religious experience.* New York: New American Library (original work published 1902).

James, W. (1976). *Essays in radical empiricism.* Cambridge, MA: Harvard University Press (original work published 1912).

Josephson, B. D., & Rubik, B. A. (1992). The challenge of consciousness research. *Frontier Perspectives*, 3(1), 15-19.

Kabat-Zinn, J. (1994). *Wherever you go, there you are: Mindfulness meditation in everyday life.* New York: Hyperion.

Langone, M. (Ed.). (1993). *Recovery from cults.* New York: Norton.

Muster, N. (1997). *Betrayal of the spirit.* Chicago: University of Illinois Press.

Sela-Smith, S. (2002). Heuristic research: A review and critique of Moustakas' method. *Journal of Humanistic Psychology, 42*(3), 53-88.

Singer, M., & Lalich, J. (1996). *Cults in Our Midst.* San Francisco: Jossey-Bass.

van Kaam, A. (1966). *Existential foundations of psychology.* New York: University Press of America.

Wilber, K. (2001). *Eye to eye. The quest for the new paradigm.* Boston: Shambhala (original work published 1983).

PART 4: NEOPAGAN RITUALS: AN EXPERIENTIAL ACCOUNT

(April, 2010)

NOTE: This article is essentially the same as the published version of my article (see [82] in Chapter One Notes), except for updating my Bio and some minor editorial revisions.

I would like to thank Denita Benyshek, my colleague and fellow doctoral psychology candidate at Saybrook University, for editing this article with me and inducing me to portray my Neopagan experiences in a personally revealing way that was quite the stretch from my more usual experiential/academic style of writing articles for journals.

Abstract

In this article I convey some of my personally meaningful experiences at a number of Neopagan rituals, inclusive of the Starwood festival in New York State and the Twilight Covening retreat in Massachusetts. I relate my Neopagan experiences to that of "shamanistic" experience, and support my interpretation by describing various aspects of Shamanism from the perspective of a few different authors. This article is written primarily in narrative style, with academic references utilized to support some of the descriptions of Neopaganism and shamanistic experience described in these narratives.

Keywords: Neopaganism, shamanistic, altered state of consciousness, skyclad

Bio for Elliot Benjamin

Elliot Benjamin, Ph.D, Ph.D. is a philosopher, mathematician, musician, counselor, writer, and the Transpersonal Psychology Program Director at Akamai University. He is the author of three self-published books and over a hundred published articles in the fields of humanistic and transpersonal psychology, spirituality and awareness of cult dangers, art and mental disturbance, parapsychology, progressive politics, pure mathematics, and mathematics enrichment. Elliot lives in Maine and enjoys playing the piano, tennis, and ballroom dancing.

Neopagan Rituals: An Experiential Account

When I was forty-seven years old I met an attractive woman at a "personal growth" workshop, with whom I shared the experience of participating in a nude group massage, and I soon visited her at her home in New Jersey. The "personal growth" workshop I attended was a "polyamory" event. Polyamory is a philosophy that is based upon the idea that it is natural to have more than one committed loving sexual relationship at the same time, while being completely honest with everyone you are involved with (Anapol, 1997) [1].

My polyamory workshop followed twelve years of romantic relationships that lasted generally six months to two years, and prior to that, fifteen years of marriage. Nevertheless, I yearned for a lifelong soul mate, and I began to wonder if I were capable of fulfilling this dream. Because of my self-doubts about ever finding the monogamous intimate relationship I truly wanted, I explored various polyamory events. Although I eventually learned that polyamory was not the answer for me, polyamory played an important role in my personal growth and development—aided by the polyamorous woman I visited in New Jersey. She urged me to meet a very special group of people who would change my life forever and propel me on a lifelong path of finding my true self. In 1997 I decided to follow her advice, which led me to the special pagans at the Starwood festival, my first Neopagan festival [2]. Neopagans are "people in modern times who consider themselves to be practicing Paganism with present day adaptations" (Benjamin, 2004, p. 12).

At Starwood, I was surprised by how comfortable I felt participating in opening circle. I could easily acknowledge water, earth, fire, and sky through simple recitations of respect that beautifully expressed my love of nature. I liked the priest and priestess who sincerely led two hundred participants through the ritual. Admittedly, the people at opening circle looked rather weird to me. Some of them were "skyclad" (naked). Many of them had tattoos and/or painted bodies with body piercings in various places that I think I will leave to your imagination. Starwood was an uncanny combination of bikers and hippies and ex-hippies. A number of the men wore robes and skirts of colorful material (they were "sarongs").

The priestess and priest led people through the "spiral dance" (Starhawk, 1979) [3], an interesting and fun experience for me. Everyone held hands. Being quickly pulled in and out of spirals, I found myself face to face with the strange looking people. I gazed into the eyes of naked people, now all smiling and laughing, and I was smiling and laughing too! I had always loved to dance, although I felt inhibited when dancing in groups. But somehow, in the spiral dance, my inhibitions disappeared. Drum rhythms went through me. My body moved in a free and cathartic way. That night, I was amazed to find myself dancing near the stage in the midst of the dancing enthusiasts, most of whom were at least twenty years younger than me. Was I really a forty seven year old mathematics professor? I felt ageless at the Starwood fountain of youth, on some strange but delightful whole other planet.

The live concert and dancing ended near midnight. Then, the stream of people flowed past the vendors' booths, which offered a colorful array of everything from home-made jewelry to safe sex products to Reiki and massage sessions. The stream flowed past Pagan clothing, costumes for witches and wizards, musical instruments, and books about Paganism, Wicca, esoteric philosophy, and various other subjects. Lo and behold, I found myself joining the stream that flowed towards the sound of drumming, louder and louder, incessantly rhythmic, to a great bonfire. I have always had quite the shy streak in me and it took me a while to fully participate. However, the intense drum rhythms and people dancing around the bonfire captivated me, loosening my inhibitions and making my body move of its own accord. For the next three nights, my new ritual was to dance around the bonfire until around 3:00 a.m. Many people danced skyclad—though I stopped short of the full skyclad experience myself—well at the bonfires, anyway.

The nightly drumming and dancing around the bonfires sent me into an altered state of consciousness (ASC). ASC is described as "stable patterns of physiological, cognitive, and experiential events different from those of the ordinary waking state" (Baruss, 2003, p. 7). My mind and my body moved in a continuous flow of energy. A more real and deeper me was emerging.

A particularly vivid altered state of consciousness occurred at one of the midnight Voudoun ceremonies [4]. The group danced continuously, forming spirals. Stimulated by continuous rhythmic drumming, an extreme energy filled me. We stood. A strange looking, long haired man in a grotesque looking mask and a tuxedo walked up to each one of us, offered some kind of alcoholic beverage, and blew incense into our faces.

Events felt more and more eerie, more and more unreal. Our Voudoun priestess instructed us to put intention into our deepest wishes as we danced and whirled, around the forest enclosure under the light of the moon. After many hours, I became very tired, my feet ached, and I didn't think I could continue to move. Then, something snapped inside of me. I found myself in a fast moving small group, holding hands with a young African American man and young, attractive Euro-American woman. My energy transformed into a youthful, rigorous, interactive, and playful dance with my two partners, seemingly going on and on without ending. When the dancing and Voodoo ceremony ended, I again felt ageless, as if I had climbed out of a veritable fountain of youth.

This kind of intensive and extensive physical endurance is a common feature of shamanic activity in indigenous societies. Scott (2002) described the powerful energies that dancing may stimulate in a person:

> Dancing is tremendously powerful in helping to speed up the receptive state, either by raising the energy or by leading the shaman and other dancers to feel a kind of exhaustion that leads to trance. It can also help lead to the sense of merging with the spirits, particularly when combined with masks. (p. 134).

Every day, there were live concerts and five workshops, including magic, Witchcraft, massage, psychedelics, movement, yoga, acting, drumming, Paganism, and batik dyeing. I found myself becoming more and more comfortable with the people at the workshops, letting down my guard, moving to dance music and yoga, enjoying participation in improvisational theatre and drumming, and learning about the roots of Paganism. I was initiated into the skyclad experience during a communication workshop.

At the Starwood festival it was not uncommon to find workshops led by modern day shamans. The terms "modern day shamans" (Scott, 2002) and "shamanistic" practitioners (Krippner, 2008) refer to contemporary adaptations of Shamanism developed from indigenous Shamanism, similar to how Neopaganism evolved from Paganism. I attended a shamanic healing ritual in which we initially were told to identify our selves with our "power animals." I chose a bird as my power animal, symbolizing freedom to me. Walsh (2007) described a shaman's transformation into an animal:

She may see herself turned into an eagle and soar into the sky, or become a wolf and feel infused with its power. After returning from the journey she may perform her "power animal dance," moving and sounding like the animal, as a way of experiencing and maintaining its presence. (p. 134).

Although for the indigenous shaman the power animal is real (Walsh, 2007, p. 135), Scott focused upon the modern shamanic practice of using power animals symbolically to delve into one's deep inner psychic processes (Scott, 2002, pp. 92-103). We were instructed to merge with our chosen power animals, becoming them in our very beings. I flapped my arms and ran in the grass, making the sounds of birds, enjoying this freedom while being fully conscious that this was, to me, just "pretending."

Subsequent to these power animal enactments, I witnessed our young, long haired and bearded, raggedly-dressed modern day shaman perform a long, intensive shamanic healing upon a volunteer from our group. This shamanic healing involved continuous blowing of cigar smoke all over the client, spitting out some kind of liquid onto his body, and sucking out the purported "evil spirit" from the client's leg. The shamanic techniques that this modern shaman performed were quite similar to the techniques performed by indigenous shamans (Harner, 1980; Scott, 2002; Walsh, 2007).

Indeed, by the end of the session, the client looked like a great burden had been removed from him. But, in my opinion, well known psychological and social mechanisms, such as the placebo effect and self-fulfilling prophecy, could easily explain the healing. As described by Walsh (2007):

Research shows that the expectations of both patient and therapist tend to become self-fulfilling prophesies and that faith in a physician can exert a powerful placebo effect. Indeed, the environment, the physician's status, and the rituals involved in giving and taking medicine can sometimes be as the drug itself. (p. 118).

Achterberg (1985) explicitly summarized the various medical healing effects of placebos as follows: "The placebo is actually granting permission to heal; it is a symbol the imagination can incorporate and translate into wondrous biochemical changes that are as yet beyond the comprehension of the finest scientific minds." (p. 85).

372   *Modern Religions: An Experiential Analysis And Exposé*

Symbol or placebo, prophesy or imagination, throughout this well-designed festival, mind, body, and spirit were integrated in an exceptionally harmonious way. I found myself re-immersed in spiritual exploration. Gradually, during the five day festival, I became a Neopagan.

Many families attended Starwood every summer. I saw teenagers walking together and laughing in small groups. Toward the festival's end I conversed over dinner with a mother and daughter. They described the wonders of sharing the Starwood experience with young children.

At that time, my son Jeremy was nearly sixteen. I knew that my son had a great deal of artistic and creative potential inside of him, but he was also very inhibited in some fundamental ways. I knew I wanted to bring him to Starwood the next summer. I hoped that Starwood would loosen him up and allow his true self to emerge.

Starwood became a special and rejuvenating father/son tradition for us, where time and the world were on hold, where our free selves emerged in the captivating sounds of the electrifying bands, with the nightly bonfire drumming as our companion. We first attended Starwood together in 1998, and returned again in 2000, 2001, 2002, and 2003, and for logistics reasons we attended the Rites of Spring Pagan festival (instead of Starwood) in Massachusetts in 2004. I can still remember the chant from the enormous theatrical last night bonfire event that my son and I sang during our thirteen hour drive home from our first Starwood festival: "We are a circle—we are moving together—we are in one another—we are one. I am spirit—I am in you; you are spirit—you are in me...."

When someone asks if I have any particular religious affiliation I say that I was brought up Jewish, but that I do not identify myself with being Jewish. For me, finding value and meaning from rituals necessitates my understanding and believing in what these rituals were originally based upon. I do not believe in or relate to the Bible, either *Old Testament* or *New Testament*. I am not comfortable with Jewish rituals or holidays. I am even more uncomfortable with Christian rituals and holidays, especially after the horrors of the Holocaust, as I do feel an ingrained cultural connection with Judaism. I became a Neopagan without conflict between my background in Judaism and my exploration of new age spirituality. The freedom to think, feel, and live the way you want to, as long as you are not harming others, is an essential ingredient in Neopaganism—and Neopagans practice what they preach, at least from my experiences at the Starwood festival.

By far the most spectacular ritual at the Starwood festival occurred annually on the last night of the festival, with choreographed dancers, theatrical performances, continuous chanting, endless drumming, and dancing around the enormous bonfire into the wee hours of the morning. The bonfire was lit by ceremonious fire-dancers, and it looked like it would reach the sky, with ecstatic people dancing in huge circles around this amazing spectacle throughout the night. To feel part of any kind of ritual, much less a major theatrically staged ritual with over a thousand persons, was unusual for me; but somehow it happened. Entranced, in some kind of altered state of consciousness, I danced round and round and round the bonfire with my people, the Neopagans, some skyclad and some clothed, everyone under the Starwood spell, including me.

The use of hallucinogens to accelerate the experience of altered states of consciousness is generally recognized as an age-old fundamental aspect of Shamanism (Achterberg, 1985; Harner, 1980; Scott, 2002; Walsh, 2007). Many people at Starwood used hallucinogens to achieve altered states. I did not.

Ritual experiences at Starwood led to my most intense Neopagan/shamanistic experience: my "vision ritual" at the Fall, 2004 Twilight Covening. "Covening" refers traditionally to a gathering of "witches." Neopaganism is closely linked with the religion of Wicca, which denotes witchcraft in its positive, extrasensory, personal power elements (Adler, 1979; Curot, 2001; Starhawk, 1979). A weekend retreat gathering, Twilight Covening is the Fall counterpart to the Rites of Spring Neopagan festival.

At the time of the Twilight Covening event, I was at a major crossroads in my 55th year of life. I had recently ended my three year romantic relationship with a Reiki master. In my 20th year as a mathematics professor at a small college in rural Maine, I felt like a failure in life. My high level spiritual/philosophical calling was faltering. It was quickly becoming too late for me to experience the harmonious life-long romantic relationship that I so much yearned for. I was unhappy.

I joined a "clan" [5] of Neopagans who were immersed in continuous drumming, dancing, and creative writing throughout the Twilight Covening weekend. The sleeping arrangements were stark and basic. We had to make do with sleeping bags on cold hard floors with various kinds of bugs and who knows what other kinds of creatures joining us, in crowded nooks and crannies of various dilapidated structures.

Gradually, through all the drumming, dancing, and writing, I felt myself loosen up. I took the rather unsettling living conditions in stride. As the weekend progressed, my inner strength and sense of personal freedom returned. On the last night, we gathered in the large hall to hear our instructions for the long awaited—and constantly promoted—culmination of the weekend: our "vision ritual."

Each of us was blindfolded, told to walk into the woods, and to try our best to follow the path that our intuition guided us to take. We were also told that there would be "helpers" along the way to give us various instructions and to insure that we did not venture too far off the main path. I remember the strangeness, my fear of walking blindfolded in the woods, being purposely turned around in a circle by the "helpers," and then finding myself on my own. I took one step after the other in the hope that I was on the right path, hearing the voices of others in the distance in the woods.

As my little voyage progressed, I realized that I was in a community of fellow seekers, and I knew that I was being watched to insure that I would be safe. I relaxed and enjoyed walking on a forest path in the night. When I finally arrived at my destination, I was cheerfully welcomed by my Neopagan guides, my blindfold was removed, and I witnessed a celebration of performing dancers and drummers.

Most significantly, during this vision ritual, I had once again tapped into my inner resources of strength. While gazing into a fire, I came into greater awareness. Walking blindfolded in the forest put me in touch with the reality of my life circumstances—and also with my ability to change them through self-determination and spiritual connection to the universe. A few months later, I met Dorothy. We have now been in a harmonious, romantic relationship for nearly six years.

To make changes in my job and move in the direction of my high level spiritual/philosophical calling took longer. In 1977, for five months I was a doctoral student in psychology, after having earned Masters degrees in both mathematics and counseling. I always felt deep down that I am a natural philosopher. But as I became older and older, it seemed that I had ignored what my deepest voice told me. Then, within a few years I ended my career as a mathematics professor, immersed myself in the world of mental health work, and embarked upon my new career which involves a creative combination of psychology, philosophy, and mathematics. I returned to graduate school and I am currently a Ph.D. candidate in a psychology program with a concentration in Consciousness and Spirituality at Saybrook University. This is actually the same school where I began my doctoral psychology studies thirty-three years ago, though it was then called the Humanistic Psychology Institute. I now feel like I am the philosopher I have always felt myself to be, expressing my calling in the world [6].

Perhaps it is not accurate to attribute my immense personal growth to my shamanistic visions at the Twilight Covening ritual or to my shamanistic experiences at Starwood. But my transformation from unfulfilled mathematics professor to fully alive and adventurous philosopher feels to me like I have embarked on my own shamanic path. All indigenous shamanic trials, tests, rituals, pain endurance, soul journeys, and use of hallucinogens and power animals, are part of a spiritual quest to make sense of the universe (Achterberg, 1985; Harner, 1980; Scott, 2002; Walsh, 2007). My spiritual quest, to make sense of the universe, is alive and well in me now.

As I have entered my 61th year of life, I think that my quest will eventually bring me back to a Pagan festival. This time I expect to be accompanied by my "significant other," girlfriend, lover, and soulmate, Dorothy. She is the tangible result of much of what I prayed for in the last Neopagan/shamanistic ritual that I participated in—nearly six years ago. Our harmonious relationship, my personal development, and my new career in psychology, philosophy, and mathematics are the culmination of many Neopagan rituals. Before it was too late, I found my true self and personal fulfillment found me (cf. [6]).

ENDNOTES

1) Polyamory is a minority lifestyle and viewpoint in Neopaganism. One influential Neopagan group who practices this lifestyle is the *Church of All Worlds*, a Neopagan organization with legal religious status as a church, originated by Oberon and Morning Glory Zell (http://en.wikipedia.org/wiki/Oberon_Zell Ravenheart). For more information about the *Church of All Worlds*, see *Green Egg* journal (www. greeneggzine.com). The editor of *Green Egg* journal, Diane Darling, is one of Oberon Zell's two life partners (along with Morning Glory Zell). I have participated in workshops with Oberon

and his Zell family at Starwood, and I was a member (inactive) of the *Church of All Worlds* for a year.

2)   I would like to emphasize that my portrayal of the Starwood festival is based upon my own experiences, and is described in narrative style. From attending seven Starwood festivals, I have experienced Starwood to be an authentic Neopagan festival, complete with a wide variety of Pagan workshops, rituals, chants, and ceremonies. However, this is my own experience, and others who attended the festival may have very different opinions about the authenticity of Starwood as a Neopagan festival.

3)   A "spiral dance" is a folk dance found throughout the western world and is of ancient origins. It has been adapted by Pagan (and other) groups for ritual purposes as a "greeting dance," and is a major portion of Samhain festivities held each year; see for example *Reclaiming* community in San Francisco (www.reclaiming.org).

4)   Voudoun is a native African religion that is almost universally practiced in Haiti. The central belief of the religion is in spirit possession, through which the gods speak to the devotees for a short time during the ceremonies. Magic, used for both good and evil purposes, is an integral part of Voudoun. Voudoun recognizes no dichotomy between good and evil, but sees evil as the mirror image of good (www.themystica.com/mystica/articles/ v/vodoun_also_voodoo.html). For more information about Voudon rituals, see Voudoun priestess Louisah Teish's book *Jambalaya: The Natural Woman's Book of Personal Charms and Practical Rituals* (Reish, 1985).

5)   The terms "clan" and "coven" as used in the Twilight Covening workshops are more informal than the traditional Celtic definitions of clan and coven (www.paganspath.com/magik/ coven.htm). The clans at Twilight Covening were groups of between five and twenty participants, organized around cohesive themes such as dancing and drumming, creativity and self awareness, the dark night of the soul, love and romantic relationships, etc. For a wide variety of Neopagan groups and practices in America, see Margaret Adler's book *Drawing Down the Moon: Witches, Druids, Goddess Worshippers, and Other Pagans in America Today* (Adler, 1979).

6) The following is an update of my relevant involvements and accomplishments as of February, 2013:

--Dorothy and I went to Starwood together in July, 2012.

--I received my Ph.D. in psychology from Saybrook University in May, 2012, and for the past year I have been the Transpersonal Psychology Program Director at Akamai University (www.akamaiuniversity.us).

--In May, 2012 I gave a talk at the International Congress of Qualitative Inquiry (ICQI) that was based upon my Saybrook dissertation (see Benjamin, 2012a), and in May, 2013 I will be giving another talk at ICQI; this one is entitled *The Creative Artist, Eccentricity, and Mental Disturbance: The Journal of a Struggling Actor—First Three Months: My Actor/Writer Son* (see Benjamin, 2012b).

--At the time of this writing (February, 2013), I am in the process of becoming involved with the Agents of Conscious Evolution (ACE; see http://theacetraining.com/course/AgentsofConsciousEvolution 7/homepage) which is spearheaded by the 83-year-old inspirational futurist Barbara Marx Hubbard (see [21] in Chapter Three Notes for one of her book references, and stay tuned for my future essays on ACE!).

REFERENCES

Achterberg, J. (1985). *Imagery in healing: Shamanism and modern medicine*. Boston: New Science Library/Shambhala.

Adler, M. (1979). *Drawing down the moon*. New York: Penguin.

Anapol, D. (1997). *Polyamory: The new love without limits* San Rafael, CA: Internet Resource Center.

Baruss, I. (2003). *Alterations of consciousness*. Washington DC American Psychological Association.

Benjamin, E. (2004). On Neopaganism. *PagaNet News*, *XI*(III), p. 12.

Benjamin, E. (2012a). *An experiential exploration of the possibility of life after death through the ostensible communications of mediums with deceased persons* (Doctoral Dissertation) Retrieved from ProQuest Dissertations and Thesis Database (UMI #3509443)

Benjamin, E. (2012b). *The creative artist, eccentricity, and mental disturbance: The journal of a struggling actor: Part I—m actor/writer son*. Retrieved from www.integralworld.net

Curot, P. (2001). *Witchcrafting: A spiritual guide to modern magic*. New York: Broadway Books.

Harner, M. (1980). *The way of the shaman: A guide to power and healing*. San Francisco: Harper & Row.

Krippner, S. (2008). *Learning guide for CSP 3080: The Psychology of Shamanism*. Saybrook University.

Scott, G. G. (2002). *The complete idiot's guide to Shamanism* Indianapolis, IN: Alpha Books.

Starhawk (1979). *The spiral dance: A rebirth of the ancient religion of the great goddess*. San Francisco: HarperSanFrancisco.

Tart, C. T. (Ed.). (1972). *Altered states of consciousness*. Garden City NY: Anchor.

Teish, L. (1985). *Jambalaya: The natural woman's book of persona charms and practica rituals*. New York: Harper Collins.

Walsh, R. (2007). *The world of Shamanism: New views of an ancien tradition*. Woodbury, MN: Llewellyn.

CPSIA information can be obtained at www.ICGtesting.com
Printed in the USA
LVOW081724210613

339728LV00003B/421/P